Face-to-Face in Shakespearean Drama

Face-to-Face in Shakespearean Drama

Ethics, Performance, Philosophy

Edited by Matthew James Smith and Julia Reinhard Lupton

EDINBURGH
University Press

Edinburgh University Press is one of the leading university presses in the UK. We publish academic books and journals in our selected subject areas across the humanities and social sciences, combining cutting-edge scholarship with high editorial and production values to produce academic works of lasting importance. For more information visit our website: edinburghuniversitypress.com

Edinburgh University Press Ltd
The Tun – Holyrood Road
12(2f) Jackson's Entry
Edinburgh EH8 8PJ

Typeset in 11/13 Adobe Sabon by
IDSUK (DataConnection) Ltd, and
printed and bound in Great Britain.

A CIP record for this book is available from the British Library

ISBN 978 1 4744 3568 0 (hardback)
ISBN 978 1 4744 3570 3 (webready PDF)
ISBN 978 1 4744 3571 0 (epub)

Contents

Part IV: Moving Pictures

List of Illustrations

Acknowledgements

This collection began, as so many volumes in our field do, as a Shakespeare Association of America seminar, held in New Orleans in 2016, organised by Matthew Smith. We would like to thank the original participants as well as the newcomers to the conversation. Special thanks to Bruce R. Smith, who has been a mentor and friend to both of us. We are delighted to feature his essay in this volume. A generous gift from Dr Marilyn Sutton to the UCI Shakespeare Center allowed us to hire Laura Hatch as a research assistant and to subsidise images for this volume. This volume is the fruit of a special friendship between the two editors, composed over several years out of face-to-face conversation, the liberal exchange of research and shared theatrical experiences. Stanley Cavell (1926–18) passed away while we were editing the completed manuscript. His influence is everywhere evident in these pages, and we would like to honour his memory in this volume.

Matthew James Smith   Julia Reinhard Lupton
Azusa Pacific University   University of California, Irvine

Introduction

Matthew James Smith and Julia Reinhard Lupton

Figure I.1 Beth Lopes directs Jesse Sharp (Leontes) and Meg Evans (Camillo) in *The Winter's Tale* in a 'spacing rehearsal' at New Swan Shakespeare Festival, University of California, Irvine, June 2018. Photo by Julia Lupton.

Rehearsal notes: spacing/facing

'Camillo, you are disturbed by the way Leontes says the word "business". Leontes, you are ticked off by the word "satisfy". Try opening up when you hear those words.' Beth Lopes is directing Act One, Scene Two of *The Winter's Tale* for a production at the University of California, Irvine.[1] The actors are roughing out their lines in preparation for a performance in the round that will open in a few weeks. Here's the passage:

> *Leontes:*   Lower messes
> are to this **business** purblind? Say.
> *Camillo:* **Business**, my lord? I think most understand
> Bohemia stays here longer.
> *Leontes:* Ha?

> *Camillo:* Stays here longer.
> *Leontes:* Ay, but why?
> *Camillo:* To **satisfy** your highness, and the entreaties
> Of our most gracious mistress.
> *Leontes:*   **Satisfy?**
> Th'entreaties of your mistress? **Satisfy?**
> Let that **suffice.**
>
>   (I, ii, 225–35; emphasis added)

This exchange is part of an emotionally charged and morally vola-
tile conversation between a king and his counsellor. In real life, the
two speakers would likely face each other through most of the discussion: Camillo might look away in distress, bow his head in his
hand or even briefly walk away to buy time to process his shock and
decide on a strategy while Leontes might close his eyes in mortified
rage or begin to look beyond Camillo towards the imagined trans-
gressors or the whispering court. By and large, however, the cognitive requirements and social conventions of conversation would limit
lengthy deviations from face-to-face discussion. On stage, however,
as Bernard Beckerman points out, actors must continually navigate
between the 'actor-to-actor exchange' that constitutes the substance
of so many scenes in classical Western theatre and the 'frontal orientation' that both proscenium and thrust stages require.[2] Actors can
only face each other in close proximity for brief moments or risk
losing the attention of the audience. As a result, they must continually find ways to 'open up' their actions while remaining attuned to
the demands of the conversation on stage.

In the blocking of some hundred lines of text, the actors playing
Leontes and Camillo had recourse to many different movements.
Camillo stood still and Leontes moved in a half circle while pointing at his steward and recriminating him for complicity in the adul-
terous liaison (I, ii, 239–49). Camillo stood in place while Leontes
spun out his rumination on the theme 'Is whispering nothing?' to
an audience of possible whisperers who also serve as proxies for
his own agonised consciousness before returning to face Camillo at
the end of the conceit (I, ii, 284–96). The actors approached each
other as the prospect of poisoning Polixenes crawled into direct
speech out of the cup of innuendo (I, ii, 313–26). None of these
manoeuvres felt forced or distracting, since the actors motivated
their movements in response to cues in the text. Charged words
like 'business' and 'satisfy' prompt the actors to initiate new spatial
configurations while also knitting their exchange together through

repetition. Phil Thompson, a speech coach for the Utah Shake-speare Festival, explained to us that such switch words are 'action cues': as soon as Camillo hears the word 'business', he should take a sharp breath and prepare to speak. Whereas an inexperienced actor might respectfully wait until his partner has finished his line, it's closer to real conversation to begin responding as soon as the action cue has sounded. As Thompson put it, 'Think about inhalation as the wind-up before we throw a ball. That action is as necessary and natural a part of the action as the throwing.'[3] 'Business' and 'satisfy' are balls thrown by the actors to each other, and the dynamic distances that emerge between the speakers enhance the legibility and amplify the impact of the volley. Such mobile blockings of face-to-face conversation provide opportunities for frontal orientation without breaking the flow and intimacy of speech, and they help 'crystallize intentions and responses' by articulating words and actions in patterns that diagram the shifting relationship of the speakers.[4] These orchestrations of distances make sense of, and with, the text in a continuous mutual refocusing of meanings and motives.

Leontes comments on face-to-face communication as a form of heightened reflexive responsiveness to spontaneous changes in the aspect of the other:

> Good Camillo,
> Your changed complexions are to me a mirror
> Which shows me mine changed, too.
>
> (I, ii, 378–80)

He verbalises what usually goes without notice in daily speech, in which the face of our conversation partner acts as a mirror that prompts us to understand and refine our own performance. One way to understand Leontes's jealousy is as a result of his forgetting about the reciprocity of the face to face, instead finding in the frontality of the other a reflection and confirmation of what he takes to be 'certain', in the sense described by Stanley Cavell: such perspectives in ordinary language use 'take a claim to obviousness as a claim to certainty, and they take the claim to totality as a claim to exhaustiveness.'[5] In the beginning of *The Winter's Tale*, Leontes's claim to exhaustiveness occurs through his failure to acknowledge his own reciprocity in the imagined crime, breeding new duets and new confrontations. His accusations do not expose the face to face nor are they privations of it; rather, they contort and usurp it.

In other words, Leontes treats the face as static and absorptive rather than dynamic and reflective. The somatic and spatial contortions of the face – masquerading as retreats of the face – is particularly clear in Shakespearean ballet. Here the face appears as an articulation in itself, always on the cusp of but never crossing into verbal speech, and so relying forthrightly on the audience's active interpretation of gesture, prop, musical movement and pantomime.

In the Royal Ballet's production of *The Winter's Tale*, choreographed by Christopher Wheeldon, the dancer playing Leontes interrupts Hermione and Polixenes in a gesture of accusation (Figure I.2). Hermione and Polixenes face one another, while Leontes stands between them. But Leontes cannot face both characters at once, and Wheeldon emphasises this physical limitation. Leontes stands with his back to the audience, pointing a finger in either direction, his head turning to the left to face Polixenes, revealing a side profile of Leontes's face. The other half of his face remains hidden, presumably shadowed by the stage lighting, dramatising his own inevitable self-constitution through the theatrical faces and facings of others.

Figure I.2 *The Winter's Tale*: Federico Bonelli (Polixenes), Edward Watson (Leontes) and Lauren Cuthbertson (Hermione) at The Royal Ballet, at the Royal Opera House, London, UK, 9 April 2014 © Marilyn Kingwill/ArenaPAL.

This scene does not have an obvious correlative in the play. Instead it choreographs how jealousy takes the form of a false medium that Shakespeare represents in Leontes's rejections of Mamillius, Camillo and Paulina. Leontes does not connect the accused lovers in any simple way; he twists himself between them, crosses his arms to point at them, juts his neck, strains and contorts his face. 'Affection!', Leontes shouts at Mamillius, voicing in a word his shock at the procreative capacities of the human mind. His rant converges on the rich etymological relation between thought and sexual reproduction, playing on the maternity (*mammalis*) in Mammalius's name, the 'hardening of [Leontes's] brows' into cuckold horns, the 'possible' sexual affair between his wife and his friend turned 'very credent' and the mutual entanglement of the reproductive vocabulary of *conceit* with terms for copresence – 'communicat'st', 'coactive', 'co-join'.

> Thou dost make possible things not so held,
> Communicat'st with dreams – how can this be? –
> With what's unreal thou coactive art,
> And fellow'st nothing: then 'tis very credent
> Thou mayst co-join with something;
>
> (I, ii, 138–43)

Rebounding these linkages between the self and others in the mind's conceit, Wheeldon renders Leontes's accusations as projections not only of sexual betrayal but also of self-betrayal. The choreography reinforces the fact that in the theatre the face cannot merely be glimpsed but must turn towards the other and must be turned towards by the other.[6] As Leontes turns his waist, his shoulders and his head, and as the tail of his coat whips around in pursuit, his face enters a new duet, ironically giving itself to rather than retreating from the moral demand of the other. The momentum of the face in the theatre, as in ballet, is away from abstraction.

The face to face is not just about the interpersonal drama of one person facing down another but entails an original acceptance or rejection of reciprocity. In his lead essay for this volume, Bruce Smith cites art historian James Elkins: '"Speaking is like making ripples in a pool of water, and a face is like the wall that sends the ripples back," Elkins says. "If we speak forcefully, we send waves out toward the other face, and in a moment we can expect to feel the response. Faces move in this way even when they are not speaking."'[7] Sociologist Anthony Giddens, drawing on Irving Goffman, argues that co-presence involves a 'continuous reflexive monitoring of action which human beings display and expect others to display',[8] and he argues that 'modalities of co-presence, mediated directly by the body, are clearly different from social ties and forms of social interaction established with others absent in time or in space.'[9] James Thompson and Hans Ulricht Gumbrecht develop the idea of 'presence-effects' to capture the range of pre-semantic, rhythmic, affective, gestural, respiratory and other embodied aspects of face-to-face encounters that actors realise on stage.[10] Such presence-effects, we are suggesting, incorporate an elastic range of distances within them: this is the pregnant, pivotal space between 'I' and 'thou' and the indexical 'to' in the 'face-to-face'. These distances do not challenge the immediacy of co-presence by insisting, say, on the prison houses of language and subjectivity, but rather approach the composition of co-presence out of variable intensities and punctuating abruptions of thought and affect that issue in reaction, reflection and evaluation. In this volume, Kevin Curran demonstrates that the 'face of judgment' in *Measure for Measure* is 'part of a dynamic, dimensional process of knowledge-making and knowledge management', manifested in shifting spatial dispositions and the continual reorganisation of proximity, and Akihiko Shimizu shows how Renaissance decorum trained social actors to adjust their own behaviour in response to micro-changes in the aspects and comportments of others.

Such matters are not merely technical. To face, to circle, to point, to reflect, to listen, to turn, to attend, to adjust, to judge: these postures all imply plastic attitudes towards self, other and world that resonate with the larger philosophical questions raised by drama as an art form and by Shakespeare as a dramatic poet. The distances that open up within face-to-face interactions on Shakespeare's stage need be neither naturalistic nor defamiliarising; instead, they embody and conceptualise the shifting tactics, reflexive monitoring and ebb and flow of attention that belong to face-to-face communication. In confronting one another, actors elaborate their own knowledge of interpersonal relationships into a moving repertoire of presence-effects. Turning toward the audience, actors solicit everyone gathered in the theatre to draw on their own histories of interaction, from the conventions of etiquette ('little ethics') to the muscle memory, affective rush and cognitive alertness that accompany scenes of shame, distress, arousal, disgust, contempt, surprise, anger and fear.[11] How a scene manages the audience's self-conscious sensitivity to such affects is largely an effect of the audience's feeling of being seen themselves – through dramatic irony, theatricality, rhetorical and poetic form, and asides. Theatre incorporates the interactivity of everyday life while stylising those forms of encounter in a manner that renders them legible and memorable, inviting new evaluative, reflective and definitional work on the part of actors, viewers and readers. Such stylisation evokes pre-dramatic celebrations and rituals of co-presence, such as children's games, sportive fighting, social dancing, clowning, table fellowship, trials and hearings, street-corner ballading and parental benediction, as well as the interlocutory rhythms and performance disciplines of schooling, sermonising and catechism.[12] And in contemporary theatrical practice, such as the Schaubühne production of *Hamlet* analysed in this volume by W. B. Worthen, these pre-dramatic vocabularies feed post-dramatic repertoires of technological remediation, so that drama, which places faces at a distance, can incorporate cinematic close-ups through the use of projection.

The forms of intimacy, conflict, cognition and re-cognition that animate the choreography of co-presence are the matter of this collection. Drama is the art of co-presence par excellence, the only art form that convenes speaking beings in conversation and conflict with each other as its essential expressive medium.[13] Beckerman has demonstrated how classical drama composed its actions out of a series of duets, sometimes simple ones involving two characters alone on stage, as in the exchange between Leontes and Camillo, and sometimes complex ones in which the vector of dialogue shifts from one pair of actors on stage to another over the course of the scene, as when the dancer of Leontes interrupts the *pas de deux* of Hermione and Polixenes.[14] The duet is fraternal twin to the duel, each predicated on forms of cooperative competition that marry sport to music and warfare to love-making and the pursuit of acknowledgement. Face-to-face interactions on stage borrow from the scripts of everyday experience, but operate under very different conditions of visibility and audibility. Those conditions produce technical problems that in turn yield both inventive artistic solutions and new matter for thought. This collection addresses the duets and duels, the bed tricks and stool shticks, the blessings and curses, and the portraits and projections that bring actors face-to-face with each other and us on the Shakespearean stage and in scenes of reading.

Face-to-face in Shakespearean drama: three moments and one milieu

In the next few pages of this introduction, we sketch three exemplary kinds of face-to-face engagement, the duet of *falling in love*, the duel of *conflict and rivalry* and the rapprochement of *recognition and acknowledgement*, milestones of interaction in the unfolding of Shakespearean drama as an art of co-presence. The first foregrounds *proximity*, the second *distance*, and the third a special emulsion of the two, but all three work with distance and closeness as malleable measures that are constantly in play in face-to-face events. We end with a consideration of trust as the ambient milieu or affective climate cultivated by childhood play, attenuated and extended in the networks of dependency that make social life possible and elaborated by theatrical work as a cooperative enterprise.[15]

First encounters: Shakespeare's most exquisite and iconic dramatisation of an initial conversation between strangers occurs in *Romeo and Juliet*. The lovers' initial conversation at the Capulet ball unfolds not only face to face, but also palm to palm and lip to lip. Drawing on courtly dance, pilgrim's postures and the dialogic musicality of the sonnet, the lovers' exchange composes speech, touch, gaze, audition and taste into a symphony of meanings and motions, at once mystical and profane. In this volume, Lawrence Manley characterises the scene as a duet 'in a nearly musical sense', aglow with echolalia and echopraxia.[16] David Schalkwyk, in his new work on love and language in Shakespeare, emphasises the conversational and co-creative rhythm of the exchange: they 'forge a *dialogue* of embodied and requited love that moves beyond Petrarchan desire.'[17] That Romeo wears the half-mask of the carnival reveller increases the intensity by de-inhibiting the erotic performances of both players in the scene. A reference to the *commedia dell'arte* and its female actors, the half-mask suggests that the part being played may be more than professional, that the female or potentially feminised actor might feel real desire and with his or her words might express it. The mask activates a philosophy of theatrical desire, as Tzachi Zamir puts it, by paradoxically making Romeo anonymous while also overtly theatricalising the player's 'committed manifestation of the desire to be' Romeo, not hiding what's real but 'revealing hidden dimensions of the living process'.[18] On stage, half a face is not less of a face; instead, the mask becomes a tool for shaping co-presence and intensifying its impact and energy.[19] As a device of artificial concealment, Romeo's mask creates the opportunity for the ebb and flow of want and reception, desire and fulfilment. He expresses this consummation – both sacramental and sexual – as the performative answer to his own prayer: 'Then move not while my prayer's effect I take' (I, v, 102). The sonnet form also aurally introduces delay into this progress towards the kiss, and Juliet uses her parts of the song first to slow Romeo down, but ultimately to invite the action that replaces the metaphor: 'Saints do not move, though grant for prayers' sake' (101). Their duet stages the ecstasy of union, yet the measured sonnet they build together also leaves a margin for subjective freedom to be born in their exchange, as Paul Kottman has argued.[20]

Conflict and rivalry: Conflict moves us from the duet to the duel: the face-to-face combat, crystallised in the *aristeia* of the classical heroes. The *aristeia* discloses the hero's *arete* (virtue, excellence): not only his skill as a fighter, but his courageous affirmation of human freedom from necessity, expressed by his willingness to risk his life. According to Paul Kottman, in the duel from Homer to Hegel, 'one fights to prove one's humanity – and, by the same token, only in such an active demonstration does one come to have the standing (for oneself and for others) as human, as part of history.'[21] In Shakespeare, however, the duel is undone, displaced, extended and particularised: supplanted by bedtime assassination or poisoned foils (*Macbeth*, *Hamlet*); corroded by reflections and contextualisations that challenge honour as a value (*Henry IV*, *All's Well*); or relocated onto linguistic, legal, sexual or intergenerational scenarios that rewire the rules of engagement (*Shrew*, *Merchant of Venice*, *Othello*, *Lear*). In each case, the face-to-face combat of classical epic is also stretched and shaken, rendered freshly 'transforming and transformable, replayable, re-enactable, rethinkable'.[22]

Whereas falling in love begins from the standpoint of intimacy, conflict expresses distance, both psychological and physical. Warring parties often enter from different doors, as when fairy king greets fairy queen across the facade of the tiring house: 'Ill met by moonlight, proud Titania' (III, i, 6). Macduff, on the other hand, may chase Macbeth onto the stage from the same door, as he demands that Macbeth face him for their final combat: 'Turn, hell-hound, turn' (V, x, 4). Hand-to-hand or sword-to-sword combat, as we see at the beginning of *As You Like It* or the end of *Hamlet*, are forms of contact sport: conflict mobilises real and subjective distances in order to bridge them through both physical impact and acts of verbal and non-verbal mirroring, assessment, adjustment and recognition. Macduff's directive completes a half line of Macbeth's, conjoining the two characters through the verse form itself. In *The Taming of the Shrew* the great verbal match between Katherine and Petruccio in Act Two has the character of a game: competitive, yes, but also drawn out by the two players for the purpose of displaying and enjoying their skills as they take turns driving the jokes. Game theorist Eric Leifer discovered in his studies of chess masters that, contrary to the reigning wisdom, players do not always take the swiftest path to victory; instead, they often work to equalise the match in order to extend the interaction.[23] In this volume, Emily Shortslef reaches conclusions similar to those of Leifer in her analysis of Hamlet and Laertes' management of 'situational deficits or advantages of knowledge, skill or fault'. Fight choreography uses the skills of dance, tumbling and sport to create the appearance of violence, yet face-to-face fighting such as wrestling, fencing and swordsmanship also includes cooperative elements, formalised in the rules of the game and honour codes. Between faces in conflict, there is no strict divide between form and content, intention and constraint. On stage, the conflicts that appear most threatening and risky to the characters are those that require the most trust, timing and non-verbal communication on the part of the actors, as both Shortslef and Waldron explore in this volume. Put otherwise, the *distance* (in outlooks, family allegiances, resentment or accumulated grievance) expressed by conflict as an aversive relationship leverages surprising forms of *intimacy* handled at the level of touch, movement, gaze and linguistic play.

Rosalind and Orlando fall in love across a scene of wrestling, combining duel and duet in an exquisite form exemplary for much of Shakespearean drama: not only the sparring matches of warring lovers such as Katherine and Petruccio and Beatrice and Benedick, but the more Socratic exchange of Marina and Lysimachus in *Pericles*, or the self- and other-disclosing interview between Olivia and Viola in *Twelfth Night*, or the cagey, post-ironic love of Antony and Cleopatra.[24] Sanford Budick turns to Husserlian psychoanalyst Daniel Stern to gloss the chiastic rhythms that organise the contact improvisations of Rosalind and Orlando as both courtship and wrestling match:

> 'Each relational move and present moment', Stern says, 'is designed to express an intention relative to the inferred intention of the other. The two end up seeking, chasing, missing, finding, and shaping each other's intentionality.' Stern's account is striking but it lacks the peril entailed by this 'shaping of each other's intentionalities' when full responsibility for each other is a condition of such 'seeking'. Rosalind knows that the game of chasing after each other in which she engages with Orlando is fraught with multiple perils. It is perilous not only because the world does not kindly wait upon lovers taking their exploratory time and not only because the outcome of the game of reciprocal play-acting can easily be a bitter, all-devouring scepticism of the possibility of any love.[25]

Such perils, of course, are the matter of Desdemona's failed advocacy for Cassio in *Othello* or Hermione's coerced invitation to Polixenes in Act One of *The Winter's Tale*. In both cases, marital duets lead to martial law and 'the outcome of the game' is not the forgiveness exchanged by Hamlet and Laertes at the end of their duel, but 'a bitter, all-devouring scepticism' that threatens to decreate the world itself.[26]

Recognition and acknowledgement: If falling in love sometimes initiates the action of a play and if conflict often drives that action forward, many Shakespearean dramas end with moments of recognition that bring characters face to face with each other after a traumatic separation and temporal dilation (shipwreck in *The Comedy of Errors* and *Twelfth Night*; disinheritance and exile in *King Lear* and *The Tempest*; kidnapping in *Pericles* and *Cymbeline*). As Matthew James Smith discusses in this volume, such reunions rely on overtly theatrical devices, the rings and birthmarks that give romance *anagnorisis* its capricious character. Yet like Romeo's half-mask, the fortuitous occasions of recognition accentuate the faces that they mediate. In Shakespeare's plays, the restoration of a lost face requires more than mere reception of the other's reappearing; these reunions expose the fragility of the relation between the middle prepositional term in the face *to* face, or what William N. West calls in his Afterword 'not a catching-sight-of but a moment of address towards'.[27] According to many of the major accounts of the ethics of recognition by Kant, Hegel, Merleau-Ponty, Levinas, Honneth, Ricoeur and others, the identity and sometimes even the being of the self is tied to the presence of the other, interfaced through a kind of social proprioception: I feel myself when I feel you. Rather than championing one such philosophical explanation of this transaction as the key to co-presence, the essays in this volume work from the performances outward, testing explanations from Wittgenstein, Arendt, Levinas and Hegel as Shakespeare's plays create amenable conditions for them.

Although recognition implies mutuality and has become identical with the ideal of formal equality in post-Kantian ethics, many scenes of recognition, especially when coupled with acts of benediction, pardon or forgiveness, incorporate words and gestures of supplication in which one person consciously lowers himself in response to another, rendering tangible the asymmetry between them. The child kneels for the parent's blessing, while the transgressor faces the injured party or officiating judge but lowers his gaze, head or body.[28] The recognition scene between Lear and Cordelia combines both gestures in an affective choreography of mutual supplication. Lear lowers himself because of his paternal failures, Cordelia because of the inefficacy of her filial love. Leontes wants to burn the infant Perdita alive in order precisely to avoid such a scene: 'Shall I live on, to see this bastard kneel / And call me father? Better burn it now / Than curse it then' (II, iii, 153–5). Here and elsewhere, Shakespeare builds the infinitely deep ethical, legal and theological scripts of forgiveness upon the simplest bodily comportments.

Why do some recognition scenes end in the warm embrace and verbal acknowledgement of parents, children or lovers while in others touch is either deferred (Viola and Sebastian) or takes the form of a push or shove (Posthumus and Innogen; Pericles and Marina) or allows for touch but not speech (Leontes and Hermione)?[29] These are questions for actors and for readers, which in turn become questions for us as agents in our own scenes of reconciliation and return. We had an opportunity to read the end of *The Winter's Tale* with two pioneering social workers in the open adoption movement, who shared that reunions between adult adopted children and their birth parents are often fraught with overwhelming experiences of erotic confusion, the upswell of resentment and a sense of haunting by the ghosts of absent persons and missed experiences: Shakespearean through and through.[30]

The very phrase 'face-to-face' measures a distance – the ethico-symbolic distance between persons – within the conversational closeness that allows personhood to be recognised and cultivated. That distance is constituent of compassion. Martha Nussbaum differentiates between compassion and empathy, comparing a claim to empathy to 'the mental preparation of a skilled (Method) actor'. Many of Shakespeare's most powerful scenes of face-to-face encounter not only restore co-presence between characters but brim with a desire to witness their compassion for one another, an acknowledgement of the other's suffering and a sharing of her passion. Yet just as such anagnoritic reunions garner their power from former scenes of loss and confusion, so does the compassion of coming together require a certain distance, not of empathetically feeling *within* another but of feeling *with* another. In Nussbaum's judgement, 'If one really had the experience of feeling the pain [of another] in one's own body, then one would precisely have failed to comprehend the pain of another *as other*.'[31]

The distance within the face to face measured by acts of recognition is linked to the virtues of respect, dignity and reverence, attitudes that incorporate bodily, affective and cognitive orientations towards the subjective autonomy and mysterious excess of others into their scripts of approach and withdrawal.[32] Hannah Arendt contrasts respect and love: 'What love is in its own, narrowly circumscribed sphere, respect is in the larger domain of human affairs. Respect, not unlike the Aristotelian *philia politikē*, is a kind of "friendship" without intimacy and without closeness; it is a regard for the person from the distance which the space of the world puts between us.'[33] Whereas Romeo and Juliet's love duet composes intimacy out of mask, game and dance, the respect that might be exchanged by the Duke and Isabella at the end of *Measure for Measure*, by Hermione and Leontes at the close of *The Winter's Tale* or by Caliban and Prospero at the edges of *The Tempest* demands a very different kind of face-to-face encounter, one chastened by an accounting of failures and uneasily keyed to the mystery of other souls.

Trust in theatre: Philosophers, psychologists and sociologists of trust emphasise the genesis of trust in early childhood experiences, when babies and toddlers learn to tolerate the absence of a caregiver through the use of symbolising tools such as security blankets, teddy bears and simple games like peekaboo and hide and seek. Philosopher Jay Bernstein describes trust as 'radiating out from the body as our original vulnerability to others' and tending to 'be implicit, casually spread out (like an atmosphere or mood)' (2015: 226–7). Philosopher Sverre Raffnsøe emphasises the gift character of trust: when we delegate a task or act on a recommendation, both partners extend their capacities.[34] Trust takes root in the deep co-presence of pregnancy, feeding and rocking, and mixes it with what we might call *co-absence*: a cooperative sojourning that tolerates uncertainty and accepts risk as the condition of action. In a trusting relationship, I cannot know what you are thinking, but I trust that your intentions are good, and I may not know where you are or what you are doing, but I trust that you are pursuing our common projects. In such examples, trust not only differentiates itself from knowledge, but one's use of knowledge is also reframed by an experience of trust, as one rethinks what it means to subject another person to the risks of one's own knowledge claims. Without trust the world is harsh and lonely, and each person's reach and capacities are severely truncated; trust involves letting others go in order to be and do more, a lesson hard won by Posthumus and Leontes and realised by Othello only when his actions have allowed chaos to come again.

Shakespeare often presents the face as a deceptive mask that hides bad intentions within, leading to scenes of conscious physiognomic reading so hermeneutically heightened that Shakespeare is often led to compare the face to a book, whether open or closed.[35] In their exchange before the banquet scene, Lady Macbeth advises Macbeth to present a pleasing aspect to their company: 'Sleek o'er your rugged looks, / be bright and jovial / Among your guests tonight' (III, ii, 29–30). As the two proceed to talk around the matter of Banquo's murder, the trust that remains within the marriage offers a strangely tender under-song to the distrust they have unleashed in the state of Scotland. Macbeth's references to the thickening ambient light, his loving pet name ('dearest chuck'), the lullaby-like character of his lyric flights and his desire to protect Lady Macbeth from specific knowledge of the deed, all communicate a trust between the couple that flows beneath and around the overt theatricality introduced by the metaphor of the mask.[36] In the Trevor Nunn video of 1978, based on the 1976 production at The Other Place, Ian McKellen whispers the sounds of bat and beetle into the ear of Judi Dench, at once comforting and chilling her. In their dialogue, the hard bright mask of dissimulation is supplemented by aural and haptic assurances that Dench and McKellen, climatologists of trust, brilliantly communicate through the hushed play of their pressed bodies and turned faces. 'Presence effects' oscillate with 'meaning effects', to use the parlance of James Thompson and Hans Ulricht Gumbrecht.[37] The result is the hatching of an uncanny climate of trust, an atmosphere of soothed nerves and tender mercies knit around a fundamental tear in the social fabric.

The rogue Autolycus's sardonic commentary in *The Winter's Tale*, 'What a fool honesty is, and trust – his sworn brother – a very simple fellow' (IV, iv, 574–5), should not be taken as Shakespeare's last word on trust. If the Shepherd is the honest fool and his son the Clown the very simple fellow, their pursuit of 'charity' and a 'good deed' at the sea's margin (III, iii, 97, 114) bespeaks a world in which trust is a fragile commodity requiring acts of courage and a generous judgement. Trust belongs in a fundamental way to the practices of theatre. Sustained by the cooperative co-presence of the actors in the specialised environment of the stage, theatre engages the acting ensemble, the audience and the performance setting in feedback loops of laughter, attention, suspense and emotional mirroring. In no way is the reciprocation of trust inevitable. In fact, it is a theme of the face to face in Shakespearean drama that the closer, more exposed and more recognisable one is, the less determined the relation to the other will be. Consider the facelessness of the bed trick in *Measure for Measure*, as Devin Byker discusses in this volume, or the reduction of Innogen into Giacomo's report of an intimate mole as Matthew Smith discusses. These elaborate omissions of face-to-face interaction result in a new and terrible determinacy of events – a forced marriage in the one case and a murder plot in the other. Trust is thus a principal component of the face to face as a virtue that positions free will as the prepositional medium of mutual risk and reception.

The full-frontal love of Romeo and Juliet is direct, immediate and ecstatic, yet composed of inherited routines of social interaction and enhanced by the presence of the half-mask and the artful orchestration of delay. The duel between Hamlet and Laertes is a fight to the death, but also a choreography of handicaps that extend the contest to allow for recognition and forgiveness (Shortslef). The respect that remarries Hermione and Leontes 'as over a vast' and 'as it were from the ends of opposed winds' acknowledges their deep history of love and attachment but refuses to disavow the losses and misprisions that have led to their divorce and the scattering of their family. Warmer than respect but less absolute than love, the *trust* that Caliban extends to Trinculo and Stephano when he first encounters them is misplaced and potentially endangering, yet it is also required if they are to become 'strange bedfellows' in a brave new political project. Love, rivalry, respect and trust are forms of co-presence that combine bodily, affective and cognitive capacities in uniquely human, and distinctively dramatic, ensembles. They are among the many forms of face-to-face interaction that Shakespeare explores in his dramas.

This book: orienting goals, virtuous properties and the order of essays

From these brief readings (there are many more ahead), we hope that several key propositions have emerged. First, our subject matter, *face to face in Shakespeare*, does not involve the face alone or abstracted; our focus, rather, is on the dynamism of the face to face, an improvisational composition always ripe with movement and consequence. The face taken by itself can trigger narcissistic, idolatrous and imaginary forms of identification, as emblematised today by emoji, Instagram, Facebook and the newly termed condition of 'selfitis' and the celebrity portrait. The interpersonal and contingent character of the face to face as a moment in real time and space, on the other hand, concerns what Arendt called 'the web of human relationships' which originates in moments of co-presence and cultivates forms of listening, attention and improvised response that draw on multiple forms of perception and cognition, including sound, touch, smell, movement and proprioceptive adjustments to changes in other persons and the environment.

Second, we aim to read philosophy and performance in a continuum. What happens when a character on stage turns to face another? This usually indicates an interaction *to come*, a sign that points to what we expect to appear in dialogue or paraphrasable action. Yet a dramatised face-to-face encounter is not only a medium for scripted conversation but also a form of philosophical content in and of itself. With or without words, face-to-face encounters can initiate love affairs, demand acknowledgement, deliver or refuse a gift, request forgiveness, offer obsequy, spawn rivalry, witness crime or trigger shame. In each of these instances, facing another person is an embodied, spatially situated and transactional event involving gesture and posture, orientation and disposition, evaluation and adjustment. Flattery, disguise and dissimulation test the plastic properties of facial encounters in ways that bear directly on theatre as a medium. The art and style of facing empowers the give and take of conversation, the affront of argument and the miracle of the kiss, and is essential to the action of drama. In the age of the smart phone and news incrementally published on social media, understanding the special dynamism and essential elements of face-to-face exchange, including its mutations, migrations and disavowals, is a matter of new interest and urgency, in the contexts of both university instruction and contemporary social life.

Third, we aim to avoid opposing distance and proximity, and surface and depth, instead seeking the ways in which the face-to-face encounter unfolds across these divides and integrates them into moving composites of relationality and rationality, embodiment and exchange. At stake in all scenes of face-to-face encounter, from the lightning rush of first love to the travails of reunion, redress and repair, is the fragile, shifting balance between immediacy and reserve, intimacy and distance, freedom and dependency, that all relationships after earliest infancy require. Devin Byker cites Toril Moi on Wittgenstein, who wants us to 'stop thinking of the body as something that hides the soul, and to make us realize that the body is expressive of soul, which means that it is expressive also of our attempts to hide, disguise, or mask our feelings and reactions.'[38] The face is *not* a mask, at least not in the reductive sense that the image usually carries: most adults are equipped to sense when someone is lying, and actors learn to express and communicate such signals to their audiences and fellow actors.

We also want to avoid identifying face-to-face encounters exclusively with vision and sight. Avoiding the gaze of the other usually signals an ethical failure: when Hermione demands that Leontes 'behold' her in court, directors often infer that he has turned his back on her and must be called to account. Yet face-to-face encounters need not enlist the gaze at all. When Gloucester blesses Edgar at the edge of the imaginary Dover Cliff, his blind benediction dramatises the vulnerability of human actors in an ecology of mutual dependencies. Shakespeare's bed tricks are unusual examples of faceless co-presence, as Devin Byker describes them in this volume. Isabella refers to the bed trick with Angelo as a 'repair i'the dark' (IV, i, 40): to repair is to journey, return or resort to a place (*OED*, v^1 1), but also to mend, fix or restore a damaged thing (*OED*, v^2 1). To attempt a repair in the dark is to undergo a certain blindness, take a moral risk, tap the other senses and accept subjective undoing as the basis of renewal. In his account of 'dorsality' or the backward turn, David Wills pushes Levinas into motion – into forms of turning away that isolate the special asymmetry of the face-to-back.[39] When Lear curses Goneril with sterility, or when Hal in the person of his father promises to banish old Jack Falstaff, the receivers of these verbal assaults often face the audience rather than their accusers.[40] Saying such things face-to-face would be much harder than addressing the back of one's interlocuter (or sending a text message). Yet say these things friends and fathers do, and 'opening up' the dialogue into a frontal presentation allows the faces of Falstaff and Goneril to reveal the impact of speech on their persons in a manner that is central to the plays' investigation of speech-acts.[41]

Philosophies of the face to face can be understood on a spectrum ranging from the phenomena of one's own eidetic reduction, at the one end, to the objective and infinite demand of the bare presence of the other, at the other end. A Husserlian approach, for example, attempts to learn about the other by varying perceptual and imaginative orientations toward it and thus by forming empathy with the other. The other is potentially a stranger but through intersubjective reflection appears also as an alter ego – I may be an apperception of hers just as she is one for me. We can position Levinas on the opposite end of this spectrum. Levinas holds that the other's being-there produces an ethical demand that precedes any internal reflection that leads to viewing the other as an alter ego; in the horror of the infinite other, as Stephen Shankman describes it, 'the subject is stripped of his subjectivity, of his power to have private existence'.[42] The face of the other is an affective 'interruption', showing the subject that its own thoughts and even its being proceed from the initial ethical fact of the other.[43] Each position – the phenomenological and the ethical – involves a distance and asymmetry between the self and the other and also an attempt to use face-to-face encounters in order to hold unique persons accountable to the moral demand of the other. Ricoeur observes that these two poles mirror one another in their attempt to account for the opposite perspective: 'Whether one starts from the pole of the ego or the pole of the other, in each case it is a question of comparing incomparables and hence of equalizing them.'[44] How to accomplish this ethical bridging without compromising the integrity of one's respective starting point – the self or the other – has been the challenge of such philosophy.

The essays here land at varying points on this face-to-face spectrum and for the most part declare no strict allegiance. This is because their readings are to a significant extent *about* the spectrum itself, the various conflicts involved in differentiating between faces and yet holding them answerable to one another. Theatre, in this way, is 'the occasion for . . . the comparison between incomparables'.[45] Shakespeare's characters themselves sometimes seem conscious of their roles in testing moral parameters with one another for the sake of each other. In drama, faces always appear as facings, shaped by the rift between the other as absolute or as alter ego, energised and often distorted by the effort to detect the other's willingness to move forward together. Shakespeare's faces undulate toward and away from one another, pulling tension and giving slack depending on the particular affect of a scene. Theatrical faces emerge within the conditions of plot, stage technology, emotion, occasion, grammar and ecology. And so even when an actor's face is unadorned, its countenance is always like that of a half-mask, never simply representing itself but continuously giving and rescinding what it purports to cover. 'The face is not a *simulacrum*, in the sense that it is something dissimulating or hiding the truth: the face is the *simultas*, the being-together of manifold visages constituting it.'[46] In short, the face to face is never only first-personal; it manifests within acts of desire, trust, suspicion and judgement, and one of this volume's aims is to explicate the ways that theatre reports such often idealised phenomena as interfaces of society and ethics.

If drama is largely composed out of dialogue, what in theatre is *not* a face-to-face encounter? We would submit that to qualify as a face-to-face moment, an interaction should:

1. Unfold between two persons or parties at a time, even if more are present.
2. Raise questions or prompt reflection on the quality and nature of the interaction.

3. Touch on something fundamental in human relationships.
4. Advance the plot or reveal something substantial about the affective relations among characters.
5. Refuse to sublimate its personnel and their faces to an idea, institution or single theory.

This is not an absolute or exclusive list of properties, but it describes the cases convened in this book. The emphasis of our authors is on human interaction. Although Jennifer Waldron takes up the face-to-face communion with God imagined by St Paul as the time of apocalypse, a spectre that emerges with paranoiac force when human trust has been violated, she would likely agree with William West that 'Shakespeare lets us look through a glass darkly, but has the advantage of really showing us that dark glass, really letting us examine it, rather than waiting for the differently conceived otherworldliness of either Paul or Levinas.'[47] Both Waldron and Worthen introduce questions of technology into the apparent directness of face-to-face communication. Our authors are theoretical pluralists as well as practising humanists. Influenced especially by the work of Emmanuel Levinas, volumes such as *Shakespeare and the Power of the Face* and *Of Levinas and Shakespeare* have treated Shakespearean drama as an art form that makes special use of the human face's ability to capture, affect and obligate beholders.[48] And yet to apply Levinas to theatre is necessarily to move beyond Levinas, beyond imagining the infinite demand of the other in the appearance of the face, and to re-instantiate the troubled subject, the ego.[49] Is there a first philosophy in theatre, an event that precedes genre and plot, the emotions and rationalities created by actors and characters, between persons in acts of desire, exclusion, aggression and invitation? The theatrical face, in short, is always foremost a product of the conjunctional and prepositional movements of faces *to* faces. Early modern drama, in particular, wavers 'between a belief in the ability to witness identity in the face and an acknowledgement of the face's inability to convey eternal truths'.[50] Drama scholars have also turned to Hannah Arendt's political phenomenology, which places self-disclosing speech in the presence of others at the heart of political and dramatic action.[51] Theatre research in proxemics, contact improvisation, trust exercises and embodied cognition intersect in productive ways with the phenomenology of Merleau-Ponty and the ordinary language philosophy of Ludwig Wittgenstein, J. L. Austin and Stanley Cavell. Recent studies on the soliloquies of characters like Hamlet have acknowledged the determining presence of the audience and the remarkable performativity of this most private form of monologue.[52] Even soliloquy, we find, appears among faces facing one another. This volume investigates how a spatial configuration of persons that might ordinarily be considered a mere support for communication becomes – in theatre – weighted with the essential content of human relationships. Our broadly phenomenological perspective addresses theatre as an environment that uses spaces, bodies and immanent social conditions to create a heightened awareness of other persons.

Part I, 'Foundational Face Work', establishes key terms and approaches for the study of dramatic proximity in Shakespeare. In 'Outface and Interface'. Bruce R. Smith takes up 'face' as verb rather than noun in order to disclose the active and interactive character of facing in Shakespeare – to face, outface, interface, efface, deface, sur-face. Larry Manley traces the evolution of the love duet in Shakespeare from its early form, 'the unchaperoned duet', in which the absence of witnesses encourages intimate exchange, to the more sophisticated 'occulted duet' in which inhibiting factors such as separation or the presence of bystanders reshape the nature of exchange between romantic partners. In 'The Course of Recognition in *Cymbeline*', Matthew James Smith compares and differentiates the overlapping face-to-face concepts of classical *anagnorisis* and modern *Anerkennung* or mutual recognition. He argues that the final return to the caprice of *anagnorisis* in the recognition scene of *Cymbeline* re-emphasises the middle term in the face *to* face for establishing moral norms after a society has undergone self-inflicted suffering.

Part II, 'Composing Intimacy and Conflict', looks at iconic scenes in Shakespearean drama where proximity becomes problem. In 'Face to Face, Hand to Hand: Relations of Exchange in *Hamlet*', Emily Shortslef turns to the scenes in which Hamlet and Laertes face and outface each other. Shortslef focuses on the ethical dimensions of stage fighting, which builds on the collaborative give-and-take of dance. In 'Bed Tricks and Fantasies of Facelessness'. Devin Byker shows how one of Renaissance drama's most artificial dramatic devices, the bed-trick, revolves around an aversion to facing one's partner, a paradigm he extends from the sexual instances staged in *Measure for Measure* and *All's Well That Ends Well* to the bedtime murder of Duncan in *Macbeth*.

Part III, 'Facing Judgement', looks at scenes of divine and human judgement as moments of face-to-face encounter. In 'The Face of Judgement in *Measure for Measure*', Kevin Curran shows how the spatial and revelatory dynamics of facing one's accuser, unmasking one's victim and standing before the law in the presence of witnesses gives judgement its dramatic energy and theatrical character. In 'Then

Face to Face: Timing Trust in *Macbeth*', Jennifer Waldron explores the interferences among the personal trust networks of hospitality, the face-to-face with God promised by apocalypse, and the theatrical trust required by trust falls and slapstick.

Part IV, 'Moving Pictures', looks at the face as image – from sacred icon to profane cosmetics to media projection – within the three-dimensional dynamics of Shakespearean theatre. In 'The Man of Sorrows: Edgar's Disguise and Dürer's Self-portraits', Hanna Scolnicov takes up one of art history's most iconic faces, the Man of Sorrows, in order to draw compelling comparisons between Shakespeare's Edgar and Dürer's self-portrait. In 'The Face as Rhetorical Self in Ben Jonson's Literature', Akihiko Shimizu argues that Jonson's characters are not 'flat' so much as transactional and performative, presented self-consciously to others through face-painting (another form of icon-making) or rhetorical self-amplification. Finally, in 'Hamlet's Face', W. B. Worthen turns to the role of technology in contemporary theatre, in which projected images mix with and separate from acting, speaking bodies to create new ethical complexes.

Will West's Afterword concludes this collection by elaborating on the Pauline theme of seeing through a glass darkly: 'but then shall we see face to face.' Paul's statement is deeply dramatic, West suggests. It implicates the actor, character and audience member in dual acts of searching and anticipating, working towards a discovery of the other in fuller clarity and preparing for this event as an epiphany. In a sense, Levinas serves as just such a dark glass. At the risk of abstraction, he focalises ideas of being and epistemology into the infinity of the other's face. And the face-to-face in Shakespeare criticism, West suggests, both follows and resists Levinas by retethering the face to its theatrical turns and affronts, ultimately dwelling in a double mind about what the 'first philosophy' really is.

Together, the essays that comprise *Face to Face in Shakespearean Drama* investigate the physicality and theatricality of persons as they appear to each other in moments of co-presence. These essays also challenge the appearance–reality binary sometimes implied in interpretations of the face by refusing to stabilise the face as such, instead restoring human phenomena like sympathy, trust, risk and rebuke to their found states of reverberant exchange. These essays argue that the performative and phenomenologically demanding frames of drama test the meanings and affordances of the face-to-face in order to offer varieties of co-presence up for judgement and redeployment in the theatre of life. That was a very long wind-up for our pitch. Let the game begin! We hope the business is satisfying.

Notes

1. New Swan Shakespeare Festival, Summer 2018, University of California, Irvine.
2. Bernard Beckerman, *Theatrical Presentation: Performer, Audience, Act*, p. 132.
3. Phil Thompson, personal communication, Utah Shakespeare Festival, June 2018.
4. Beckerman, *Theatrical Presentation*, p. 132.
5. Stanley Cavell, *Disowning Knowledge: In Seven Plays by Shakespeare*, p. 83.
6. David Wills refers to this as a 'dorsal turn', where 'The Other doesn't appear in front of me, facing me, so much as turn or incline itself toward me, summoning me as responsible from outside my consciousness or perception', *Dorsality: Thinking Back through Technology and Politics*, p. 45.
7. Bruce R. Smith, citing James Elkins, *The Object Stares Back: On the Nature of Seeing*, p. 107.
8. Anthony Giddens, *Constitution of Society*, p. 3.
9. *Constitution of Society*, p. xxv.
10. On presence-effects, see James Thompson, *Performance Affects: Applied Theatre and the End of Effect*, p. 121. Thompson is drawing on Hans Ulrich Gumbrecht, *Production of Presence: What Meaning Cannot Convey*.
11. This list is based on Sylvan Tompkin's core affects: the three positive affects of interest, enjoyment and surprise; and the six negative affects of fear, anger, distress, shame, contempt and disgust. *Exploring Affect: The Selected Writings of Silvan S. Tomkins*. See also Paul Ekman (ed.), *Emotion in the Human Face* for a classic empirical study of the judgement of emotions.
12. See Matthew James Smith, *Performance and Religion in Early Modern England: Stage, Cathedral, Wagon, Street*; Erika T. Lin, *Shakespeare and the Materiality of Performance*; and Henry S. Turner (ed.), *Early Modern Theatricality*.
13. See Paul Kottman, 'Duel', on drama as the mimesis of the action of speaking beings. In Henry S. Turner (ed.), *Early Modern Theatricality*, pp. 402–22. We are speaking here of the classical drama of the West and not of other post-dramatic or non-mimetic traditions.
14. For an application of Beckerman's argument, see the essay by Lawrence Manley in this volume.
15. Julia Reinhard Lupton, 'Trust in Theater'.
16. Lawrence Manley, this volume.
17. David Schalkwyck, *Love and Language in Shakespeare*, p. 203.
18. Tzachi Zamir, *Acts: Theater, Philosophy, and the Performing Self*, p. 218.

19. Eli Simon, *Masking Unmasked: Four Approaches to Basic Acting*, pp. 139–41.
20. Paul A. Kottman, *Love as Human Freedom*, pp. 60–70.
21. Kottman, 'Duel', p. 414.
22. Kottman, 'Duel', p. 420.
23. Leifer argues, 'Skill and equality are thoroughly interdependent. While rationality produces disengagement, skill fuels involvement by sustaining equality.' *Actors as Observers: A Theory of Skill in Social Relationships*, p. 7. Russel Bodi applies Leifer's theory to street-fighting in *Romeo and Juliet*, 'Lessons from a Street-fighter: Reconsidering *Romeo and Juliet*'.
24. On the wilful suspension of doubt and ambivalence by the mature lovers Antony and Cleopatra, see Tzachi Zamir, *Double Vision: Moral Philosophy and Shakespearean Drama*, pp. 131–41.
25. Sanford Budick, 'Wrestling, Death and Intersubjectivity in *As You Like It*' (unpublished manuscript, cited courtesy of the author); citing Daniel Stern, *The Present Moment in Psychotherapy and Everyday Life*, p. 146.
26. On scepticism in Shakespeare, see the work of Stanley Cavell, especially *Disowning Knowledge*.
27. William H. West, 'Theater and Speculation'.
28. See Sarah Beckwith, *Shakespeare and the Grammar of Forgiveness*, and Leah Wittington, *Renaissance Suppliants: Poetry, Antiquity, Reconciliation*.
29. Yu Jin Ko, 'The Comic Close of *Twelfth Night* and Viola's *Noli me Tangere*'.
30. Sharon Kaplan Roszia and Deborah N. Silverstein and, Laguna Woods, California, May 2017. Silverstein and Roszia are authors of the 1982 article 'Seven Core Issues in Adoption', distributed on many adoption websites and published as 'Adoptees and the Seven Core Issues of Adoption', *Adoptive Families* 32 (1999): 8–13. See also Julia Reinhard Lupton, 'Shakespeare's Social Work: From Displacement to Placement in *Twelfth Night*',
31. Martha Nussbaum, *Upheavals of Thought*, pp. 327–8.
32. On reverence, see Paul Woodruff, *Reverence: Renewing a Forgotten Virtue*. On dignity, see *Dignity: A History*, ed. Remy Debes, especially Patrice Rankine, 'Dignity in Homer and Classical Greece', pp. 19–46. Rankine's central example is the face-to-face encounter between Achilles and Priam at the end of the *Iliad*. On respect for the alterity of persons in the romances, see Donald Wehrs, 'Ethical Ambiguity of the Maternal in Shakespeare's First Romances'.
33. Arendt, *The Human Condition*, p. 243.
34. Sverre Raffnsøe, 'Beyond Rule: Trust and Power as Capacities'.
35. On the face as book in Shakespeare, see Sibylle Baumbach, '"Thy face is mine": Faces and Fascination in Shakespeare's Plays', p. 19.

36. Masks in practice, as we noted above, actually function very differently; in performance, masks help actors with 'specifying moments, pursuing objectives, articulating actions, listening and responding, and freeing creative impulses', Eli Simon, *Masking Unmasked*, ix. For an example of the mask's de-inhibiting effects in Shakespearean drama, see Bottom's translation.
37. Thompson, p. 121; Gumbrecht, p. 108.
38. Cited by Byker, this volume.
39. Wills, *Dorsality*, 46.
40. *Henry IV*, directed by Daniel Sullivan, Tom Hanks as Falstaff, Harry Groener as Hal, Shakespeare Center LA, June 2018.
41. On the performative theology of curses in *King Lear*, see Björn Quiring, *Shakespeare's Curse: The Aporias of Ritual Exclusion in Early Modern Royal Drama*.
42. *Of Levinas and Shakespeare*, p. 172.
43. On the Saying and the Said, Levinas writes: 'For the saying is both an affirmation and a retraction of the said. The reduction could not be effected simply by parentheses which, on the contrary, are an effect of writing. It is the ethical interruption of essence that energizes the reduction.' *Otherwise than Being or Beyond Essence*, p. 44.
44. Ricoeur, *Course of Recognition*, p. 161.
45. Ricoeur, *Course of Recognition*, p. 161.
46. Giorgio Agamben, *Means without End: Notes on Politics*, p. 98.
47. William N. West, 'Afterword', this volume. For more on facing God, see Maurice Hunt, *The Divine Face in Four Writers: Shakespeare, Dostoevsky, Hesse, and C. S. Lewis*.
48. James A. Knapp (ed.), *Shakespeare and the Power of the Face*; Moshe Gold, Sandor Goodhart and Kent Lehnhof (eds), *Of Levinas and Shakespeare: 'To See Another Thus'*.
49. *Of Levinas and Shakespeare* (Gold et al.) addresses the problem through the ambiguity of the preposition 'of' in Levinas's statement in *Time and the Other* that 'The whole of philosophy is only a meditation of Shakespeare'. Levinas and Shakespeare share what several essays in that volume describe as a midrash relation. *Of Levinas and Shakespeare*, p. 1.
50. Knapp (ed.), *Shakespeare and the Power of the Face*, p. 2.
51. Julia Reinhard Lupton, *Thinking with Shakespeare: Essays on Politics and Life*.
52. Brian Cummings, *Mortal Thoughts: Religion, Secularity and Identity in Shakespeare and Early Modern Culture*, p. 173; David Schalkwyk, *Speech and Performance in Shakespeare's Sonnets and Plays*, p. 106.

Part I

Foundational Face Work

Chapter 1

Outface and Interface

Bruce R. Smith

Lacking Madame Toussaud's waxworks (it didn't open until 1835), Shakespeare's London offered two places for face-to-face encounters with personages from the past. One was the long gallery of Whitehall Palace, hung with painted portraits of English monarchs and foreign potentates, interspersed with a few depictions of battles and scenes from classical history and mythology. The other place for face-to-face encounters with historical personages was the theatre. Thomas Platter, visiting in 1599, saw both places. Some idea of the space Platter visited in Whitehall Palace (the edifice was demolished in 1698) can be witnessed today in the Long Gallery at Hardwick Hall, Derbyshire, which happens to be furnished with many of the paintings catalogued in an early seventeenth-century inventory (Figure 1.1).[1] Platter locates his encounter with one Whitehall picture in particular 'in the long hall' (*im langen saal*).[2] As for the theatres where Platter took in performances, the reconstructed Shakespeare's Globe in London lets us not only see a similar space but move around in it.

Just one of the pictures in the Whitehall long gallery is singled out by Platter in his travel journal: 'a face [*angesicht*, literally 'on-face' or perhaps 'at-face'] painted with very artfully lengthened perspective, a copper engraving of which I took back with me to Basle'.[3] (The German idiom for 'face to face' is *von Angesicht zu Angesicht*.) From the long room Platter moved on to 'the queen's library, in which there were many books in Latin that she had written out cleanly in her own hand. For besides Latin she can speak well French, Italian, and Spanish.'[4] Perhaps because he had just seen at least two portraits of Elizabeth in the long gallery – other visitors testify to their existence even though Platter doesn't mention them – he reads the library as synecdoche for a personage behind, or perhaps within, the books that were shown to him. That synecdoche he finds in Elizabeth's writing hand and in her polyglot tongue. One thinks of the ears and

Figure 1.1 Hardwick Hall, Derbyshire, the Long Gallery, built 1590–7.
Source: © National Trust Images/Andreas von Einsiedel.

eyes on Elizabeth's gown in Isaac Oliver's rainbow portrait in the 1611 Marble Hall at Hatfield House, Hertfordshire.[5] In his juxtaposition of picture gallery and library Platter establishes a connection between paintings and books that will concern us towards the end of this chapter.

Two hundred words later in his journal, after his notes on the Whitehall gallery and library, Platter recollects his two visits to London theatres: one to 'the thatch-roofed house on the South Bank', where he saw a production of *Julius Caesar* (almost certainly Shakespeare's, which had just been added to the company's repertory) and one to a theatre outside Bishopsgate (likely the Curtain in Shoreditch), where he enjoyed a raucous comedy and paid close attention to views from different spots in the theatre. The theatres are so constructed, Platter notes, that the actors play on a raised platform (Platter calls it a *bruge*, or bridge), and everyone can see everything well. There are also, however, 'different gangways and levels [*gäng unndt stände*]' where one can pay a little more, sit down, and get a 'jollier' (*lustiger*) view. From the 'jolliest place' (*am lustigesten ort*) – perhaps an arcaded gallery above the stage platform as shown in the Swan drawing, perhaps stools set out on the platform itself) – 'one not only sees everything well, but

can also be seen.'⁶ People in those jolly locations found themselves
face to face with the rest of the spectators as well as with the actors,
at least when the actors turned around or to the side.

For Platter both the Whitehall long gallery and the public theatres were viewing-places. *Théatron* in ancient Greek, like *theatrum*
in Latin, literally means that: 'a place for viewing'.⁷ What Platter saw
in the Whitehall long room was not a portrait (*Bildness* or *Portrait*
would be the expected term in modern German) but a face (*angesicht*). At the Curtain as well it was faces he attended to, at least the
eyes in faces. The difference between the two venues seems to turn
on who is doing the moving about: the spectators (in the Whitehall long room) or the actors (on the theatre's raised platform). If
Gina Bloom is right about early modern theatre-going as competitive game-playing, spectators at the Globe, the Curtain and the Rose
may have been quite mobile as they jockeyed for what Platter calls
'jolly' viewing spots.⁸ In early modern English the root meaning of
the word *gallery* was 'a covered space for walking in'. *Gallery* in the
sense of 'a platform, supported by columns or brackets, projecting
from the interior wall of a building, and serving e.g. to provide additional room for an audience' is an eighteenth-century idiom.⁹ Long
galleries were spaces for taking walks in bad weather as well as for
hanging painted panels, mirrors and tapestries – items that might be
regarded as amusements for passing walkers. Picture gallery, library,
theatre: Platter's itinerary lays out three interconnected venues for
face-to-face encounters in late-sixteenth-century London.

The 'face painted with very artfully lengthened perspective'
mentioned by Platter is described in more detail by a visitor to the
Whitehall long gallery the next year, Paul Hentzner, who was touring
Germany, France, England and Italy as tutor to the young Silesian
nobleman Christoph von Rehdiger. Perhaps befitting his role as a
tutor, Hentzner in his published *Itinerarium* pays more attention than
Platter does to the other portraits he passes in the Whitehall gallery –
'Queen Elizabeth, at sixteen years old; Henry [the VII and/or the
VIII, according to other witnesses], Richard [presumably the II not
the III], Edward, Kings of England; Rosamond; Lucrece, a Grecian
bride, in her nuptial habit' – before he arrives at 'a picture of King
Edward VI, representing at first sight something quite deformed, till
by looking through a small hole in the cover which is put over it, you
see it in its true proportion'. And on from there to the Holy Roman
Emperor Charles V, Ferdinand Duke of Florence and King Philip of
Spain, 'besides many more illustrious men and women; and a picture
of the Siege of Malta'.¹⁰ Since the portraits were likely hung from

Figure 1.2 Anamorphic portrait of Edward VI, oil on panel, attributed to John Scrots, 1546.

Source: © National Portrait Gallery, London, NPG 1299.

floor to ceiling as they are at Hardwick Hall, some walking about and standing back would have been required for anything like a face-to-face view, but Edward VI's portrait, usually on display in Room 1 of the National Portrait Gallery in London, demands more radical moves (Figure 1.2). The 'cover' Hentzner describes was a metal viewing-device fitted to the right-hand side of the frame. The notch still to be seen today on the unusually deep frame was placed there to give viewers a sight-line when they looked through the hole in the device.[11]

Standing before Edward VI's portrait in 1613, Johann Ernst I, the nineteen-year-old Duke of Saxe-Weimar, describes his own adjustment in perspective not in terms of a viewing-hole or a notch in the frame but as a movement he makes in the space between himself and the picture. The portrait is given pride of place in Saxe-Weimar's remarkably full catalogue of the room's pictures: 'Portrait of King Edward VI, perspectively painted [*prospectivisch gemahlet*]. In front one cannot distinguish what it is meant for, but from the side the portrait is seen quite clearly.'[12] In general, Saxe-Weimar is very attentive to space and his relationship to the pictures on the walls, noting which portraits are full-length, which pictures are large and which small. Next to 'A small Portrait of Louis XII. King of France', for example, he catalogues 'Julius Caesar, also small – a fine picture'.[13]

Visitors to Room 1 in the National Portrait Gallery today are invited to follow in the Saxe-Weimar's footsteps. Look at Edward straight on, face to face, and you see a distorted image. Move to your right, and Edward's face begins to assume a recognisable shape. A startling effect of looking through the notch is that Edward's face starts floating free of the panel background, assuming a life-like three-dimensionality. Amid that virtual reality you might expect Edward's eyes to catch yours, but what you finally see is Edward's face in profile. When seen *properly*, as it were, royal Edward refuses to return your gaze however much you stare at him. He keeps his royal distance and puts you in your place. In a word, he 'outfaces' you, in the literal sense of turning aside and staring you down with his left eye.[14]

Getting a perspective

The three early observers of Edward VI's portrait all speak of the relationship between viewer and picture in terms of perspective. Platter's 'artfully lengthened by perspective', Hentzner's 'true proportion' and Saxe-Weimar's *prospectivisch gemahlet* imply the same understanding of perspective we assume today: a rationalised geometric relationship between viewed object and viewing subject. Within such a schema, object and subject figure as opposites. *En face*: the French phrase for 'opposite' captures this relationship precisely. The strategies of movement necessary to align the faces in the Whitehall long gallery suggest, however, a more dynamic situation. So, too, do the viewing arrangements that Platter describes in London's public theatres. What we confront in all these situations is something more fluid than stationary perspectival geometry. We find ourselves in a space of possibilities, resistances and negotiations of power between the viewer and the viewed.

Coming face to face with portraits we can perhaps appreciate these negotiations more readily than in the theatre. Pictures hanging on a wall are said to 'face out' into the room, but how the viewer faces the pictures is another matter. Portraits can be full-length, half length or face only in what we might regard as the vertical dimension. The horizontal dimension is determined by whether the persons being depicted are single (as in most Tudor and Stuart portraits) or double (as in portraits of married couples, parent and child, two friends or master and servant) or multiple (as in portraits of two parents with their children or in Antony van Dyke's famous oil sketch of Charles I's face, neck and shoulders seen from three different angles).[15] The third dimension, the extension of the persons depicted into the viewer's space, is determined in part by whether the face or faces are represented full face, turned slightly or turned 45 degrees to show a profile. No less important is where the face or faces in the portrait turn their eyes, making eye contact with the viewer or averting their eyes away from the viewer, as Edward VI does when seen from the right. The most powerful among the famous royal portraits of Henry VIII and Elizabeth I are full-length, single and full-face or slightly turned. These images are designed to outface the viewer, to inspire awe. Profile portraits like Edward VI's are more complex in orientation and effect on the viewer. The sitter is facing in another direction, situated against a background into which (or onto which in the case of the originally blue colour-field behind Edward VI) the viewer also has access. The effect is more equivocal than in a full-face portrait. With or without a hole or a notch, with or without a trick in perspective, the viewer is drawn in, creating an interface between sitter and viewer. Those dynamics work also in stage plays. Outface and interface define two extreme situations within a range of inter- mediate possibilities.

In both portrait galleries and the theatre a fourth dimension is introduced by time. With the exception of Queen Elizabeth and a few foreign rulers, the portraits in the Whitehall long gallery all depicted personages from the past. Edward VI is typical: he had died in 1553, forty-five years before Platter set foot in the long room. Even the still-living personages in other paintings were, for the most part, geo- graphically remote from Whitehall Palace. To view these likenesses was to come face to face with the past, or if not with the past with the physically distant. The coming-to-life of the personages in the paintings happened in the interface between the face in the portrait and the eyes of the viewer. With respect to time, the encounter could be momentary or it could last for minutes, as it seems to have done in the cases of Hentzner and Saxe-Weimar. None of these witnesses mentions a looking-glass among the furnishings of the Whitehall gallery, but other such rooms had them, including the High Great Chamber at Hardwick Hall, where in 1601 'a looking glass painted with the arms of England' shared wall space with some of the paint- ings that now hang in the Long Gallery.[16] In such cases viewers could also come face to face with their own visages alongside personages from the past. Henry VIII, Richard II, Lucrece, Julius Caesar: over- laps between the repertory of personages in the Whitehall long gal- lery and in Shakespeare's plays and poems reinforce the connection between the two sorts of galleries as sites of face-to-face interactions. In the theatre face-to-face encounters lasted not minutes but two hours or more, and they involved movement on the part of both actors and spectators/listeners.

To face: shifting attention from the noun to the verb points up the power dynamics involved in looking. To face a person, an object or a situation is an act of volition, a show of power. The dynamics of the verb *to face* are registered in the prepositions that get added to it: *to face up* to a situation, *to face down* an adversary, *to face out* toward what's in front of you. Two prepositions in particular will concern us in this chapter: *out-* and *inter-*. Shakespeare himself gives us the first one: 'outface' is a verb he uses many times. The second preposition, *inter-*, captures the (literally) *pro-visional* quality of face-to-face situations: the possible shifts in subject/object relationships and the opportunities for finding inter-subjectivity.

Phenomenological thinking capitalises on the interface between the observing subject and the observed object. Eight of George Lakoff and Mark Johnson's 'primary metaphors' are at least partly frontal and volitional: 'Intimacy is closeness', 'Actions are self-propelled motions', 'Causes are physical forces', 'Relationships are enclosures', 'Control is up', 'Knowing is seeing', 'Seeing is touching'.[17] David Morris describes 'facing' in syntactical terms: 'Our sense of orientation . . . is rooted in a way of moving and grasping the world, and in a deep grammar of the body, a topo-logic of the body that can face or not face itself, and thereby (conversely) not face or face others and its place.'[18] As we shall see toward the end of this chapter, Ben Jonson in *The English Grammar* makes a similar move in explaining how verbs express agency and passivity. With respect to drama we can distinguish four types of face-to-face situations: (1) between characters within fictions; (2) between actors on stage; (3) between actors and spectator/listeners; and (4) between readers and texts both visual and verbal. Let us consider each in turn.

Characters within fictions

Richard II facing up to his fate as he looks in a mirror is a spatially and temporally complex scene:

> Was this face the face
> That every day under his household roof
> Did keep ten thousand men? Was this the face
> That like the sun did make beholders wink?
> Is this the face which faced so many follies,
> That was at last outfaced by Bolingbroke?
>
> (IV, i, 145.A127–32)[19]

Richard can no longer face himself. He has been outfaced by Bolingbroke earlier in the same scene. The royal gaze that Richard has lost can be witnessed in several surviving portraits from the sixteenth century. Perhaps the portrait in Figure 1.3, which usually hangs with Edward VI's distorted portrait in Room 1 of the National Portrait Gallery, is the very 'Richard' seen by Hentzner in the Whitehall gallery in 1598. If not, it nonetheless represents a widely copied prototype, usually face-forward, in suites of royal portraits commissioned in the sixteenth and seventeenth centuries for long galleries all over England. The Dulwich Picture Gallery preserves sixteen such portraits purchased by the actor Edward Alleyn between 1618 and 1620. One of them, showing Henry V in profile, depicts a monarch that Alleyn himself likely played onstage in *The Famous Victories of Henry V*.[20] Alleyn, coming face to face with his portrait of Henry V more than ten years after his retirement from the stage, might have experienced the same temporal distancing effect as Shakespeare's Richard II staring at his face in the mirror.

Richard II is not the only character in Shakespeare's plays who reads faces as texts. Cassius is another, and much more politically

Figure 1.3 Portrait of Richard II, oil on panel, by an unknown artist, 1597–1618, based on a full-length lifetime portrait from the 1390s in Westminster Abbey.

Source: © National Portrait Gallery, London, NPG 4980(8).

astute he is than Richard. In *Julius Caesar* I, ii, just after Caesar has
summoned the Soothsayer into his presence ('Set him before me; let
me see his face' (I, ii, 22)) and summarily dismissed both the speaker
and his prophetic warning about the ides of March, Cassius reads the
troubled look in Brutus's face and confronts his friend:

> CASSIUS
>   Tell me, good Brutus, can you see your face?
> BRUTUS No, Cassius: for the eye sees not itself
>   But by reflection, by some other things.
> CASSIUS 'Tis just;
>   And it is very much lamented, Brutus,
>   That you have no such mirrors as will turn
>   Your hidden worthiness into your eye,
>   That you might see your shadow.
>
>   (I, ii, 53–60)

In particular, the shadow he casts among 'many of the best respect in
Rome', who wish that Brutus could see Caesar's offenses with *their*
eyes and take action (I, ii, 61). Caesar, told of the ill auguries, at first
resolves to go to the Capitol anyway:

> Caesar shall forth. The things that threated me
> Ne'er looked but on my back; when they shall see
> The face of Caesar, they are vanishèd.
>
>   (II, ii, 10–12)

He would, that is, outface the auguries as he has always outfaced his
enemies. The suicides of Cassius and Brutus later in the play, let it be
noted, both involve averted faces.

Cleopatra is another astute reader of faces. When a messenger
from Italy enters in II, v, Cleopatra tries to read the news in the messenger's face: 'there's no goodness in thy face' (II, v, 37). When the
messenger, many times interrupted, is finally able to blurt out the
news that Antony has married Octavia, Cleopatra invokes one genre
of the paintings on display in the Whitehall long gallery mythologi-
cal scenes: 'Hadst thou Narcissus in thy face, to me / Thou wouldst
appear most ugly. He is married?' (II, v, 97–8). She angrily sends the
messenger away, then abruptly asks for him to be called back: 'bid
him / Report the feature of Octavia; her years, / Her inclination;
let him not leave out / The colour of her hair' (II, v, 112–15). In
the meantime, Cleopatra tries, unsuccessfully to close her mind's

eye on Antony: 'Though he be painted one way like a Gorgon, / The other way's a Mars' (II, v, 117–18). The messenger comes back several scenes later to report and verify his verbal portrait of Octavia: 'Madam, in Rome. / I looked her in the face' (III, iii, 8–9). He tactfully presents Octavia in terms that recall Hentzner's description of Edward VI's portrait as 'something quite deformed'. Toward the end of the play, when her military forces have been defeated, Cleopatra wishes to outface Caesar even as she expresses defeat. 'Pray you, tell him / I am his fortune's vassal', she tells Caesar's emissary

> and I send him
> The greatness he has got. I hourly learn
> A doctrine of obedience, and would gladly
> Look him i'th' face.
>
> (V, ii, 28–32)

What Caesar sees when he arrives, after Cleopatra's suicide, is a tomb-like effigy: 'she looks like sleep' (V, ii, 335). Perhaps, indeed, like a famous piece of Roman statuary, the sleeping Ariadne with a snake-like bracelet, known in Shakespeare's day as Cleopatra through Giovanni Battista de'Cavaliere's engraving in *Antiquarum Statuarum Urbis Romae* (successive editions from 1561 to 1594).[21] Cleopatra has outfaced Caesar by becoming, in her own words, 'marble-constant', a funerary portrait in stone (V, ii, 236).

Other Shakespearean characters who study faces include Othello ('Let me see your eyes. Look in my face', he demands of Desdemona (IV, ii, 23)) and, most notably perhaps, Hamlet. Horatio's report of the Ghost's appearance in I, ii is prompted by Hamlet's startling declaration 'methinks I see my father'. Where, exclaims Horatio, likely looking around the stage. 'In my mind's eye', Hamlet quips. When Horatio reports the appearance of an armored figure like his father – an event spectator/listeners have witnessed in the play's first scene – Hamlet is eager to know whether or not they saw the armored figure's face:

HAMLET   Then saw you not his face.
HORATIO   O yes, my lord, he wore his beaver up.
HAMLET   What looked he, frowningly?
HORATIO   A countenance more in sorrow than in anger.
HAMLET   Pale, or red?
HORATIO   Nay, very pale.

```
HAMLET      And fixed his eyes upon you?
HORATIO     Most constantly.
HAMLET      I would I had been there.
```

(I, ii, 183–4, 227–35)

When Hamlet becomes suspicious of Ophelia's sincerity, he reads her face like a picture. According to Ophelia's report to her father, Hamlet

> took me by the wrist and held me hard.
> Then goes he to the length of all his arm,
> And with his other hand thus o'er his brow
> He falls to such perusal of my face
> As 'a would draw it. Long stayed he so.

(II, i, 85–9)

In setting up 'The Mousetrap' as a ploy to discover Claudius's guilt, Hamlet urges Horatio to 'give him heedful note' during the performance. 'For I mine eyes will rivet to his face, / And after we will both our judgements join / In censure of his seeming' (III, ii, 72–4). After Claudius has evinced his guilt, presumably in his face as well as by rushing out, Hamlet presents to Gertrude two painted faces, 'the counterfeit presentment of two brothers' (III, iv, 52) and demands that she see the elder Hamlet's portrait as Hyperion, Claudius's as a satyr. The language of portraiture guides Hamlet's scrutiny of faces.

Particularly in Shakespeare's history plays and Roman plays, interfaces are staged as political confrontations, in challenges to combat, in battles. Take, for example, the 'bar and royal interview' that Burgundy sets up between King Harry and King Charles at the end of *Henry V*:

> Since, then, my office hath so far prevailed
> That face to face, and royal eye to eye
> You have congreeted, let it not disgrace me
> If I demand, before this royal view,
> What rub or what impediment there is
> Why that the naked, poor, and mangled peace,
> Dear nurse of arts, plenties, and joyful births,
> Should not in this best garden of the world,
> Our fertile France, put up her lovely visage?

(V, ii, 27, 29–37)

Multiple faces are involved in this particular interface: those of King Harry and King Charles, of Burgundy (he hopes he will not lose face by proposing peace talks), of Peace. In the background, imaginatively at least, is a battle view like the 'picture of the Siege of Malta' that Saxe-Weimar saw in the Whitehall long gallery. Among the Roman plays *Julius Caesar*, *Antony and Cleopatra*, and *Coriolanus* are full of such scenes of outfacing and saving face.

Macduff's exchange with Macbeth in their final battle is a particularly forceful example. 'Tyrant, show thy face', Macduff yells amid the noise and rapid entrances and exits of the battle sequence:

> either thou, Macbeth,
> Or else my sword with an unbattered edge
> I sheathe again undeeded. There thou shouldst be;
> By this great clatter, one of greatest note
> Seems bruited. Let me find him, fortune,
> And more I beg not.
>
> (V, viii, 1, 5–10)

Find him Macduff does, from behind. Macduff's command 'Turn, hell-hound, turn' (V, x, 3) creates the interface that ends in Macduff's outfacing of Macbeth, after Macbeth has first attempted to outface Macduff: 'I will not yield, / To kiss the ground before young Malcolm's feet / . . . Lay on, MacDuff, / And damned be him that first cries "Hold, enough!"' (V, x, 28–9, 34–5). Thinking of the interface between Macduff and Macbeth in this literal, physical way makes the spectator/listeners' final vision of Macbeth's face chillingly visceral. After the stage direction '*Enter MacDuff with Macbeth's head*' (V, xi, 20 *s.d.*) Macduff directs Malcolm's vision – and the spectator/listeners': 'Behold where stands / Th'usurper's cursèd head' (V, xi, 20–1). That surely indicates that Macbeth's head is placed on a pike, not brought onstage in a bag as in many modern productions. Malcolm, like Macduff, outfaces Macbeth and undoes him.

In comic situations to outface is not only to challenge but to feign, to take on a disguise. Holofernes in *Love's Labour's Lost* complains that the quipping young lords have undone the actors' heroic impersonations of the classical Worthies and stopped the show. 'You have put me out of countenance', Holofernes complains. Berowne counters, 'False, we have given thee faces' – meaning the young lords have grimaced at the actors. 'But you have outfaced them all', Holofernes answers back (V, ii, 603–5). Prince Harry in *1 Henry IV* explodes Falstaff's bragging about the Gad's Hill robbery by ripping off Falstaff's mask: 'Then did we two set on you four, and with a word outfaced you from your prize' (II, v, 212–13). 'We'll have a swashing and a martial outside', Rosalind tells Celia in *As You Like It* as they plan their escape from the court, 'As many other mannish cowards have, / That do outface it with their semblances' (I, iii, 109–11). 'We shall have old swearing', the disguised Portia counsels the disguised Nerissa in *The Merchant of Venice* after they have successfully begged their husbands' rings, 'That they did give the rings away to men. / But we'll outface them, and outswear them too' (IV, ii, 15–17).

All of these instances – Richard II, Burgundy, Macbeth, Macduff, Caesar, Cleopatra, and Hamlet in their tragic situations as well as Holofernes, Prince Harry, Rosalind and Portia in their comic situations – invite us to consider the face as a mask, part of a costume. The connection between mask and costume is secured by the pun of *to face* as to appliqué fabric on a garment.[22] Challenge becomes seaming when Grumio outfaces Petruccio's bill-bearing tailor in *The Taming of the Shrew* with puns not only on 'facing' as added fabric but on 'braving' as decking out: 'Face not me. Thou hast braved many men. Brave not me; I will neither be faced nor braved' (VI, iii, 123–4). Dismissing Worcester's reasons for rebelling, King Henry in *1 Henry IV* declares, 'These things indeed you have articulate, / Proclaimed at market crosses, read in churches, / To face the garment of rebellion' (V, i, 72–4). In *Measure for Measure* Pompey laments that ''Twas never merry world' since sumptuary laws allowed 'the worser' sort of usurer 'a furred gown to keep him warm – and furred with fox on lambskins too, to signify that craft, being richer than innocency, stands for the facing' (III, i, 250–3).

Putting on a face is not limited to comedy, and the object being outfaced need not be a person. Turning his back on the infamy Edmund has created, Edgar in *King Lear* puts on a different face so as to outface the play's inimical heavens:

> My face I'll grime with filth,
> Blanket my loins, elf all my hair in knots,
> And with presented nakedness outface
> The winds and persecutions of the sky.
>
> (II, ii, 165–8)

For Lear madness works the same effect as Edgar's beggary: 'Was this a face / To be opposed against the warring winds', Cordelia exclaims when Lear has been rescued from the storm (IV, vii, 29–30).

Actors on stage

On the stage outfaces and interfaces between characters within the fiction become physical actions. With respect to the tiring house, the entire stage was referred to as 'out' in stage directions, so it can be said that every actor made an entrance with an 'out face' on.[23] What happened then was choreography in which one actor's out face was adjusted and readjusted to other actors' out faces. The fixity of geometric perspective is constantly being altered as actors move toward, away from, around, next to, above and below each other. The most frequent use of the word *face* in stage directions refers to something being put on or over a face.[24] When that something is a mask an actor's out face is covered by a second out face – a situation that can be played out to hilarious effect in comedies but to disastrous ends in tragedies.

The fluid stage dynamics that Bernard Beckerman has outlined – particularly asides, soliloquies and observation scenes – bring actors together in ever-shifting relationships of faces.[25] *Richard II* offers an array of examples of choreography with faces. A scene of outfacing begins the play: Bolingbroke and Mowbray face off with one another, but in the face of King Richard, who outfaces both of them. He turns their quarrel into ritual armed combat that two scenes later brings the opposing lords, armed with lances, face to face at opposite sides of the stage, *en face* in every sense of the word. The stage direction in the 1597 quarto makes it clear that before the combat is to begin the king and his nobles are seated, most likely close to the tiring house wall – 'upstage' in later terminology – with Richard's chair placed in the position of greatest power, perhaps raised on a portable dais. Richard and his nobles are positioned to oversee the face-off. In terms of political power they see all, but unlike Foucault's prison wardens they are also seen. In the event Richard again exerts control over both Bolingbroke and Mowbray by stopping the combat and banishing Bolingbroke. In those actions Richard outfaces Bolingbroke, setting up the banished lord's revenge.

In their next face-off, when Bolingbroke returns to Britain in the middle of the play, Richard's position of power is further enhanced by his entering 'above', while Bolingbroke enters 'below'. At first the two adversaries communicate via a third party, Northumberland, who does the work of face-to-face communication for them. Richard's *de*-position as king is literally a coming down to face Bolingbroke, this time with no intermediary but face on face, eye to eye. 'In the base court: base court where kings grow base, / To come at traitors' calls, and do them grace', Richard laments (III, iii, 179–80).

Surprisingly, it is Bolingbroke who kneels and does Richard grace when the deposed king arrives on the platform, but Richard perforce must yield the military victor's lands and titles. In starkly physical terms Richard outfaces Bolingbroke at the play's start; in even more starkly physical terms, Bolingbroke outfaces Richard at the play's turning point. If there is an interface, a shared subjectivity created by the actors in *Richard II*, it happens in the scene in which Richard and his Queen take leave of one another in a London street as Richard is being escorted to the Tower. The highly wrought speeches they exchange, face to face, dissolve into stichomythia that implies face-to-face immediacy – 'And must we be divided? must we part?' / 'Ay, hand from hand, my love, and heart from heart' – before ending in two explicitly cued kisses: 'One kiss shall stop our mouths, and dumbly part. / Thus give I mine, and thus take I thy heart' (V, i, 81–2, 95–6). In none of Shakespeare's history plays is the juxtaposition of outface and interface so blatant.

Among the tragedies *Romeo and Juliet* comes close, with its shifts from the public face-off between Benvolio and Tybalt in the first scene to the dancing maskers Romeo and Juliet coyly outfacing one another in sonnet stanzas and exchanging two kisses in the fifth scene to the vertical choreography of their moonlit tryst in the sixth scene to the horizontal choreography of the public face-off between Mercutio and Benvolio in the eighth scene to Juliet and Romeo in the pose of two funerary statues facing up on chest-tombs in the play's last scene. Such brutal contrasts between public outface and intimate interface are not really resolved in the pronouncements of Capulet and Montague at the play's end. Turning the dead body of Juliet into a 'statue in pure gold' (V, iii, 298) and Romeo's into a statue 'as rich' (V, iii, 303) are acts of facing out as one might see in a chapel or gallery of paintings. Juliet and Romeo, whose stilled bodies remain on display to the scene's end, are turned into posthumous portraits before the spectators' eyes.

Among Shakespeare's comedies the choreography of facing is especially complex and varied in *Much Ado About Nothing*. Beatrice and Benedick face off in the first scene of the play, when Beatrice exclaims how happy she is that she does not have a suitor.

> BENEDICK God keep your ladyship still in that mind! So some gentleman or other shall scape a predestinate scratched face.
>
> BEATRICE Scratching could not make it worse, an 'twere such a face as yours were.
>
> (I, i, 98–101)

As comic figures Beatrice and Benedick keep their eyes trained not only on each other but on other characters on stage – and of course on the spectator/listeners beyond the platform. In the intrigues that follow there are multiple outfacings: Beatrice and Benedick being tricked into thinking they have misread each other's words and faces ('Signor Leonato, truth it is, good Signor, / Your niece regards me with an eye of favour . . . And I do with an eye of love requite her' (V, iv, 21–2, 24)), Claudio's jealous misapprehension of whose face he sees leaning out of Hero's chamber window the night before the wedding ('Is this face Hero's? Are our eyes our own?' (IV, i, 67)), Hero's feigned death and entombment ('Done to death by slanderous tongues, / Was the Hero that here lies' (V, iii, 3–4)), Leonato's trick of persuading Claudio to marry a veiled surrogate bride ('Which is the lady I must seize upon?' (V, iv, 53)), the unveiling of the bride to reveal the face of Hero ('Sweet, let me see your face' (V, iv, 55)). Such maskings, veilings and mistaking of identities confirm the argument that the 'nothing' in the play's title can be heard as 'noting'. The rectifying of these multiple mistakes in noting come in face-to-face encounters in the play's last scene: Claudio with Hero, Benedick with Beatrice. The contrivance of these revelations has left some twentieth- and twenty-first-century readers and spectator/listeners uneasy as to the interfaces into which these outfaces are transformed.

The same is true of the resolution of *The Winter's Tale* when Leontes in a scene reminiscent of Claudio's visit to Hero's tomb, is scripted to come face to face with an effigy of the wife he has wronged. Claudio speaks to Hero's tomb by reading aloud from a scroll; Leontes would go so far as to kiss Hermione's effigy after exclaiming, 'The fixture of her eye has motion in't, / As we are mocked with art' (V, iii, 67–8). The fictional setting for this face-to-face encounter is referred to by Paulina as a 'chapel' (V, iii, 86) but by Leontes as a 'gallery', a space not unlike the long gallery in Whitehall Palace as described by Platter, Hentzner and Saxe-Weimar:

> we came
> To see the statue of our queen. Your gallery
> Have we passed through, not without much content
> In many singularities; but we saw not
> That which my daughter came to look upon,
> The statue of her mother.
>
> (V, iii, 9–13)

Reference in the previous scene to Hermione's statue as 'a piece many years in doing, and now newly performed by that rare Italian master,

Julio Romano' (V, ii, 75–6), establishes the convergence of chapel, picture-gallery and stage play.

That event happens in the moment Hermione's carved and painted portrait descends and speaks: actors do what statues and painted portraits cannot. The dynamics of face-to-face encounters in both media are formulated by the art historian James Elkins in a chapter on 'What Is a Face?' in his book *The Object Stares Back*. Elkins's larger point is that objects of all kinds – animals and plants as well as man-made artefacts – read us just as we read them. They demand to be looked at in certain ways. That is particularly true of faces. 'Speaking is like making ripples in a pool of water, and a face is like the wall that sends the ripples back', Elkins says. 'If we speak forcefully, we send waves out toward the other face, and in a moment we can expect to feel the response. Faces move in this way even when they are not speaking.'[26] Elkins's observation applies to faces in all the guises we are considering in these pages: viewer to portrait, character to character, actor to actor, spectator/listener to actor, reader to text. In the interface objects can become subjects, and subjects objects.

Actors and spectator/listeners

It could be argued that the strongest interface in *Richard II* happens, not within the fiction or even between Richard and the Queen, but between Richard and the spectator/listeners. As a rhetorical set-piece, Richard's ekphrasis of his image in the mirror is pitched as much to the house as to the actors onstage. What is probably his most famous speech – 'I have been studying how I may compare / This prison where I live unto the world' (V, v, 1–2) – follows the stage direction '*Enter Richard alone*'. The 'royal view' that Burgundy invokes in *Henry V* may well embrace the entire onstage assembly of noble personages. If so, that embrace includes the faces of the spectator/listeners in the theatre. One did not, in fact, have to occupy the 'jolliest place' to be seen as well as to see. In live performance the bodily dynamics of the actor/spectator interface are patent. The actor's face becomes several things at once: an exteriorisation of the actor's will, for the spectators an optical effect to be looked at and through, a text to be read. The traffic of the stage moves in two directions. It requires the spectator/listeners' participation.

The face of the Chorus in the Folio version of *Henry V* looks out at the faces of the spectators and instructs them how to read the ciphers they are about to see. 'There is the playhouse now', the Chorus gestures in the prologue to the second act, 'there you

must sit' (II, 0, 36), presumably gesturing toward the entire interface between the spectator/listeners and the actors who, with their
powers, will transport them to France. During the performance
the actors 'move' the spectator/listeners in more ways than one.
Early modern understandings of the actors' power located it in fiery
beams shooting from the actors' eyes and from the *energia* of their
verbal rhetoric.[27] In modern performances those physical forces
may not be foremost in the participants' imaginations, sight and
sound may be mediated electronically, but the physical presence
of the actors that the spectator/listeners face endow the interface
between them with visceral power.

The to and fro of the performative interface is at its most obvious, perhaps, in the face-to-face transactions between Shakespeare's clowns and the crowds that face them. Richard Tarleton
could make the crowd roar with delight merely by showing his face
from behind a curtain. Will Kemp, who is cued by name in early
printings of *Romeo and Juliet* in the fictional role of Peter and in
Much Ado About Nothing in the fictional role of Dogberry, was a
physical comedian who seems to have traversed the interface of the
stage just as he later traversed the road from London to Norwich
while dancing a jig. Both Peter and Dogberry, let it be noted, have
fraught relationships with writing. Face-to-face transactions were
Robert Armin's stock-in-trade. In his jest book *Quips upon Questions* he takes cues from the spectator/listeners and develops them
into shticks.

A second situation occurs in soliloquies which put the actor as
he voices the lines in the position of addressing two people at once:
on the one hand each of the spectator/listeners and on the other
himself. Among the phenomena that the psychologist and novel-
ist Charles Fernyhough studies in *The Voices Within: The History
and Science of How We Talk to Ourselves* is the role of language
in thought. Thinking to oneself, Fernyhough argues, is conscious,
linguistic, private, coherent, and active. Brain scans show activity
in language areas of the brain as people think.[28] Soliloquies share
all the qualities that Fernyhough enumerates, but they make the
private public. Hamlet in the act of thinking – or at least the actor
playing Hamlet in the theatre – is talking not only to himself but
to *us*. The actor makes eye contact with us as he casts the speech in
our direction.

There is a third situation, in which an onstage figure who alternately faces his fellow actors on the stage and us as onlookers sets
up an interface in two directions. Hamlet in his snide asides in

I, ii is a perfect example. 'A little more than kin, and less than kind' (I, ii, 65) is a warm-up for the soliloquy that closes the scene: 'O that this too too sullied flesh would melt' (I, ii, 129). The multiple foci in *Troilus and Cressida* V, ii are another virtuoso instance. Diomedes outfaces Cressida, while Troilus and Ulysses, observing the scene from elsewhere on the platform, alternately face each other and almost certainly in their asides also face the spectator/ listeners. Especially in situations like these the spectator/listeners are put in the position of visitors to an early modern picture gallery like the Long Gallery at Whitehall. Soliloquies correspond to face-front portraits, asides to profiles, back-and-forth turnings like those of Troilus and Ulysses to turnings of less than 45 degrees. In all these performance situations spectator/listeners have to get their bearings, just as spectators do with Scrots's Edward VI portrait. Intersubjectivity requires movements of attention on the reader/spectator/listeners' part as much as shifts in the angle of delivery on the actors' part.

In a live performance the power dynamics of face-to-face encounters might seem to be just the reverse of reading typeface. In the theatre you choose to face the actors who are speaking and moving the lines, but the power seems to emanate from them, not you. On occasion in the course of performance the actors turn from their stage business and face you physically. That is certainly the case in soliloquies, asides and speeches made by Chorus figures, but it can happen other times as well, with a mere glance from one of the actors in your direction, with a gesture *within* the fiction that acknowledges your presence *outside* the fiction. In acting practices from the sixteenth to the early twentieth centuries face-to-face encounters with spectator/listeners were what actors *did*.[29] Even today, after Stanislavsky, after Brecht, after Robert Wilson, even when you are seated at a distance, it can seem as if the actors are looking you in the eye: taking your measure, impressing you with their physical being, filling you with their psychic presence. Through it all, however, *you* wield power as well. The best in this kind are but shadows unless imagination, *your* imagination, mend them by putting the pieces together. The actors are crooked figures, ciphers; you must piece out their imperfections with your thoughts, eke out their performance with your mind. You do much the same with typeface letters as you read between and across them. Without you, texts and actors alike are indecipherable. Deciphering happens in the interface between you and the actors, between you and the text.

Readers and texts

Richard II's gaze into the mirror is cast by Richard himself as an act of reading. Northumberland has tried to hand Richard a paper on which are written the crimes that have led to his arrest. Richard refuses the paper and waits for the mirror to be brought.

> I'll read enough
> When I do see the very book indeed
> Where all my sins are writ, and that's myself.
> *Enter one with a glass.*
> Give me that glass, and therein will I read.
>
> (4, i, 145. A119–22)

For spectator/listeners in the theatre the actor playing Richard turns the image in the mirror into an oral text in the speech that follows. For readers of printed texts of the play the process is repeated – but in reverse. Readers must turn the written text into a visual image: they must imagine the face that Richard sees in the mirror. Readers face the printed text no less physically than spectator/listeners face the actor playing Richard. In both situations there is an interface: no more than fifty feet between spectator/listeners in the theatre and actors on the platform, 18 to 24 inches between a reader's eyes and book in hand.[30] Of the four types of face-to-face encounters considered in this chapter, that between readers and written texts is the most elusive, but fundamentally the most important, since actors themselves begin with written texts.

You yourself have been experiencing this fourth interface even as you have read my writing. Whether you're holding a printed book in your hands or reading the text online, you are facing the text and the text is facing you. Either way, you're looking at a type*face* of a certain font and size. If, instead of reading *Face-to-Face in Shakespearean Drama*, you were reading *M[aste]r William Shakespeare's Comedies, Histories, & Tragedies*, you could have begun on signature πA1+1-recto with the engraved portrait of the author and found yourself face to face with a visual image, in this case an engraved portrait. Ben Jonson's verses on the facing page (signature πA1-verso) elide verbal text and visual text. The face-to-face pairing of 'To the Reader' and Martin Droeshout's engraved portrait turn the comedies, histories and tragedies into synecdoche for the historical personage William Shakespeare, seven years deceased when the folio was published in 1623.

Despite Jonson's reference to 'gentle Shakespeare', it is hard to read the staring eyes in Droueshout's engraving. According to some viewers, the eyes confronting you are two *left* eyes, so it is no wonder if you find yourself not quite knowing how to look back. Let us assume, however, that you've heeded Jonson's advice 'Reader, looke / Not on his Picture, but his Booke' and have turned the pages, perhaps to signature d2-verso where you can come face to face with Richard's face-to-face encounter with the mirror.[31] In turning from Shakespeare's portrait to his written text, you have repeated Platter's transition from picture-gallery to library. As Elizabeth's face may have haunted Platter when he noticed the neat character of the queen's handwriting, so the fame of Droueshout's engraving has made it all but impossible for readers to forget Shakespeare's face, even as they come face to face with his dramatic characters on the printed page or in the theatre. The printed and the performed texts function as synecdoche for the man William Shakespeare, even as Elizabeth's handwritten books did for Platter.

In your encounters with verbal texts, the greater power would seem to be on your side: it is you who is doing the looking, the reading and the interpreting. But the typeface remains stubbornly impassive. It says what it wants to say, again and again, not what you want it to say. It would just as soon be looked at by someone else. It glares back. It stares you down. It outfaces you. The page's clean, confident Pica Roman will face many more readers when you have vacated the reading-space. The impassivity of the typeface would seem to illustrate perfectly the idea of 'surface reading' that, at the time of this writing, was a controversy in literary studies. According to Stephen Burt and Sharon Marcus in their manifesto 'Surface Reading: An Introduction', a text has no 'interior':

> We take surface to mean what is evident, perceptible, apprehensible in texts; what is neither hidden nor hiding; what, in the geometrical sense, has length and breadth but no thickness, and therefore covers no depth. A surface is what insists on being looked at rather than what we must train ourselves to see *through*.[32]

Nancy Armstrong and Warren Montag's critique of this proposition can be verified in your own negotiations with signature d2-verso.[33] The stage directions alone invite you to look *through* the printed text, to project yourself into the interspace. In that act of self-projection you enter into a kind of *ménage à trois*. You face Richard and the mirror even as they face each other. Your entrance

into the interspace, via an act of reading, creates a zone of intersubjectivity.

In his chapter 'What Is a Face?' Elkins cites E. H. Gombrich
to the effect that we read art works in the same way that we read
faces: in pieces, in details, incrementally. Mouth, eyes, hairstyle and
other details are assembled into the image of a unified character,
just as our 'reading' of a painting is assembled from individually
observed details. From this proposition Elkins reflects on the elu-
siveness of saying something coherent about faces – or about art.
Gombrich's theory, he says, 'explains why faces are so difficult to
understand and describe: because they are at the very beginning
of our understanding of unity and coherence.'[34] If portrait-faces
abound in Shakespeare's history plays and Roman plays, one reason might be the prevalence of historical and classical portraits in
collections of paintings like that in the Whitehall long gallery. There
is more traffic between long galleries and theatre galleries than we
might suppose. In *Twelfth Night* Olivia presents the removal of her
mourning veil as being like the pulling back of a curtain in front
of a painted portrait. 'Have you any commission from your lord to
negotiate with my face?' Olivia asks Viola in her guise as Orsino's
servant Cesario. 'You are now out of your text. But we will draw
the curtain and show you the picture. [*She unveils*] Look you, sir,
such a one I was this present. Is't not well done?' (I, v, 188–90).
Beyond Bardolph's red face, the butt of jokes across three plays, it
is remarkable how little information about faces is actually encoded
in Shakespeare's texts. Bodies, including faces, must be supplied by
readers of the text, along with the three other elements missing on
the page: sound, space and time.

Inhabiting the four dimensions

In 'the long room' at Whitehall Palace and in the Curtain Theatre
in Shoreditch, Thomas Platter helped us situate ourselves in four
dimensions vis-à-vis faces: horizontally in terms of the number of
faces in front of us, vertically in terms of how much of the body
below the face we get to see, three-dimensionally vis-à-vis ourselves
as viewing subjects and the faces as viewed objects, and temporally
as we, in the act of viewing, bring to life personages from the past.
Ben Jonson in *The English Grammar* proves to be an unlikely but
provocative guide to the dynamics of what happens when the noun
face is turned into the verb *to face*. To modern linguists Jonson may

seem wrong-headed in trying to apply Latin rules to English speech, but his insistence that verbs have 'number', 'person' and 'time' helps us appreciate the transitivity of *to face*. Whether a verb is coordinated with a singular or a plural subject determines, in early modern English, its 'number' and its endings: *I face, we face, thou facest, you face, he faceth, they face*. Jonson laments that beginning a century earlier, during the reign of Henry VIII, the distinctive ending of third-person-plural verbs had been cut off: *they facen* became *they face*, and precision was lost.

When tense ('time') is added to person and number, verbs assume an almost bodily power. They have hands, legs, feet. In a final gambit, Jonson classifies all verbs into two groups: 'active' and 'neuter'. (Curiously, to me at least, he calls these two groups 'times'.) The difference turns, for Jonson, on whether the past participle can be coupled with *am*. If it can, the verb is 'active'. If not, the verb is 'neuter'. Jonson's examples of the latter case are *pertain, die* and *live*.[35] I wonder if Jonson is not flirting here with English vestiges of the 'middle voice' in ancient Greek and of deponent verbs in Latin. As Émile Benveniste reveals, these verbs tend to refer to actions that I can do but that can also be done to me.[36] By Jonson's criterion, *to face* is most definitely an active verb. I can *face*, even as I *am faced*. Active verbs set up an interface between subject and object, the possibility that the subject can become an object and the object a subject.

With respect to space and time, interface as we have been considering it in this chapter, can be identified with what Gilles Deleuze and Félix Guattari call *assemblage*, the space between two 'territories': in our case, the territories behind individual faces, the territories dominated by particular media and the territories policed by different academic disciplines.[37] For Deleuze and Guattari it is in this in-between space that creativity happens. Learning to inhabit the versions of interfaces explored in this chapter perhaps offers a way out of, or at least a way across, the disciplinary divide between art history and performance studies as well as the page-versus-stage dichotomy that has dominated Shakespeare studies since the eighteenth century. That is a jolly place to be.

Acknowledgements

I am grateful to Julia Lupton, Lawrence Manley and Matthew Smith for making connections where I first saw isolated episodes.

Notes

1. Santina M. Levey and Peter Thornton, *Of Household Stuff: The 1601 Inventories of Bess of Hardwick.*
2. Thomas Platter, *Englandfahrt im Jahre 1599*, p. 35, my translation. For the purposes of this chapter the translation usually cited in scholarship on Shakespeare and London's playhouses, *Thomas Platter's Travels in England 1599*, trans. Clare Williams (London: Cape, 1937), is not exact enough in details. Hence my own translations of all passages quoted from Platter.
3. Platter, p. 35, my translation.
4. Platter, p. 35, my translation.
5. See http://www.hatfield-house.co.uk/house-park-garden/the-house/the-marble-hall/ (last accessed 29 November 2017).
6. Platter, pp. 36–7, my translation.
7. William N. West, 'The Idea of a Theatre: Humanist Ideology and the Imaginary Stage in Early Modern Europe'.
8. Gina Bloom, *Gaming the Stage: Playable Media and the Rise of English Commercial Theatre.*
9. 'gallery, *n.*, 1, 3.a', *Oxford English Dictionary Online* (http://www.oed.com/view/Entry/76266 (last accessed 29 November 2017).
10. Paul Hentzner, *Itinerarium Germaniae, Galliae, Angliae, Italiae . . . ,* p. 32.
11. See https://www.npg.org.uk/collections/, NPG 1299, Edward VI, note to image 2 (last accessed 29 November 2017).
12. Johann Ernst I, 'Pictures and Other Works of Art in the Royal Palaces, in the Year 1613', p. 159.
13. Ernst, 'Pictures', p. 159.
14. 'outface, *v.*' 1.a, *OED Online.*
15. Examples of single, double, and multiple portraits hang in Rooms 1 and 2 of the National Portrait Gallery in London, https://www.npg.org.uk/collections/explore/discover-the-tudors/on-display (last accessed 29 November 2017). Van Dyck's oil sketch, a model for a carved bust by Lorenzo Bernini, is in the British Royal Collection, https://www.royalcollection.org.uk/ (last accessed 29 November 2017).
16. Levey and Thornton, pp. 46–7.
17. George Lakoff and Mark Johnson, *Philosophy in the Flesh: The Embodied Mind and Its Challenge to Western Thought*, pp. 50–4.
18. David Morris, *The Sense of Space*, p. 157. I am grateful to Matt Smith for this reference.
19. William Shakespeare, all citations of Shakespeare are from *The New Oxford Shakespeare: Modern Critical Edition*, ed. Gary Taylor et al.
20. http://www.dulwichpicturegallery.org.uk/explore-the-collection/501-550/henry-v/, with note (last accessed 29 November 2017); S. P. Cerasano, 'Edward Alleyn, the New Model Actor, and the Rise of the Celebrity in the 1590s'.

21. Bruce R. Smith, 'Sermons in Stones: Shakespeare and Renaissance Sculpture'. An image of the statue today in the Vatican Museums can be seen at http://museivaticani.va/ (last accessed 29 November 2017).

22. 'face, *v*' II.7.a, *OED Online*.

23. Alan C. Dessen and Leslie Thomson, *A Dictionary of Stage Directions in English Drama, 1580–1642*, 'out', pp. 155–6.

24. Dessen and Thomson, 'face', p. 87.

25. Bernard Beckerman, *Shakespeare at the Globe, 1599–1609*, pp. 157–213.

26. James Elkins, *The Object Stares Back: On the Nature of Seeing*, p. 107.

27. Joseph Roach, *The Player's Passion: Studies in the Science of Acting*, pp. 23–57.

28. Charles Fernyhough, *The Voices Within: The History and Science of How We Talk to Ourselves*, pp. 8–9.

29. Roach, *The Player's Passion*, pp. 23–57; Sharon Marie Carnicke, 'Acting Techniques', pp. 1430–43.

30. My estimate of fifty feet is based on the reconstructed Shakespeare's Globe in London. On the distance between a reader's eyes and a book you can make your own measurement. Eighteen inches is mine.

31. William Shakespeare, *Comedies, Histories, & Tragedies,* sigs. ᵖA1ᵛ, ᵖA1+1ʳ, d2ᵛ.

32. Stephen Best and Sharon Marcus, 'Surface Reading: An Introduction', p. 9.

33. Nancy Armstrong and Warren Montag, '"The Figure in the Carpet"'.

34. Elkins, *The Object Stares Back*, p. 105.

35. Ben Jonson, *The English Grammar*, Chapter 16 ('Of a Verb').

36. Émile Benveniste, 'Active and Middle Voice in the Verb'.

37. Gilles Deleuze and Félix Guattari, '1837: The Refrain'.

Chapter 2

'Everybody's Somebody's Fool': *Folie à Deux* in Shakespeare's Love Duets

Lawrence Manley

There are no exceptions to the rule,
Everybody's somebody's fool.

to be wise and love
Exceeds man's might; that dwells with the gods above.
(*Troilus and Cressida*, III, ii, 136–7)

Of the myriad versions of face-to-faceness in Shakespeare, an elementary case is what might be called the 'love duet'. Appearing frequently enough in Shakespeare's comedies and love tragedies to be one of their distinct conventions, these are also a special instance of the actor-to-actor work that Bernard Beckerman considered both fundamental to performance and pervasive as a unit of Shakespearean composition. Distinguished by Beckerman from the solo actor-audience relation and from the complex ensemble scene, the actor-actor 'duet' was for Beckerman (especially in early Shakespeare) the elemental building block from which larger, multi-actor scenes are constructed.[1]

Beckerman's broader sense that actor-actor duets can occur in the course of scenes where additional actors share the stage is one that I shall ultimately retain for the case of the love duet. But as my interest is in the way that duets function in erotic contexts between lovers or married couples (and thus in Shakespeare's ways of depicting and understanding couples), I will begin with the more restricted instance I will call the 'unchaperoned duet', a scene or portion of a scene in which the absence of third parties is a theatrical pre-condition and a token for the absence of inhibitions to erotic face-to-face encounter (such as those advantaging one of the parties by means of disguise, privileged knowledge, ulterior motives or other forms of insincerity). It is in the nature of face-to-faceness, of course, that complete disinhibition is neither possible nor (in life or in the theatre) desirable. And so I will end this essay by attending to the ways that the presence of inhibiting factors can support face-to-faceness in its more interesting, occulted forms.

I have arrived at this formalistic topic by following the thematic associations in Shakespeare's mind (and not in his alone) between love and folly. Many quotations might be adduced, but the heart of the matter is to be found where the paradoxical relations of folly to wisdom intersect with commonplaces about love's transvaluation of value and, from Plato's *Symposium* onward, its power to transform the self by way of relation to another. There would be little drama in this transformative power if it were not dangerous to the self and to the conventional terms by which the world values things. *Romeo and Juliet, Othello, Antony and Cleopatra* and *Macbeth* depict the straits of folly into which Shakespeare's couples are led by love. The French *folie* captures better than the English 'folly' the danger – theatrically, the unstable generic potential – surrounding Shakespeare's couples. So does the psychiatric diagnosis of *folie à deux* or 'Shared Psychotic Disorder' in the fourth edition of the American Psychiatric Association's *Diagnostic and Statistical Manual of Mental Disorders*, according to which (a) 'a delusion . . . develops in an individual who is involved in a close relationship with another person' and (b) 'the individual comes to share the delusional beliefs' of the other.[2] Sir Kenelm Digby, who is credited with the earliest description of *folie à deux* in English, placed phenomena like echopraxia and suggestibility among the occulted 'antipathies and sympathies' between persons; he explained 'contagion of the imagination' by observing 'that when two Lutes, or two Harps, near one another, both set to the same tune, if you touch the strings of the one, the other consonant harp will sound at the same time, though no body touch it.'[3]

The song quoted as my epigraph – made most famous by Connie Francis's hit single of 1961 – illuminates the paradox in Shakespeare's sense of love's folly. First credited to Ace Johnson and Lionel Hampton and originally sung by Little Jimmy Scott in the late 1940s, 'Everybody's Somebody's Fool' has proven popular as a 'cheating song' among rhythm and blues vocalists and country and western vocalists. Their way of construing love's folly – as a matter of victims falling prey to an endless *ronde* of betrayals – sticks close to the story the song's lyrics tell. That sort of story is never far out of sight in the scenes we're about to consider: Cressida, for example, declares it is 'an unkind self, that itself will leave / To be another's fool' (III, ii, 129–30).[4] But the tune's plangent refrain (which is also its title) becomes richer and more complex where it breaks free of the lyrics in the work of instrumental jazz improvisers (the stretched-out version of Dexter Gordon comes especially to mind) as multiple changes and inflections can vary the phrasal emphasis between 'everybody's' and 'somebody's' and develop, in an almost Empsonian way, myriad resonances for 'fool'.[5] Shakespeare's comedies of course favour the happier, wiser resonances of 'fool' (not as dupe or exploited victim but as free soul, loving collaborator and blessed beneficiary of madness), just as they also combine an insistence on the universal power of nature in 'everybody's' – in nature's law there are 'no exceptions to the rule' – with a nearly Miltonic awareness that the self becomes most truly 'individual' through belonging to 'somebody'.[6] As Scully tells Mulder in an episode of *The X-Files* titled 'Folie à Deux', 'You're my one in . . . five billion.'

To skip way ahead and risk confusion by working backward, as Shakespeare might have done, from ideas of marriage to romantic courtship, there is in Shakespeare's sense of sympathetic vibration a resemblance to the *homosophryne* or like-mindedness that Odysseus commends when he wishes Nausikaa might find 'a husband, a home, and like-mindedness (*homosophryne*), for nothing is stronger . . . than when a man and a woman hold a house, both thinking alike in their thoughts' (*homophroneonte noemasin*)' (6.181–4).[7] This 'thinking alike', which can anticipate speech or even amount to occulted dialogue (one place, we'll see, where Shakespeare eventually goes with his duets), links the key married couples in *The Odyssey*. Arete and Alkinoos, perhaps the most fortunate of these pairs, are paragons of gracious hospitality who, while harbouring no malicious thoughts, together and separately manage their unspoken concerns about the strange guest and his intentions toward their daughter (there are few such married couples in Shakespeare). The hospitable Helen and Menelaos are equally deft negotiators of the unspoken; in their case, the unspoken is their mutual mistrust and sense of grievance (the Macbeths are closer analogues than the more voluble Antony and Cleopatra). Penelope and Odysseus also find their way (asymmetrically, given the disguise of Odysseus) toward their concluding dialogues by means of occulted sympathies. Telemachus's sneeze at the mention of the name of Odysseus, for example, provokes Penelope to laugh and then to summon the ragged stranger; her laughter at her own sudden impulse to show herself attractively to the suitors is answered by the laughter in

Odysseus's heart when he sees her descending the stairs like Artemis from heaven and hears her solicitation of gifts from the suitors and her call for more feasting on the following day (in this occulted communication we might again think of the Macbeths). Later that night, when Penelope is alone with the stranger, the two speak of Odysseus and of his possible return; Penelope then shares with the stranger her plans for the test of the bow, and the stranger approves. On the day of reckoning, Penelope unbidden fetches the bow, carrying the quiver of arrows on her shoulder, and goads the suitors with the insult that the stranger might best them and take her for his bride.

This like-mindedness is formed against a background of striking unlikeness, in particular the implication of a social mismatch between the aristocratic Spartan Penelope (daughter of Ikarios, brother of Tyndareos and thus cousin to the queens Helen and Clytemnestra) and the roughneck stranger from remote, rocky, and rustic Ithaka, where kings, little better than peasants, consort with shepherds and the swineherds who are their adopted brothers.[8] The one wooer of Helen to have brought no gifts, Odysseus was said to have won Penelope by besting her father in a foot-race, and against Ikarios's wishes he insisted on taking Penelope back to Ithaka instead of remaining in Sparta.[9] Menelaos tells Telemachus of his plan to have resettled Odysseus and his family into a proper life in Sparta, where there is space and use for horses, as there is not in Ithaka (4, 175–80). Athena tells Telemachus, plausibly enough, that Ikarios and his kinsmen are planning to marry Penelope to the highest bidder, Eurymakos, whose gifts are double those of the other suitors (15, 17–20).

There may be a precedent here for Shakespeare's own 'madly mated' couples, at least if *The Taming of the Shrew*'s apparent allusions to *The Odyssey* are any guide.[10] Shakespeare, as William Kerrigan has noted, 'is the supreme artist of the improbable love match, concerned over and over again with the attraction between antagonists, foreigners, disparates – people on either side of a difference, border or firing line.'[11] The extreme cases, where political, racial, religious or cultural differences become crucial to the dramatic focus (as in *The Merchant of Venice, Troilus and Cressida, Othello* or *Antony and Cleopatra*), are dire extensions of the simpler comic potential Shakespeare always finds in the nature of exogamy, where the necessity of seeking a spouse among strangers results in the binds and quandaries of encountering an other in the heterogeneous nature of loving.[12] Erotic heterogeneity (for Shakespeare by no means limited to heterosexuality) creates the necessity for the harmonising influences that Erasmus's Folly attributes to erotic foolishness, the mutual 'flattery, joking, complaisance, illusions, and deceptions' that, against all reason, bind couples together.[13] While an ill-omened mismatch like that between Touchstone and Audrey might best be characterised in Samuel Johnson's dour assessment that 'love is the wisdom of a fool and the folly of the wise',[14] the happier effects of erotic folly and its shared delusions are summed up in Erasmus's neo-Platonic claim that 'the madness of lovers is the highest form of happiness . . . The more perfect the love, the greater the madness, and the happier.'[15]

In his early works, the love duet is one innovative means by which Shakespeare represents lovers contracting such madness. Unchaperoned face-to-face encounters between lovers in Shakespeare's earlier plays are relatively rare and brief, and they are remarkably alike. Important examples are the litany of Lysander and Hermia on the vexed course of true love (*A Midsummer Night's Dream*, I, i, 128–79), the dialogue between Jessica and Lorenzo on 'such a night' as theirs in Portia's garden (*The Merchant of Venice*, V, i, 1–88), and the duets of Romeo and Juliet, including the sonnet scene (I, v, 89–106), the balcony scene (II, ii, 52–177) and the aubade (III, iii, 1–59). All of these duets are highly formal and symmetrical, marked by the sort of echolalia and echopraxia suggestive of shared illusion and collaboration. They are 'duets' in a nearly musical sense. (It is worth remembering that the duet, as opposed to the more common lute song and madrigal, is itself a relatively rare form in Elizabethan music, and that it was just being invented with Thomas Morley's suggestively contemporaneous *First Booke of Canzonets to Two Voyces* (1595). In close harmonies, the singers of Morley's *Canzonets* share identical text, leading and following in imitative form, though the following singer usually overtakes the lead before the two arrive simultaneously at the close of phrases.)[16]

It is probably not accidental that in the formal patterns of their first duet, Lysander and Hermia jointly compose, from a whole tradition of tales and histories, a catalogue of the ways in which lovers are thematically ill-matched or crossed by circumstance:

> *Lys.* How now, my love? Why is your cheek so pale?
> How chance the roses there do fade so fast?
>   *Her.* Belike for want of rain, which I could well
> Beteem them from the tempest of my eyes.
>   *Lys.* Ay me! For aught that I could ever read,
> Could ever hear by tale or history,

The course of true love never did run smooth,
But either it was different in blood –
   Her. O cross! Too high to be enthralled to low.
   Lys. Or else misgrafted in respect of years –
   Her. O spite! – too old to be engaged to young.
   Lys. Or else it stood upon the choice of friends –
   Her. O hell! – to choose love by another's eyes.
   Lys. Or if there were a sympathy in choice,
War, death, or sickness did lay siege to it,
Making it momentary as a sound,
Swift as a shadow, short as any dream,
Brief as the lightning in the collied night,
That, in a spleen, unfolds both heaven and earth,
And, ere a man hath power to say 'Behold!',
The jaws of darkness do devour it up.
So quick bright things come to confusïon.
   Her. If then true lovers have been ever crossed,
It stands as an edict in destiny.
Then let us teach our trial patïence,
Because it is a customary cross,
As due to love as thoughts and dreams and sighs,
Wishes and tears, poor fancy's followers.
   Lys. A good persuasion . . .
          (*A Midsummer Night's Dream* I, i, 128–55)

Licensed by the exit of Helena, Hermia and Lysander begin their eloquent encounter immediately, face to face, with Lysander's question about Hermia's pale cheek and with her mention of her tears, both signalling her appearance to Lysander in all her vulnerability as an other in distress. During the first portion of the exchange, Lysander leads and Helena follows, but at the end of the selection I have quoted, the lead changes with Helena's 'If then' exhortation to patience, which she clinches by returning to her opening mention of tears. It is a nice question whether Lysander's final 'or' (I, i, 141) marks merely another item in an anaphoric list or an emphatic, bifurcating turn in the catalogue, from cases where lovers, mismatched by their poor choices with regard to status, age or parental wishes to cases where they are well-matched in these ways but crossed by chance mishaps. It is possible that by 'sympathy in choice' Lysander means something like the ideal of homogeneity invoked by Portia when she says that if 'souls do bear an equal yoke of love, / There must be needs a like proportïon / Of lineaments, of manners, and of spirit' (III, iv, 13–15). If so, it is an even nicer question (indeed, it is the primary question of

A Midsummer Night's Dream) whether such 'sympathy' is an objective condition or a matter of perception. Helena's claim that 'Love looks not with the eyes but with the mind' (I, i, 234), to say nothing of Titania's fondness for Bottom and other events in the forest, suggests that it is the mind that makes 'sympathy' between lovers.[17] That same idea is being reinforced by the lyrical forms and harmonies of the duet itself.

It is commonplace to say this duet, like those between Juliet and Romeo or Jessica and Lorenzo, reveals its participants to be bookishly imitative or immature in ways that will be tested as the drama uncovers the yet unspoken discords beneath apparent concordancy. Shakespeare, as C. L. Barber noted, leaves 'the judgment free to mock what the heart embraces',[18] and certainly in the external system of communication (involving what the play communicates to its audience), the patterns of speech into which Shakespeare's lovers fall betoken their subjection to compulsion and mutually created illusion. But equally it must be said that the patterns of expression in these duets are powerfully lyrical for reasons that become more apparent if we consider Beckerman's models for actor-to-actor performance:

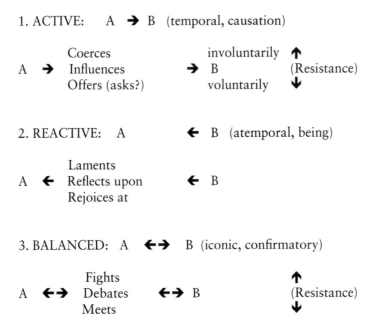

Rather than quarrel over Beckerman's nomenclature for the individual speech-acts in his schema, let us merely note that these acts support his categorisation of the three basic duet types: the 'Active' (which is primarily temporal and causal in nature, supportive of narrative, conflict, uncertainty and the directorial sensibility); the 'Reactive' (which retards time and narrative, tending toward lyric, and expressing being rather than effecting causation); and the 'Balanced' (where the parties are 'virtually matched' and 'the pressures . . . are so nearly the same that one cannot say either figure is the mover or the moved').[19] Beckerman's second or 'Reactive' category corresponds in many respects to what Roman Jakobson labels the 'Expressive' function of communication, centred on the sender, while Beckerman's first and third categories, the 'Active' and the 'Balanced,' might be said to encompass different ranges of Jakobson's 'Appellative' function, which lays greater stress on the receiver of a message.[20] To the right-hand side of the diagram I have added to Beckerman's model a visual reminder of a vector of 'Resistance' that is pertinent to the first and third types of duet and especially to the differences between them – between, that is, the greater instrumentality of the 'Active' type and the more dialogical nature of the 'Balanced' type. It should be clear (if it is not simply the case that different distributions of all three types are always implicit in all duets), that the love duets mentioned so far involve all three types (the 'Active' type, perhaps least relevant to the duet of Hermia and Lysander, will be more important to cases ahead of us) and that they tend to operate toward the lower ranges of resistance (other Shakespearean couples will operate in the higher ranges; Antony and Cleopatra perhaps transit them all). The early love duets, in other words, actively initiate mutual, voluntary undertakings, they confirm them by lyrical reaction and they bring both parties into balanced meeting. The lyrical quality of responsiveness in such duets draws on the 'phatic' aspects of communication, on those features that first establish and maintain the communicative channel between interlocutors. Hermia and Lysander entwine themselves phatically around the anaphoric 'O/Or,' and they collaborate in such an extensive and elaborate pattern primarily (and quite amusingly) because they are wanting, like Romeo and Juliet at the balcony, to prolong their conversation.

Our familiarity with the technique of Shakespearean love duets, reinforced by its pervasive influence on the subsequent history of romantic drama, should not prevent us from recognising how hard it actually is to find precedents for them in previous dramatic literature. Few precedents are to be found, for example, in Roman comedy or the *commedia erudita*, where strong romantic currents are relatively rare and desires are usually expressed to or through intermediaries.[21] One of the closer contemporary analogues to the echolalia and stichomythic construction of Shakespeare's love duets is to be found in powerfully 'Active' scenes of seduction or tyrannical ravishment, derived in the first instance from the Senecan precedent of Lycus's attempt on the virtue of Megara in *Hercules furens*:

> *Lycus*. You take courage from a husband sunk in the underworld?
> *Megara*. He visited the underworld to gain the upper world.
> *Lycus*. He is crushed by the weight of the vast earth.
> *Megara*. No burden will crush the one who carried the heavens.
> *Lycus*. You will be forced.
> *Megara*. One who can be forced does not know how to die.[22]

This agonistic type of duet places a heavy emphasis on the 'Appellative' function, which, as Manfred Pfister points out, increases 'to the degree the dialogue partner is involved': the more he (or she) reacts, the stronger the appellative function will be.[23] Shakespeare's closest version of the scenario and technique of *Hercules furens*, Bart van Es points out,[24] is Richard of Gloucester's seduction of the Lady Anne:

> *Glou*. Why dost thou spit at me?
> *Anne*. Would it were mortal poison for thy sake!
> *Glou*. Never came poison from so sweet a place.
> *Anne*. Never hung poison on a fouler toad.
> Out of my sight; thou dost infect mine eyes.
> *Glou*. Thine eyes, sweet lady, have infected mine.
> *Anne*. Would they were basilisks, to strike thee dead.
>   (I, ii, 143–50)

Here the stichomythic pattern of enchained verbal echoes is a function of antipathy rather than collaboration. Similar examples from earlier Elizabethan drama, van Es observes, include the stichomythic resistance of Bel-Imperia to Balthazar's advances and Sidanen's resistance to Moorton's wooing in *John a Kent and John a Cumber*.[25] Perseda's exchange with Solimon is another example.[26] None of these unpleasant exchanges strictly qualify as unchaperoned, since they all take place, even in the case of Seneca, with others in the background to reduce or increase the sense of outrageousness (it is hard to say which). On the scale of Shakespearean wooing techniques, which can range from mutual attraction through the asymmetries caused by misprision, disguise and deliberate deception toward the extreme imbalances of seduction, blackmail and force,[27] Richard's forceful seduction of Anne, backed by power and verging on coercion, ranks high on the scales of appellative force and dialogical resistance; it is (at least until Anne's resistance begins to weaken) deficient where the duet of Hermia and Lysander is strongest; in those phatic dimensions that 'create and intensify the dialogical contact' between interlocutors. On the other hand, the seduction of Anne is high in 'metalingual' reference, which occurs whenever 'the verbal code used is explicitly or implicitly developed as a central theme'. Predominance of the metalingual function, Pfister explains, may be 'motivated by a high degree of verbal virtuosity of games with rules of the code.'[28] Though metalingual wit-combat need not involve such brutal antagonism as in the case of *Richard III*, it probably does, in many Shakespearean cases, signal a measure of sceptical mockery or resistance, an awareness of possible insincerities in lovemaking or reservations about differences and discordancies that make for a potential mismatch.[29]

It is probably a mistake, though, to think of Hermia and Lysander's first duet as deliberately witty, which is a way of saying that in this early scene, before the plot thickens, they are among Shakespeare's least mismatched couples; they set the pattern for the spontaneous intimacy of other Shakespearean duets in which love is mutual, 'no seduction is necessary' and 'all that is needed is occasion and privacy.'[30] That Hermia and Lysander are making poetry is not, apart from the purely phatic functions of their collaboration, internal to what they communicate to each other; the wittiness is external, apparent mainly to the audience. Stronger precedents for their echoing, rhyming and stichomythic exchanges are found in those earlier cases where Seneca's technique has been transferred to situations of romantic lovemaking. This begins to happen in the earliest surviving English stage romances, *Common Conditions* and *Sir Clyomon and Sir Clamydes*, which Robert Y. Turner identifies as containing the earliest Elizabethan love dialogues.[31] Senecan stichomythia produces only blandly straightforward declarations in Sir Clyomon's love scene with Neronis,[32] but in the unfinished *Common Conditions*, where it remains unclear whether the apparently reluctant Nomides (the disguised prince Sedmond) is finally destined for Sabia or for someone else, the element of resistance in erotic stichomythia has yielded something like witty repartee:

> *Nomides.* I am pensiue Lady but yet welcome to me as any one.
> *Sabia.* Not so sir knight, I thinke you beare to Ladies no such loue,
> *Nomides.* My Lady how know you that, you did me neuer proue.

> *Sabia.* She y^t should proue I thinke should finde in you sum suttel gyle.
> *Nomides.* You weemen sure are ful of y^t though oftentimes you smile.
> *Sabia.* We wemen? nay, in men you would say for wemen mean to true.
> *Nomides.* Say you so Lady? for experience then mark what woords ensue.
> *Sabia.* Speake forth your minde I am content if so you will not faine.
> *Nomides.* If so I do Lady, I doubt not, but you will reply againe.
> *Sabia.* And reason good if wrongfully you wemen would disproue.[33]

Because Balthazar's unwanted advances with Bel-Imperia are so clearly styled by Kyd's Senecanism, it is worth speculating that Kyd's juxtaposition of this predatory scene against Bel-Imperia's subsequent dialogue with her lover Horatio helped to transform Senecan stichomythia into what looks like a key precedent for Shakespeare's early love duets:

> *Horatio.* . . . . fair fortune is our friend,
> And heavens have shut up day to pleasure us.
> *Bel-Imperia.* . . . .Why sit we not? For pleasure asketh ease.
> *Horatio.* The more thou sit'st within these leafy bowers,
> The more will Flora deck it with her flowers.
> *Bel-Imperia.* Ay, but if Flora spy Horatio here,
> Her jealous eye will think I sit too near.
> *Horatio.* Hark, madam, how the birds record by night,
> For joy that Bel-Imperia sits in sight.
> *Bel-Imperia.* No, Cupid counterfeits the nightingale,
> To frame sweet music to Horatio's tale.
> *Horatio.* If Cupid sing, then Venus is not far,
> Ay, thou art Venus, or some fairer star.
> *Bel-Imperia.* If I be Venus thou must needs be Mars,
> And where Mars reigneth there must needs be wars.
> *Horatio.* Then thus begin our wars: put forth thy hand,
> That it may combat with my ruder hand.
> *Bel-Imperia.* Set forth thy foot to try the push of mine.
> *Horatio.* But first my looks shall combat against thine.
> *Bel-Imperia.* Then ward thyself. I dart this kiss at thee.
> *Horatio.* Thus I retort the dart thou threw'st at me. [*They kiss.*]
> (II, iv, 19–41)

Strong resonances with elements in the duets of Romeo and Juliet or with Jessica and Lorenzo's duet in Portia's garden suggest that

Kyd's duet was a prominent model for those of Shakespeare. While Shakespeare never did to his lovers anything quite so cruel as what the Senecan Kyd does to Horatio and Bel-Imperia (Horatio has been hanged in the arbour stabbed to death just six lines after the duet is interrupted), Kyd's nighttime setting and his ominous references to Cupid, Mars and Venus may have combined with the tragic outcome in Hieronymo's garden to lend some darker shading to the duets in *Romeo and Juliet* and *The Merchant of Venice*. Far more important, however, are the uses of echolalia and echopraxia in a game of love-making that turns heavy irony or Senecan defiance into witty and responsive playfulness.[34]

The prominence of similarly reactive or lyrically responsive expressions in love duets like those in *A Midsummer Night's Dream*, *Romeo and Juliet*, or *The Merchant of Venice* seems linked to the fact that in addition to using echolalia they also involve transactions that qualify in several senses as 'performatives'. First of all, just as the actor-audience relation can be reduplicated in the actor-actor relation, with the second actor serving as audience to the first, so it is possible for the actor to display as well as interact, to 'show' as well as tell. These duets are, first of all, courtship displays. I suspect Beckermann might find Shakespeare's love duets 'iconic' and 'confirmatory' in the same way he says a patriotic parade confirms the patriotism of its spectators – they do not so much prove or persuade as they confirm what the lovers already believe.[35] The love duets I've mentioned hover first of all around the display of the face and body (Lysander launches off the question of Hermia's pale cheek; Romeo and Juliet are all wrapped up in hands and lips; in Belmont, Lorenzo and Jessica zero in on memories of their earlier duet, the elopement scene and its concern with shame and hidden faces). All three duets reactively demonstrate appreciation in exclamations and interjections; they display the sympathies of the lovers in phatic responsiveness, and they demonstrate the fitness of each party (potentially or actually) for gamesome folly by using formal wordplay (such as shared diction, schemes, metre and rhyme) to secure the communication channel.

The erotic displays and protestations in Shakespeare's duets are linked, however, to the specifically Austinian ways in which these duets (unlike the one in *The Spanish Tragedy*) involve performative undertakings: they contain promises and commitments sealed by vows and oaths. Functioning in the same manner as echolalia, reciprocal promises are first of all a form of echopraxia; even as they contribute in the manner of echolalia to the immediate binding effects of 'flirtatious wordplay' they further bind the present to continuing commitments.[36] Like collaboration in the making of verbal patterns, which externalises emotion in a form the audience objectively perceives as love poems, promising is perhaps one of the few 'actions' that, by externalising emotion, can render mutual declarations of love dramatic to an audience.[37] Once again, Shakespeare's earliest precedents may have been those eventful mid-Elizabethan stage romances. In the key duet of *Sir Clyomon and Sir Clamydes*, Neronis reciprocates Clyomon's pledge of his heart with a love-token jewel (l. 1105), while in *Common Conditions* Clarisia and Lamphedon conclude their lengthy duet with an elaborate set of mutual pledges, tokens and invocations of legendary lovers:

> *Lamphedon.* And therfore Lady, here is my hande, eke faith and trouth I giue,
> To rest and be thy louing knight, whilst I haue day to liue.
> In signe wherof take here this gim, and weare it for my sake.
> *Clarisia.* Upon condicion noble knight, the same of thee I take.
> But yet receiue of Lady thine a pledge for pledge agayne,
> In token that for aye I rest thy loue without disdayne.
> The whiche Bracelet is made of golde, receaue that with good wil
> And all that doth belong to me, shall rest as thine owne still.
> Wherfore syr knight receiue the same of me thy lady deare.
> *Lamphedon.* I shall O Lady for your sake euen place it present here.
> And till I die I surely will weare it for loue of thine,
> *Clarisia.* And this shall rest in keping mine till dayes my life define.
> *Lamphedon.* Well Lady then, my wife you are before the gods you see,
> *Clarisia.* I am and will remaine my deare a true Penelopee.
> Though I for thy sweete sake my knight a thousand woes should proue:
> I would remaine as true to thee as shee did to her loue.
> *Lamphedon.* And Lady, as true will I still rest to thee,
> As Leander did that swome ouer the sea.
>
> (ll. 651–68)

Less than 200 lines later, these lovers' allusions to Penelope and Odysseus and Hero and Leander are answered much more ominously by Nomides and Sabia in a lengthy duet (805–902) that invokes the names of Helen and Menalaos, Cressida and Troilus, Ariadne and Theseus, Dido and Aeneas – many of the names that Shakespeare's lovers will reckon with.

In the romance worlds of these precedent-setting mid-Elizabethan plays, faithful lovers' vows are tested by wholly external misfortunes such as capture by pirates or flight from tyrants (*Solimon and Perseda*, too, begins in the manner of a romance, with courtly pledges and tokens between the lovers). But in Shakespeare's comedies the plot immediately thickens around the fact that in their promises Shakespeare's lovers are committing themselves to the necessarily clandestine acts and histrionic subterfuges that follow from their fates of being mismatched or otherwise crossed in love.[38] The lyrical sonnet scene between Romeo and Juliet only prepares for the emergence of their vows in their second duet at Juliet's balcony, while Jessica and Lorenzo's lyrical duet in Belmont, occurring late in the play, looks back on their first duet in the elopement scene ('In such a night / Did young Lorenzo swear he loved her well, / Stealing her soul with many vows of faith, / And ne'er a true one' (V, i, 18–20).[39] Hermia closes her litany with Lysander by swearing, ominously, to elope

> By Cupid's strongest bow,
> By his best arrow with the golden head,
> By the simplicity of Venus's doves,
> By that which knitteth souls and prospers loves,
> By that fire which burned the Carthage queen
> When the false Trojan under sail was seen,
> By all the vows that ever men have broke – [40]
>
> (I, i, 169–75)

Perhaps reflecting roots in chivalric stage romance, the echolalia and echopraxis of promising bestows upon Shakespeare's duets a quasi-liturgical quality (in fact, just as *A Midsummer Night's Dream* invokes the Litany, *The Merchant of Venice* evokes the Easter Vigil and *Romeo and Juliet* the rites of religious pilgrimage). This liturgical quality confirms the status of the duets as performatives in the Austinian sense. Promises rendered are accompanied by lyrical displays and extravagant professions of love, the purpose of which is not to secure the formal legitimacy of the performative procedures themselves, thus preventing what Austin calls 'misfires'. The procedures performed by Shakespeare's lovers are for the most part formally illegitimate, rash or rebellious 'misfires' of the proper conventional procedures. Lyrical displays of affection in Shakespeare serve to confirm instead that there are no 'abuses' (for example, insincere or hollow promises) that would render the undertakings 'infelicitous'.[41] In other words, the performatives of Shakespeare's youthful lovers tend to be so unconventional as to be procedurally invalid from the standpoint of society – they involve 'misinvocations' or 'misexecutions' of correct procedures – but they are otherwise 'felicitous' (they are sincerely loving misinvocations or misexecutions of the socially accepted procedures). The promises undertaken, with the possible exception of Lorenzo's oath to Jessica, are not instrumental, conditional or otherwise manipulative. They prolong communication and connection, but more importantly they are unconditional offers or uncompelled gifts, despite being mutually rendered. By contrast, the later 'broken nuptials' plays and problem comedies deal more with performatives that are formally correct, alas even binding, but otherwise 'infelicitous' (they involve insincere, hollow or otherwise abusive executions of correct and binding procedures – such as Angelo's promises, or Bertram's, or Troilus and Cressida's vows to each other).

Although the vows and promises in Shakespeare's early duets are seldom insincere in this later way, they are often, as Juliet says, 'rash' in ways that threaten to render their intended sincerity subsequently hollow. In the little duet between Proteus and Julia, for example (*The Two Gentlemen of Verona*, II, ii), a conspicuous dearth of rhyming and gamesome protestation augurs poorly for their performative exchange of rings and kisses; just four scenes later, having become jealous of Valentine's love for Silvia, Proteus blithely declares 'Unheedful vows may heedfully be broken' (II, vi, 11). In most of Shakespeare's early plays, however, reactive and balanced lyricism lends strong illocutionary support (by attesting to the fact of sincerity) to perlocutionary commitments sincerely undertaken. This makes it important to remember that Shakespeare's precedent for these quasi-liturgical commitments was very possibly the tradition of performing chivalric pledges on the stage a generation earlier.

It is of course ironic that in Shakespeare's duets pledges are so frequently overshadowed by the ominous precedents of legendarily infelicitous couples. Just 140 lines before Romeo and Juliet meet at the cell of Friar Laurence to take their formal vows, Mercutio mocks that compared to Romeo's Juliet Petrarch's Laura was 'a kitchen wench, . . . Dido a dowdy, Cleopatra a gipsy, Helen and Hero / hildings and harlots, Thisbe a grey eye or so; but not to the purpose' (II, iii, 33–5). Lorenzo and Jessica weave their duet in Belmont around a similar catalogue invoking Troilus and Cressida, Pyramus and Thisby, Aeneas and Dido, Jason and Medea.

Hermia's vows by Cupid's best arrow, the tawdry doves of Venus and 'that fire which burned the Carthage queen / When the false Trojan under sail was seen' fittingly conclude a duet that began with a catalogue of all the ways that lovers can be mismatched.[42] But even while these catalogues cast Shakespeare's lovers in an ironic light, they powerfully attest to his deeply literary-historical interest in mismatched couples as such, to his interest in the undertakings of love duets and to his interest in the problem of *folie à deux*. So powerful is this preoccupation that in *Troilus and Cressida* and *Antony and Cleopatra* (whose protagonists also channel Aeneas and Dido) Shakespeare actually revisits the scenes of the original crimes.

The risk of infelicity in erotic commitments and shared illusions also helps explain why Shakespeare's love duets, though short and relatively rare, are seldom solitary. Like the ghost of revenge tragedy, they tend to reappear strategically, partly as a simple matter of the plot's testing of commitments, but just as importantly to yoke the desire of the couple to that of the audience in something like the way a *da capo* aria (or duet) in baroque opera answers everyone's desire and suspense (both singers' and audience's) by reprising its opening theme. Hermia and Lysander's second brief duet, for example, finds them testing whether there might be a lie hidden in Lysander's pretty riddling over the 'One heart, one bed, two bosoms, and one troth' that will bed them on 'one turf' (an arrangement in which Hermia declines to participate) (II, ii, 47–8). The duet ends with a formal reconfirmation – Hermia's wish 'Thy life ne'er alter till thy sweet life end' is answered, liturgically, by Lysander's 'Amen, amen to that fair prayer' (II, ii, 79–80) – but this is just before Puck's application of love-in-idleness begins to hollow out the promises and shared illusions with a growing sense of differences. Jessica and Lorenzo's Act V duet is actually their second, a late-hour check-in on their earlier elopement scene, revisiting Lorenzo's swearing 'he loved her well / Stealing her soul with many vows of faith.' Up until its first interruption by a messenger, this duet remains a reciprocal and balanced lyrical game, though perhaps an increasingly mean or melancholy one; when it resumes with the departure of the Clown and Messenger, it shifts from balance and reciprocity to a more 'Active' mode, and Lorenzo's thirty-three insistent lines to Jessica's single-line declaration ('I am never merry when I hear sweet music' (V, i, 68)) may signal upward movement on the scale of resistance, pitting voluble coercion against silent opposition. Further off in the direction indicated by these hints of regret and reservation lie

the greater perversities of Shakespeare's more coercive love duets –
Gloucester's with the Lady Anne, Angelo's with Isabella, Bertram's
with Diana, or Lysimachus's with Marina.

Like those of Hermia and Lysander and Jessica and Lorenzo, the
several duets of Romeo and Juliet contend with a widening sense of
differences (beginning with the discovery of Juliet's name at the end
of the first). The last of these, the aubade scene, plays beautifully
by the formal rules of the lyrical duet, as night and day, nightingale
and lark, contend harmoniously even as they shift between the two
voices. But the lovers' final lines together, following the entry and
departure of the nurse (and thus forming a reprise of a reprise), take
the duet into a different domain altogether:

> *Jul.* O God, I have an ill-divining soul!
> Methinks I see thee now; thou art so low
> As one dead in the bottom of a tomb.
> Either my eyesight fails, or thou look'st pale.
>   *Rom.* And trust me, love, in my eye so do you;
> Dry sorrow drinks our blood. Adieu, adieu.
>
>   (III, v, 54–9)

'Methinks' is a Shakespearean dream-formula, and here the duet and
its shared illusions, though still pale face-to-pale face, are beginning
to enter the realm of joint hallucination and psychosomatic contagion. The passage throws into question my special case at the beginning for the 'unchaperoned duet', since it marks one beginning of
what might be called the 'occulted duet' in this play and in Shakespeare's subsequent work.

In *Romeo and Juliet*, the occulted duet is conducted, in the second
half of the play, mainly through the sympathetic vibrations between
the lovers' separate fears and dreams – a case in point is Romeo's
realisation that *even before* learning of Juliet's supposed death (and
without knowing of the friar's plan or the potion) he had *already
intuited*, just seeing the apothecary's shop, the desperation of a man
who would seek poison there. Juliet's ever-handy dagger is her sympathetic vibration with Romeo's malaise. The separate hallucina-
tions of the Macbeths perhaps make theirs an increasingly occulted
duet, as may the separate hyperbolical imaginings of Antony and
Cleopatra. Occulted intuitions may also be at work in Orlando's
only strictly unchaperoned duet with Rosalind, when both parties
(perhaps) hover around the question of Rosalind's faint in ways that
can (in performance) verge on unspoken recognition.

A second type of occulted duet arises from a second question begged by my initial proposition: must encounters be unchaperoned to qualify as duets, or can they occur in the presence of third parties? Simple cases like the self-betrothal of Ferdinand and Miranda in the unperceived presence of Prospero (III, i) – a duet that otherwise looks much like the early, symmetrical lyric performances with which I began – suggests that of course they can. By these terms, Orlando's handfasting with Rosalind in the presence of Celia might also qualify, especially if there is unspoken work to be done with perceptions arising from Orlando's holding of Rosalind's feminine hand. Antony and Cleopatra, often apart, are in fact never in the play 'alone together' but a case might be made for the play as an extended duet conducted entirely in and through the presence of others.

Another type of occulted duet is the one that involves strong currents of unspoken subtext. With Jessica and Lorenzo, this subtext emerges after the fact of their initial encounter, as a sense of possible regret or developing friction. Stripped of their carnival masks and the ducats and the jewels, they have arrived in Belmont, as Gratiano's earlier characterisation of desire perhaps predicts, like the prodigal 'scarfed bark' returning from sea 'With over-weathered ribs and ragged sails, / Lean, rent, and beggared by the strumpet wind' (II, vi, 18–19). More common in the early courtship plays, however, is occultation of an opposite sort, in which a powerful unspoken subtext at first outweighs the formal dance of the initial encounter, launching a complicated duet before the two parties are fully aware of its having begun or before they are willing or able to say openly how far things have already gone. A key precedent for such heavily subtextual duets, as Robert Turner observed, may have been the suggestion-heavy dialogues of John Lyly, where self-imposed inhibitions, whether in the form of external restraints internalised or of self-created fears, protect against the serious dangers of mismatch by means of wary games and thinly veiled innuendo. Prime examples are the duets between the painter Apelles and Campaspe, the Theban captive of Alexander (*Campaspe*, IV, iii, 1–55; IV, ii, 21–50) and between Sappho the Princess of Syracuse and the ferryman Phao, a mismatch destined not to be (*Sappho and Phao*, III, iv, 43–90).

Self-protective courtship fashioned in Lyly's arch, knowing vein tends to misfire in Shakespeare, as the damp squibs of *Love's Labour's Lost* or Beatrice's brief flirtation with the uncomprehending or unreceptive Don Pedro attest. Nevertheless, in keeping with the spirit of Lyly's example, old Capulet suggests that a 'visor' makes it easier at first to 'tell / A whispering tale in a fair lady's ear' (I, v, 19–20).

Shakespeare often uses the literal theatrical device of the mask (for example, in *Love's Labour's Lost*, *Romeo and Juliet*, *The Merchant of Venice* and *Much Ado about Nothing*) or the metaphorical masking of faces by the shadows of night in what might be deemed a Lylyian way, in order to establish those conditions of simultaneous licensure and inhibition, vulnerability and defensiveness, in which subtextual exchange can flourish in face-to-face encounter. In comedy, Shakespeare's preference is that the enabling masks should eventually come off, that the face should cease to function as a mask, and that the encounter should finally be open and on equal footing. This is why, even at the furthest extremes of veiled courtship, found in the deliberate assymmetries and deceptions of disguising in plays like *As You Like It* and *Twelfth Night* (where there is plenty of subtext but a dearth of unguarded and fully reciprocal duets) the ending lies in the explicitness of mutual exposure and recognition.

Perhaps the most interesting cases of subtext-heavy duets in the early corpus are the formal one-on-ones of Katherine and Petrucchio and of Beatrice and Benedick, both of which initially develop the subtext below the threshold of the participants' consciousness and much higher up on the scale of resistance (with 'fighting', for example), and in the former case with perhaps less balance and lyrical reactivity than active force, before arriving at rapprochements more like the more reciprocal and lyrical duets of *A Midsummer Night's Dream*, *Romeo and Juliet* or *The Merchant of Venice*. If it is not read as a scene of crude sexual harassment on the part of Petrucchio, the wit-combat of his first duet with Katherina – with its bawdy, tumbling double entendres of join-stool, bearing ass, mounted jade, tail-stinger and tongue in tail – may be seen as a still occulted (but perhaps already mutual) expression of sexual attraction and temperamental likeness despite the odds. Not all would agree that this scene or the sun vs. moon game (applauded by Hortensio as Petrucchio's victory) or the kiss in the street in Padua (where Grumio stands by to support Petrucchio's possibly extortionate threat to return home) can qualify as balanced or lyrical, or even as duets, but it can be argued that in both scenes the husband and wife share, romantically, in illusions and games – conjured up at the expense of others and over their heads – in ways that verge on the collaboratively metalingual and the theatrically performative. The submission of Katherina in the play's final scene can certainly be read as a collaborative theatrical performance, the conclusion of an occulted duet that perhaps recalls the one performed by Penelope and Odysseus just before the contest of the bow and the slaughter of the suitors.

Perhaps less controversial is the principal duet in *Much Ado About Nothing*, for which the audience as well as Beatrice and Benedick, prepared by their previous encounters, have been waiting until the moment when the stage is finally vacated for their most intimate duet in the aborted wedding scene. The silent interval (on the page, the white space) between the exits of the wedding party and Benedick's first words to Beatrice mark one of the most decisive of Shakespeare's romantic commitments, as Benedick remains onstage to share with Beatrice a root conviction of Hero's innocence. The two begin to commit themselves, in the symmetries of a prose (part of Shakespeare's Lylyian heritage) that combines performatives with lyrical protestations:

> *Bene.* By my sword, Beatrice, thou lovest me.
> *Beat.* Do not swear and eat it.
> *Bene.* I will swear by it that you love me, and I will make him eat it that says not I love you.
> *Beat.* Will you not eat your word?
> *Bene.* With no sauce that can be devised to it. I protest I love thee.
> *Beat.* Why then, God forgive me!
> *Bene.* What offense, sweet Beatrice?
> *Beat.* You have stayed me in a happy hour, I was about to protest I loved you.
> *Bene.* And do it with all thy heart.
> *Beat.* I love you with so much of my heart that none is left to protest.
> *Bene.* Come, bid me do anything for thee.
> *Beat.* Kill Claudio.
>
> (IV, iv, 272–82)

The lyrical reactivity and balance established by Beatrice and Benedick is capacious enough to accommodate both sceptical resistance and forceful persuasion of the strongly active, appellative type. In appellative force, Beatrice quickly overtakes Benedick's initial lead in the duet, inducing shock with a blunt proposal that swiftly carries them from those chivalric oathtaking love dialogues of the mid-Elizabethan period toward the mad project of the Macbeths. In Beatrice's subsequent attack on Benedick's manhood and in Benedick's capitulation, that resemblance is confirmed, as joint madness and folly, despite its foundation in strong moral instincts, threatens to prevail. To reverse the sequence in which

Erasmus's Folly presents her case, there are two kinds of madness: the madness that frees the mind and restores the soul and the madness that leads to blood-soaked crime.[43] Benedick, in all seriousness, actually delivers his mortal challenge to Claudio, though a scene revealing the constabulary's discoveries intervenes, thereby casting a comic light on Benedick's next attempt, against his better nature, to harden his murderous resolve and undermining his already self-undermined lament of his distracted state: 'in loving, Leander the good swimmer, Troilus the first employer of panders, and a whole book full of these quondam carpet-mongers whose names yet run smoothly in the even road of a blank verse, why they were never so truly turned over and over as my poor self in love' (V. ii. 22–6). 'Turned over and over': Benedick nods less than half-seriously toward famously tragic victims of *folie à deux* and toward places where the later Shakespeare will be more inclined to go. But Benedick's scenes with Beatrice, in their echoes and debts to plays like *The Taming of the Shrew*, *A Midsummer Night's Dream*, *Romeo and Juliet* and *The Merchant of Venice*, suggest that the matrix for Shakespeare's treatment of erotic mania was the early and innovative love duet.

Notes

1. Bernard Beckerman, 'Shakespeare's Industrious Scenes', *Shakespeare Quarterly*, especially pp. 144, 150; Beckerman, 'Shakespeare's Dramaturgy and Binary Form'.
2. 297.3: 'Shared Psychotic Disorder (Folie à Deux)', *Diagnostic and Statistical Manual of Mental Disorders: DSM-IV*, 4th edn (Washington, DC: American Psychiatric Association, 1994). Carrying further the preference of the *DSM-IV* for *folie imposée* over *folie simultanée* and thus retaining its emphasis on the source of delusion in the 'inducer' or 'primary case', the new DSM-5 relegates to the category of 'other' the diagnosis of 'delusional symptoms in partner of individual with [the now primary case of] delusional disorder' (298.8), *Diagnostic and Statistical Manual of Mental Disorders: DSM-5*, 5th edn (Washington, DC: American Psychiatric Publishing, 2013).
3. *Two treatises* (1644) and *A late discourse . . . Touching the cure of wounds by the powder of sympathy* (1658), selections anthologised in Richard Hunter and Ida Macalpine (eds), *Three Hundred Years of Psychiatry, 1535–1860* (London: Oxford University Press), pp. 124–7.
4. William Shakespeare, all citations of Shakespeare are from *The New Oxford Shakespeare: Modern Critical Edition*, ed. Gary Taylor et al.

5. See William Empson, 'The Praise of Folly' and 'Fool in Lear', in *The Structure of Complex Words*, pp. 107–74.

6. See John Milton, *Paradise Lost*, 4, 481–6.

7. The translation is by Norman Austin in his *Archery at the Dark of the Moon: Poetic Problems in Homer's Odyssey*, p. 181; I am indebted throughout this paragraph to Austin's account of marriage in *The Odyssey*, pp. 179–238.

8. On the view that Helen and Menelaos regard the marriage of Penelope and Odysseus as a mismatch, see especially Eva Brann, *Homeric Moments: Clues to Delight in Reading 'The Odyssey' and 'The Iliad'*, Ch. 24.

9. Hesiod, *Catalogues of Women, fragment 68.21–7, in Homeric Hymns, Epic Cycle, Homerica*; Pausanias, *The Description of Greece*, III, xii, 2; III, xx, 10–11.

10. *The Taming of the Shrew*, III, ii, 244. The play's most overt allusion to *The Odyssey* – a work that many experts doubt that Shakespeare knew – is indirect, channelled through Lucentio's and Bianca's use of two slightly misquoted lines from Penelope's letter to Odysseus in Ovid's *Heroides*: '*Hic ibat Simois; hic est Sigeia tellus; Hic stererat Priami regia celsa senis*' (III, I, 28–9; cf *Heroides* 1.33–4 in *Ovid: Heroides and Amores*). On the significance of this allusion, see Heather James, 'Shakespeare's Learned Heroines in Ovid's Schoolroom', and Margaret Ferguson, 'Translation and Homeland Insecurity in Shakespeare's *The Taming of the Shrew*'. My summary of the Penelope-Odysseus mismatch above and my allusion below to the contest of the bow and the slaughter of the suitors are meant to raise the question of whether, by the time he wrote *The Taming of the Shrew*, Shakespeare had a more direct acquaintance with Homer, perhaps through the same Greek-Latin edition by Spondanus (*Homeri Quae Extant Omnia*, Basel, 1583) used by George Chapman. On Shakespeare's possible familiarity with this text, see A. D. Nuttall, 'Action at a Distance: Shakespeare and the Greeks', and Paul A. Olson, *Beyond a Common Joy: An Introduction to Shakespearean Comedy*, p. 114.

11. William Kerrigan, 'The Personal Shakespeare', in *Shakespeare's Personality*, p. 178.

12. See my 'Shakespeare and the Golden Fleece'.

13. Erasmus, *The Praise of Folly*, in *Collected Works*, 27: 97. For an essay linking both Erasmus and Shakespeare to Levinasian ethics, see Donald R. Wehrs, 'Touching Words: Embodying Ethics in Erasmus, Shakespearean Comedy, and Contemporary Theory'.

14. In William Cooke, *Memoirs of Samuel Foote, Esq. with A Collection of His Genuine Bon-Mots, Anecdotes, Opinions, &c.* (2 vols) (New York, 1806), 2: 78.

15. Erasmus, *The Praise of Folly*, in *Collected Works*, 2: 152.

16. Morley makes great fun with imitative form in the fifth canzonet: 'I goe before my darling, / Follow thou to the bowre in the close alley, / Ther wee will together, / Sweetly kisse each eyther, / And like two wantons, / Dally, dally, dally, dally, dally, dally, dally, dally, dally, dally, dally, dally, dally, dally'. Canzonet V in *The First Booke of Canzonets to Two Voyces* (1595), sig. B3v.

    In Morley's *A Plaine and Easie Introduction to Practicall Musicke* (1597) (accessed at http://tei.it.ox.ac.uk/tcp/Texts-HTML/free/A07/A07753.html), the music master prefers, as 'songes wherein to exercise', songs 'of two parts, which I haue made of purpose, that when you haue any friend to sing with you, you may practice together, which wil sooner make you perfect than if you should studie neuer so much by your selfe' (p. 55). In connection with this pedagogy inherent in the duet form, it seems worth recalling the structure of apprenticeship built into Shakespeare's love duets: beneath the (usually) opposite-gendered roles in Shakespeare's love duets lies the instructional relationship between master actor and his boy apprentice. See especially Scott McMillin, 'The Sharer and His Boy: Rehearsing Shakespeare's Women'.

17. Helena's claim, and indeed Shakespeare's habitual juxtapositions of love with folly, may have been influenced not only by Erasmus but by Robert Greene's translation of the first two discourses of Louise Labé's *Débat de folie at d'amour* (1556) as *The debate betweene Folly and Loue* (1584). While the sighted Cupid once made proper matches, joining like with like, Folly, responsible for the matches of Venus with Mars, Helen with Paris and Dido with Aeneas, blinds Cupid, covers his eyes and gives him wings to show that it is she who 'gouerneth the heart, the braine, and the minde'. While Apollo laments on the 'confused inequalities' resulting from Folly's influence over Love, Mercury defends Folly's claims that 'Loue should be of no force without her' (*Gwyndonus. The Carde of Fancie* (1584), sigs. T3v, U4).

18. C. L. Barber, *Shakespeare's Festive* Comedy, p. 233.

19. Beckerman, *Theatrical Presentation: Performer, Audience, and Act*, pp. 138–45.

20. See Roman Jakobson, 'Linguistics and Poetics'.

21. The dialogues between Lelia and Flammino in *Gli Ingannati*, where Lelia (like her descendant, Shakespeare's *Viola*) remains in male disguise with her employer, are perhaps the closest thing in the *commedia* to the exposures and intimacies in Shakespeare's undisguised duets.

22. *Seneca. Vol. VIII: Tragedies*, ll. 422–7.

23. Manfred Pfister, *The Theory and Analysis of Drama*, p. 111.

24. Bart van Es, *Shakespeare in Company*, pp. 67–71.

25. *Shakespeare in Company*, p. 68. See Kyd, *The Spanish Tragedy*, ed. David Bevington, 1.4.80.99; Munday, *John a Kent and John a Cumber*, ll.175–80.

26. See Kyd, *Solimon and Perseda*, IV, I, 90–114.

27. This range is succinctly described by Paul Budra, 'Affecting Desire in Shakespeare's Comedies of Love', pp. 98–109.
28. Pfister, *Theory and Analysis of Drama*, pp. 113, 115.
29. A dialogue that might have contributed to elements of scepticism and mockery in Shakepearean love dialogues is Erasmus's colloquy *Proci et puella*, translated by Nicholas Leigh as *A Modest Mean to Marriage, pleasantly set forth by That Famous Clerk Erasmus Roterdamus* (1568). See Susan Snyder's 'Introduction' and 'Erasmus' Colloquies', pp. 6–8, 233–9.
30. Budra, 'Affecting Desire', p. 98.
31. Robert Y. Turner, 'Some Dialogues of Love in Lyly's Comedies', pp. 276–88; without making the connection to Seneca, Turner identifies the dialogues in *Common Conditions* and *Sir Clyomon and Sir Clamydes* as the earliest examples in the Elizabethan period.
32. *Clyomon and Clamydes: A Critical Edition*, ll. 1048–1109 (pp. 111–13).
33. *Common Conditions*, ll. 806–15 (pp. 24–5).
34. *Solimon and Perseda* perhaps anticipated *The Spanish Tragedy* in this regard, since there, too, a stichomythic agon between Perseda and the tyrannical Soliman (IV, i, 91–114) is juxtaposed against a subsequent love duet between Perseda and Erastus (V, i, 1–19) just moments before he is strangled. This precedent is acknowledged in *The Spanish Tragedy* (ed. Bevington) itself, IV, i, 13–66.
35. Beckerman, *Theatrical Presentation*, p. 81.
36. See John Kerrigan, *Shakespeare's Binding Language*, pp. 32–3.
37. See Turner, 'Some Dialogues of Love', p. 277.
38. Thus William Kerrigan connects the predilection of Shakespeare's lovers for acting, pretence and feigning to the problem of erotic heterogeneity: 'They have chosen unconventional roles for themselves and must improvise unwritten scripts for the conduct of their lives,' 'The Personal Shakespeare', p. 180.
39. Beckerman observes that 'the reactive structure' helps with 'recalling the past, focusing on the present, and imagining a future', *Theatrical Presentation*, p. 144.
40. She is probably recalling promises that were never made by Virgil's hero but prominently featured in a scene of *Dido Queen of Carthage* (III, ix, 40–50); both because of its duet form and because of its classical prestige, the scene must also count as another key precedent for the unchaperoned duets of Shakespeare.
41. I am departing here from Austin's terminology. For Austin, 'infelicitousness' is a generic quality common to the two species of 'misfires' (incorrect procedures) and 'abuses' (insincere or hollow performances of correct procedures). For me, and I think for Shakespeare, a 'misfire' can be 'felicitous' in the broader sense (if not in Austin's sense specifically) when it entails no abuses or hollowness. See *How to Do Things with Words*, pp. 12–24.

42. In this regard, too, there is a precedent for Shakespeare's technique in *Common Conditions*, where Sabia and Nomides precede their own vows with an ominous catalogue of dubious couples: Helen and Paris, Troilus and Cressida, Phaedra and Hippolytus, Jason and Medea, Dido and Aeneas, Ariadne and Theseus, ll. 781–810.
43. Erasmus, *The Praise of Folly*, in *Collected Works*, p. 111.

Chapter 3

The Course of Recognition in *Cymbeline*

Matthew James Smith

One of the stated aims of this collection of essays is to bring some of the offerings of performance studies to bear on matters of ethics in Shakespearean drama. Thinking with the preposition – face *to* face, intentionally omitting the hyphens in noun and adverb forms – invites us to consider, for instance, how certain phenomenological approaches to the human face both inform and change when subjected to the performativity of theatre. The appearance of a face in Shakespeare's plays differs in important ways from the appearance of a face in philosophical reflection. When a face features in drama it does not simply appear but comes before characters and audiences in a conspicuous aspect. That is to say, in Richard II's reflection in his mirror, in Mariana's resolution to 'unmask' before Angelo, in Hamlet's sympathy for the 'portraiture' of Laertes's 'cause', and in all of the face-to-face scenes considered in this volume, the face features as the frontal aspect not only of a person but also, and perhaps primarily, of a relation to the other. One of the more prominent of such relational aspects is found in the recognition scene, a device that has long been associated with drama's moral revelations, and one question to ask of recognition scenes is how the reciprocity of face-to-face encounters enables moments of otherwise circumstantial reunion between characters to establish or correct real social relationships, such that the face to face fashions a kind of grace out of capricious materials, though in some ways it may not be said to *cause* it. Or, put in performative terms, how do such scenes and the unexpected reversals of action that often accompany them serve to imbue the new or desired social conditions that recognition scenes create with accepted moral authority? An answer, I believe, is found not in any qualities of the face as imagined abstractly or ideally but in the process of its appearing and performance, in the often extraordinary circumstances that enable a scene of mutual presence.

The reunion of Posthumus and Innogen at the end of Shakespeare's late play, *Cymbeline*, demonstrates ways that recognition scenes can sometimes follow a theatrical logic of the face to face toward the mutual acceptance of a normative moral agreement. In Act V we find Posthumus despairingly listening to Giacomo's confession, despite Posthumus's best efforts to make himself a casualty of war. Giacomo, he learns, had not seduced Innogen after all. Instead, having been 'thus quenched / Of hope' in his intention to sleep with Innogen, he reveals how he presented 'simular proof enough / To make the noble Leonatus mad / . . . / With tokens thus and thus' (V, xi, 195, 200–1, 203).[1] Posthumus, taking responsibility for falling victim to Giacomo's ploy, responds to his story with his own confession to Cymbeline:

> Thou, King, send out
> For torturers ingenious. It is I
> That all th'abhorred things o'th' earth amend
> By being worse than they. I am Posthumus,
> That killed thy daughter –
>
> (V, vi, 214–18)

Innogen and Pisanio restively hear Posthumus's lament – 'O Innogen! / My queen, my life, my wife, O Innogen, / Innogen, Innogen!' – but it is Innogen, up until now disguised as Fidele, that first answers: 'Peace, my lord, hear, hear –' (V, vi, 225–7). Taking her for a 'page', Posthumus strikes Innogen, and the ensuing eruption of voices suddenly breaks the perceptual focus caused by Giacomo's and Posthumus's confessions and scatters it among several characters' individual expressions of surprise and confusion:

> POSTHUMUS   Shall's have a play of this? Thou scornful page,
> There lie thy part!
>   [*He strikes her and she falls.*]
> PISANIO   O gentlemen, help!
> Mine and your mistress! O my lord Posthumus,
> You ne'er killed Innogen till now. Help, help!
> Mine honored lady.
> CYMBELINE   Does the world go round?
> POSTHUMUS   How comes these staggers on me?
> PISANIO   Wake, my mistress.
> CYMBELINE   If this be so, the gods do mean to strike me
> To death with mortal joy.
>
> (V, vi, 228–34)

What had been a series of notably focused monologues breaks into dizzying aural chaos. Almost everyone is at fault. And so with this dispersal of attention and with Posthumus's shocking display of violence comes the need for a new sensory principle to mediate the characters, especially in the absence of a full understanding of the events that have led to this moment. This principle cannot be a simplistic notion of Innogen's identity – for we've already seen how the question of identity can be falsified through bracelets and rings, 'tokens thus and thus'. The characters sound out for a new stabilising echo, a point of view, sound and sight that might allow them to move forward together.

We can glimpse Shakespeare's suggestion of a way forward through the scene's use of metatheatrical imagery to bring Innogen back to presence. Posthumus accuses her of having a 'play' and lying in her 'part', in an analogy that invokes antitheatrical attacks that denounced stage players as hypocrites. Cymbeline's expression of the world as 'round' acknowledges the ring-like circumference of playhouses like the Globe, where Simon Forman recorded attending a performance in 1611.[2] This description of the scene as 'round' also describes the circular or regressive quality of recognition in the form of *anagnorisis* – returning to knowledge or knowing again. And perhaps the fact that in Forman's account of the plot he paraphrases the final events of *anagnorisis* with a cursory '&c' punctuates the scene's predictable, or even cyclical, impression. Moreover, with this word Cymbeline also acknowledges the call-and-response, songlike rhythm of Innogen's interruption of Posthumus, Posthumus's interruption of Innogen and Pisanio's interruption of Posthumus, echoing the sound of popular music sung in the 'round'. Cymbeline continues to record the impression of Innogen's reappearance as music just moments later when he characterises hearing her voice in the manner of popular ballad tunes, exclaiming, 'The tune of Innogen' (V, vi, 238). And after impatiently witnessing the reunion of Innogen to her betrothed, Cymbeline turns again to theatrical metaphors, complaining that Innogen has delayed too long in attending to him, in recognising him, and he accuses her of making him 'a dullard in this act', here employing a term sometimes used to characterise audiences who are insensitive to the nuances of drama and poetry (V, vi, 265).

These musical and theatrical patterns emphasise the preposition of face-*to*-face recognition. *To* is a directional preposition. A face – even Innogen's face – is not quite good enough for the desperate characters of *Cymbeline*. What they need is a connection, a direction to face and someone to be faced by. Michel Serres compares prepositions to angels, winged messengers who create meaning by making such connections. 'Already present – always and everywhere – when the need of a transformation begins to be felt. Weaving space, constructing time, they are the precursors of every presence . . . In fact, dare I say it, the *pré-posés* are there even before the fact of being there.'[3] *Cymbeline*'s characters gradually but decidedly build toward the 'need of a transformation', a way out of impending tragedy. This transformation is discovered, and tragedy is averted, in recognition – not *through* recognition, but *in* recognition, what Paul Ricoeur describes as a 'festive' quality, a celebration of recognition as a meaning-making act.[4] It could be argued that Shakespeare's late romances, including *Cymbeline*, are distinctively simple in this regard. They threaten to turn towards tragedy through a failure of recognition, a cancelling of the middle term in the face-to-face, and then, through a second turning as in the 'round', they offer grace by restoring the theatrical middle term that was lost.

In this essay I want to unpack some seldom examined implications involved in treating recognition as a key moral component to tragic and post-tragic plays. Influenced especially by the philosophical criticism of Stanley Cavell, as well as by Hannah Arendt, Ludwig Wittgenstein and Emmanuel Levinas, it is now common for scholars to describe Shakespeare's tragic situations as failures of recognition. In this vein, a character refuses to acknowledge the mediation of others insofar as they might both challenge and enable that character's sense of autonomy and self-consciousness. Such readings have their roots – even if they ultimately fall far from the tree – in Fichte's and Hegel's notion of *Anerkennung*, or mutual recognition. More often than not, these readings focus on scenes of dramatic recognition, but this habit is not as straightforward as it may seem. For in so doing, scholars inadvertently conflate two overlapping yet distinct forms of recognition – *Anerkennung* and the classical device of *anagnorisis*, a character's movement from a state of ignorance to knowledge.

While it may seem natural to look to moments when characters discover or fail to discover each other's true identities in order to examine breakdowns in social recognition, this convergence of classical and modern notions of recognition is tenuous – and yet potentially promising – both as a practice of literary criticism and as moral philosophy. In literary criticism, there is no reason to think that playwrights would dramatise the historical achievement of reciprocal recognition through scenes in which one character discovers the true nominal identity of another. Moreover, classical and modern forms of recognition would seem to inform divergent systems of moral philosophy. As characterised by Aristotle, *anagnorisis* serves to produce certain socially productive emotions, such as a feeling of shame excited by witnessing the extreme actions of the tragic character. Likewise, as adapted by Seneca, scenes of *anagnorisis* (using the cognate, *agnoscere*) operate as a kind of mirror, showing spectators the consequences of unruly passions.[5] *Anerkennung*, on the other hand, is a historical accomplishment and as such, in Hegel's ethical thought, relocates the notion of normative moral rules from metaphysics to social achievement.

In Shakespeare studies, this confusion may explain in part the difficulty scholars have had in accounting for Shakespeare's romances or post-tragic plays.[6] Presumably, we call these late plays 'post-tragic' not simply because Shakespeare writes them after he writes his tragedies but because their plots progress through a seemingly permanent tragic situation towards some form of conciliation or repair. And insofar as recognition is a pivotal element to what this 'moving through' entails – recognition as the establishment or re-establishment of continuity – explanations of the post-tragic will vary depending on whether one is talking about *anagnorisis*, *Anerkennung* or a further response to *Anerkennung* in the phenomenological tradition. This essay resumes its reading of *Cymbeline* in order to advance the promising study of recognition in Shakespeare criticism by first disambiguating the dramatic and moral distinctives of several classical and modern forms of recognition and then by suggesting one way that they might be seen to intersect productively. The two broad forms of nominal and mutual recognition indeed converge, namely, as some of the philosophical underpinnings of mutual recognition are embedded in the very theatricality that makes outlandish scenes of *anagnorisis* possible. My ultimate aim is to introduce the notion that *Cymbeline* demonstrates a conspicuous return to *anagnorisis* and to the face-to-face as a mode of what Paul Ricoeur calls 'the festive'. In this usage, the festive refers to the ability of drama to imbue the act of recognising, the very celebration of recognition and the face to face, with the power to repair and even to evolve the moral foundations of society. The grace that is exchanged at the end of *Cymbeline* is founded on just such a celebration of the surrogating power of the theatrical aspects of *anagnorisis* to re-establish the middle term of the face *to* face.

Choosing the right participle

In writing on *Cymbeline* it is common to find a list of the final scene's extraordinarily elaborate serial and interconnected recognitions and tale-tellings. Fidele recognises Posthumus's ring on Giacomo's hand. Giacomo confesses to his wager with Posthumus. Posthumus discloses his own identity. Fidele reveals herself to be Innogen. And on and on until the soothsayer revises his reading of the signs, Cymbeline renews his tribute to Rome and all are reconciled. It also typically does not go without mentioning that this recognition sequence is the longest of any in Shakespeare's plays, 539 lines in the First Folio, counting from the announcement of the queen's death.

It is reasonable, therefore, to assume that Shakespeare is particularly interested in exploring recognition as a tragic and post-tragic device in *Cymbeline*. As a post-tragic play, *Cymbeline* arguably uses recognitions for moving beyond the tragic situation. And a host of philosophically and theologically laden options for describing this act of 'moving beyond' the tragic situation is available. Through recognition the character could be *transcending*, *negating*, *overcoming*, *surviving*, *adapting to* or *redeeming* tragedy, and from the perspective of the critic, each participle reflects a corresponding philosophy of moral action.[7] In fact, it could be argued that one of the distinct challenges facing the play's characters is the very struggle to make sense of their efforts to avoid tragic calamity – the quandary of choosing the right participle.

For example, having found it within himself to forgive Innogen without any essential change in his knowledge of her – that is, without *anagnorisis* – Posthumus bemoans the irony of his 'noble misery': 'I, in mine own woe charmed, / Could not find death where I did hear him groan, / Nor feel him where he struck' (V, v, 64, 68–70). Shall we say that Posthumus has survived the justice he deserves? Or, has he found himself on the losing side of a struggle to the death, prompting him to assume the identity of a Roman prisoner? One thing is certain: while something has led Posthumus to contrition, he is no freer for it: 'My conscience, thou art fettered / More than my shanks and wrists' (V, v, 102–3). Principles like moral duty, social contract and autonomy of will have lost their meaning for Posthumus, and all he can think to do is ransom himself for a return that is already forfeited:

> For me, my ransom's death;
> On either side I come to spend my breath,
> Which neither here I'll keep nor bear again,
> But end it by some means for Innogen.
>
> (V, v, 80–3)

Maybe Posthumus imagines himself as a kind of scapegoat. If so, his efforts at self-sacrifice put him in a different category from Agamemnon and Iphigenia: there is no purchase on Posthumus's death, since he himself already committed the act of betrayal that renders doing anything 'for Innogen' impossible. Nor is Posthumus's desired sacrifice like that of Abraham and Isaac, since, as Kierkegaard would say, his self-martyrdom lacks 'concealment' – an essential requirement for an act of faith.[8] As far as Posthumus knows, there is nothing hidden from him; there are only the consequences of his actions laid bare and yet wrenchingly ineffectual.

In short, Posthumus finds himself not at the beginning of a tragic plot – like Agamemnon who must choose between two terrible paths – but at the end of one. What comes after and saves both him and Innogen is one of the many nominal recognitions that populate the final scene. It is a moment of *anagnorisis*, like the others, but also like the others – and, I argue, problematically if we want to consider the question of recognition as making sense of the post-tragic – Posthumus's recognition of Innogen is excessively circumstantial. If we recall, for a moment, Aristotle's list of types of recognition catalogued in the *Poetics*, which includes recognition by signs, tokens, through the author's intervention and through reasoning and paralogism, we note that not one of *Cymbeline*'s final recognitions is 'brought about directly by the incidents, the surprise being produced by means of what is likely.'[9] Whereas recognition from the action itself is ideal, the other forms are less artful, meaning they succeed less in holding together the opposing forces of the marvellous with the inevitable that are thought to propel *catharsis*. In this particular case recognition comes through Giacomo's voluntary confession. Like Posthumus, Giacomo's contrition is not instigated by a change in knowledge and actually precedes *anagnorisis*. Recognition, here, fits Aristotle's category of those that are 'manufactured by the poet', caused by 'what the poet wants and not what the plot requires'.[10] Thus, so the theory goes, the sequence of events that leads to Innogen's restoration appears less caused, is less transferable and fails to meet the force of the play's tragic inevitability.

In one way, this incidental quality of recognition is no surprise. After all, Terence Cave wrote a nearly comprehensive volume on recognition in which he describes it as a 'scandal', 'characteristically juxtapos[ing] two moments of fictional biography . . . sketching the structure of a life and in many cases suggesting the precariousness of the structure, its proneness to collapse.'[11] Recognition scenes in the classical mode of *anagnorisis* buckle under the weight of the extreme

circumstantiality of various spyings of bracelets, birthmarks, foot-
prints, locks of hair and vocal accents. Cave finds value, however, in
this problem of the superficiality of recognition in that such scenes
help us understand how 'fictions as such are constituted, the way in
which they play with and on the reader, their distinctive marks *as*
fictions – untruth, disguise, trickery, "suspense" or deferment, the
creation of effects of shock or amazement, and so on.'[12] While this
may be true, it is a far cry from Aristotle's reliance on the primacy
and cohesion of tragic action as the heuristic machine that produces
the kinds of healthy shame that discourage social disruption and that
befit a good citizen.[13]

Piero Boitani, who also has written extensively on dramatic recognition, offers a strikingly different explanation of the narrative
gaps that are manifest in the practices of recognition. 'To recognize
those we love is a god', he quotes from Euripides's account of Menelaos's recognition of Helen after the fall of Troy.[14] Viewed as a form
of grace, recognition functions like J. L. Austin's notion of the 'perlocutionary act' and what Cavell subsequently terms 'passionate utterance'.[15] To recognise someone we love simultaneously activates that
love, both describing and enabling the love that motivates it. This
characterisation of *anagnorisis* as an occurrence of grace attributes
heightened spiritual and moral significance to the continuity of relationships. When one who is lost is recognised, their reappearance
becomes relational; it affects others through the act of recognition.
Sanford Budick's Kantian treatment of tragedy locates a similar form
of grace that he terms 'benediction' in the turn from the tragic recognition of the 'endlessness' of suffering to the 'moral feeling' that
one finds in this place of desolation (Lear in the wilderness, Oedipus
at Colonus).[16] It is in the experience of 'nothing' that one glimpses
a moral duty toward others as mere humans, and for Budick Shakespeare conditions this transformation by harnessing 'the magic of
presence and disappearance in tragic theater'.[17] While this characterisation of moral feeling differs acutely from Hegelian readings
of morality as a historical achievement occasioned by recognition,
both Budick and Boitani locate a kind of grace or blessing in the
re-establishment of a character's moral connection to or continuity
with others. In fact, the rediscovery of the other can even create or
build upon a moral relation that may have only been inchoate. These
examples show *anagnorisis* using continuity to traverse the divide
between merely nominal recognition and a more existential event.

Does this characterise our experience of *Cymbeline*, though? Do
we, as readers and audience members, *use* Guiderius's birthmark,

Posthumus's ring, Innogen's bracelet, Giacomo's confession and Cornelius's corrective story as opportunities to reflect on the blessing of recognition and on the grace that such contingent factors might be thought to effect through continuity? The reason I am raising these questions is not to say that recognition is a cheap narrative trick and that attempts to make sense of it predictably strain our belief. Quite the opposite: classical recognition in the form of *anagnorisis* is powerful, I believe, for the same reason that Aristotle describes it as the pivotal catalyst producing tragic emotion. For Aristotle, recognition is tasked with holding together the naturally repelling magnetic charges of the inevitable and the marvellous. But in practice, as in *Cymbeline*, recognition fails to do this, and most often it favours the marvellous to the neglect or even outright eschewal of the inevitable.

From *anagnorisis* to a failure of recognition

In the preceding section I've been referring to recognition as a device of poetics. Yet scholars of Shakespeare will be quick to point to another perspective on dramatic recognition that seems to escape the circumstantiality and over-cooked plot turns of many instances of *anagnorisis*. I'm referring, of course, to the rich and influential work done in the vein of Fichte's and Hegel's *Anerkennung* – understood in different situations as mutual recognition, acknowledgement and intersubjectivity. This way of reading Shakespearean tragedy, championed especially by Cavell, is familiar to us – but I wonder if it has become too familiar. It is easy to interpret the tragic situation as a loss of acknowledgement, but the inverse interpretation has been slower to gain traction. I mean the relative absence of explanations that attribute the overcoming of a potentially tragic situation to the achievement of mutual recognition. Cavell's readings are persuasive to many of us, but little has been said to clarify how the two forms of recognition – *anagnorisis* and *Anerkennung* – differ and overlap.[18] At stake in discerning the relation between classical recognition and mutual recognition is not so much the question of the past but of the future – a vision of the cause-and-effect that might be said to characterise the unlikely endings of *Cymbeline*, *Pericles*, *The Winter's Tale* and *The Tempest*.

One central difference between mutual recognition and *anagnorisis* is that mutual recognition cannot be merely nominal, discursive or conventional. Mutual recognition must entail understanding one's being *for* oneself through the mediation of another. It involves a subject-subject relation rather than a one-directional recognition of a thing's or person's identity – or *Wiedererkennung*, a term indicating one's reliance on past experience in order to correctly identify another.[19] Mutual recognition, *Anerkennung*, seeing the self in the other, is intersubjective and, according to Hegel, achieving it requires that the parties involved move through a dialectical struggle to the death. For, understood as 'absolute self-assertion', freedom, 'when confronted by another, seeks the death of the other, and in doing so "I" must risk what I intend, namely, instead of enjoying my life and possessions, I risk their utter loss.'[20] Viewed this way, an act of intersubjective recognition must confront the other first through an encounter governed by a feeling of inevitability in order to subsequently experience the other in a spirit of possibility. By contrast, through *anagnorisis* a character may learn something, namely something about the past and one's agency in it, or perhaps about one's own or another's true identity, but descriptions of such discoveries as existential in various senses tend to involve an element of metaphysical rather than historical revelation. For example, Electra's self-understanding may change when she learns that her brother is alive and nearby after identifying his footprint and a lock of his hair, but this sort of recognition, while powerful, is somewhat distinct from the process of mutual recognition that has influenced readings of a Hegel-inspired acknowledgement in Shakespeare. This latter process is one wherein an individual risks death in facing the other and, ideally, comes to learn that she needs to be recognised reciprocally by others in order to experience freedom in society. It is this sense that freedom can be a historical achievement over and against presumptions of natural or *a priori* freedom of the will that differentiates *Anerkennung* from the potentially existential deliverances of classical *anagnorisis*.

To follow through with the terminology I've been using, where *anagnorisis* attempts to hold together the opposing forces of the inevitable and the marvellous, mutual recognition proposes to collapse this opposition by taking responsibility – not responsibility as duty to others viewed in their irreducible humanity that we find in the metaphysics Kant but a kind of responsibility that is achieved by relinquishing one's claim to be irreducible to or autonomous from others. It is chosen with a clear-eyed view of one's past, of the risks involved with moving beyond it and of the transformative possibilities of one's future. As Cavell says of modern tragedy: 'we became responsible for the meaning of the suffering itself, indeed for the very fact that the world is to be comprehended under the rule of causation at all.'[21]

In my view the modern notion of mutual recognition, understood broadly, has enormous explanatory power for the tragic situations we find in Shakespeare. That is, tragic situations like Posthumus's often fit the description of a disastrous struggle to the death, a misguided pursuit of freedom or domination. Still, I think that there is something lacking in accounts of mutual recognition's ability to carry characters beyond the tragic situation, for explaining how they take responsibility for the meaning and causes of suffering itself. After all, Hegel himself spends far more time describing the master–bondsman scenario – which is a compromised and thus ultimately failed version of mutual recognition – than he does prescribing the way out of it.

Anagnorisis, on the other hand, has been used to explain the reversal of tragic conflict with more promise, yet less precision. One reason for the aptitude of *anagnorsisis* in this regard is the way in which scenes of recognition tend to embrace the grace of the circumstantial. *Anagnorisis* is inherently festive in that it celebrates the accidental, fictive and sometimes ceremonial contingencies of the face to face. What I want to propose here is a return to *anagnorisis* as a supplement for mutual recognition and as a mode of drama that accumulates new moral capabilities in forms of early modern theatrical festiveness. If scholars have been right in describing Shakespeare's tragic situations as failures of recognition, that is as refusals to acknowledge 'the fact and true cause of [another's] suffering', and as psychological and sometimes even social appropriations of the inevitability of tragic cause and effect – if we're right, in short, that the cause of tragedy is a character's attempt to make his actions inevitable, then maybe the defusing of tragedy comes not through a rerouting of tragic causation but through a refusal or circumvention of it altogether, through a mutual agreement to choose an alternative experience of time and agency. Plays like *Cymbeline* demonstrate that the solution is not symmetrical with the problem. And, as I briefly discuss here, *anagnorisis* becomes for Shakespeare a useful theatrical occasion – even if, and perhaps precisely because, it is conspicuous in its occasionality. Shakespeare knows that recognition will break under the weight of its responsibility to the genre, and, in fact, he counts on it.

Cymbeline demonstrates an interest specifically in the relation between *anagnorisis* and modern recognition. This plays out in two ways, first negatively through characters' over-reliance on tokens of recognition, almost as talismans of a sort, that present characters with false myths about the mind's power of immediate access to other characters. This can be described as a failure in the anagnoritic movement from ignorance to knowledge and, thus, as the failure of mutual recognition with which we often characterise the tragic situation. The second intersection of *anagnorisis* and mutual recognition is positive, as the relation reverses when characters like Posthumus discover that they are unable to free themselves from cycles of domination and in particular from the domination enacted by knowledge. And in consequence these characters ultimately return to the circumstantiality of knowledge, its instantiation in signs, tokens and other 'scandalous' forms of recognition – the other's appearance in her own particularity in a gesture of mutual graciousness. Such a return to *anagnorisis*, as I will discuss later, is in the spirit of the festive.

We might describe the first of these two movements – from *anagnorisis* to a failure of recognition – as a movement from the present to the past, or from possibility to determinism. Consider, for example, Giacomo's description of Innogen's birthmark, 'Under her breast – / Worthy the pressing – lies a mole, right proud / Of that most delicate lodging' (II, iv, 134–6). In an illuminating essay on this bedroom scene, J. K. Barret says that Giacomo's descriptive report uses allusion and ekphrasis to lure Posthumus into a mindset of always-present possibility. The scene 'prompts ethical judgment because it sponsors the multiple, the possible, and the uncertain, rather than the fixed, determinate, ossified, or singular.'[22] I question, though, whether Posthumus experiences a movement from the determinate to the possible rather than other way around. What I see is not a movement away from the determinism of the past but, instead, a situation in which one's actions are determined by the actions of the other because one's operative understanding of freedom implies freedom *from* the other. Posthumus still understands the present reality to be determined by the past, but now the past under question is his own rather than Innogen's. Giacomo's description of Innogen's actions indicates not only her agency, what she putatively chose to do, but also Posthumus's agency, what he must do. Which is to say, it isn't really about the knowledge he has as much as it is about his having of knowledge – framed as knowledge possession – a kind of certainty gained through the negation of others. Posthumus might be able to imagine some reasonable explanations for Giacomo's knowledge of Innogen's bedroom, but actual knowledge of her body is secondary to the feeling of confidence that empowers what *he* can imagine. The problem, of course, is that there happened to be a true explanation for that knowledge as well. Hence, as David Schalkwyk remarks, for all of its numerous stagings of 'mistaking, misprision, misrecognition, and misrepresentation' in *Cymbeline*, 'the resolution of these misses is not based upon knowledge.'[23] For instance, despite the intimate visual account of Innogen's body that Giacomo provides, it's notable that Innogen's identity and virtue are never really under scrutiny in the sense that they are never directly the objects of recognition. Moreover, there is no effective difference between alternative explanations that are available: maybe Giacomo slept with a different person, or maybe he made up the story altogether. Regardless, this *false* recognition is not really of Innogen at all but of Posthumus's criteria, in a sense, of Posthumus himself and the forensic media that he takes as immediate (without mediation) and therefore as threatening his own freedom.

This helps to explain the bizarre reunion of Posthumus and Innogen in the final scene. The certainty of Posthumus's belief in the birthmark evidence of Innogen's guilt reincarnates here as an attitude of control over the content of his own recognition, when he silences Innogen in the very moments during which she occupies his thoughts – 'O Innogen, / Innogen, Innogen!' (V, vi, 226–7). What or who indeed is Posthumus thinking of if he cannot recognise the person he names as she answers his call face to face before him? Given that Giacomo has just confessed to describing 'some marks / Of secret on her person, that he could not / But think her bond of chastity quite cracked', it may be that the birthmark, as an icon of an erotic encounter, or the birthmark's abstract quasi-forensic symbolism, rather than Innogen's face, is what Posthumus pictures when he utters her name (V, vi, 205–7). Even at this point in the play, Posthumus is still seeking to recognise himself in the other. How ironic then that the conjured-up image of the mole situated intimately on Innogen's body becomes the very thing that strips her of her freedom – and, as eventuates in her disguise as Fidele, strips her also of her nominal identity.

The affective shudder that sweeps through the audience when Posthumus strikes Innogen, leaving only Posthumus himself unmoved, is evidence enough that the true depravity of his wager with Giacomo is its effect in compressing Innogen into a determining event of his own history. She is merely part of his own identity. Thus, ironically, it is when Posthumus creates a wager that subjects Innogen to a form of sexual domination and moral judgement that he loses freedom himself.[24] This process, I want to say, is facilitated by the first intersection of *anagnorisis* and the failure of recognition, where circumstantial signs of Innogen – her bracelet and birthmark – are taken to be direct representations of Innogen herself and thus accumulate the force of inevitable conflict with Posthumus. Shakespeare draws our attention to this movement through Posthumus's initial rejection of Giacomo's comparison of Innogen to the diamond ring: 'You are mistaken. The one may be sold or given, or if there were wealth enough for the purchase or merit for the gift. The other is not a thing for sale, and only the gift of the gods' (I, iv, 64–6). Innogen, says Posthumus, cannot be reduced to comparison with a 'trifle'. But Giacomo changes his tack and succeeds in engaging Posthumus by pretending to remove Innogen from the equation and claiming to wager only against Posthumus's 'confidence': 'But I make my wager rather against your confidence than her reputation, and to bar your offence herein to, I durst attempt it against any lady in the world' (I, iv, 86–8). That Giacomo gives Posthumus the option to choose another woman for him to seduce is immaterial. Rather, the attitude of fidelity-by-trial that Posthumus adopts toward Innogen removes her identity from the universal category of 'the gift of the gods', in which she is mediated to him by what he imagines to be a transcendent otherness, instead subjugating Innogen to the mastership of his own 'confidence'.

Posthumus's attitude is a species of what Francis Bacon, in his essay on the topic, terms 'suspicion'. Suspicions 'are defects, not in the heart, but in the brain.'[25] But whereas, according to Bacon, 'There is nothing [that] makes a man suspect much, more than to know little,' Posthumus's suspicion is grounded in a kind of knowledge that is, as it were, too much at hand in the forms of tokens, ekphrasis, and tales. Confronting the bracelet that Giacomo stole from Innogen, Posthumus determines, 'The cognizance of her incontinency / Is this', that is this bracelet, that has become much more than a trifle after all (II, iv, 27–8). In endowing 'this' bracelet – with emphasis on the demonstrative – Posthumus adds to a scene that already abundantly features characters pointing to physical and imaginary objects. Just seconds earlier, for instance, in response to Giacomo's account of the Cupids 'fretted' on the roof of Innogen's bedroom, Posthumus rejects the story with the sarcastic demonstrative – 'This is her honour!' – as if the problem isn't in the materiality of the proof but in the very idea of proving Innogen at all (II, iv, 91). Of course, we know that the wager is based on the question of proof from the beginning, but interestingly Giacomo agrees to what seems to be a rather subjective and negotiated process of deciding after the fact what kind of evidence will, indeed, be treated as demonstrative. Certainty and suspicion are bedfellows in this sense.

Echoing Bacon, Cavell writes that suspicion is caused by 'an ignorance which is not to be cured by information (because it is not caused by a lack of information)'.[26] But if not misinformation, then what causes certainty of this sort? One reason why this question is difficult is that the information available never seems to add up to enough. It always appears to be too circumstantial, transactional, capricious and, in a word, anagnoritic. This paradoxical ability of objects like the bracelet to incite, as efficient causes, a character's over-confidence is suggested in Posthumus's term, 'cognizance'. 'Cognizance' commonly denotes a kind of identifying object or badge; one's cognisance is a socially recognised verification of one's identity. But this usage historically overlaps with its more psychological meanings as observational knowledge and recognition – a cognisance of mind. Posthumus's demonstrative assertion – 'The cognizance of her incontinency / Is this' – blends the two definitions and thus makes the bracelet into a talisman of Posthumus's certainty. We can note, for instance, that a ritual equivalence has already been drawn between a ring and a life. The power that Posthumus attributes to this object, in Hegelian terms, cancels the mediation between Innogen and himself, and she becomes immediate to him. Which, on the one hand, is to say that she becomes wagerable and unacknowledged by him, but on the other hand, her immediacy is literally just that, a self-sameness, an accessibility – a mere possibility that nonetheless determines his actions.

Posthumus's anti-theatrical attitude

The language of mediation and immediacy helps to clarify how *anagnorisis* and *Anerkennung* converge uniquely in post-tragic plays like *Cymbeline*. For Johann Fichte, from whom Hegel adapted his notion of mutual recognition, the kind of immediate knowledge presumed by ahistorical claims to transcendental philosophy and culminating in Kant's metaphysics of morality is based on self-enclosed first principles and so has the effect of encircling, even binding, the ego. Fichte writes, 'There is nothing in the ego but its actions, and the ego itself is nothing other than action reverting upon itself.'[27] Building on Fichte, Hegel thinks that to claim transcendental morality is to reduce the other to the status of a variable that supports one's own invariable – or categorical – freedom of will. To claim transcendental volition likewise – the idea that my will can be determining for itself – is to believe that I can introduce a moral relation to another not by interacting with her but by finishing Descartes's experiment, by retreating into my mind, as she retreats into hers, while we negate one another's actual presence by classifying it as incidental, empirical or circumstantial – in a sense, 'the mind's retreat from the face'.[28] Instead, Hegel believes, to be truly free is not accomplished by imagining one's will to be untouched by alien causes, such as the will of another, but rather through coming to grips with the social and historical conditioning of freedom, where 'Freedom becomes explicit only as the result of intersubjective mediation.'[29] We can begin to sense in this description the outline of a convergence or reconvergence of Hegel's concept of intersubjective recognition with the overt contingencies and capriciousness of classical *anagnorisis*.

Shakespeare makes the question of mediation central to *Cymbeline* by placing so much psychological and even semantic pressure on the wager. In one way the wager is full of mediating objects and stories, but insofar as these anagnoritic signs fuel a crucial failure in recognition, I view the wager also as a fight over who will be the master and who the bondsman.

Giacomo, we recall, targets Posthumus in the first place because he hears from the Frenchman that Posthumus has a history of duelling in defence of Innogen's reputation, leading him to believe that Posthumus will be easy prey. Paul Kottman's essay on the Shakespearean duel is instructive for understanding the wager itself as a kind of duel, and one that Posthumus loses. Kottman suggests that Shakespeare's duels are like the duels of Hobbes and Hegel insofar as they dramatise the struggle to the death through which 'the achievement of our humanity is on display', that is through which one's humanity strives to become meaningful for and to oneself.[30] To adapt Fichte's words, such a struggle makes the very process of the ego reverting upon itself intelligible to itself. Yet Kottman avers that Shakespeare's use of the duel differs from the understandings of Hobbes and Hegel in that Shakespeare does not attribute to the duel the power of a primal and therefore authoritative historical precedent that allegedly illustrates the original transcendence of the human above the animal, the social and normative above the state of war. Instead, Shakespeare's duels contribute to the same ends as do all of his theatrical events – as 'test[s] of our historical understanding . . . with all its attendant baggage and precise conundrums.'[31] What I find especially salient in Kottman's argument is his understanding of the tragic struggle as a specifically theatrical fight to the death, where 'theatrical' here behaves like a mirror – a mirror wherein 'we see our sociality most clearly',

when we attend 'to its expressions as if they were theatrical performances'.[32]

Cavell characterises tragedy in a similar way in 'The Avoidance
of Love' when he says that 'acknowledging in a theater shows what
acknowledgement in actuality is'. Posthumus's wager is a reflection
of how acknowledgement actually fails. Giacomo intuits that Posthumus would fail to notice the parallels between the theatricality of
the wager event and the theatricality of the forensic event. Giacomo
thus constructs a theatricalised version of Innogen that induces
a failure of recognition inspired by a myth of immediacy, that is
instigated by Posthumus's blindness to the theatrical as a form of
mediation. Such a failure of recognition, as Shakespeare shows us,
causes Posthumus to view Innogen as historically determined while
projecting a view of himself, the one who thinks about and articulates her determinism, as someone who is therefore free and – in
the vein of Kant – transcendentally free by virtue of this very act of
judgement. It is through the wager with Giacomo that Posthumus
becomes Innogen's master.

We can contrast Posthumus's attitude with that which Cavell
says characterises the practice of mutual recognition, an attitude of
'continuous presentness'. Interestingly, Cavell depicts such continuity as a 'spiritual exercise':

> To let the past go and to let the future take its time; so that we not
> allow the past to determine the meaning of what is now happening
> (something else may have come of it) and that we not anticipate what
> will come of what has come. Not that anything is possible (though it is)
> but that we do not know what is, and is not, next.[33]

There is something resonant between Cavell's description of 'continuous presentness' and characterisations of the grace found in
the continuity re-established by *anagnorisis* in the work of scholars such as Boitani and Budick. For Cavell, to live in a state of
mindfulness is to grasp the fact that only the present is continuous
with itself; it is, in short, to realise that determining factors garner
much of their force through the explanations of their determining power that we hold for them. Such continuity, he says, is a
kind of 'spiritual exercise'. Similarly, Boitani's reading of *Cymbeline* locates something spiritual in the continuity of the human
through face-to-face encounters as a corrective to the fragmented
account of social life introduced through behaviours such as Posthumus's suspicion. Recognitions such as those that occur in the

rapid-fire sequence at the end of *Cymbeline* are more than mere passages 'from ignorance to knowledge' but, in fact, provide 'a new, more profound, and more vital trajectory of knowledge already possessed'.[34] The reason why such critics gravitate toward 'continuity' of what is 'already possessed' as a mark of the existential and grace-bestowing properties of recognition has to do with the ways that recognition pulls characters away from an illusion of the immediate and bridges relationships as an intermediary, in some ways working to circumvent the struggle or duel. As we've seen, the binding exchange of the wager in the end is reversed by a giving-over to the overt theatricality of *anagnorisis*. The wager is a tragic duel which Posthumus loses precisely because he doesn't see it as a game, a form of theatre and a play of signs and storytelling, as Giacomo does.

Posthumus's wager thus enacts an anti-theatrical attitude. It is similar to the phenomenon of iconophobia where radical reformers deface spiritual images ostensibly for fear that they'll lead worshippers to superstition. This same act of iconoclastic violence betrays an acknowledgement that such images indeed have real power over worshippers; that they *must* be destroyed. And thus the fear of an iconophobic is also a kind of belief in the immediacy and determinacy of the very images he destroys.[35] Just so with Posthumus's 'confidence' and 'cognizance'. Posthumus misappropriates the instruments of *anagnorisis* and, essentially, demands of the bracelet the same inevitability that Aristotle asks of recognition, namely the power of the marvellous to determine events. The post-tragic release, as we will see, requires freeing such anagnoritic devices of their absolutely determining power.

In characterising Posthumus's tragic mistake as anti-theatrical, I'm suggesting that the way he might overcome, negate, survive or otherwise 'move beyond' the tragic consequences of his action is through a positive recognition not of the other directly but of the other as theatricalised, met face to face. In what follows I briefly describe what I mean by 'the theatrical' in the context of recognition – namely, a return to *anagnorisis* with its overt reliance on signs, tokens and human will to re-plot dramatic action. Acknowledging a theatricalised other, one who is overtly mediated, highlights the other in a festive orientation and creates new ways of seeing old paths to mutual reconciliation.

The parallel I'm drawing between the tragic attitude and the anti-theatrical (iconophobic) attitude is that both presume immediate knowledge of the other and also that both eventuate in violence.

Writing on Hegel's 'mutual recognition', Robert Williams attributes the problem of immediacy to the absence of an 'emergent middle'. In the struggle to the death, he says, 'there is no emergent middle, and each is unable to find self-recognition in the other. Thus, the social order comes into tragic conflict with itself.'[36] This leads to what I think is a key question raised by the problem of Shakespearean tragedy: *How can drama use the tools of the tragic tradition to re-cultivate the emergent middle of mutual recognition?* It is important, moreover, to focus our search on the tragic tradition if we want to maintain a view of Shakespeare's late Romances as post-tragic, as moving beyond the tragic by moving through it.

By 'middle', I'm referring to something between two extremes of human encounter. On the one side is the absolute opaqueness of the other, the negation of circumstance and particularity. This is arguably what Othello is so afraid of in Desdemona according to Cavell's reading of *Othello* as it draws on Hegel – his fear of Desdemona's desires as an alien cause that threatens his own freedom and in particular his possession of her.[37] 'O curse of marriage', says Othello, just when Iago plants the seed of suspicion in his mind, 'That we can call these delicate creatures ours / And not their appetites!' (III, iii, 262–4). Desdemona's appetites ought to belong to him, Othello reasons, because he cannot freely possess what is his – cannot experience free will – if Desdemona has desires of her own. On the other extreme is the absolute self-sameness of the other. This is, I have argued, how Posthumus comes to view Innogen, as a mirror to his own honour and immediate knowledge. The first extreme, illustrated by Othello, is one of too much ownership of the other. The second is of a stale and overly materialised reciprocity, relationships falsely mediated through an over-reliance on exchange, hence the importance of Posthumus's wager. An emergent middle would be between and among these two extremes, in a relationship of mutuality as opposed to one exclusively of exchange.

At first glance, the recognitions at the end of *Cymbeline* appear to be superficial attempts at resolution and thus do nothing to bridge these two extremes in an emergent middle. We see the restoration of institutions, such as marriage, religion and Roman protection, the kind of restoration that often features at the end of Shakespeare's comedies. As Schalkwyk has discussed, these institutions are forms of the master–bondsman scenario, where 'erotic relationships are displaced onto master–servant relationships so that each turns into but also allows for the transformation of the other.'[38] Schalkwyk points to the trend among *Cymbeline's* characters to adopt identities of servitude and to the transformations they experience as a result. Still, such mutuality is limited. For example, Janet Adelman has observed that Cymbeline's recognition of his lost sons initiates a re-transition of inheritance and power from the female, in Innogen, back to the male, thus potentially inhibiting whatever progress Innogen had hoped to make with regard to her father and her marriage to Posthumus.[39]

To my mind none of these recognitions are 'brought about directly by the incidents' themselves but, instead, are introduced by Aristotle's lower-hanging forms of *anagnorisis*, and in particular by recognition proceeding from the invention of the poet, 'what the poet wants and not what the plot requires'. Recall Giacomo's sudden confession and Posthumus's sudden contrition. Their humility is not necessarily caused by the material suffering that they experience as a result of their own action. Like Leontes sixteen years after discrediting Hermione, the story requires that the characters simply realise and repent of their mistakes. Nevertheless, Posthumus's and Giacomo's respective decisions to repent move us closer to something like an emergent middle, not anything that transcends social practices of gender hierarchy, paternal authority, Roman rule, or other forms of the master–bondsman relation, but something that begins to bridge it. They both risk death, but rather than doing so out of an inevitable effort to protect their autonomy, they do so freely, where the likely outcome is more suffering and the only possible positive outcome is grace.

Returning to *anagnorisis* in the spirit of the festive

In his final book, *The Course of Recognition*, the philosopher Paul Ricoeur draws a connection between festivity and dramatic recognition. In the concept of the 'festive' Ricoeur seeks to reconcile differing definitions of recognition and to explain the historical transition from recognition as identifying to a passive form of self-recognition or receiving recognition – from *to recognise* to *being recognised*. The difference between the active and passive forms is problematically unreconciled in Aristotle's *Poetics*, and the pervasive attempt in the *Poetics* to hold together the inevitable with the marvellous maps onto its efforts to bridge these two forms of recognition.[40] In the examples given in the *Poetics* the paradox of *anagnorisis* is its putative capacity to denote two radically different recollective acts in the same event: nominal recognition of another and a profounder form of self-discovery. The latter form of recognition as self-discovery, a version of *being-recognised*, has been adopted by Shakespeare critics in various adaptations of a politics of recognition in the vein of Hegel and his interlocutors. But can a recognition scene perform both of these acts and, if so, must there not be a medium between the two, something that causes or allows the reappearance of the other to integrally affect one's own philosophical or social outlook at its core? Must not the appearance of the other also create an existential demand on the self? In other words, can recognising the other reciprocate in an act of being recognised and thus reinvigorate the middle term in the face to face?

Ricoeur's terming of the 'course' of recognition is meant to mediate *anagnorisis* and *Anerkennung* in this way. By 'course', he explains, 'I mean the passage from recognition-identification, where the thinking subject claims to master meaning, to mutual recognition, where the subject places himself or herself under the tutelage of a relationship of reciprocity, in passing through self-recognition in the variety of capacities that modulate one's ability to act, one's "agency".'[41] In Ricoeur's account – which, it should be said, alongside Axel Honneth's, may be the most extensive treatment of mutual recognition with a view of its pre-modern history to date – the institutions that mediate and help mitigate the struggle for recognition create dissymmetrical relationships.[42] Relations between subjects, and namely between their respective self-consciousness of freedom, are dissymmetrical in the sense that one subject acts more in the role of the recogniser, while the other subject more fully adopts the passive role of being recognised. This is a master–bondsman relation stated in grammatical terms of active versus passive recognition, and it pervades dramatic scenarios like those of *Cymbeline*'s various judgements and confessions.

Whereas for Cavell this sort of dissymmetry is conclusive and tragic, Ricoeur thinks that its conclusion is not, in fact, inevitable. The problem that we face, he says, isn't that we exist in these dissymmetrical relations – or what I want to depict as a family of relations, between recogniser and recognised, *anagnorisis* and *Anerkennung*, the marvellous and the inevitable, and between the master and the bondsman. The problem is that we tend to forget about this dissymmetry and thus to become paralysed by remaining passive toward it. This forgetfulness, moreover, plays out in forms of freedom and responsibility that neglect to take into account the particularities of the other and of the occasion for recognition – even when the occasion is accidental, capricious, based on unsound reasoning, arising from chance glimpses of tokens or accents, or manufactured by the mere will of the poet. We can imagine a scenario in which Posthumus and Innogen cannot rebuild trust, in which the capriciousness of the reunion fails to change the history of the relationship, leaving things as they were, with one party dominated or injured by the other, especially if the actions that perpetrated the conflict were marked by decisive intentionality and objectification, as they were for Posthumus. The answer, Ricoeur thinks, far from forgetting one's dissymmetry with the other, is to foreground it, even to exploit it, and this happens by attending explicitly to the symbolism and, in a word, festiveness of one's face-to-face encounter with the other in an attitude of receptivity and gratitude:

> In receiving, the place of gratitude, the dissymmetry between the giver and the receiver is affirmed twice over: other is the one who gives and the one who receives; other is the one who receives and the one who gives in return. This twofold alterity is preserved in the act of receiving and in the gratitude it gives rise to.[43]

There is something ceremonial and festal about this exchange of mutual recognition insofar as it exploits the occasion for the purposes of reinstating the other in her unique history, particularity, otherness and dissymmetry. Presiding over the final scene, Cymbeline himself adopts the attitude of an emotionally compelled play-goer. He is eager to hear the many circuitous circumstances of the various reunions, but this knowledge is far from necessary. He speaks to Innogen:

>   O rare instinct!
> When shall I hear all through? This fierce abridgment
> Hath to it circumstantial branches which
> Distinction should be rich in. Where? How lived you?
> And when came you to serve our Roman captive?
> How parted with your brothers? How first met them?
> Why fled you form the court, and whither? These,
> And your three motives to the battle, with
> I know not how much more should be demanded,
> And all the other by-dependences,
> From chance to chance.
>   (V, xi, 382–92)

The occasion – imagined as anagnoritic moment, 'From chance to chance', a ritual – thus becomes a theatre for the other, where the other is re-collected and given new life in the vertical time of the festival, 'cloth[ing] itself and convey[ing] itself in the exchange'.[44] In the spirit of the festive, a social relationship's past has no absolute hold on its future, and the normative responsibilities between two parties are refigured in the ritual time of the theatrical moment. One character's acceptance of the other, and vice versa, does not occur directly but is facilitated through the intermediary step of each character's decision to countenance the power of the occasion. Shakespeare conveys this freedom as distinctively face-to-face when Cymbeline describes his view of Posthumus and Innogen at their reunion:

> Posthumus anchors upon Innogen,
> And she, like harmless lightning, throws her eye
> On him, her brothers, me, her master, hitting
> Each object with a joy: the counterchange
> Is severally in all.
>
> (V, vi, 394–8)

Innogen's lightening-like gaze is infectious, almost violently so, and it becomes an occasion for others to experience a 'counterchange' as well. The way in which attention is called to her face as it blends into the theatricality of the scene grants her an extra measure of personal freedom. As Kevin Curran puts it elsewhere in this volume, Innogen's face is instrumentalised, a metonym-in-motion for the recognition scene as a whole, simultaneously discovering and performing its capacity to create and renew social realities. Donald Wehrs describes the transformative power of Innogen's gaze as causing Posthumous to begin 'a new life through losing his sense of male sovereign entitlement'. Drawing on Levinas's notion of the 'maternal', Wehrs characterises the 'signature implausibility' of Shakespeare's romances as offering a felicitous regression that moves away from the self; 'nature, via the gracious maternity embedded within it, produces the second chances from which culture renews its capacity to battle' its various narcissisms.[45] Though I am not elaborating on this connection here, it is not difficult to imagine how the tradition of holiday entertainments and religious festivals from which Shakespeare culled much of his theatrical awareness provided him with a ready understanding of the performative power of the festive, importantly, bridging the active and the passive forms of recognition in a rich mutual symbolism. Shakespeare's post-tragic drama exhibits a return to the anagnoritic paradigm in this way, particularly through the medieval valences informing aspects of these late plays' distinctive theatricality – gods descending, resurrections, mysterious music, masques and unlikely reunions. We can remember especially similar characteristics in morality drama, the court masque, the postlude jig, pastorals, and Christmas and Epiphany season festivals of misrule that indeed wear the terms of social exchange on their sleeves and by calling attention to how such terms performatively reject their determining influence.

And for Ricoeur, as we've seen for others, this manner of returning to *anagnorisis* – a re-appropriation of *non*-inevitable recognition – enables grace in the restoration of continuity even if such continuity is seen to be theatrical. Like the lost sons of Cymbeline and the reappearance of Innogen, when someone is absent for a time and then later is recognised, Ricoeur finds a small triumph over death. Ricoeur perceives something spiritual about the paradox of re-establishing continuity. The acts of recognising and being recognised that such disappearances occasion give 'to perceptual identity an aspect of assurance' and a kind of grace or blessing. 'The temporal distance that disappearance stretches and distends is integrated into such identity through the very grace of otherness. Something escaping the continuity of our gaze for a time makes the reappearance of the same a small miracle.'[46] Ricoeur isn't thinking of religious or tribal rituals but is explicitly attempting to rectify injustice, visions of the other as subaltern or disenfranchised. How might we opt to view the reappearance of the other in such gestures toward justice as a gift rather than merely as the effect of a person's actions? In recognising another there is not only a reunion but an act of deliberate acknowledgement of mutuality akin to the ritual gift offered in a benediction.

Translated into the poetics of tragedy, the festive is represented by all of the anagnoritic circumstances that Aristotle relegates to second-rate drama. A festive recognition is one that purposely eschews the inevitability implied by forms of *anagnorisis* that are thought to arise purely from the action itself, as if fated or prophesied – although few historical examples of this exist. Giacomo's contrition is an instance of such a festive recognition. Having remained silent for nearly 250 lines since his initial confession, Giacomo answers Posthumus's demand that he admit to having been defeated by him in battle, a report that is intended to confirm the nominal recognition of Posthumus as the disguised British soldier. Kneeling, Giacomo replies:

> I am down again,
> But now my heavy conscience sinks my knee
> As then your force did. Take that life, beseech you,
> Which I so often owe; but your ring first;
> And here the bracelet of the truest princess
> That ever swore her faith.
>
> (V, vi, 413–18)

Posthumus responds with an act of forgiveness, manifestly invented by the will of the poet:

> Kneel not to me.
> The power that I have on you is to spare you,
> The malice towards you to forgive you. Live,
> And deal with others better.
>
> (V, vi, 418–21)

Giacomo provides no explanation for why he is now so contrite, except perhaps for shame of being identified while wearing Innogen's ring. In fact, in this moment he returns the ring and the bracelet to Posthumus. It is unimaginable that this is intended as a gift of reciprocity or exchange, though it may be one of obligation. More likely, it is given out of fear. These infamous anagnoritic tokens, the ring and the bracelet, re-emerge here to announce themselves as mere efficient causes, lacking the power to determine or compel anyone. And yet Posthumus's response disavows his own claim to act out of the inevitability of past events. He acknowledges the dissymmetry of their respective circumstances – the 'power that I have on you' – only to forgive Giacomo in a conspicuously lopsided self-description: 'The malice toward you to spare you.'

What has become of Posthumus's certainty? Moreover, where is his sense of duty, an ethical obligation answerable only to himself as the sole acknowledger of right? As Robert Brandom writes, paraphrasing Hegel, 'The content [of responsibility] itself must have an *authority* that is independent of the *responsibility* that the judger [or recogniser] takes for it.'[47] In other words, the possibility of escaping death and bondage begins by acknowledging that my claim on another is only as binding as the other's claim on me. This realisation reveals the limits of reciprocity and the seeds of mutual moral recognition. Giacomo's unnecessary confession renounces the reciprocity of the tokens he returns to Posthumus, performing their non-determining status and effectively reversing Posthumus's earlier tragic mistake. And in turn – where correlation does not imply causation – Posthumus responds to this overt acknowledgement of the dissymmetry of their relation to one another and chooses – by the wilful invention of the poet and by the refiguration of the wager into the festive – to acknowledge his own dissymmetry in the eyes of Giacomo and others: 'Kneel not to me.' The normative implications of Posthumus's action prompts Cymbeline to take it as a lesson of sorts: 'We'll learn our freeness of a son-in-law', followed by his own universal pardoning of all offenders.

We can notice here the grace of continuity. By the rules that seem to govern many of Shakespeare's tragedies, the marvellous in this final scene would have been held in check by the inevitable and catastrophic. But just as Posthumus is released from the self-determining consequences of his social domination of Innogen, so does he release Giacomo from any self-determining effects of Giacomo's own actions. Notice the social logic whereby a character's acknowledgement of another, in a sense, frees that other from the rules of determinism that they imposed on themselves. This can be theorised, as I've suggested, in a refiguration of exchange and gifting. Recognition takes on a 'symbolic' function, as Ricoeur says, when Posthumus chooses to imagine the event as symbolic, when he chooses to accept Giacomo's tokens as symbols, releasing them from their overdetermining tragic effects. And yet in this same act of imagining, the symbolic becomes a real social achievement capable of a new conscious form of free action in society.

I don't mean to argue that this final scene of serial *anagnorisis* is a fully developed scene of mutual recognition, but it is a reversal of what I began this essay by describing as the first intersection of classical and modern recognition. It reverses the transition from *anagnorisis* to a failure of recognition – again, not through the empirical acquisition of knowledge, nor through a self-discovery of transcendent duty, but through a face-to-face encounter with the other embraced as both alien and historically constitutive of one's own moral action. Shakespeare shows us a return to *anagnorisis* in the spirit of the festive, where freedom, especially in the form of forgiveness, becomes explicit through the tokens and tools of the occasion itself, allowing the occasion to re-present them through the giver's self-conscious disavowal of immediacy and predetermined exchange.

Notes

1. All citations of Shakespeare are from *The New Oxford Shakespeare: Modern Critical Edition*, ed. Gary Taylor et al.
2. Simon Forman, 'The Bocke of Plaies and Notes therof per forman for Common Pollicie', 1611. Accessed at www.shakespearedocumented. org. Regarding Cymbeline's theatrical reference to 'globe' as 'round', see the Prologue to John Marston's *Antonio's Revenge*: 'Therefore we proclaime, / If any spirit breathes within this round / . . . / We shall affright their eyes.' Accessed at Early English Books Online, https:// quod.lib.umich.edu/e/eebogroup/.
3. Michel Serres, *Angels: A Modern Myth*, p. 146.
4. Paul Ricoeur, *The Course of Recognition*, p. 244.
5. Gregory A. Staley, *Seneca and the Idea of Tragedy*, p. 93.
6. I mean 'post-tragic' in the sense described by Beckwith, plays that 'work through the failures of acknowledgement that form Shakespearean tragic action' (6). Sarah Beckwith, *Shakespeare and the Grammar of Forgiveness*.
7. For example, in addition to a host of medieval Christian and Reformation paradigms, we might coordinate 'transcending', 'negating' and 'overcoming' respectively to the moral thought of Kant, Hegel and Nietzsche.
8. 'Wherever it is possible to speak of recognition, for that very reason a prior concealment is implied' (Søren Kierkegaard, *Fear and Trembling*, p. 76). Kierkegaard offers a brief reflection on *anagnorisis* and excludes it from his analysis of Abraham as an example of faith.
9. Aristotle, *Aristotle in 23 Volumes*, vol. 23, *Perseus Digital Library*, ed. Gregory R. Crane. Tufts University. Online http://www.perseus.tufts. edu (accessed 5 August 2017), 1455a.
10. Aristotle, *Poetics*, 1454b.
11. Terence Cave, *Recognitions: A Study in Poetics*, pp. 1, 23.
12. Cave, *Recognitions*, p. 46.
13. I am influenced in this description by Elizabeth Belfiore's discussion of Aristotle's tragic emotions as allopathic: *Tragic Pleasures: Aristotle on Plot and Emotion* (Princeton: Princeton University Press, 1992).
14. Piero Boitani, *The Gospel According to Shakespeare*, p. 8.
15. J. L. Austin, *How to Do Things with Words* (Cambridge, MA: Harvard University Press, 1975), p. 101. Stanley Cavell, *Philosophy the Day after Tomorrow*, p. 19.
16. Sanford Budick, 'Shakespeare's Secular Benediction: The Language of Tragic Community in *King Lear*', pp. 330, 335.
17. Budick, 'Shakespeare's Secular Benediction', p. 345.
18. The most direct examination of these two forms of recognition is by Simon Haines, 'Recognition in Shakespeare and Hegel'. Others who have addressed this include Paul Kottman, *Tragic Conditions in Shakespeare:*

Disinheriting the Globe and *Love as Human Freedom*; Sarah Beckwith, *Shakespeare and the Grammar of Forgiveness*; David Schalkwyk, 'Cavell, Wittgenstein, Shakespeare, and Skepticism: *Othello* vs. *Cymbeline*'; Jennifer Bates, *Hegel and Shakespeare on Moral Imagination*.

19. My thanks to Paul Kottman for helpful discussion about *Wiedererkennung*.

20. Robert R. Williams, *Recognition: Fichte and Hegel on the Other*, p. 88.

21. Stanley Cavell, 'The Avoidance of Love: A Reading of *King Lear*', p. 318.

22. J. K. Barret, 'The Crowd in Imogen's Bedroom: Allusion and Ethics in *Cymbeline*', p. 442.

23. Schalkwyk, 'Cavell, Wittgenstein, Shakespeare, and Skepticism', p. 623.

24. In stating the matter in terms of sexual domination, I am influenced by Kottman's book, *Love as Human Freedom* where Kottman traces freedom through historical and literary instances of risking life in the hope of achieving a love relationship outside of the status quo.

25. Francis Bacon, *The Major Works*, p. 405.

26. Cavell, *'The Avoidance of Love'*, p. 314.

27. Quoted in Williams, *Recognition*, p. 36.

28. Borrowing from Fergus Kerr's analysis of Wittgenstein, Beckwith uses the phrase as a chapter title in *Shakespeare and the Grammar of Forgiveness*, pp. 15–33.

29. Williams, *Recognition*, p. 50.

30. Paul A. Kottman, 'Duel', p. 415.

31. Kottman, 'Duel', p. 421.

32. Kottman, 'Duel', pp. 421–2.

33. Cavell, 'The Avoidance of Love', p. 322.

34. Boitani, *The Gospel According to Shakespeare*, p. 69.

35. A similar argument has been put forward by David Freedberg, *The Power of Images: Studies in the History and Theory of Response*. See also Joseph Leo Koerner, *The Reformation of the Image*, pp. 105–9.

36. Williams, *Recognition*, p. 204.

37. See Stanley Cavell, 'Othello and the Stake of the Other', pp. 125–42.

38. Schalkwyk, 'Cavell, Wittgenstein, Shakespeare, and Skepticism', p. 624.

39. Janet Adelman, *Suffocating Mothers: Fantasies of Maternal Origin in Shakespeare's Plays*, Hamlet *to* The Tempest, pp. 193–238.

40. I have written about this tension/convergence in Matthew James Smith, 'Tragedy *before* Pity and Fear', pp. 391–412.

41. Ricoeur, *The Course of Recognition*, p. 248.

42. Axel Honneth, *The Struggle for Recognition: The Moral Grammar of Social Conflicts*; Ricoeur, *The Course of Recognition*, p. 262.

43. Ricoeur, *The Course of Recognition*, p. 263.

44. Ricoeur, *The Course of Recognition*, p. 244.
45. Donald R. Wehrs, 'Ethical Ambiguity of the Maternal in Shakespeare's First Romances', in *Of Levinas and Shakespeare: "To See Another Thus"*,' pp. 216, 225–6.
46. Ricoeur, *The Course of Recognition*, p. 65.
47. Robert Brandom, 'From Autonomy to Recognition', pp. 58–9.

Part II

Composing Intimacy and Conflict

Chapter 4

Face to Face, Hand to Hand: Relations of Exchange in *Hamlet*

Emily Shortslef

As he and Laertes are forcibly separated from each other beside Ophelia's grave, their fight broken up by their companions, Hamlet flings a question at his opponent: 'Dost thou come here to whine, / To outface me with leaping in her grave?'[1] The verb 'outface', which means not only to defy and defeat but also to contradict and deny, is the kernel of Hamlet's haughty rhetorical question – how dare you think your mourning to surpass mine? – as well as a less self-assured demand the lines also articulate: do you mean to negate my grief, to cancel me out?[2] With its evocation of the contiguity between out-doing and undoing, Hamlet's reference to *outfacing* suggests what this essay will describe as the risks attendant upon *facing*, where the face is imagined as the site of the self's exposure – its disclosure and its vulnerability – to the other. In *Hamlet*, Shakespeare represents the face-to-face encounter as a scene of agonistic interaction with existential stakes. Yet the play also suggests, just as insistently, that the possibility of ethical relation hinges on a willingness to risk being outfaced.

Taking as my subject the exchanges between Hamlet and Laertes in Act V of *Hamlet*, from Ophelia's grave to Claudius's court, I make two intertwined arguments about these encounters.[3] First, I suggest that they unfold the play's ethical themes, which I propose extend beyond a concern with what critics have called the 'ethics of revenge' (the relationship of vengeance to justice, as delimited by particular legal, religious and moral codes) to articulate more reparative modes of responding to, and taking responsibility for, injuries received and inflicted.[4] Secondly – despite the symmetry that this essay's title may imply – I suggest that these exchanges are insistently marked by an asymmetry that is inextricable from their ethical charge. I use the term asymmetry capaciously, to describe situational deficits or advantages of knowledge, skill or fault that put Hamlet and Laertes on uneven ground; rhetorical surpluses that are generated by, left over from or posited through verbal exchanges (as when Hamlet proposes to imitate Laertes, action for action, at Ophelia's grave, but also declares that 'forty thousand brothers / Could not with all their quantity of love / Make up my sum' (V, i, 265–7)); or, finally, to gesture to what Emmanuel Levinas, Stanley Cavell and other philosophers have described as the intrinsic excess of another person, the way that the other, in its separateness, exceeds the full comprehension of the self.[5] The asymmetry that characterises the Hamlet–Laertes relationship appears in all these forms in the play, falling on one or the other side and always falling between them, as palpable a phenomenological object for the theatrical audience as it is for the characters.

If it is typical for asymmetry to drive the plots of vengeance that revenge tragedies traverse, what interests me here is its persistence across the contrapuntal arc of forgiveness also charted by the encounters between Hamlet and Laertes. As I will show, the asymmetry that underpins the affronted aggression and self-assertion that characterises these encounters also manifests in the twinges of ethical regard that appear in their exchanges. Consider Hamlet's admission-accusation to Laertes after the fight at the grave that 'I loved you ever' (V, i, 286), or the aside Laertes speaks as he prepares to strike with the poisoned rapier ('My lord, I'll hit him now . . . And yet 'tis almost 'gainst my conscience' (V, ii, 248, 249)). In each case, one person's regard for the other exceeds – possibly to their embarrassment, annoyance or peril – the mutual antagonism that otherwise permeates the encounter: Hamlet's admission of love goes unanswered by Laertes while Laertes's conscience inconveniently re-emerges after we have seen it 'seal' Claudius's 'acquittance' by sentencing Hamlet to death for the killing of Polonius (IV, iii, 1). Indeed, the play makes asymmetry the mark of the ethical, showing how the self is interrupted, called into question or thrown off balance by the other. By attending to the shifting forms in which Shakespeare keeps this asymmetry before his audience, I want to put pressure on the familiar understanding of Hamlet and Laertes as doubles or foils – characters who are structurally alike – and more importantly, to challenge the concomitant assumption that their reconciliation at the end of the play stems from their recognition of this fundamental similarity.[6] On the contrary, *Hamlet* aligns the ethical with the asymmetrical, and in so doing points away from an ethical relation grounded in likeness.

In what follows I trace the thread of that ethical solicitude for the other through Hamlet and Laertes's asymmetrical interactions to its culmination in the exchange of apology and forgiveness that serves as a counterpoint to Laertes's revenge plot. These speech acts perform reparative work in a manner resonant with Hannah Arendt's description of forgiving as 'the exact opposite of vengeance', but reading them as such has tended to involve overlooking or smoothing over a certain asymmetry that here too presents itself (namely, the questions the play raises as to whether Hamlet 'really' apologises or grants Laertes's request that they 'exchange forgiveness', which go to the heart of the performative force of these speech acts).[7] Can their asymmetry and their reparative work not merely coexist but be mutually reinforcing? To address this question I turn to the climactic fencing match, the site of asymmetry, revenge and repair alike. *Hamlet*'s other play-within-a-play, the fencing match that these speech acts of apologising and forgiving frame, is also a frame for them, illuminating their dynamics through its own nature as an inset theatrical performance – a form of reciprocal engagement that depends on self-disclosure, vulnerability and exposure, cultivates attunement and responsiveness to the other and risks injury for the sake of collaborative creation.[8] Reading the fencing match as performance, I argue that in tandem with those speech acts, and in distinction to the action of revenge, Shakespeare uses it to stage an ethical exchange and relation across various forms of ineradicable asymmetry, and to suggest how the asymmetry that so often sparks revenge might also have a role to play in its repair.

Face to face

In Act V, scene ii of the Folio text of *Hamlet*, just before he will be invited to the fatal fencing match, Hamlet admits regret for having fought with Laertes at Ophelia's grave:

> But I am very sorry, good Horatio,
> That to Laertes I forgot myself,
> For by the image of my cause I see
> The portraiture of his. I'll count his favours;
> But sure the bravery of his grief did put me
> Into a towering passion.
>
> (V, ii, 75–80)

The crossroads between these two scenes of physical rivalry, this moment introduces an ethical dimension to the relationship between Hamlet and Laertes, insofar as it constitutes a reflective pause in which Hamlet shows concern for Laertes. At its core is the image of Laertes's face. This face appears in Hamlet's memory, as he recalls the 'bravery' of Laertes's mourning for Ophelia, the ostentatious signs of grief that have not only provoked Hamlet himself to the heights of passion but into the very depths of Ophelia's grave, where he has followed Laertes so as not to be 'outface[d]' by him (V, i, 274). So too, his description of the 'portraiture' of Laertes's cause metonymically evokes Laertes' countenance. In contrast to Claudius, who has goaded Laertes to vengeance by asking if he is 'like the painting of a sorrow: / A face without a heart', Hamlet's figurative language skims over the distinction and potential disjunction between exterior appearance and interior reality that has elsewhere in the play preoccupied him ('one may smile and smile and be a villain' (IV, iii, 91–2; I, v, 108)). Here he privileges the representation, the visage: it is as a 'portrait' that Laertes's cause manifests for Hamlet, who can be sorry precisely to the extent that he can visualise that cause as a reflection of the image in which his own 'motive and . . . cue for passion' have been captured (II, ii, 555).[9]

This speech, in which Hamlet describes the arc of his insight moving from himself to Laertes, reverses the dynamics of the graveside encounter it recalls. In the earlier scene, it is the literal sight of the grieving Laertes that compels Hamlet's self-disclosure:

> [*Comes forward.*] What is he whose griefs
> Bears such an emphasis, whose phrase of sorrow
> Conjures the wandering stars and makes them stand
> Like wonder-wounded hearers? This is I,
> Hamlet the Dane.
>
> (V, i, 251–5)

Critics have long read this encounter as crucial to the way Hamlet assumes his identity as his father's son and revenger, with Laertes's mourning serving as a catalyst for what David Scott Kastan has called Hamlet's 'most determined assertion of self'.[10] The coupling of question and assertion in Hamlet's outcry ('What is he whose grief / Bears such an emphasis . . . This is I, / Hamlet the Dane') demonstrates how Hamlet's identification of himself is underwritten by his identification with Laertes.[11] When he recalls the incident to Horatio, Hamlet simply rescripts this narcissistic projection as an empathetic one, recasting his identification with Laertes as the achievement of his retrospective, rational and reflective thought.

But if Laertes's face initially appears in Hamlet's speech to Horatio as a figure for his likeness to Hamlet, I want to suggest that Shakespeare calls attention to a surplus that exceeds and eludes Hamlet's identificatory operations, a surplus that is reified in Laertes's face *qua* face. The memory of that impassioned face returns to puncture the very speech in which Hamlet distances himself from its power, a disruption evident in the way his measured acknowledgement of responsibility ('I am very sorry' (V, ii, 75)) is suddenly broken up by defensive excuse ('But sure the bravery of his grief . . .' (V, ii, 79)). Returning as an echo of his earlier question at the grave – 'What is he whose grief / Bears such an emphasis' – Hamlet's unbidden recollection of the extravagance of Laertes's mourning interrupts his reflective thought and ruptures the analogy that he has drawn between himself and Laertes (V, i, 251–2). It retroactively points to, and embodies in the present, something in excess of the identity he has posited between them, a 'bravery' (daring, splendour) that Hamlet describes as having 'put me / Into a towering passion' (V, ii, 79, 79–80).[12] This admission of passivity in the face of Laertes's action reiterates the profound asymmetry that underlies Hamlet's identification with Laertes in the graveyard, the sense of threatening difference and separation that initiates and haunts his (mis)recognition of himself in the other. Just as he experiences the Player's tears for Hecuba as an indictment of his own inaction, Hamlet hears Laertes's 'phrase of sorrow' that 'Conjures the wandering stars and makes them stand / Like wonder-wounded hearers' as a reproach, an address that singles him out (V, i, 252, 253–4). We can see his self-nomination ('This is I, / Hamlet the Dane') as an attempt to account for himself before the enigma of Laertes's outrageous grief ('What is he whose griefs / Bears such an emphasis [?]' (V, i, 254–5, 251–2)). Like his turn to analogy in the speech to Horatio, Hamlet's proposal to imitate each of Laertes's actions in order to 'fight with him upon [the] theme' of his love for Ophelia (V, i, 262) similarly attempts to eradicate the excess that Laertes's grief constitutes by asserting symmetry between them:

> Come, show me what thou'lt do.
> Woul't weep? Woul't fight? Woul't tear thyself?
> Woul't drink up eisel, eat a crocodile?
> I'll do't! Dost thou come here to whine,
> To outface me with leaping in her grave?

Be buried quick with her, and so will I.

　. . .

　　　　　Nay, an thou'lt mouth,
I'll rant as well as thou.

　　　　　　　　　　　　　　　　　(V, i, 270–80)

If Hamlet's claim to have loved Ophelia more than 'forty thousand brothers' (V, i, 265) aims to match in its hyperbole Laertes's rhetorical ostentation, his strange but telling suggestion that Laertes has come 'To outface me' (V, i, 274) indexes what is at stake in this desire to measure up to, and exceed, 'the bravery of [Laertes's] grief' (V, ii, 79). In the flesh, Laertes's face is no static 'portrait' that reflects Hamlet's own image. Rather, it is an event, an experience of sublimity that provokes and confounds Hamlet, confronting him with what he experiences as a threat to his very being.[13]

Thus far I have been suggesting that Laertes's face focalises a challenge that his otherness presents for Hamlet, a challenge whose dimensions are at once epistemological, existential and ethical. This claim evokes and draws upon Levinas's famous description of the Other as a 'face' whose expression of absolute alterity calls the self into an asymmetrical, non-reciprocal relation of absolute responsibility for the Other. This relation, which Levinas calls 'ethical' and posits as preontological, preconscious and constitutive of subjectivity itself, makes itself felt in the way that the 'I' experiences itself as an ethical subject, addressed by and obligated to another whose demands compel a response and set limits on the self's freedom. As many critics have shown, Levinas's account of the face-to-face encounter – an incipiently dramatic scene itself – resonates with the ethical inquiries of Shakespearean drama, which likewise does much of its philosophising in the mode of phenomenology, presenting one character's face as a catalyst for what David B. Goldstein describes as another's 'apprehending of ethical relation and responsibility'.[14]

For Hamlet and Laertes, such apprehension follows from an initially more antagonistic reaction to each other. For Laertes this antagonism arises from Hamlet's role in the deaths of Polonius and Ophelia, but Hamlet experiences the asymmetry that structures their encounter at Ophelia's grave in terms that are not immediately those of responsibility. Levinas's account of the Other's alterity as that which 'puts the I in question' is useful for articulating the sense of affronted bewilderment that Hamlet displays here.[15] For Levinas, the primary ethical relation governs the very terms in which the 'I' experiences itself. In the oppositional orientations of facing and speaking – Levinas describes 'conversation' as co-extensive with the face – the 'I' senses its indebtedness to the Other.[16] Thus he speaks of 'the ethical exigency of the face' as 'tear[ing] consciousness up from its center'.[17] This refers to the self's sense of itself as being split from the start by the Other, consciousness traversed from without and within by otherness it cannot assimilate to itself.[18] What Levinas's 'ethics as first philosophy' insists is that the 'I' cannot be the centre of its universe, the primary point of reference. In her reading of Levinas, Judith Butler refers to this as the self's 'dispossession' by the other.[19] Hamlet cannot comprehend Laertes's grief, as we have seen, but the play insists that his own is indelibly shaped by it. He can only express his love for Ophelia in relation to Laertes, as a 'quantity of love' greater than that of 'forty thousand brothers' (V, i, 266, 265). As a measure of his love, Laertes's grief sets the terms for Hamlet's love, so that his grief becomes, quite literally, a *response* to Laertes.[20] This encounter, their first, thus exemplifies the dispossession intrinsic to the orientations of facing and speaking.

This dispossession is fundamentally at odds with the Hegelian synthesis by which thought assimilates its objects, a conceptual 'grasping', 'seizing' and 'possessing' of alterity that Levinas argues the face renders impossible.[21] He writes, 'The face resists possession, resists my powers. In its epiphany, in expression, the sensible, still graspable, turns into total resistance to the grasp.'[22] As it does so, 'the I loses its hold before the absolutely Other, the human Other, and, unjustified, can no longer be powerful.'[23] In contrast to philosophical and phenomenological projects in which 'It is the Same that rediscovers itself in the Other', for Levinas the ethical call the face issues is inseparable from its resistance to the conceptual categories by which consciousness assimilates phenomena.[24] The Other 'shows a face and opens the dimension of height, that is to say, it infinitely overflows the bounds of knowledge.'[25] We might see the physical 'grappl[ing]' that Hamlet and Laertes engage in during the graveyard scene as tracking the same kind of conceptual grasping that Levinas describes (V, i, 255SD). Recall that the encounter begins with Hamlet's question: 'What is he [?]' (V, i, 251). It has often been observed that despite warning Rosencrantz and Guildenstern against the arrogance of thinking they could 'pluck out the heart of my mystery', Hamlet is bent on uncovering what in others resists his full knowledge (III, ii, 355–6). His plan to 'rivet' his eyes to Claudius's face during *The Mousetrap* treats the face as a surface that might give away the secrets of its bearer's heart. But what has been less noted is the way that Hamlet also describes various kinds of external objects, including representations of faces, as having the capacity to reveal the interiority of *other people* who face them. It is to this end that he 'set[s] up' the portraits of Claudius and his father ('the counterfeit presentment of two brothers') as the 'glass' wherein Gertrude might 'see [her] inmost part' – and wherein he, watching her look, might also see into her soul (III, iv, 20, 54, 21). Just as he uses literal portraits to demand of Gertrude the motives of her remarriage, so he speaks to Horatio of Laertes' 'cause' as something revealed by his 'portraiture' – in this case, not an actual portrait, but an imagined reflection of another object, 'the image of *my* cause' (V, ii, 78, 77, italics mine). It is by acting as Laertes does at the grave, imitating his motions ('actions that a man might play'), that Hamlet turns himself into this object that faces Laertes and shows his hitherto unknown 'cause' (I, ii, 82). As his words to Horatio indicate, he also imagines himself as the spectator of this reflection: 'by the image of my cause, / I see the portraiture of his'.[26] But to borrow Levinas's words, 'The face with which the Other turns to me is not reabsorbed in a representation of the face' but rather 'overflow[s] the sphere of the same'.[27]

If Levinas's point is the impossibility of this attempt to grasp the Other through reference to the self, Shakespeare directs us to what is lost in that attempt. Hamlet's claim to see the portraiture of Laertes's cause in his own image may well be a citation of a face-to-face encounter in Thomas Kyd's *Spanish Tragedy* in which the play's revenger Hieronimo, who has been grieving the murder of his son Horatio, is approached in his office as Knight Marshal by Bazulto, an old man seeking justice for his own murdered son. After a series of misrecognitions – Hieronimo describes Bazulto first as 'the lively portrait of my dying self' (III, i, 129), then mistakes him for the ghost of Horatio, then an avenging fury – Hieronimo claims to finally know who Bazulto is:

> Ay, now I know thee, now thy namest thy son.
> Thou art the lively image of my grief.
> Within thy face, my sorrows I may see.[28]
> (III, xiii, 158–60)

The stage instructions specify that Hieronimo speaks these lines while 'staring him in the face' (III, xiii, 129). In Hieronimo's solipsistic failure to see the man who stands before him, the theatrical audience thus bears witness to precisely the experience that Levinas terms the face-to-face: 'the way in which the other presents himself, exceeding *the idea of the other in me*'.[29] Unable to recognise Bazulto as a person distinct from himself, Hieronimo ignores his petition and tears up the other supplications presented to him. More than simply an instance of literal misrecognition, then, the scene is one of failed recognition, both in the legal sense as well as the ethical sense that Stanley Cavell describes as requiring the acknowledgement of 'the sheer existence of the other, its separateness'.[30] Levinas and Cavell each suggest that the ethical recognition or acknowledgement of the other is bound up with the recognition of the limitations of one's own knowledge, or what Cavell calls the acceptance of 'metaphysical finitude'.[31] Levinas writes that 'For the claim of realism – the recognition of another than I – to be possible, it is necessary that I myself am not originally what I remain even in my explorations of the obscure or the unknown: the peaceful and sovereign identification of the self with itself and the source of adequate ideas.' That is, the experience of the Other gives the lie to my most deeply held notions of my own autonomy and conceptual mastery.[32] While *The Spanish Tragedy* gives no indication that Hieronimo experiences this challenge, Hamlet does.

To be clear, I am not arguing that *Hamlet* locates the other beyond all comprehension, nor am I claiming that Shakespeare suggests (as Levinas does) that the 'surplus' that attends upon the face-to-face encounter expresses an 'idea of infinity' that points to a transcendent realm beyond totality.[33] What I am suggesting is that the graveyard encounter between Hamlet and Laertes, with its presentation of their 'grappling', can be illuminated by the twinned dynamics of the face-to-face encounter as Levinas understands it: the negative movement of putting the 'I' into question, which I have been exploring, and the positive movement in which the ethical relation is announced, which I will consider shortly. For Levinas, the two are intertwined, the latter depending on the former; 'putting [the I] into question binds it to the Other in an incomparable and unique way' that he describes as a 'commitment' and 'promotion'.[34] If their grappling registers Hamlet's response to the asymmetry embodied in Laertes's excessive and enigmatic grief, it also performs this binding work, demonstrating how, as Levinas puts it, 'the facing position, opposition par excellence, can be only as a moral summons.'[35] The putting into question of Hamlet's powers that Laertes's face generates also confronts him with his responsibility, albeit one that is situational rather than essential or primary. We will see him acknowledge this responsibility the next time they meet, in the apology he offers to Laertes's face, in the presence of others, before the fencing match.

I will turn to this apology momentarily, but I want to close this section by returning briefly to the speech with which it began, Hamlet's expression of remorse to Horatio for having 'forgot[ten] myself' to Laertes (V, ii, 76). I have been speaking of Hamlet's identification with Laertes as an attempt to level the asymmetry between them, to eradicate the surplus that Laertes's grief constitutes – as, in short, a knee-jerk reaction to finding himself put into question. Similarly, I've aligned Hamlet's drawing of a correspondence between them with his more overtly aggressive attempts to assert mastery over Laertes's otherness, or gain the upper hand over him. But we might also hear in this speech Hamlet's shameful regret for having allowed himself to become so exposed, for having in his 'towering passion' (V, ii, 80) revealed himself to Laertes and before others, and for disclosing a love that he had once declared only so he could disavow it:

> HAMLET   I did love you once.
> OPHELIA   Indeed, my lord, you made me believe so.
> HAMLET   You should not have believed me . . . I loved you
> not.
>   (III, i, 115–19)

In claiming that 'I loved Ophelia', Hamlet says to Laertes's face what he can no longer say to hers, belatedly retracting his self-protective lie (V, i, 265). In her Cavellian reading of the play, Sarah Beckwith argues that such exposure is so horrifying to Hamlet that he would prefer to think his own grief categorically inexpressible than confront, in her words, the 'terrible responsibility for having to account for yourself and the relentless exposure to others' that such responsibility involves.[36] If Hamlet's fear of being 'outfaced' by Laertes momentarily trumps his desire to avoid such exposure, in Laertes's absence, alone with Horatio, Hamlet retreats from that self-disclosure, obscuring not only Laertes's particularity but his own singularity too in the positing of their likeness (V, i, 274).[37] But, as we will see, the taking up of responsibility when they come face to face again requires precisely this self-disclosure. In the last scene of *Hamlet*, this exposure to the other, with all the attendant risks and structural and situational asymmetries, plays out in apologising and forgiving – forms of action through which, as Hannah Arendt argues, distinct selves make themselves known to each other, however imperfectly.

Hand to hand

When, at Claudius's urging, Hamlet takes Laertes's hand and requests his pardon, he also takes up the ethical summons of the face. Given its public nature, apparent orchestration by others and seeming evasions, the question as to whether this apology is genuine or illustrates sufficient contrition has been a matter of some critical debate.[38] But what has struck some as Hamlet's avoidance of responsibility, I read in terms of the experience Levinas describes as the 'I' coming to 'coincide less and less with itself', as an effect of his earlier encounter with Laertes.[39] The apology is worth quoting in full, for it demonstrates the excess that is at once Hamlet's theme and his rhetorical mode.

> Give me your pardon, sir. I've done you wrong,
> But pardon't as you are a gentleman.
> This presence knows, and you must needs have heard,
> How I am punished with sore distraction.
> What I have done
> That might your nature, honour and exception
> Roughly awake, I here proclaim was madness.
> Was't Hamlet that wronged Laertes? Never Hamlet.
> If Hamlet from himself be ta'en away
> And when he's not himself does wrong Laertes,
> Then Hamlet does it not; Hamlet denies it.
> Who does it then? His madness? If't be so
> Hamlet is of the faction that is wronged –
> His madness is poor Hamlet's enemy.
> Sir, in this audience,
> Let my disclaiming from a purposed evil
> Free me so far in your most generous thoughts
> That I have shot mine arrow o'er the house
> And hurt my mother.
>
> (V, ii, 172–91)

Referring to himself in the third person and delineating a difference between 'Hamlet' and 'his madness', 'himself' and 'not himself', Hamlet speaks of himself as another whose enigmatic excess eludes his comprehension. Dodge or no, his claim that he cannot tell Laertes 'who does it' except to say that the 'evil' was not 'purposed' articulates a truth in its admission that the wrong committed was beyond any kind of intention for which he could, narratively speaking, account. This is not to say that Hamlet refuses responsibility for Polonius's death: indeed, the apology begins with the acknowledgement that 'I have done you wrong' (V, ii, 172). Rather, it is to suggest that Hamlet sees his ethical responsibility as extending to the unintended and opaque, that which exceeds his intention and full comprehension alike.[40] The figure of speech through which he acknowledges the injury he has committed – the suggestion that he has 'shot mine arrow o'er the house / And hurt my mother' – at once echoes Aristotle's notion of *hamartia*, or the 'missing of the mark' that constitutes error, and a description of a different kind of excess in Roger Ascham's archery discourse *Toxophilus* (1545), whose prefatory epistle refers to those who shoot with bows too strong for them and consequently 'overshoote the mark . . . and perchance hurt some that look on'.[41] With their reference to an 'excessive' action whose injurious effects are in excess of the doer's 'mark' or intention, Hamlet's words point proleptically to Gertrude's death by the poisoned goblet that Claudius, in his own act of excess, has arranged as 'a back or second' to 'this project' (IV, iii, 126, 125).[42] They also recall, through the figure of the overshot arrow, the 'wandering stars' that Laertes's grief has made 'stand, / Like wonder-wounded hearers' (V, i, 253, 253–4). The apology thus repeats what it recalls, the risks of being exposed to another's excess. At the same time, it suggests that assuming responsibility for the other entails this kind of exposure, insofar as responsibility means being exposed *as responsible*, and therefore subject to the vagaries of the other's response.

Arendt's account of the unpredictability or surplus inherent to action offers a useful framework for highlighting the exposure bound up in Hamlet's acknowledgement of responsibility and his request for pardon. Describing the 'irreversibility and unpredictability of the process started by action' – the risks inherent in the very nature of action as the initiation of something new – she argues that forgiving, itself a 'potentiality' of action, offers 'possible redemption from the predicament of unpredictability – of being unable to undo what one has done though one did not, and could not, have known what he was doing'.[43] For Arendt, it is precisely the unintended, unforeseen consequences of action that the act of forgiving addresses and from which it releases the doer. Indeed, she suggests that 'Without being forgiven, released from the consequences of what we have done, our capacity to act would, as it were, be confined to one single deed from which we could never recover; we would remain the victims of its consequences forever.'[44] Situating his killing of Polonius as beyond his intentions and performed in madness, Hamlet describes the wrong he has done as exactly the kind of 'trespass' to which Arendt argues the act of forgiving may be applied, and it is this 'release' that he requests when he asks Laertes to 'Free me'.[45] But apologising requires what Arendt describes as the particular kind of courage on which all forms of action depend, the courage of 'leaving one's private hiding place and showing who one is . . . disclosing and exposing one's self'.[46] In disclosing himself in this way, Hamlet also opens himself up to the uncertainties of Laertes's response, exposing himself to more consequences that are beyond his control and prediction. Arendt writes, 'In contrast to revenge, which is the natural, automatic reaction to transgression and which because of the action process can be expected and even calculated, the act of forgiving can never be predicted.'[47] In entering into the ethical relation, taking up his responsibility for Laertes, Hamlet leaves himself open to Laertes, at the mercy of his freedom to grant, or deny, forgiveness. The framing of his request for forgiveness in the subjunctive mood – 'Let my disclaiming from a purposed evil / Free me' – foregrounds that the release he desires is dependent on another (and another's) speech act. As Arendt writes, forgiveness 'depend[s] on plurality, on the presence and acting of others, for no one can forgive himself.'[48]

In keeping with the asymmetry that I have been suggesting marks the encounters between Hamlet and Laertes, Laertes' response only partially grants this release, explicitly leaving an unanswered remainder:

> I am satisfied in nature,
> Whose motive in this case should stir me most
> To my revenge. But in my terms of honour
> I stand aloof and will no reconcilement
> Till by some elder masters of known honour
> I have a voice and precedent of peace
> To keep my name ungorged. But till that time
> I do receive your offered love like love
> And will not wrong it.
>
> (V, ii, 191–9)

Laertes's words, disingenuously, suggest a time to come when full 'reconcilement' between himself and Hamlet may be possible. For the time being, however, he and Hamlet will meet on uneven ground.

I want to suggest that Shakespeare draws a parallel between this rhetorical and affective asymmetry and the other asymmetries that more obviously structure Hamlet's entry into the fencing match. Indeed, the event is overladen with asymmetries marked as such:

Laertes's complicity in (and Hamlet's ignorance of) Claudius's plot; the general assumption of Laertes's greater skill at the rapier; the odds Claudius has laid on what Hamlet calls 'th' weaker side' (V, ii, 209); the foils that are identical but for one crucial difference. The repetition of the word 'foil' as they prepare to play highlights Hamlet's vulnerability. Punning on 'foil' as the background that offsets a gem, Hamlet contrasts himself with Laertes:

> I'll be your foil, Laertes. In mine ignorance
> Your skill shall like a star i'th' darkest night
> Stick fiery off indeed.
>
> (V, ii, 202–4)

Opposing Laertes's 'skill' to his own 'ignorance', Hamlet's description of himself as Laertes's ignorant foil gestures, like his apology, to his lack of self-knowledge – knowledge of 'your foil' that, in this case, simultaneously highlights the information he lacks concerning Laertes's literal foil. His description of himself as Laertes's foil also anticipates the way that he, like it, will become 'envenomed' (V, ii, 272). The talk of foils before the match ('Give us the foils. Come on'; 'Give them the foils;' 'These foils have all a length?') also draws attention to the rapiers themselves, a weapon that for early modern audiences connoted acute danger (V, ii, 201, 205, 212).[49] In short, Shakespeare emphasises the risk to which Hamlet is exposing himself here in a manner that suggests that on some level Hamlet himself senses it too, as his declaration to Horatio that 'the readiness is all' implies (V, ii, 170). Thus I would suggest that his entry into the match demonstrates – in a different register to his apology – his taking up of the ethical command of the face, his assumption of responsibility to Laertes. By framing the match as so obviously weighted in Laertes's favour, the play calls attention to what is at stake in apology as a form of exposure too, which involves a risking of oneself in the face of known or potential asymmetries, entrusting oneself to the other in good faith.[50]

As a performance within the play's narrative, then – a representation of fencing-as-performance – the match directs us to think about the wilful assumption of risk. At the same time, as a performance whose presentational dimensions exceed the play's representational frame, the match also models an idealised ethical relationality, depicting through its very different kinds of exchanges the same capacities that the speech acts of apologising and forgiving engage. Shakespeare's theatrical audience is fully cognisant of Laertes's plot against Hamlet and the danger that Hamlet faces, but as a large body of scholarship on the ubiquity of fencing performances in early modern England has shown, these same audiences would have been equally aware of the great care taken by the actors playing Laertes and Hamlet to avoid injuring each other.[51] Evelyn Tribble and Stuart Hampton-Reeves emphasise that the intent to commit violence is what distinguishes a fight or duel from a performance of fencing: '"playing" was on the one hand a serious exhibition of skill, but was on the other hand not fully in earnest – that is, not entered into with the direct aim of injuring, maiming or killing', Tribble writes, while Hampton-Reeves suggests that fencing matches like those between Hamlet and Laertes transform the codes associated with duelling 'into a formal game, a play, in which it is essential to observe the etiquette of the duel without the actual violence'.[52] If, as Mary McElroy and Kent Cartwright suggest, the fencing match 'celebrated the power and danger of the human body', the power consists in harnessing the danger.[53] Here it is important to think about skill, to which Hamlet's words to Laertes have already called our attention. Tribble describes skill as embodied knowledge shaped through a range of sensations and practices 'link[ing] mind, body, and affect in intelligent action'.[54] The skill necessary to fence with another without causing or sustaining injury involves an attunement to the space of performance, the movements of the other, and the capacities of one's own body that Tribble likens to the intricacy, agility and improvisational skill necessary for dance, a form of 'mindful movement' in relation to others and to one's environment.[55] By watching the actors playing Hamlet and Laertes take care to avoid injury while also exposing themselves to its possibility, the theatrical audience witnesses a form of solicitude for the other, an ethical regard that keeps the surplus of the other always in play, insofar as there always remains a certain unpredictability about the other's movements.[56] As Tribble argues, early modern writers of 'manuals of skill' insist that the skills they teach – fencing, dancing, archery – have the potential to transform one's comportment more generally. From this perspective, the fencing match might not simply represent a model of relationality analogical to an ethical one, but rather represent a set of practices that actually cultivate an ethical disposition.[57] From this perspective, Laertes's acknowledgement that it is 'almost 'gainst my conscience' (V, ii, 249) to strike Hamlet reflects the way that playing has transformed him: his crisis of conscience is less an internal phenomenon than a response to this interaction that has exposed him to Hamlet's exposure. Notice that he speaks these words as Gertrude beckons Hamlet to 'let me wipe thy face' (V, ii, 247). As Hamlet's face becomes the object of her concern, so it appears to Laertes as posing an ethical command.

When Laertes does at last hit Hamlet on the third pass, following a taunt that suggests he has in fact been holding back ('Come for the third, Laertes, you do but dally. / I pray you pass with your best violence' (V, ii, 280–1)), the exchange highlights the unpredictability and contingency that Arendt ascribes to action:

> LAERTES   Say you so? Come on. [*They play*].
> OSRICKE   Nothing neither way.
> LAERTES   Have at you now! [*In scuffling they change rapiers.*]
> KING   Part them – they are incensed.
> HAMLET   Nay, come – again. [*Queen falls.*]
> OSRICKE   Look to the Queen there, ho!
> HORATIO   They bleed on both sides, How is it, my lord?
> (V, ii, 253–9)

Laertes's wounding, which follows from the unplanned exchange of rapiers, turns on an action that in the play's plot (that is, Claudius's plot) is unscripted. For Michael Witmore, this accidental exchange exemplifies the 'eventuality' in which theatre specialises: it is an event or moment that happens through 'an unforeseen meeting of causal lines of action' and as such is easier to recognise than to explain.[58] Laertes's injury – the way that he becomes, as he puts it, 'as a wood-cock to mine own springe' (V, ii, 261) – thus reflects the inherent riskiness of even the most careful performance, theatrical and social alike.[59] Every scene of plurality is one of risk. The fencing match is thus the privileged means by which the play exposes its audience to the exposure of others – to their susceptibility to chance and contingency, the bad intentions of others, the unintended consequences of actions and the unpredictability of actions and others alike. Here that risk touches Hamlet and Laertes both, so that 'they bleed on both sides' (V, ii, 259). This is about as much symmetry as we get.

Witmore links the contingency and unpredictability of the eventuality to the phenomenological experience that theatre fosters. Because the eventuality is 'rooted in the immanent fact of performance itself', tied to its ephemerality, it indexes theatrical drama's ability 'to engage participants precisely on the basis of what they cannot already know or expect'.[60] He writes, 'Eventualities are witnessed rather than understood; they are more seen than foreseen.'[61] Building on this point, I want to suggest that the phenomenon Witmore describes as characteristic of eventuality – the heightening of awareness to the fact *that* something has happened, without the accompanying knowledge of exactly *how and why* it happened – might apply not only to the way that 'in scuffling they change rapiers', but to Laertes's striking of Hamlet as well. Hampton-Reeves, for one, notes that this question is one that Shakespeare's spare stage directions simply do not answer.[62] In Laertes's action too, then, we are presented with a wrong that cannot be completely accounted for, an injury for which the play does not script a full narrative (or dramatic) representation. The fact that Gertrude falls while they fight recalls Hamlet's apology, with its suggestion of injury beyond intention, the figure of the over-shot arrow that 'hurt my mother' (V, ii, 191). Thus this moment not only fulfils the prolepsis of the Folio's surprising use of 'mother' – the First and Second Quartos each have 'brother' – but also reiterates, by repeating, the intimate connection between the extra-intentional woundings of an opponent-'brother' and a spectator-'mother'. This nod to Hamlet's apology in Gertrude's fall codes Laertes's treacherous pass as something more akin to Arendt's notion of the 'trespass', a missing of the mark. Indeed, Laertes announces the news of both his and Hamlet's imminent deaths by pointing to the poisoned foil that has exceeded the purpose for which it was intended:

> It is here, Hamlet – Hamlet, thou art slain.
> . . .
> The treacherous instrument is in thy hand
> Unbated and envenomed. The foul practice
> Hath turned itself on me.
>
> (V, ii, 268–73)

My point, however, is not to insist that Laertes does not mean to strike Hamlet, but rather to suggest that the play leaves open the possibility that he does so (in the execution, if not the planning of the act) with something less than full intentionality. Nor am I suggesting that Laertes denies his responsibility. On the contrary, his request for forgiveness, like Hamlet's before him, speaks to the need for release from the consequences of his action:

> LAERTES   Exchange forgiveness with me, noble Hamlet,
> Mine and my father's death come not upon thee,
> Nor thine on me.   *Dies.*
> HAMLET   Heaven make thee free of it. I follow thee.
>
> (5.2.283–6)

From one perspective, this exchange looks like the complete reconciliation without remainder that Laertes has earlier denied Hamlet, as if here they have come full circle. That forgiveness is broached in the same site as the injury was committed marks this as a scene of reparation, just as (but in opposition to) the way in which, as John Kerrigan argues, revenge tragedies re-enact vengeance at spatial locations on the stage that recall the original offence.[63] Here, perhaps the audience recalls Hamlet's stabbing of Polonius, reiterated with Laertes's stabbing of Hamlet and now overwritten with their exchange of forgiveness. This is, I think, the ground of reparation. But it is asymmetrical, as here too the play calls attentions to asymmetries it refuses to resolve. By suggesting that his own imminent death will 'come not upon' Hamlet, Laertes offers Hamlet release above and beyond what he has requested. And, like Hamlet's earlier request to be 'free[d]' in Laertes' thoughts from his action (V, ii, 189), so Laertes's speech act is caught somewhere between a performative utterance that in the act of speaking removes the consequences from Hamlet and a subjunctive, merely a wish that it may be so. Hamlet's response sparks similar questions. Is it a wish, a prayer of sorts that offers his assent to whatever release heaven might grant Laertes? Does he grant Laertes forgiveness, or defer it, redirecting the request to another judge? These questions lead to larger ones: to what extent do these asymmetries, these unfinished or imbalanced acts of apologising and forgiving, undermine or negate the ethical, reparative arc they limn? Why does Shakespeare emphasise the asymmetry of these speech acts?

The answer I want to propose in closing is a simple one. It has to do with another address. The exchanges of apology and forgiveness that frame this encounter begin, and end, by invoking the theatrical audience. Hamlet's apology, his request for release, addresses Laertes, but it addresses us too:

> This presence knows, and you must needs have heard,
> How I am punished with sore distraction.
> . . .
> Sir, in this audience,
> Let my disclaiming from a purposed evil
> Free me so far in your most generous thoughts [.]
>
> (V, ii, 175–89)

So too at the end, Hamlet turns to the entire 'presence', those who remain:

You that look pale and tremble at this chance,
That are but mutes or audience to this act,
Had I but time (as this fell sergeant Death
Is strict in his arrest) – O, I could tell you –
But let it be.

                                        (V, ii, 288–92)

Each of these addresses includes the theatrical audience in its circle, appealing to our knowledge, our judgement, our witness, our experience, our faces. This is the arena in which these speech acts of exposure occur. As Julia Reinhard Lupton suggests, for Shakespeare and Arendt alike, 'forgiving happens in the presence of others, engaging not only forgiver and forgiven, but also a larger public assembly, whether the circle of family and friends or the court of opinion.'[64] Hamlet takes his leave of us, preparing to 'follow' Laertes to another scene of encounter. We remain on asymmetrical ground because the play's holding out of symmetry as a desired but never promised end is integral to its own ethical work. Revenge tragedy is characterised by the relentless pursuit of impossible symmetry (moral, legal, aesthetic) in the form of satisfaction for offences committed, leading to one after another act of violence that outdoes the excess of the one before.[65] By refusing to make these exchanges of speech acts symmetrical, Shakespeare exposes his audience to a very different kind of excess, the asymmetries crucial to repairing the ravages of vengeance: the acknowledgement of alterity and unpredictability, the assumption of responsibility, the taking on of risk and vulnerability, the exposure of oneself to the possibility of injury. This, the play suggests, is what the ethical relation entails. Against the compulsive repetitions of revenge tragedy, where the greatest fear is of sustaining the greater injury, *Hamlet*, through the exchange of apology and forgiveness, reconfigures asymmetry – in the form of the apology that may be unaccepted, the gift of forgiveness that may be refused – as a thing to be risked.

Acknowledgements

I would like to thank Julia Reinhard Lupton and Frederick Bengtsson for their generous and helpful comments on this essay. I am also grateful to Matthew James Smith and the participants of the 2016 Shakespeare Association of America seminar on 'The Face-to-Face in Shakespearean Drama'.

Notes

1. *Hamlet*, V, i, 274–5. Unless otherwise noted all citations of *Hamlet* are from the 1623 Folio text printed in *Hamlet: The Texts of 1603 and 1623*, ed. Thompson and Taylor. Hereafter cited parenthetically.
2. *OED*, *outface, v.*
3. These are in fact their only encounters in the play, as the only other time Laertes and Hamlet have been on stage together is in Act I, scene ii, when they each appear before Claudius and Gertrude to seek permission to leave Elsinore, and in this scene they do not speak to or interact with each other.
4. On the tension between the popular obligation to revenge and religious and legal codes of Elizabethan England, see Kerrigan, *Revenge Tragedy*; Prosser; *Hamlet and Revenge*.
5. For an overview of the complicated textual history of the three early modern versions of the play, and critical debates regarding their transmission, see the editors' introduction to *Hamlet: The Texts of 1603 and 1623*, pp. 8–12.
6. See, for example, Levin, 'Hamlet'.
7. See Arendt, *The Human Condition*, p. 240.
8. On the fencing match as a play-within-a-play that constructs a 'fictional, ritualized world', see Hampton-Reeves, 'Fighting', p. 152.
9. In his *Art of English Poesy* (1589), George Puttenham classifies figurative language that 'liken[s] a human person to another in countenance, stature, speech, or other quality' as 'Resemblance by Portrait or Imagery'. By suggesting that one person's 'portrait' reflects another's 'image', Hamlet thus doubles down on the resemblance between himself and Laertes he posits, using words that not only denote the reproduction of an 'original' but were also associated with the figurative comparison of one person to another. See Puttenham, *The Art of English Poesy*, p. 329.
10. Kastan, '"His semblable is his mirror"', p. 111. Girard suggests that Laertes is Hamlet's 'mimetic model' because his situation parallels that of Hamlet. Girard, 'Hamlet's Dull Revenge', pp. 276, 277.
11. In Lacan's influential reading, Laertes is the imaginary, specular double in whose mourning Hamlet finds at last the coordinates of his desire. See Lacan, 'Desire and the Interpretation of Desire', pp. 31, 36.
12. *OED*, *bravery, n.*
13. In one of the passages present only in Q2, Hamlet responds to Osric's effusive praise of Laertes by suggesting that 'his semblable is his mirror and who else would trace him, his umbrage, nothing more' (V, ii, 104–5). Cited from *Hamlet*, ed. Ann Thompson and Neil Taylor. Hamlet is mocking Osric, but his suggestion that to compare himself to Laertes would make him 'nothing' also acknowledges the lesson of the encounter at the grave.

14. Goldstein, 'Facing *King Lear*', p. 79. For recent Levinasian readings of Shakespeare's plays see also Kearney, '"This is above all strangeness"'; Lawrence, 'The Two Faces of Othello'; and Lehnhof, 'Relation and Responsibility'.
15. Levinas, *Totality and Infinity*, p. 195.
16. 'The event proper to expression consists in bearing witness to oneself, and guaranteeing this witness. This attestation of oneself is possible only as a face, that is, as speech.' Levinas, *Totality and Infinity*, p. 201.
17. Ibid., p. 207.
18. Ibid., p. 207.
19. Butler, *Giving an Account of Oneself*, p. 54.
20. Peter Sacks likens the two to the singers of ancient, antiphonal Greek lamentations, who would stand on either side of the grave. Sacks, 'Where Words Prevail Not', p. 596.
21. On Levinas's association of conceptual grasping with physical violence, see Critchley, *The Problem with Levinas*, p. 22.
22. Levinas, *Totality and Infinity*, p. 197.
23. Levinas, 'Transcendence and Height', p. 17.
24. Levinas, *Entre Nous*, p. 126.
25. Levinas, 'Transcendence and Height', p. 12.
26. On the use of visual tropes (images, portraits, mirrors) to describe the conceptual inextricability of 'self' and 'other' in early modern literature, see Selleck, *The Interpersonal Idiom*, pp. 89–122.
27. Levinas, *Totality and Infinity*, pp. 215, 195.
28. Citations of *The Spanish Tragedy* are from *The Spanish Tragedy*, ed. Calvo and Tronch.
29. Levinas, *Totality and Infinity*, p. 50 (author's italics).
30. Cavell, *Disowning Knowledge*, p. 9.
31. Ibid., 11. On the continuities and divergences between Cavell and Levinas, see Cavell, 'Philosophy the Day After Tomorrow'.
32. See Levinas, *Totality and Infinity*, p. 194; 'Transcendence and Height', p. 14.
33. Levinas, 'Transcendence and Height', p. 19; *Totality and Infinity*, p. 197.
34. Levinas, 'Transcendence and Height', p. 17. 'The putting in question of the I – which coincides with the nonallergic presence of the Other – does not consist simply in its losing its natural foundation and confidence but in an elevation; consciousness finds in itself more than it can contain, the commitment is a promotion.' 'Transcendence and Height', p. 18.
35. Levinas, *Totality and Infinity*, p. 196.
36. Beckwith, *Shakespeare and the Grammar of Forgiveness*, p. 19.
37. On Hamlet's horror at being known to others even as he attempts to know them, see Travis, 'Wordplay', who argues that the play links words that share the Latin root *fendere*, to strike, with characters' attempts to expose the secrets of others (p. 46).

38. Strier points out that Laertes's acceptance of the apology 'means that he feels the force of what Hamlet has said'. See Strier, 'Excuses', p. 57. On the awkward coexistence of confession and petition in this apology, and its relevance to larger philosophical debates about apologising, see Escobedo, 'On Sincere Apologies'.
39. Levinas, 'Transcendence and Height', p. 12.
40. As Escobedo and Strier each note, the account of involuntary actions in Aristotle's *Nicomachean Ethics* suggests that an action that results in harm to another can be both unintentional and blameworthy. Actions done 'in ignorance' – that is, without evil intention but with a certain carelessness or lack of discipline – are errors for which the agent should indeed feel regret. See Escobedo, 'Unlucky Deeds', p. 161, and Strier, 'Excuses'.
41. On *hamartia* see Book 13 of the *Poetics*. Ascham's use of 'perchance' indicates the dual kinds of unpredictability attached to such an occurrence, as it signifies both the potentiality of injury to occur – its hypothetical status – and the chance nature of any such actually occurring event.
42. In Q2 it is 'brother', but 'mother' – in conjunction with the notion of accidentally injuring onlookers that Ascham mentions – seems to neatly anticipate Gertrude's death.
43. Arendt, *The Human Condition*, pp. 236–7.
44. Ibid., p. 237.
45. In her description of the model of forgiveness established in the gospel of Luke, Arendt notes that one of the Greek words translated as forgiveness is *hamartanein*, or 'to miss'. There is thus a connection between Arendt's model of forgiveness as pertaining to 'trespasses', Aristotle's *hamartia* and Hamlet's description of his wrong as shooting an arrow over the house. See Arendt, *The Human Condition*, p. 240, note 78.
46. Ibid., p. 186.
47. Ibid., p. 241.
48. Ibid., p. 237. On Arendt's understanding of forgiveness, particularly its intimate relation to the act of judgement and its dialogue with Shakespearean drama, see Julia Reinhard Lupton, 'Judging Forgiveness'.
49. In his *Paradoxes of Defence* (1599), a polemic against the popularity of Italian rapiers, George Silver warns that 'there is no certaine defence in the Rapier' (A6r). Tribble notes of the rapier that 'it was deadlier than other weapons in one-on-one encounters'. See Tribble, *Early Modern Actors*, p. 71.
50. My account of the apology has some commonalities with Sterrett's discussion of confession in *Hamlet* as an act that requires 'the reciprocal assent of those who hear'. See Sterrett, 'Confessing Claudius', p. 754.
51. On the multiple kinds of fencing performances common in early modern England and the skill necessary to perform these feats on stage,

see Tribble, *Early Modern Actors* and 'Skill'; McElroy and Cartwright, 'Public Fencing Contests'; and Hampton-Reeves, 'Fighting'. McElroy and Cartwright argue that at the theatre and in other displays of fencing, 'Elizabethans watched the style and execution of the sword play with keen interest and considerable knowledge' (p. 209).

52. Tribble, *Early Modern Actors*, pp. 73–4; Hampton-Reeves, 'Fighting', p. 153.
53. McElroy and Cartwright, 'Public Fencing Contests', p. 203.
54. Tribble, *Early Modern Actors*, p. 5.
55. Ibid., p. 102.
56. Hampton-Reeves notes that the precautions against injury are greatest precisely when the performance calls for the actors to feign injury. See 'Fighting', p. 146.
57. Tribble, *Early Modern Actors*, p. 69.
58. Witmore, 'Eventuality', p. 387.
59. On the risks associated with theatrical performance, see Hampton-Reeves, 'Fighting', p. 147, and Ellen MacKay, *Persecution, Plague, and Fire*.
60. Witmore, 'Eventuality', pp. 387, 388.
61. Ibid., p. 387.
62. Hampton-Reeves, 'Fighting', p. 152.
63. Kerrigan, *Revenge Tragedy*, p. 4.
64. Lupton, 'Judging Forgiveness', p. 646.
65. On this pursuit of symmetry, see Kerrigan, *Revenge Tragedy*, pp. 3–29.

Chapter 5

Bed Tricks and Fantasies of Facelessness: *All's Well that Ends Well* and *Macbeth* in the Dark

Devin Byker

What would it mean to imagine a human without a face? Where we would normally find eyes, a nose and mouth, for example, we instead might be confronted with a neutral, blank canvas of skin. If we were to interact with such a human, what differences would mark our encounter? Some tasks would certainly be more difficult, such as any attempt at basic communication, or efforts at empathy, mind-reading or anticipation. But other tasks might in fact be easier. It might feel less difficult to deliver bad news to this person, to reprimand her for something, to ignore her altogether, or even to steal her wallet. But why might this be the case? The human face, we might say, places particular demands upon us and, in these circumstances, whatever demands those might be would be absent.

Although this mental exercise may seem rather bizarre, it is one that Shakespeare may have found himself undertaking through bed trick conventions, and other bedtime scenes, employed in *All's Well That Ends Well*, *Measure for Measure* and *Macbeth*. Long observed to be a 'cheap theatrical gimmick or an archaic dramatic device', as Marliss Desens has noted, the bed trick's peculiar dynamics nevertheless continue to receive scrutiny and attention.[1] In *All's Well* and *Measure for Measure*, the bed trick emerges as a pressing concomitant to questions about the human face and its absence, because the bed trick presents female bodies with imperceptible faces with whom male protagonists have sex. When such bodies have their faces restored in the spectacular fifth acts of both plays – when, for example, Helena who is thought dead returns both alive and pregnant, or when Mariana declares, 'This is that face, thou cruel

Angelo, / Which once thou swor'st was worth the looking on' (V, I, 201–3) – the male protagonists are overcome with shame: Bertram cries, 'O, pardon!' (V, i, 298) while Angelo laments his desire '[t]o think I can be undiscernible' (V, i, 353).[2] These plays not only express a preoccupation with faces but locate their theatricality within a drama of faces lost and restored. *Macbeth*, meanwhile, transposes this comic device onto a tragic setting, in which the darkened bed chamber becomes a site not for sex without faces but for faceless murder. Through these comic and tragic juxtapositions, Shakespeare explores both the epistemological and ethical force of the claims of the face and the consequences of a fantasy that wishes to ignore such claims.

Shakespeare's illustrative bed tricks give flesh and bone to the concerns of a particular philosopher of the face, Ludwig Wittgenstein. Wittgenstein wrote frequently about the human face, and he littered his remarks on faces with little doodles of them to show how even the most primitive illustration of a face extends its particular grip toward us (Figure 5.1).[3] For Wittgenstein, the face embodied his enduring concerns with the relationship between inner experience and external expression, and his remarks frequently counter the idea that our inner lives, or a private, internal language of thought (a 'private language'), could exist independently from the

Figure 5.1 Illustration, p. 162 from *The Blue and Brown Books* by Ludwig Wittgenstein. Copyright © 1958 by Basil Blackwell. Copyright © renewed 1986 by Basil Blackwell Limited. Reprinted by permission of HarperCollins Publishers and Wiley-Blackwell, Inc.

exterior, public and shared world. In *Philosophical Investigations*, for example, he expresses his scepticism toward such a notion by addressing the concept of 'essence':

> When philosophers use a word – 'knowledge', 'being', 'object', 'I', 'proposition', 'name' – and try to grasp the *essence* of the thing, one must always ask oneself: is the word ever actually used in this way in the language-game which is its original home? – What *we* do is to bring words back from their metaphysical to their everyday use.[4]

For Wittgenstein, the best way to know the meaning of a word involves not attempting to penetrate its metaphysical essence but understanding the manner in which it is used in the world. Thus when he elsewhere writes not about words but about bodies, claiming that '[t]he human body is the best picture of the human soul', or that '[t]he face is the soul of the body', we can identify a similar logic at work.[5] As Toril Moi writes, Wittgenstein's statements about the body are 'an attempt to make us stop thinking of the body as something that *hides* the soul, and to make us realize that the body is *expressive* of soul, which means that it is expressive also of our attempts to hide, disguise, or mask our feelings and reactions.'[6] Our 'essence' or 'soul' is best apprehended through the human body in general and the human face in particular, for the face of another can ultimately tell us much more than an elusive and immaterial 'soul'.

In his interpretation of Wittgenstein, Stanley Cavell takes this formulation as his starting point, yet he widens his inquiry to explore how this relation influences our response to the presence and faces of others. His remarks clarify the manner in which faces, expressive by nature, do not represent neutral phenomena that we are equally free to entertain or to overlook, but instead place a claim on those who view them. In regard to witnessing the (face of the) other, Cavell writes:

> My condition is not exactly that I have to *put* the other's life there; and not exactly that I have to *leave* it there either. I (have to) *respond* to it, or refuse to respond. It calls upon me; it calls me out. I have to acknowledge it. I am as fated to that as I am to my body; it is as natural to me. In everyday life the lives of others are neither here nor there; they drift between their own inexpressiveness and my inaccuracy in responding to them.[7]

Responding to the sceptic's dilemma, in which one wonders if other minds truly exist, Cavell argues that the other cannot be animated merely by our decision that she exists, nor is her existence something we can simply and passively neglect. Rather, the face of the other places a demand of acknowledgement upon us, one that we must respond to or ignore.

Although Wittgenstein and Cavell root their descriptions of expressiveness and acknowledgement in the scenes of everyday language use, their observations are particularly suited for considering the medium of theatre, which constructs and expresses itself via the faces and bodies of actors. As Moi observes:

> This is why ordinary language philosophy is so relevant for theater, for theater presents this aspect of the human condition in pure form: to understand the characters on stage, all we have to go on are their actions and expressions, in this particular setting, at this particular time. Theater teaches us how much we can tell about the mind from paying attention to the expressive body.[8]

If the grammar of theatre necessarily consists of 'how much we can tell about the mind' through our scrutiny of 'the expressive body', Shakespeare's repeated returns to a dark bedchamber that occludes the body and face only magnifies these interests. This recurring circumstance fosters dramatic investigations into the attractions and disavowals that a faceless environment might engender.

The shadow of a wife: wedded and bedded in *All's Well that Ends Well*

Through their participation in Shakespeare's bed tricks, both Bertram and Angelo seek to escape and even to dissolve the claims that a face places upon them. Although these tricks are devised by others with the intent to deceive them, Bertram and Angelo nevertheless each readily consent to a sexual encounter cloaked in darkness. The setting of *Measure*'s bed trick, for example – a 'garden circummured with brick' in the '[h]eavy middle of the night' – is arranged not by the bed trick's architects but by 'the news from this good deputy', Angelo himself (IV, i, 25, 32, 24). The darkness in which the bed tricks occur not only blots out the faces of those involved but reduces the exchangeable female bodies, by virtue of their exchangeability, to facelessness. Janet Adelman's reading of the bed trick has made apparent how the bed trick harnesses a fantasy of depersonalisation:

[T]he bed trick is thus the primary device through which desire is regulated, both legitimized and relocated in the socially sanctioned bond of marriage. [. . .] The bed tricks thus offer to save Bertram and Angelo from their own fantasies: presented with legitimate sexuality as a *fait accompli*, they might go on to accept the possibility that they have been tricked into the possibility of desire within marriage. [. . .] And insofar as the bed tricks betray the desires of the male protagonists in curing them, they tend to become less a vehicle for the working out of impediments to marriage than a forced and conspicuous emblem for what needs working out. [. . .] [I]t becomes the epitome not only of the dark waywardness of desire but also of its depersonalization, the interchangeability of the bodies with which lust plays.[9]

While Adelman argues that the bed trick, although betraying the desires of Bertram and Angelo, attempts to save these figures from their fantasies by orchestrating legitimate sex between husband and wife, I contend that the bed trick in fact realises their fantasies by creating conditions of facelessness that indulge their latent desires.[10] In *All's Well* in particular, the bed trick is but one of many faceless relations, including the Countess's adoption and imagined enwombment of Helena as well as Parolles's kidnapping by his fellow soldiers. These various relations create a constellation of inquiries into the human face that surrounds the bed trick at the play's centre.

For Bertram, faces present an epistemological demand, entreating him to a recognition of knowledge that he desires not to have. When the King honours Helena's request to marry Bertram, Bertram responds with incredulity:

> But follows it, my lord, to bring me down
> Must answer for your raising? I know her well;
> She had her breeding at my father's charge.
> A poor physician's daughter my wife? Disdain
> Rather corrupt me ever.
>
> (II, iii, 104–8)

When Bertram states to the King that he knows Helena well, his admission of knowledge is nowhere neutral or strictly cognitive. This lack of neutrality is often the case with superficially objective declarations of fact: for example, even statements such as 'I know that my son comes home tomorrow' or 'I know that money's running low' may be animated by particularly forceful intonations and sentiments. Bertram's 'I know her well', too, is saturated in negative affect. This knowledge, linked closely with what Bertram calls disdain, offers little justification for itself beyond Helena's inferior social position, yet its grip is so strong and its affect so comprehensive that Bertram both abdicates the King's favour and abandons his home to escape the consequences of this knowledge. Seeking to annul both his betrothal to Helena and his abiding knowledge of her that might also render him a fitting companion to her, Bertram quickly turns away from her face, avoiding both her presence and even her request for a parting kiss ('I pray you, stay not, but in haste to horse' (II, v, 81)). In the letter that he writes to Helena – itself an avoidance of her face – he casts his conditions of marriage in terms of impersonal exchanges that elide the face-to-face encounters that would typically facilitate these exchanges: 'When thou canst get the ring upon my finger, which never shall come off, and show me a child begotten of thy body that I am father to, then call me husband. But in such a "then" I write a "never"' (III, ii, 50–3). Relentlessly unwilling to countenance Helena's face, Bertram can only bring his impossible conditions to mention non-agentive objects – a ring and a child – while omitting the face-to-face actions that procure or produce these entities. By strategically avoiding Helena's face after their vows, Bertram reinforces his understanding that marriage is secured and sustained through face-to-face intimacy. Bertram's jittery flight from Helena suggests that any further shared presence with her might certify their incipient marriage in irrevocable ways.

Of course, the elisions specified in Bertram's letter are also what makes Helena's bed trick plot possible; Kathryn Schwarz succinctly observes that Helena 'acts according to the letter'.[11] When Helena's surrogate, Diana, proposes the conditions of darkness and silence for their rendezvous with Bertram, she does so in a manner that diminishes both future face and identity in favour of the objects that will mark their encounter:

> When midnight comes, knock at my chamber window.
> I'll order take my mother shall not hear.
> Now will I charge you in the band of truth,
> When you have conquered my yet maiden bed,
> Remain there but an hour, nor speak to me.
> My reasons are most strong, and you shall know them,
> When back again this ring shall be delivered.
> And on your finger in the night I'll put
> Another ring, that what in time proceeds,
> May token to the future our past deeds.
>
> (IV, ii, 54–63)

While Diana's instructions are littered with the pronominal markers of face-to-face interaction, 'you' and 'I', she nevertheless insists that, in the darkness of midnight, Bertram must remain 'but an hour, nor speak to me'. These conditions of speechlessness and sightlessness dissolve the stability of concrete identities. The rationale for the exchange of rings, too, is postponed; what instead receives emphasis is the choreography of how the rings are transferred: Bertram shall know Diana's reasons 'When back again this ring shall be delivered. / And on your finger in the night I'll put / Another ring'. Although these rings are well-established markers of familial identity that extend far beyond the span of a single human life (Bertram's ring 'downward hath succeeded in his house / From son to son, some four or five descents / Since the first father wore it' (III, vii, 23–5)), their meanings, like faces, are obscured and exchangeable within the matrix of their dark encounter.

While one might expect that Diana's elaborate instructions would elicit questions or suspicion from Bertram, such instructions do not inspire the least bit of confusion, doubt or even a sense of concession. Instead, they appeal rather neatly to Bertram's logic of effacement expressed in his letter to Helena: all that will survive this encounter is a mere object, a ring that '[m]ay token to the future our past deeds' (IV, ii, 63). Bertram's elated response, 'A heaven on earth I have won by wooing thee', only clarifies his attraction to this faceless encounter, for the ephemeral event will be outlasted by materials whose meanings he believes can be defined and redefined independently of the events in which they partook (IV, ii, 66).

While the marital act of consummation is centred on a face-to-face encounter that Bertram intentionally works to avoid ('Although before the solemn priest I have sworn, / I will not bed her' (II, iii, 244–5)), the bed trick as Helena, Diana and Bertram have mutually arranged it manages to invert the marital act's conditions while ensuring its outcome, legitimising the marriage rite through a faceless encounter. As Sasha Roberts notes, 'The culmination of wedding day celebrations was the bedding ceremony which, in cases of dispute, was used as evidence of marriage: performing the ritual of the bedding ceremony was akin to signing a marriage contract.'[12] After the bed trick, however, Helena identifies Bertram's disconcerting attraction to the faceless darkness:

> But O, strange men,
> That can such sweet use make of what they hate,
> When saucy trusting of the cozened thoughts
> Defiles the pitchy night; So lust doth play
> With what it loathes for that which is away.
>
> (IV, iv, 21–5)

In the 'pitchy night', Bertram is able to channel both sweetness and hate toward one whom he does not have to face and therefore need not know. Helena's assessment that 'lust doth play / With what it loathes for that which is away' speaks to the displacement at the heart of the bed trick, not merely Diana for Helena, or Helena for Diana, but the faceless for the human.

As Helena expresses discomfort with Bertram's loathing lust, her ambivalence invites reflection upon the ethical ambiguity of her orchestration of the bed trick itself. The bed trick, after all, is Helena's scheme: does not her 'sinful fact' suggest that she herself bears an attraction to the faceless fantasies attributed to Bertram (III, vii, 47)? Troubling as Helena's actions might be, her interventions fall within a series of unwilled moral interventions, repeated 'repair[s] i' the' dark', to use Isabella's phrase, that confront facelessness, agency and self-knowledge in *All's Well*. Schwarz suggests that Helena might be found unsettling because of her acts of critical exposure and reflection: 'Structurally, Helena does not upset conventional arrangements: she speaks in the name of custom, asserting that kings should govern subjects, husbands master wives, and fathers determine children. But she is upsetting in that other, affective sense, exposing natural order as an engineered set of parts.'[13] Like her unveiling of early modern hierarchies, Helena's strategies of effacement evoke discomfort by undertaking extreme means to expose, in caricatured and alarming form, a conventionally latent desire. Like her, the Countess and even Bertram himself employ similarly startling strategies to unearth in others self-knowledge that is previously disavowed.

Indeed, the bed trick is not the only faceless relation put forth by *All's Well*. When, near the beginning of the play, the Countess announces her desire to adopt Helena, she draws attention to a human relation that often begins in a faceless manner; in so doing, she augments our understanding of the scope of facelessness within human relations:

> You know, Helen,
> I am a mother to you.
> [. . .] I say I am your mother,
> And put you in the catalogue of those
> That were enwombèd mine. 'Tis often seen
> Adoption strives with nature, and choice breeds
> A native slip to us from foreign seeds.
> You ne'er oppressed me with a mother's groan,
> Yet I express to you a mother's care.
>
> (I, iii, 109–10, 114–20)

Although the Countess here seeks to become Helena's mother through adoption, she nevertheless draws on the biological, maternal imagery of the womb as a symbol of her care for Helena. Imagining Helena as belonging to the 'catalogue of those / That were enwombèd mine', the Countess draws attention to the intimate relation between mother and child that is not only faceless but in fact founded before faces, facilitating a relation into which the child and mother will grow. In such an encounter, the mother both develops and anticipates the face of a child whose significance will be further defined through the forms of bodily contact and privilege that mark early infancy. The child itself is thus initiated into a nurturing face-to-face relation even before it can recognise and claim the relation as such. Yet this biological relation, of course, is precisely the mutual origin that Helena and the Countess do not share. Nevertheless, Erin Ellerbeck notes that the Countess 'blur[s] the boundaries of biological and adoptive parent-child relations' by drawing on 'the horticulturalist's art of grafting': Helena evolves into a 'native slip' despite arriving from 'foreign seeds'.[14] An adoptive parent, who never having seen the face of her child, first greets the child and beholds his face within a parent–child relation that has already been initiated. Thus the claims that we recognise the face to make are first iterated and reiterated within a range of parent–child relationships, in which the face comes to embody an originary nurturing relation. As Cavell's earlier remarks suggest, the belated emergence of faces within parent-child relationships indicate that we do not bestow or determine the meaning of a face, as the sceptic would have it (we do not '*put* the other's life there'), but we must instead 'respond, or refuse to respond', to the claims of the face with which we are, by virtue of being born, already deeply acquainted.

Both Parolles and Bertram wish to ignore these claims as they flee the French court to join the wars in Florence. When Parolles is kidnapped, blindfolded and denied the faces of his captors, he encounters his own faceless relation that parallels Bertram's involvement in the bed trick.[15] Although Parolles is taken captive against his will, he, like Bertram, nevertheless both seeks and enjoys the faceless relation with which he is presented. Before Parolles is taken captive, he confesses the difficulty of disguising his own military cowardice:

> What shall I say I have done? It must be a very plausive invention that carries it. They begin to smoke me, and disgraces have of late knocked too often at my door. I find my tongue is too foolhardy, but my heart hath the fear of Mars before it, and of his creatures, not daring the reports of my tongue. (IV, i, 20–4)

In the midst of his endeavours to counterfeit his involvement in battle, he is suddenly seized by his fellow soldiers, blindfolded, and kept 'dark and safely locked' (IV, i, 83). In the literal and epistemological darkness of his captivity, Parolles finds an escape from his own cowardice.

Although his captors speak in a nonsense language intended to elude Parolles's 'smack of all neighboring languages', Parolles nevertheless quickly declares, 'I know you are the Moscows regiment' (IV, i, 12, 56). Such an assertion of certainty rings hollow in light of the farcical language being spoken; at the very least, Parolles's linguistic prowess seems suspect. Instead, it seems more likely that Parolles embraces his blindfolded opportunity to remain unknowing, disavowing his knowledge of who is interrogating him and of the responsibilities such knowledge may demand of him. Within this environment of faceless men, Parolles is simultaneously relieved of the burden of seeming, yet also afforded the occasion to become, militarily valiant:

> O, let me live,
> And all the secrets of our camp I'll show,
> Their force, their purposes. Nay, I'll speak that
> Which you will wonder at.
>
> (IV, i, 71–4)

In these circumstances, Parolles's secrets of his camp become prized military intelligence that he takes pleasure in sharing with his captors: 'I will confess what I know without constraint. If you pinch me like a pasty, I can say no more' (IV, iii, 95–6). Parolles's pledge to confess alludes to an office that he cannot properly undertake: as Sarah Beckwith has shown, one cannot confess to those whom one cannot acknowledge. Beckwith observes:

> The mutuality [of confession] is key; to tell someone something one must have something to tell, something the other must be in a position to be struck by. [. . .] The relief is of a mutual intelligibility that restores a sense that their lives are common, shared, and no longer uniquely isolating.[16]

As Parolles evades the claims of the human face, he necessarily forfeits his acknowledgement of the other, of himself and of the deeds that both he and his military camp have done. Parolles's words, so easily spoken to those without faces, become inert in their force and cannot serve in the self-defining and self-absolving capacity inherent to the form of confession.

Instead, in his blindfolded capacity, Parolles situates himself within an altered theatrical environment unfamiliar to early modern spectators. Speaking to a faceless audience that, from Parolles's perspective, is shrouded in darkness, Parolles no longer speaks with or to anyone in particular, but instead performs for imperceptible spectators, substituting face-to-face conversation with marvellous orations '[w]hich you will wonder at' (IV, i, 74). To modern theatregoers, a darkened theatre is a familiar experience, and Cavell claims that this particular theatrical environment, of 'keep[ing] ourselves in the dark', spells out problems when adopted in our daily lives:

> We must learn to reveal ourselves, to allow ourselves to be seen. When we do not, when we keep ourselves in the dark, the consequence is that we convert the other into a character and make the world a stage for him. [. . .] The conditions of theater literalize the conditions we exact for existence outside – hiddenness, silence, isolation – hence make that existence plain.[17]

For Cavell, to keep ourselves in the dark is to theatricalise our relations. As Beckwith elaborates, 'Theatricalization is here understood as any act that makes my face or yours a mask. If I withhold my emotions from my face, and from my language, I am presenting you with a role. If I also refuse to grant that your expressions are yours, I do the same thing, make a role for you.'[18] To put it another way, Parolles's wilful blindness removes the fundamental element of exposure and visibility that structures both early modern theatre as well as human interaction, allowing him instead to imagine different, any or no persons on the other side of his mask.

It is only when the faces of Parolles's captors are restored and revealed that Parolles, the allegorical embodiment of Speech, becomes at last silent in their presence and returns to a theatre of self-revelation and acknowledgement.[19] When a soldier removes his blindfold and asks, 'So, look about you. Know you any here?', his inquiry links the act of looking (of perceiving the faces of others) and of knowing (of enduring the recognition of others). Parolles silently witnesses each soldier as they greet him, compelled to acknowledge them one by one, face to face: 'Good morrow, noble captain', 'God bless you, Captain Paroles', 'God save you, noble captain', and so forth (IV, iii, 255–7). After all have left him, Parolles finally accepts the truth he had sought to evade:

> Simply the thing I am
> Shall make me live. Who knows himself a braggart,
> Let him fear this, for it will come to pass
> That every braggart shall be found an ass.
> Rust, sword; cool, blushes; and Paroles live
> Safest in shame!
>
> (IV, iii, 272–7)

Rather than endeavour to cloak his cowardice or to attain military prowess, Parolles suddenly sees himself in plain light, as '[s]imply the thing I am', purged of his faceless fantasies. This revelatory statement of self-acknowledgement, one that is echoed many times over in Shakespeare's plays, abandons the theatre of darkness and instead recovers the self-revealing properties of a theatre situated in broad daylight.[20] Such a vision of himself is neither comforting nor reassuring (Parolles identifies as a 'braggart', vowing to 'live / Safest in shame' (IV, iii, 276–7)), yet it accepts the faces of others in their capacity to reveal and confirm to us the thing we are. The gulling of Parolles, despite its unwilled application or endurance, is nevertheless the moral corrective or repair that reorients Parolles to the claims of his community; it enacts in miniature what Helena's bed trick works to accomplish within Bertram.

When Helena at last reemerges in the King's court, dispelling the rumour of her death and revealing her identity as Bertram's bed trick partner, she, too, suddenly appears as 'simply the thing that I am' (IV, iii, 272). As Helena silently comes into view, the inscrutability of faceless darkness is replaced with the wonder of lucid vision:

> KING
>   Is there no exorcist
> Beguiles the truer office of mine eyes?
> Is 't real that I see?
>
> HELENA
>   No, my good lord,
> 'Tis but the shadow of a wife you see,
> The name and not the thing.
>
> BERTRAM
> Both, both. O, pardon!
>
> (V, iii, 294–8)

Describing herself as 'but the shadow of a wife you see', Helena recalls not only the shadowy circumstances of the bed trick but also

Bertram's disavowed 'I know her well' (II, iii, 105) and his efforts both to escape and to blot out her face. She produces the ring and the child required by Bertram's original letter, and the irrevocable impression of action and identity upon the ring is ultimately what catches Bertram in his own lies when the ring's identity is variously confirmed. This consequence further attests to the inescapability of faces, which reassert themselves even through a non-agentive object. When Bertram cries that Helena is 'both' name and thing, he calls Helena out of the faceless shadows that denied her both personhood and wifehood. Here, he at last acknowledges Helena as both she who has fulfilled his conditions of marriage as set out in his letter and she who has taken all pains to face him when he would deny such an encounter. While infamous for its ambiguity, Bertram's final condition, 'If she, my liege, can make me know this clearly, / I'll love her dearly, ever, ever dearly', nevertheless revisits his earlier 'I know her well' by commissioning Helena as one who 'can make me know', revealing Helena both as the architect of his faceless indulgences as well as the necessary antidote to such fantasies (V, iii, 305–6).

Thus *All's Well* explores the meaning of the human face through variously dramatising a fantasy of facelessness, investigating both the consequences and the antidote to such fantasies. While, as the Countess suggests, we acquire our understanding of faces through various parent–child relations into which we are initiated, both Parolles and Bertram seek to evade this understanding, favouring contrived circumstances in which there are no faces and thus no ethical or epistemological claims to which they must respond. While these circumstances are engineered, respectively, by Bertram and his lords and Helena in ways that deceive Parolles and Bertram, undermine their consent and exploit their desires, these artificial events of facelessness also work to transform the relationship of the deceived with their own faces and those of their community. Their faceless encounters illustrate that to repudiate the claims of the face is to yield to a fantasy of private language and private selfhood, one that forsakes a public world and disavows the claims presented by the other.

What are these faces? To bed, to bed in *Macbeth*

If the characters in *All's Well* understand the reasons they seek to avoid the face, *Macbeth*'s central characters are far less certain about the face's meaning and constitution. When, late in *Macbeth*, Lady

Macduff encounters the murderers who take the life of her son, she cries, 'What are these faces?' (IV, ii, 75). Her horrified expression gives voice to the play's persistent concern with the meaning of the face, as the Macbeths turn such a question toward each other, toward those they resolve to kill and toward themselves. While *All's Well* provides opportunities (dark bedrooms, blindfolded interrogations) to momentarily escape the face, *Macbeth* repeatedly forces its eponymous characters to encounter faces even though they most ardently wish to avoid them. The Macbeths' murder ultimately becomes a parable of faces avoided, dismantled and lost.

Like *All's Well*, this play investigates such a question in relation to beds. As Julia Reinhard Lupton has noted, *Macbeth* roots its drama in the protective, self-nurturing spaces of the *oikos* or home, spheres of biological life that foster conditions hospitable to eating, sleeping and dying – what Lupton labels a 'domain of haunted creatureliness'.[21] Thus both the bedroom and the dining room become duly important stages on which *Macbeth*'s drama unfolds. Yet unlike *All's Well*, *Macbeth*'s 'bed trick' involves a different kind of trickery: while the bed previously fosters an environment for sex, here the bed assumes its role as stage for another ritual event, death, as the Macbeths kill a king on an unwitting deathbed, whose face is not as easily submerged by the darkness of his chamber as they would like. While Schwarz remarks that *All's Well*'s bed trick 'becomes a death trick' insofar as it dissolves Helena's identity, *Macbeth* takes this premise literally, exploring the common strands between how the bed extends the opportunity to avoid faces throughout its neighbouring activities of sex and dying.[22]

Indeed, *Macbeth*'s concern about faces is initially provoked by the problem of dying. Duncan utters his famous dictum, 'There's no art / To find the mind's construction in the face' in response to the matter of an unsettling death, when Malcolm reports that the traitorous first Thane of Cawdor died '[a]s one that had been studied in his death / To throw away the dearest thing he owned / As 'twere a careless trifle' (I, iv, 11–12, 9–11). How, Duncan seems to wonder, could a duplicitous traitor like Cawdor die in such a virtuous manner? Duncan reveals an eager scrutiny of faces as media that convey the truth about one's mind, soul or interior condition, a methodology that is now destabilised by Cawdor's unsettlingly good death. Thus the play quickly insists upon not only the unpredictability and unknowability of the face, but also its irreducibility: it cannot be easily or straightforwardly linked to an authentic state of interiority.

Unlike Duncan, however, who submits faces to his careful examination, Lady Macbeth eagerly wishes faces away, yearning for a realm in which she can evade them entirely. If, as Cavell insists, 'I [have to] *respond* to [the other], or refuse to respond', Lady Macbeth incessantly searches for pathways to escape this ultimatum. As she and Macbeth calculate their plot against Duncan, she regards Macbeth's face as a legible textual surface:

> Your face, my thane, is as a book where men
> May read strange matters. To beguile the time,
> Look like the time: bear welcome in your eye,
> Your hand, your tongue. Look like th'innocent flower,
> But be the serpent under't.
>
> (I, v, 58–62)

To escape the immediacy of the face, the presence that inhabits it and the demands that such presence elicits from its viewers, Lady Macbeth frequently attempts to regard the face, instead, as a form of artifice or art – the fashioned objects that reflect and give shape to the world yet whose creation require removal from the face-to-face encounters out of which action springs.[23] In so doing, she excavates the etymological origin of 'face', a derivative of the Latin infinitive *facere*, to do or to make.[24] Here, she first observes Macbeth's face as a book, an image that other Shakespearean characters also adopt,[25] and, later, she will regard faces as pictures. Lady Macbeth's first appearance in the play, too, allows her to interact with Macbeth in just this way, reading his letter in the manner that she now reads his face. This moment will be repeated much later in the play when Lady Macbeth urges Macbeth to '[s]leek o'er your rugged looks', for her blandishment seeks to arrange, construct and make something from the raw materials of Macbeth's face (III, ii, 28–30). By translating the face first into book, then mirror ('Look like the time'), then picture, then bricolage, Lady Macbeth evades encountering the face as it is by reframing it as a form of worldly artifice.[26]

These habits of facial transposition accompany Lady Macbeth throughout the unfolding of Duncan's murder, in which she, like Bertram and Helena, is drawn to the environment of the darkened bedchamber. Lady Macbeth's affinity for the bedroom murder plot lies not only within the ease it presents for killing a sleeping person. The chamber at night provides two appealing evasions of the face: it retains the same conventional features of dark imperceptibility found in *All's Well* and, furthermore, Lady Macbeth presumes that the condition of sleep itself disables the face, rendering it another piece of neutral, unexpressive flesh like an arm or torso. When Macbeth acknowledges hesitation about their plot ('If we should fail?' (I, vii, 59)), Lady Macbeth doubles down on the fittingness of such conditions for their murder:

> We fail!
> But screw your courage to the sticking place,
> And we'll not fail. When Duncan is asleep,
> Whereto the rather shall his day's hard journey
> Soundly invite him, his two chamberlains
> Will I with wine and wassail so convince
> That memory, the warder of the brain,
> Shall be a fume, and the recept of reason
> A limbeck only. When in swinish sleep
> Their drenched natures lies as in a death,
> What cannot you and I perform upon
> Th'unguarded Duncan? What not put upon
> His spongy officers, who shall bear the guilt
> Of our great quell?
>
> (I, vii, 59–72)

Here Lady Macbeth comforts both Macbeth and herself with strategies of effacement. While the sleep that will overcome Duncan emerges as a product of his tiresome travels, his chamberlains will fall into 'swinish' sleep, an adjective of bestial degradation. This latter form of sleep in particular is the product of a kind of mental disabling: 'wine and wassail' will reduce the brain to a 'fume', its encasing head and face 'a limbeck only' (an alchemical receptacle or container). By electing an alchemical explanation of human physiognomy, Lady Macbeth supplants recognition of a face with a diagnosis of bodily processes, not only reducing the face to a mechanism of circulating fumes but also rendering the head itself an alchemical instrument. Again, Lady Macbeth turns to substitute fashioned objects for the face. Even her description of the chamberlains as 'spongy officers' seeks to remake their bodies with altered, inhuman textural surfaces, more indicative of effigies than living persons. Within these conditions of translated faces and unfamiliar bodies, Lady Macbeth proclaims a sense of unbridled possibility: 'What cannot you and I perform upon / Th'unguarded Duncan?' This exclamation is animated by an air of invincibility, a fated-ness that Macbeth himself later finds within the witches' prophecies ('I will not be afraid of death and bane, / Till Birnam forest come to Dunsinane' (V, iii, 62–3)) but, for Lady Macbeth, rests especially on the successful disabling of the faces of others. It is within the conceptual sphere of Duncan's darkened chamber that, like a heist film's museum or bank whose security systems have been effectively hacked, Lady Macbeth imagines herself to have disassembled the epistemological and ethical claims of the face and the acknowledgement these claims demand. Through the embodied instruments of wine and sleep as well as the night-vision lenses of artifice, Lady Macbeth asserts that she has crashed the mainframe of the human face.

Yet even as Lady Macbeth has achieved such intoxicating heights of liberty from the shackles of acknowledgement, once their plot begins to unfold, these consoling fictions fail to fully untether Lady Macbeth from the tug of the face. As Lady Macbeth awaits Macbeth's completion of the deed, she first confesses a fear that the disabling effects of sleep will not last:

> Alack, I am afraid they have awaked,
> And 'tis not done. [. . .]
>   Had he not resembled
> My father as he slept, I had done 't.
>
>   (II, ii, 9–10, 12–13)

Lady Macbeth not only fears that the king and his chamberlains will awake, she also finds, quite surprisingly, that sleep only heightens the similarity between the king and her father. The earlier alchemical explanations have here hit a snag; the exact and inhuman narrative of mere processes has collided against a scene of living memory. In this rare familial disclosure, sleep is no longer an inhuman mode that deactivates the other but instead recalls vivid human relations: the sleeping person before Lady Macbeth elicits a moment of irreducible human recognition, a past tableau where Lady Macbeth both faces a sleeping human and acknowledges him as her father. Just as the Countess in *All's Well* claims that the parental relation precedes faces, Lady Macbeth approaches this relation from the opposite temporal end, finding that she cannot, despite her will, efface or escape the likeness of her father.

This brief disruption in Lady Macbeth's resolution, however, dissolves when Macbeth returns. Expressing his inability to face his deed ('I am afraid to think what I have done. / Look on't again I dare

not' (II, ii, 48–9)), Lady Macbeth again chastises Macbeth's vulnerability to the face:

> Infirm of purpose!
> Give me the daggers. The sleeping and the dead
> Are but as pictures; 'tis the eye of childhood
> That fears a painted devil. If he do bleed,
> I'll gild the faces of the grooms withal,
> For it must seem their guilt.
>
> (II, ii, 49–54)

Framing the sleeping face as a picture – in particular a 'painted
devil' – Lady Macbeth insinuates that the face is a hackneyed creation that anyone but a child has learned to decipher, to recognise as
mere cartoon.[27] Associating facial fright with children, she revels in
her self-proclaimed adulthood, no longer needing to avoid faces but
instead vowing to 'gild the faces of the grooms withal'. This flagrant
act of vandalism, of defacing faces with her bloody graffiti, poses
the face once again as an artist's canvas, writer's page or street artist's wall; the chamberlains' visages become yet another book where
men may read strange matters as she inscribes onto their faces cul-
pability for Duncan's murder. Nevertheless, knowing of Lady Macbeth's brief lapse of vulnerability toward the memory of her sleeping
father, perhaps, too, this act of covering-over is also one of effacing,
ensuring that these faces, now enamelled with the opaque hues of
solidifying blood, can never return to the sentient, expressive, or live
form that once spooked her in its resemblance to her father.

While Lady Macbeth insists on the constructedness of the face,
something that humans can make and manipulate, the play does not
shy away from depicting a counterpoint to this vision, in which faces
cannot be relegated to the subservient realm of human creation but
in fact supersede and overpower human life. Unlike Lady Macbeth's
act of happy gilding, Macduff views the chamber scene with a self-
diminishing, enervating horror:

> Approach the chamber and destroy your sight
> With a new Gorgon. Do not bid me speak.
> See, and then speak yourselves.
>
> (II, iii, 64–6)

Macduff interprets the grisly scene through the lens of mythology,
drawing on the debilitating face of the Gorgon. While the Gorgon

itself is a literary creation, a fashioned object, the Gorgon's face nevertheless represents everything that Lady Macbeth's bookish and painterly faces are not; rather than a human creation that can be manipulated, controlled and mastered by its creator, the face of the supernatural Gorgon exerts power over all those who view it, robbing them of their agency and life, including their face. As Susan Zimmerman notes, '[T]he prohibition of the Medusa foregrounds the danger of apprehending that which exists outside any symbolic frame of reference[.] [. . .] To view the Medusa is to discover the indeterminacy of originary being and to lose one's "self" as a consequence.'[28] The Gorgon fittingly conveys the risks of the face that the Macbeths endeavour to minimise, for Macduff's interaction with the scene differs in every way from Lady Macbeth's earlier description of it.

Despite the destructive power of the face, Macduff nevertheless impels those around him not to evade these faces but to 'look on death itself':

> Shake off this downy sleep, death's counterfeit,
> And look on death itself. Up, up, and see
> The great doom's image. Malcolm, Banquo,
> As from your graves rise up and walk like sprites
> To countenance this horror.
>
> (II, iii, 69–73)

The bedroom homicide forces Macduff to confront not only an appalling murder but also underscores the potency of face-to-face encounters, even with faces now lifeless and covered in blood. As Macduff urges the others to 'look on death itself', the face here becomes equated with human mortality, conveying an irrepressible force beyond human control and manipulation. If Lady Macbeth seeks to nullify the heft and force of murdering a king by dismantling faces, Macduff attempts to recover the significance of murder through both the supernatural face of the Gorgon and the human act of countenancing.

While the comic unravelling of the bed trick as depicted by *All's Well* leads to resolution, restored faces and compelled mutual recognition, *Macbeth* stages the tragic consequences of the Macbeths' faceless fantasies, for Duncan's face can never return to life, nor can those of his chamberlains be ungilded. Although Lady Macbeth, like Helena, devises means to evade the face and its claims, Macbeth, unlike Bertram, cannot adopt these strategies as effectively; rather, he frequently concedes vulnerability to the faces of others. When Lady Macbeth earlier bids Macbeth to '[l]ook like the time', a performative injunction that bids Macbeth become what he mirrors, Macbeth, like Hamlet, insists on a distinction between his exterior and 'that within which passes show' (I, ii, 85), saying, 'Away, and mock the time with fairest show. / False face must hide what the false heart doth know' (I, vii, 81–2). Macbeth's mere recognition that he must put on a false face rather than perform his way to a more authentic disposition, reveals that, for Macbeth, the face can be true or false in a way that Lady Macbeth's performative and constructed visages cannot. After the murder, Macbeth confesses, 'To know my deed, / 'twere best not know myself. / Wake Duncan with thy knocking. I would thou couldst' (II, ii, 69–71). Macbeth links his deed with knowledge and acknowledgement, admitting that the epistemological cost of his deed and his avoidance of faces is the surrender of his own self-knowledge.

Despite these admissions, Macbeth nevertheless presses toward even larger spans of distance between himself and the faces of others. After Macbeth's bedroom confrontation, he plots the murder of Banquo in a way that will allow him far greater remove from facing those he seeks to kill. In his conversation with the murderers, Macbeth makes transparent excuses for his own absence from the deed:

> [A]nd, though I could
> With bare-faced power sweep him from my sight
> And bid my will avouch it, yet I must not,
> For certain friends that are both his and mine,
> Whose loves I may not drop, but wail his fall,
> Who I myself struck down. And thence it is
> That I to your assistance do make love,
> Masking the business from the common eye
> For sundry weighty reasons.
>
> (III, i, 119–27)

Although Macbeth offers a swaggering confidence in his ability to kill Banquo '[w]ith bare-faced power' – in so doing, possibly referring to the wide prerogative powers of a monarch embodied within the monarch's body and face – he nevertheless appoints others to murder Banquo and to endure Banquo's face throughout the encounter.[29] Through his false assertion of bravado, Macbeth again implicitly acknowledges the potency of the face, one that is particularly exposed in its bareness, immediacy and availability.

But why is it that the ghost who comes to haunt Macbeth is that of Banquo, not Duncan? In addition to Banquo's friendship with Macbeth ('certain friends [. . .] are both his and mine'), perhaps it is because, although Macbeth encounters Duncan's face through the diaphanously distorting layers of darkness and sleep, Macbeth places significantly greater distance between himself and Banquo's face.[30] Banquo's ghost does, after all, insistently thrust his face into Macbeth's vision: as Macbeth exclaims, 'Thou canst not say I did it. Never shake / Thy gory locks at me' and 'Avaunt and quit my sight! Let the earth hide thee', transposing the Gorgon's locks that earlier belonged to Duncan onto Banquo's ghostly countenance (III, iv, 48–9, 91). While Macbeth insists that, by having hired a murderer, he can claim independence from the deed, he nowhere summons the 'bare-faced power' of which he previously boasted. When Lady Macbeth asks him, 'Are you a man?', he replies, 'Ay, and a bold one, that dare look on that / Which might appall the devil', again pretending a boldness, assuming a false face, that he acutely lacks (III, iv, 56–8). Such claims return Macbeth and Lady Macbeth to their earlier disagreements about the face, as Lady Macbeth reiterates her artificialising mode of perception:

> O, proper stuff!
> This is the very painting of your fear.
> This is the air-drawn dagger which you said
> Led you to Duncan. O, these flaws and starts,
> Impostors to true fear, would well become
> A woman's story at a winter's fire,
> Authorized by her grandam. Shame itself!
> Why do you make such faces? When all's done,
> You look but on a stool.
>
> (III, iv, 58–66)

Lady Macbeth again invokes painting, drawing and storytelling ('[a] woman's story at a winter's fire') as a means of robbing Banquo's ghostly visage of its threatening power. Yet Macbeth cannot escape the pull of Banquo's face, accusing the ghost of having 'no speculation in those eyes / Which thou dost glare with' (III, iv, 93–4).[31] Through such an accusation, Macbeth seems to will himself to believe it is true, to convince himself that Banquo in fact is the very painting of his fear.

While the comic bed trick facilitates a sex act whose aversion to faces presumably culminates in future, face-to-face sex acts under the bond of marriage, the tragic bed trick's central faceless murder spins out to ensnare the protagonists in their own faceless deaths, for the Macbeths each lose their faces in their final moments. As V, i charts Lady Macbeth's descent into madness, the candid nature of her vivid confessions and the expressivity of her urgent gestures are nevertheless juxtaposed with a face that cannot communicate these disclosures or emotions; though the Doctor surmises optimistically, 'You see her eyes are open', the gentlewoman declares 'Ay, but their sense are shut' (V, i, 21–2). In this final appearance, Lady Macbeth ultimately inhabits the reality she has insistently sought after. Her face, too, has been decommissioned: there is no book, no painted devils, no strange matters, to be found there, only open eyes with no sense, no legibility, no meaning. Fittingly, she insists on returning to the instrument of furniture that originally granted Lady Macbeth the tools to consider facelessness, the bed: 'To bed, to bed: there's knocking at the gate. [. . .] What's done, cannot be undone. To, bed, to bed, to bed' (V, i, 54–6).

For Macbeth, too, the play's final scenes continue to feature faces that provoke and annoy him. When a servant delivers the dire news that ten thousand Englishmen stand outside the castle, Macbeth moves to attack the servant's face: 'The devil damn thee black, thou cream-faced loon! / Where gott'st thou that goose-look?' (V, iii, 11–12). Macbeth seeks to ridicule the face and thus delegitimise the threat that it conveys and contains; face-as-cream and face-as-goose are cartoonish and diminutive caricatures that Macbeth prefers to the overpowering face that, like Macduff's Gorgon, communicates his own doom. As the news that the servant delivers continues to agitate Macbeth, his assault on the face continues:

> MACBETH
> Go prick thy face and over-red thy fear,
> Thou lily-livered boy. What soldiers, patch?
> Death of thy soul! – those linen cheeks of thine
> Are counsellors to fear. What soldiers, whey-face?
>
> SERVANT
> The English force, so please you.
>
> MACBETH
> Take thy face hence.
>
> (V, iii, 16–21)

In his imperative to 'prick thy face and over-red thy fear', Macbeth wishes that the servant gild his face with blood in the same manner that Lady Macbeth earlier decorated the chamberlains' faces. The servant's 'whey-faced' visage with his 'linen cheeks' haunts Macbeth in the way his own expression once provoked Lady Macbeth, both inciting and confirming feared knowledge. The manner in which Macbeth funnels his rage and frustration explicitly toward the face – spitting out a final, monosyllabic imperative, 'Take thy face hence' – conveys the breakdown of Lady Macbeth strategies of effacement, for here is no Gorgon, nor even a Duncan or Banquo. Instead, a minor servant's visage is enough to pierce through Macbeth's defensive strategies and confront him with the knowledge he most desperately seeks to avoid.

Ultimately, the play literally defaces Macbeth, a punishment of beheading that Shakespeare had not staged since *2 Henry VI*. When Macduff enters '*with Macbeth's head*', he celebrates this beheading in a graphic and unsettling manner: 'Behold where stands / Th' usurper's cursèd head. The time is free' (V, xi, 20–1). The fantasies of facelessness entertained by the Macbeths culminate in the loss of both of their faces: Lady Macbeth's face is evacuated of sense, while Macbeth's is literally removed from his body. Yet the figure who initially spoke of the overpowering nature of the Gorgon's face now carries Macbeth's head in his hands; he no longer claims that this vision will 'destroy your sight', like the deceased Duncan, but instead insists that time is 'free'. While Marjorie Garber has noted that Macbeth's head 'is to become an object lesson, a spectacle, a warning against tyranny', Macduff's handling of this head might also represent a shift in Macduff's own relation to the face, becoming yet another attempt to show that faces can be robbed of their force.[32] This corresponds with the unsettling observation that Scotland's new king, Malcolm, has more in common with Macbeth than we may wish to admit. As Rebecca Lemon notes:

> Like Macbeth himself, the future king practices the traitor's arts of deception. [. . .] [I]n each of Malcolm's appearances between his father's murder and his own ascension as king, he increasingly exploits the opposition of 'mind' and 'face' so that, like Macbeth, he deceives his audiences onstage in order to protect himself and eventually gain the throne.[33]

Unlike Macduff's speechless witness of Duncan's deceased face, Macduff's final presentation of Macbeth's head seems more like a perverse parody of looking into the face of another as it happily manipulates Macbeth's deceased and lifeless visage. Its emergence at the play's end suggests that the strategies of facelessness first proposed by the Macbeths are in no way disavowed or eradicated.

Conclusion: beds and tricks

Across genre as well as social station, both *All's Well* and *Macbeth* root their inquiry into the meaning of the face through a scene of willed facelessness enabled by a bed. The plays link these fantasies of facelessness to two embodied activities that the bed hosts, sex and death. Where both plays feature a bedroom scene that ensnares a masculine desire of unmitigated power and manipulation, each also draws in a woman's persistent desire as well, Helena's 'constant will', as Schwarz describes it, and Lady Macbeth's originary aversion to the claims of the face. But what is it, ultimately, about beds that can foster these faceless imaginaries? The bed's horizontal plane seems to allow for the altering of the face-to-face encounter's most fundamental grammar, for its horizontality disrupts, tilts and defamiliarises these relations as it juxtaposes users and non-users into perpendicular encounters, finding in these postures new differentials of height and power. As Roberts illustrates, in the early modern period, beds owned by the wealthy (as well as beds used as stage properties) were often four-poster 'tester' beds with curtains, adding yet another way in which beds could hide the face.[34] Such arrangements are undoubtedly quotidian (no one, after all, is unfamiliar with a bed or the concept of lying within it), and they may even heighten the meeting of faces (visiting a sick grandparent, waking a child from a nap). But in circumstances when one wishes to avoid the face, the slight alteration that the bed offers may nevertheless provide a small ledge that can accommodate evasion, ceding just enough metaphysical ground to faceless fantasies in order to buoy flights into effacement.

Indeed, the bed may serve as primary the locus of effacement in these plays, but if it were not the bed, it might be (and often is) some other object that deflects attention away from faces. *All's Well* features faces supplanted by substitutionary rings that act like fetishes (another word whose etymology lies in *facere*), averting vision and drawing consciousness in ways that allows characters like Bertram and Parolles to un-know the face, to happily and temporarily forget about its grip and demands. Although *Macbeth* does not traffic in rings, it casts the vision of the Macbeths onto the face itself as a fashioned object; unlike *All's Well*, these faces receive extended scrutiny but only insofar as they no longer act like faces but instead function as drawings, pictures or pieces of writing.

Finally, if the bed is one primary object of analysis in these plays, so too is the trick, the act of deception of both lovers and hosts. In *All's Well*'s final scene, before Helena has appeared to clear up all confusion, Parolles mounts a poor defence of Bertram, proclaiming to the king, 'Tricks he hath had in him which gentlemen have' (V, iii, 237). The trick of which Parolles speaks includes not only Bertram's wilful dalliances nor his un-wilful beguilement, but also the philosophical temptation that these plays both stage in startlingly similar ways, of the desire to find pathways to escape the face and the claims it makes upon us. But the trick is ultimately on those who succumb to such fantasies of facelessness, for in the darkened chambers that these plays evoke faces may be avoided for a brief time but they are ultimately unavoidable.

Notes

1. Marliss C. Desens, *The Bed-Trick in English Renaissance Drama*, p. 17. Also see Janet Adelman, 'Marriage and the Maternal Body', pp. 76–102; Julia Briggs, 'Shakespeare's Bed-Tricks'; Julia R. Lupton, '*All's Well that Ends Well* and the Futures of Consent'; and Kathryn Schwarz, *What You Will: Gender, Contract, and Shakespearean Social Space*.
2. William Shakespeare: all citations of Shakespeare are from *The New Oxford Shakespeare: Modern Critical Edition*, ed. Gary Taylor et al.
3. Bernie Rhie has argued that Wittgenstein's exploration of the relationship between the body and the face is a means of critiquing the Cartesian subject. See Bernie Rhie, 'Wittgenstein on the Face of a Work of Art'.
4. Ludwig Wittgenstein, *Philosophical Investigations*, §116.
5. Ludwig Wittgenstein, *Philosophical Investigations*, II.iv; Ludwig Wittgenstein, *Culture and Value*, p. 23.
6. Toril Moi, *Revolution of the Ordinary: Literary Studies After Wittgenstein, Austin, and Cavell*, p. 186.
7. Stanley Cavell, *The Claim of Reason: Wittgenstein, Skepticism, Morality, and Tragedy*, p. 84.
8. Moi, *Revolution of the Ordinary*, p. 206.
9. Janet Adelman, 'Marriage and the Maternal Body', pp. 77–8.
10. For more on masculine desire in other early modern dramatic uses of the bed trick, see Marliss Desens, 'The Bed-Trick as Manifestation of Male Fantasies', in *The Bed-Trick in English Renaissance Drama*, pp. 93–115.
11. Kathryn Schwarz, *What You Will*, p. 108.

12. Sasha Roberts, '"Let Me the Curtains Draw": The Dramatic and Symbolic Properties of the Bed in Shakespeare', p. 156.

13. Schwarz, *What You Will*, p. 114.

14. Ellen Ellerbeck, 'Adoption and the Language of Horticulture in *All's Well That Ends Well*', p. 305.

15. Alexander Leggatt spells out this parallel: 'In the gulling of Parolles, though this time we see everything, Parolles is as much in the dark as Bertram. Master and man are fooled together. As identities dissolve in the darkness of the bedroom and the impersonality of sex, language for Parolles (the man of words) dissolves in the gibberish spoken by his assailants' ('Introduction', *All's Well That Ends Well* (New Cambridge Edition), p. 37).

16. Sarah Beckwith, *Shakespeare and the Grammar of Forgiveness*, p. 100. This blindfolded confession might also evoke the Catholic confessional grill separating confessor from penitent developed in the Tridentine reforms of 1545–63. But even in that relation, the penitent knows precisely to whom he or she is speaking and how such words will be received.

17. See Stanley Cavell, 'The Avoidance of Love: A Reading of *King Lear*', p. 104. Cavell's echo of Jaques's soliloquy here might suggest that the figure of the melancholic is particularly susceptible to the temptation of a darkened theatre.

18. Beckwith, *Shakespeare and the Grammar of Forgiveness*, p. 170.

19. This notion comes in part from Beckwith, who describes the ending of *The Tempest* as 'an exploration of the resources of theater in the task of acknowledgement'. See *Shakespeare and the Grammar of Forgiveness*, p. 167.

20. In *As You Like It*, Duke Senior remarks that the Forest of Arden acts as 'counsellors / That feelingly persuade me what I am' (II, i, 10–11), while Oliver confesses, 'I do not shame / To tell you what I was, since my conversion / So sweetly tastes, being the thing I am' (IV, iii, 131–3). *The Tempest*'s Miranda chastises her father, 'You have often / Begun to tell me what I am, but stopped / And left me to a bootless inquisition, / Concluding, "Stay: not yet"' (I, ii, 33–6). Othello remarks, 'I am not merry; but I do beguile / The thing I am, by seeming otherwise' (II, i, 122–3). There are additional examples in *Twelfth Night*, *Merry Wives of Windsor*, *Much Ado About Nothing* and *Coriolanus*.

21. '*Macbeth* [. . .] is most certainly a drama in which the *oikos* is key to the action, atmosphere, and image banks of the play.' See Julia Reinhard Lupton, 'Macbeth Against Dwelling', pp. 86, 116.

22. 'Helena disappears as a social subject, receding into an abnegation of self that disables the judgments of others.' Schwarz, *What You Will*, p. 124.

23. Here I follow the thought of Hannah Arendt, who distinguishes between the face-to-face, public realm of action and the workshop,

where the things that are made 'guarantee the permanence and durability without which a world would not be possible at all.' See Hannah Arendt, *The Human Condition* (1958), p. 94.

24. Kevin Curran has also noted the integral nature of 'things' to the Macbeths' world, particularly their criminality, writing, 'Macbeth presents criminal thoughts not as ontologically distinct products of the intellect or soul, but as secretions of the senses, properties of active receptive bodies moving through a world of things.' See Kevin Curran, 'Feeling Criminal in *Macbeth*', p. 391.

25. As Sandra Clark and Pamela Mason observe, 'The face/book comparison was commonplace' (*Macbeth*, Arden Shakespeare 3rd edn, p. 159, note 62). Lady Capulet asks Juliet to 'Read o'er the volume of young Paris' face, / And find delight writ there with beauty's pen' (I, iii, 82–3). In *Troilus and Cressida*, Hector exclaims, 'O, like a book of sport thou'lt read me o'er; / But there's more in me than thou understand'st' (IV, vi, 241–2).

26. There may be echoes of St Paul in this construction of face-as-mirror, for he contrasts the glass/mirror with the true face-to-face in 1 Cor. 13: 12, 'For now we see through a glass darkly [NRSV: in a mirror, dimly]: but then shall we see face to face' (Geneva Bible).

27. Claudius laments that Ophelia, 'Divided from herself and her fair judgment', sees others as 'pictures or mere beasts', suggesting that to view another as a picture is to lack a critical faculty of mind. Claudius's assessment maps nicely onto the philosophical temptation to which Lady Macbeth has succumbed (IV, ii, 81–3). One might expect pictured faces to place a claim upon us, but as this quotation from *Hamlet*, in tandem with *Macbeth*, suggests, Shakespeare seems to regard the pull of pictures as distinct from that of the living face.

28. See Susan Zimmerman. *The Early Modern Corpse and Shakespeare's Theatre*, p. 173.

29. For more on Macbeth's 'bare-faced power' and the power of prerogative, see Thomas Poole, 'Judicial Review at the Margins: Law, Power, and Prerogative,' p. 94. Poole describes Macbeth's self-described 'barefaced power' as 'a vision of prerogative as untrammeled power' (p. 94).

30. Banquo returns in another episode of facial confrontation, the show of kings, in which Macbeth responds, 'I'll see no more' and 'Horrible sight!' (IV, i, 116, 120).

31. In his essay on speed and time in *Macbeth*, Howard Marchitello writes about the banquet scene:

> What are we to make of these fits? Because Macbeth's raptures are ruptures – of time and of temporality – I see them not as manifestations of an Othello-like epilepsy, but of what Paul Virilio calls picnolepsy, a nonpathologized understanding of human perception, as well as the movement of and through time (duration) as composed of gaps, splits, and fractures.

Marchitello's notion of rupture nicely captures the manner in which Macbeth has also become ruptured from the faces of others, an event that precipitates episodes of 'gaps, splits, and fissures' of face-ghosts, such as the banquet scene and the show of kings. See Howard Marchitello, 'Speed and the Problem of Real Time in *Macbeth*', pp. 446–7.
32. See Marjorie Garber, *Shakespeare's Ghost Writers: Literature as Uncanny Causality*, p. 114. Garber also suggests that Macbeth's face represents another Medusa; I would argue conversely that Macbeth's face here is Macduff's Gorgon evacuated of its original power.
33. See Rebecca Lemon, 'Scaffolds of Treason in *Macbeth*', pp. 29, 39.
34. See Roberts, '"Let Me the Curtains Draw"', pp. 154–60.

Part III

Facing Judgement

Chapter 6

The Face of Judgement in *Measure for Measure*

Kevin Curran

As Bruce Smith points out in his lead essay to this volume, 'face' is both a noun and a verb – a thing and an action. Accordingly, the word denotes two different kinds of physicality. First, it names an object, one that can be seen, touched, listened to, even tasted (think of kissing). Second, it describes a way of orienting oneself in space and in relation to other objects (face me, face the wall, face forward, face each other). This verbal use of the word face – in which its noun-form, its thing-quality, is also always active – frequently carries some kind of ethical freight, a sense of being called to account, of taking responsibility or of acknowledging what has yet to be acknowledged. We see this most vividly in common figurative uses of the word, such as 'face the facts' or 'face the music'. In these phrases, face and facing have something to do with judgement and the kind of moral, social and practical calculus we all practise everyday, and which hopefully leads to the good, the right or at least the expedient outweighing the bad, the wrong or the undesirable.

This connection between facing and judging is central to this essay. Specifically, I am interested in how the spatial, object-oriented grammar of the face invites us to think of judgement less as an individual decision or rational cognitive procedure than as a physical, dimensional event that involves orientating oneself in space and time. I will be referring to this as the 'physics of judgment' and my case study will be Shakespeare's *Measure for Measure*, in particular Act V, scene i, in which two faces – Mariana's and Duke Vincento's – are crucial to the play's final scene of condemnation and forgiveness. The theatre provides an especially compelling locale for thinking about the physics of judgement. Indeed, judgement shares with theatre its most basic raw materials: people and things arranged in space and time.

The face is crucial to this discussion because in *Measure for Measure* it stands at the crossroads of theatre and judgement, indexing their shared fields of location and duration and their common orientation toward the future.

By following this line of inquiry, we stand to recover a version of judgement that has been largely missing from the intellectual discourse of the twentieth and twenty-first centuries, one that is positive, future-oriented and world-making. As Vivasvan Soni has shown, both Michel Foucault and Pierre Bourdieu viewed judgement as one of our most vexed inheritances from the Enlightenment – on one hand, an expression of reason and autonomy; on the other, a normative and normalising force used to police behaviour and iden-tity.[1] This account has had remarkable staying power. Even in every-day life we tend to be uncomfortable with the idea of judgement, to view it, explicitly or implicitly, as *judgemental*. Right-or-wrong/ this-or-that interpretations are unsophisticated at best, boorish or unfair at worst. Humanities classrooms are primary sites for such thinking. Since the appearance of influential New Critical work like William Empson's *Seven Types of Ambiguity*, and certainly since the rise of deconstruction, a commitment to multiplicity and open-endedness has prevailed in higher education.[2] This is hardly a prob-lem in and of itself, but there are more troubling versions of this habit of thought. For example, we have all seen in recent years how clear instances of police brutality are sometimes met with admonitions to resist judgement and avoid jumping to conclusions as there are always two sides to every story. Discomfort with judgement does not belong solely to either the political left or the political right. Hannah Arendt was famously chastised by both liberals and conservatives when she publicly condemned a range of groups and individuals for the roles they played in the Holocaust. She recalls in a subsequent essay, 'I was told that judging itself is wrong: no one can judge who had not been there.'[3]

It may seem strange to claim that a play whose final scene of judgement is known for courting darkness, irrationality and ambi-guity offers us a chance to recover a positive version of judgement. Modern critics have been uneasy about several aspects of the denoue-ment, including the arbitrary betrothal of Isabella and the Duke and the near executions of Angelo and Lucio.[4] But in arguing that the close of *Measure for Measure* models a positive version of judgement I am not suggesting that the denouement itself is uniformly positive or optimistic. More precisely, I wish to suggest that the play of faces in Act V, scene i of *Measure for Measure* usefully exposes one aspect of Renaissance theatre's unique and largely overlooked place in the history and theory of judgement. It does so by generating a choreography of adjudication grounded in the physical and ethical dynamics of mutual recognition and the corresponding possibility of new social formations.

Mariana's face and the physics of judgement

I will begin by mapping out how the physics of judgement works in Act V, scene i. The scene brings together two deception plots. In both cases, the deception is justified by the greater good for which it is committed. The first of these involves Duke Vincento who throughout the play dresses as a friar to observe the behaviour of his subjects undetected. The other involves Mariana, a woman who was betrothed to, then abandoned by, Angelo, the hypocritically puritanical deputy filling in for the Duke. Mariana, Isabella and the Duke trick Angelo into consummating his marriage to Mariana by sending her to a garden-house where Angelo thinks he is having a tryst with Isabella. The collision of these two plots in the final scene of the play leads to a series of revelations in which the face plays an essential role.

The first of these revelations occurs when, in the wake of Isabella's accusations of sexual blackmail, Mariana is led onstage, supposedly to absolve Angelo of Isabella's charges. Here is the initial part of the scene:

> DUKE: Give us some seats.
> *[Seats are brought in]*
> Come, cousin Angelo,
> In this I'll be impartial; be you judge
> Of your own cause.
> *[The Duke and Angelo sit]*
> *Enter [Friar Peter with] Mariana [veiled]*
> Is this the witness, friar?
> First let her show her face, and after speak.
> MARIANA: Pardon, my lord, I will not show my face
> Until my husband bid me.
>
> (V, i, 164–9)[5]

This is clearly a scene of arbitration. A charge has been made and a witness is being brought in to testify. The Duke even has some seats set up to make the exchange feel more like a trial with judge and jury presiding. We should also note that Mariana's face is at the centre of this judgement-event. The Duke's command, 'First let her show her face, and after speak', seems to assume that the forensic and moral evaluation integral to judgement is only possible under certain base-line conditions of collective ethical orientation: the mutual acknowledgement and recognition intrinsic to the face-to-face encounter. But Mariana refuses: 'I will not show my face / Until my husband bid me'. A little further on, Angelo echoes the Duke's request at which point Mariana finally acquiesces:

> ANGELO: This is a strange abuse. Let's see thy face.
> MARIANA: My husband bids me; now I will unmask.
> *[She shows her face]*
> This is that face, thou cruel Angelo,
> Which once thou swor'st was worth the looking on . . .
> (V, i, 200–3)

There are two aspects of this exchange that are important for understanding the physics of judgement. To begin with, the component parts of this judgement-event consist predominantly of actions and reactions centred on Mariana's veiled face. This stage business is marked verbally throughout: 'give', 'come', 'show', 'not show', 'let's see', '*shows*'. That is to say, Mariana's face indexes the way the judgement-event unfolds in space. In addition – and this is the second aspect – Mariana's face indexes the way the judgement-event unfolds through time. All terms pertaining to temporal positioning – what linguists call 'time deixis' – are used in reference to Mariana's face: 'first', 'after', 'until', 'now'.[6] Here is the relevant passage once again, this time with time deixis marked in bold and references to Mariana's face underlined:

> Is this the witness, friar?
> **First** let her show her <u>face</u>, and **after** speak.
> MARIANA: Pardon, my lord, I will not show my <u>face</u>
> **Until** my husband bid me.
> (V, i, 166–9)
>
> . . .
>
> ANGELO: This is a strange abuse. Let's see thy <u>face</u>.
> MARIANA: My husband bids me; **now** I will unmask.
> *[She shows her face]*
> (V, i, 200–1)

Marking the exchange in this way highlights the peculiar theatrical role played by the face in this scene. Though obviously part of the actor's and character's body, the face also functions almost like a prop. It is instrumentalised in a way that exceeds the demands of character in order to advance elements of plot and theme. To this extent, the face muddles some of the standard categories of theatrical semiotics established by scholars such as Patrick Pavis, Erika Fischer-Lichte and Keir Elam. Consider some basic examples of these categories: linguistic signs, paralinguistic signs, kinesic signs and proxemic signs. Linguistic signs function both rhetorically and acoustically. They comprise both the meanings of individual words spoken on stage and the tone and pace of delivery. Paralinguistic signs, meanwhile, include such things as props, music, scenery and lighting. Kinesic signs are self-contained bodily movements such as gestures. Proxemic signs, on the other hand, are movements of bodies through the space of the stage.[7]

Mariana's face does not fit in a straightforward way into any of these categories. Instead it performs two different kinds of signification simultaneously – kinesic and proxemic – while also challenging received wisdom about how these signifying units are supposed to work. Mariana's face is a kinesic sign in the way that all faces always are on stage, but the fact that it remains veiled for most of the exchange seriously undercuts its ability to do what kinesic signs are supposed to do: express or gesture. Mariana's face is a proxemic sign to the extent that it occasions the scene's primary actions and reactions. Indeed, it is at the centre of the scene's orbit of movement. And yet it does very little in the way of significant movement through space itself. A full semiotic reckoning of Mariana's face would also require the addition of a new sign-category, the 'chronemic', which would allow us to isolate the face's time-indexical function in the scene. As a chronemic sign, Mariana's face is consistently pointing to the temporal context in which it appears. It creates a scene of judgement which does not manifest itself in a flat present of decision, but rather unfolds sequentially through a linear process of action and response: '**First** let her show her face, and **after** speak'; 'I will not show my face / **Until** my husband bid me'; '**Now** I will unmask'.

The face in *Measure for Measure* bursts the seams of our received systems of theatrical interpretation. It demands a more flexible and expansive set of critical concepts. As the material anchor in the final scene's culminating moments of punishment and forgiveness, it offers a vantage point from which we can observe the physics of judgement at work, the way in which adjudication unfolds through the space and time of a mimetic environment comprised of bodies, voices and objects. From this perspective, judgement takes the form of a collaborative event. It has less to do with individual evaluation than with the collective application of knowledge toward a specific end. And as with all forms of applied knowledge – geometry, mechanics, even rhetoric – the aim of judgement is to *make* something: in this case, a livable future, a shared sense of truth and new conditions of social possibility in Vienna. We see the beginning of this process unfolding gradually during the scene of Mariana's unveiling: collective appraisal of the situation evolves as false knowledge and misperception gives way to true knowledge. The revelation of Mariana's face is the hinge on which the former swings toward the latter. Here is the scene with references to knowledge – first false, then true – set in bold:

> MARIANA: Why just, my lord, and that is Angelo,
>   Who thinks he **knows** that he ne'er **knew** my body,
>   But **knows**, he thinks, that he **knows** Isabel's.
> ANGELO: This is a strange abuse. Let's see thy face.
> MARIANA: My husband bids me; now I will unmask.
>   *[She shows her face]*
>   This is that face, thou cruel Angelo,
>   Which once thou swor'st was worth the looking on;
>   . . .
> DUKE: **Know** you this woman?
>   . . .
> ANGELO: My lord, I must confess I **know** this woman,
>   (V, i, 197–203, 208, 212)

This moment – the first phase of Act V, scene i's extended judgement-event – marks the beginning of a shared coming-into-knowledge that I will continue to trace in the next section of this essay. Mariana's unveiling and the acknowledgement it triggers – 'I know this woman' – establishes a new truth about the relations among the characters on stage that will lead eventually to fundamental changes in the social fabric of Shakespeare's Vienna. We may tend to think of judgement as a singular decision or decree, something that ends or resolves things. But the dynamics of the face in *Measure for Measure* shows us something different: a version of judgement that is collective and creative, and which has as much to do with the future as with the past.

Practical judgement: facing, managing, making

So far I have made two connected claims. The first is that in *Measure for Measure* the face is at the centre of something we might call the physics of judgement. The second is that by looking closely at how this process works on stage we can recover a version of judgement that is social and world-making. In this section, I will give more attention to the second claim. I will show, in particular, how theatrical judgement functions as a form of collective knowledge-management and conclude with some thoughts on the face as the source of judgement's future-oriented trajectory.

On the Renaissance stage, judgement forms communities of knowledge. It does so by realigning the varying levels of information possessed by characters and play-goers around a single, shared Truth. The friar is actually the Duke; there are two young men named Antipholus in town, not just one; this person who you thought was a boy is actually a young woman: these are all things that are disclosed through scenes of judgement. They constitute a specific version of the theatrical *anagnorisis* that Matthew Smith discusses in his contribution to this volume. These particular examples also indicate that creating, maintaining and finally redressing disparities in knowledge is especially important in comedy. At a basic mechanical level, humour is generated in stage comedy through the uneven evolution in the way sensory information is distributed among characters and play-goers. What makes a play like *The Comedy of Errors* funny is the disconnect between what audience members see (Antipholus of Syracuse) and what characters on stage see (Antipholus of Ephesus). The relationship between sense perception and knowledge is different for each of the two groups that together constitute theatrical experience. The same can be said for Act III, scene ii of *A Midsummer Night's Dream*, in which Robin Goodfellow hides while imitating the voices of Lysander and Demetrius. Humour, again, is generated by a simple sensory disconnect: the play-goers can hear and see everything; Demetrius and Lysander can hear but not see. Typically, this disconnect is remedied in the play's denouement. The end of *The Comedy of Errors* feels like a resolution because characters and spectators at last see and hear the same thing (*this* is Antipholus of Syracuse, *that* is Antipholus of Ephesus). Likewise at the end of *Twelfth Night* when Duke Orsino slowly comes to terms with the truth about 'Cesario', or the final act of *All's Well that Ends Well* where vision and hearing are once again revelatory. Shakespearean comedy depends for its effects on this carefully managed economy of perception and knowledge.[8]

In *Measure for Measure*, perception and knowledge are framed by the dynamics of judgement. That is, judgement is both the impetus for and the result of the facial revelations that finally distribute knowledge evenly among each character on stage and the play-goers in the audience. The faces of Act V, scene i – the first unveiled, the second unhooded – remind us that judgement is a fundamentally sensory and communal event: it begins with showing or revealing and ends with seeing, *really* seeing, together. We will recall that in the final scene of *Measure for Measure*, the Duke says of the veiled Mariana, 'First let her show her face'. Angelo agrees: 'Let's see thy face'. When Mariana concedes she says bitingly, 'This is that face, thou cruel Angelo, / Which once thou swor'st was worth the looking on.' First perception, then judgement, and somewhere in between a coming-into-knowledge for all present and the establishment of a new truth. Something similar happens when Lucio demands of the Duke (who he thinks is a friar), 'Show your knave's visage . . . Show your sheep-biting face' (V, i, 337–8). When he *'pulls off the Friar's hood, and discovers the Duke'*, the latter says, 'Thou art the first knave that e'er made'st a duke' (V, i, 340). In a brief moment that cannot quite be parsed into sequential units, judgement descends on Lucio, a shared truth is established and a new community of knowledge is formed.

In our own time, in everyday contexts, to judge is to make a decision in response to information. But what we tend to miss is the way judgement also involves managing and distributing that information. This dimension of judgement would have been familiar to many early moderns whose understanding of the concept derived primarily from the Aristotelian rhetorical tradition that was central to humanist education. In oratory, especially in legal contexts, judgement was defined as the capacity to put information in the right order. Thomas Blundeville, for example, explains in *The Art of Logicke* (1599) that once 'invention finds matter', judgement 'frameth, disposeth, and reduceth the same into due forme of argument'.[9] There are a variety of subspecies of judgement within the rhetorical tradition, some of which, like *modestia*, show us how judgement's core functions of framing and disposing, managing and curating, were not restricted to oratorical or compositional contexts, but were also essential to an orderly and ethical life-practice. In Cicero's *De Officiis*, for example – which was along with Aristotle's *Nichomachean Ethics* the most influential study of virtue in the Renaissance – *modestia* is described as 'the essence of orderliness and of right-placing'. Cicero also invokes the Stoics' definition of *modestia* as the '"science of disposing aright everything that is done or said" . . . "the arrangement of things in their suitable and appropriate places"'.[10] The term Cicero uses for 'right-placing' and '"disposing aright"' is *collocation* (*collocationis* and *collocandarum*, respectively, in Latin). For Cicero, collocation is a practice at once technical and ethical, both correct *and* good. It is essential to his notion of *modestia* as 'the science of doing the right thing at the right time'. 'Such orderliness of conduction', he continues, 'is, therefore, to be observed, that everything in the conduct of our life shall balance and harmonize.'[11] In *Measure for Measure*, the face is at the centre of a process of collocation, of setting things right. The unveiling of Mariana and the unhooding of the Duke provide object lessons in accountability and occasion the redistribution of knowledge that restores order to Vienna. This also reminds us how, in a general sense, comic *dénouements* are always moments of embodied collocation. They represent one of several ways in which the rhetorical tradition of judgement became part of the genome of theatrical form.

This much we know, then: the face of judgement in *Measure for Measure* is part of a dynamic, dimensional process of knowledge-making and knowledge-management. This process involves both actors and audience and, as such, is fundamentally collective and collaborative. I want to conclude this section by reflecting on how under these conditions judgement is also creative and future-oriented. Toward this end, I return to the exchange between Lucio and the Duke:

> LUCIO: . . . you must be hooded, must you? Show your knave's visage, with a pox to you! Show your sheep-biting face, and be hanged an hour! Will't not off?
> > *Lucio pulls off the Friar's hood, and discovers the Duke . . .*
> DUKE: Thou art the first knave that e'er mad'st a duke.
> > (V, i, 337–40)

The revelation of the Duke immediately changes the epistemological, legal and social conditions of the play-world: Mariana and Isabella are confirmed as truthful while Angelo is confirmed as false; Angelo and Lucio are promptly assigned punishments; and marriages are arranged for Angelo and Mariana, Lucio and Kate Keepdown and the Duke himself and Isabella. For the characters assembled on stage, then, the judgement occasioned by the Duke's face completely remakes the world they had known. It leads to a new truth, a new source of moral authority and a new set of social relations. Judgement takes the raw materials of one world – people, ideas, connections and obligations – and reassembles them to form another. Through an extended judgement-event that begins with showing ('let her show her face'; '*she shows her face*'; 'show your knave's visage'; 'show your sheep-biting face': '*He . . . discovers the Duke*') and ends with adjudication, condemnation and forgiveness, the lines of inclusion and exclusion are redrawn to form a version of community that did not exist when the play opened. Bastards are accommodated (the child of Lucio and Kate Keepdown), the forsaken are acknowledged (Mariana), the guilty are forgiven (Angelo), the condemned are welcomed back (Claudio) and – more dubiously – the self-exiled are reintegrated (Isabella). This is the sense in which judgement is creative and future-oriented in *Measure for Measure*. Adjudication may, in one sense, be concerned with assessing the past (past actions, past claims), but in so far as it triggers changes in behaviour, social arrangements and (in a juridical setting) legal precedent, judgement is also always directed toward the future; it is always about *making*.

The capacity of judgement to make and create, thrown into sharp relief in *Measure for Measure* by the dynamics of the face, again finds its source in the rhetorical tradition. The Blundeville quotation cited above illustrates the well-established conceptual link between judgement and invention: while 'invention finds matter', judgement 'frameth, disposeth, and reduceth the same into due forme of argument'. This formulation derives from Roman rhetorical theory which has deeper roots in Aristotle. Texts like Cicero's *De inventione*, the anonymous *Rhetorica ad Herennium* and Quintilian's *Institutio oratoria* describe invention as the skill of deciding which line of reasoning is most likely to strike a particular audience as especially compelling. Judgement's role is to break that line of reasoning down into component parts and then arrange them in a sequence calculated to achieve maximum persuasiveness. Judgement, in other words, turns ideas into arguments by lending them organisational form. Along with invention, it was an essential component of what Aristotle termed the *genus iudiciale*, the kind of speech typically found in the law courts.[12] In Shakespeare's time, anyone with a grammar school education was likely to have encountered rhetorical handbooks like *De inventione*, *Rhetorica ad Herrenium* and *Institutio oratoria*, or vernacular manuals like Thomas Wilson's *The Art of Rhetorique* (1553) which drew on the Roman handbooks.[13]

With this in mind, we can begin to see how judgement might be conceived as one crucial point along a continuum of creative endeavour.
For those with some training in rhetorical theory, judgement was a form
of production rather than a form of decision, as we would now tend to
view it. As a component of theatrical form, therefore, judgement's role
in plays like *Measure for Measure* is not simply to end things, but also
to start things anew, to plot a future course and craft another world – a
world that must finally take shape beyond the fictional parameters of
the play itself.[14]

Conclusion

My aim in this essay has been to determine what we can learn about
judgement by attending to the dynamics of the face in *Measure for
Measure*. This has involved working in the opposite direction of conventional literary criticism. That is, rather than using a concept to
give a reading of a play, I have tried to use a play to give a reading
of concept. Accordingly, the take-away is not so much a new interpretation of *Measure for Measure*, but rather a new way of thinking
about judgement and its relationship to theatricality. As we have seen,
the face in *Measure for Measure* functions as a deictic component
of judgement, an action-object whose verbal and nominal capacities
transform judgement into theatre by orienting it in time and space.
Indeed, the face reminds us that judgement is fundamentally theatrical, though not in the ways typically asserted by cultural criticism: judgement is not theatrical because courtrooms are kind of like
theatres or because juries are kind of like play audiences. Instead,
judgement is theatrical because it is constituted by the same basic
raw materials as theatre: time, space and action. The face indexes this
shared physics of experience.

When we look judgement in the face, we see that it is not simply
a unidirectional administrative procedure (as in law) or a singular
confrontation with absolute authority (as in religion). More accu-
rately, judgement is a participatory practice that forms communities
by translating common sensory experience (seeing, showing, looking, hearing) into common axes of value (a shared sense of right
and wrong, good and bad). In the arch of its unfolding, judgement
starts as *evaluation* and ends as *values*, reminding us that the etymological link between those two words finds its source in a common
conceptual space where calculation and community are neighbours.
The particular determinations of Act V, scene i – Mariana is owed

something, Lucio owes something to others, Claudio is innocent, Angelo is guilty – reinforce general ethical principles of obligation, responsibility and justice that make social life possible. The close of *Measure for Measure*, in other words, shows us how assessment can generate the shared standards that form the moral scaffolding of community. This positive and creative notion of judgement, iterated theatrically through the dynamics of the face, may have been familiar to early moderns trained in rhetoric. But it is far removed from the more punitive, categorical and normative sense of judgement that dominates the discourse of our own time.

Notes

1. Vivasvan Soni, 'Introduction: The Crisis of Judgment', in *The Eighteenth Century: Theory and Interpretation*, Special Issue on 'The Crisis of Judgment', Vivasvan Soni (ed.). See also Michel Foucault, *Discipline and Punish* and Pierre Bourdieu, *Distinction*.
2. Soni, 'Introduction: The Crisis of Judgment', pp. 66–71.
3. Hannah Arendt, 'Personal Responsibility Under Dictatorship', p. 18. See further Arendt, 'The Crisis in Culture', 'Truth and Politics', 'Some Questions of Moral Philosophy' and *The Life of the Mind*, pp. 69, 93–5, 193.
4. See, for example, Cynthia Lewis, '"Dark Deeds Darkly Answered": Duke Vincentio and Judgment in *Measure for Measure*'; Janet Adelman, 'Bed Tricks'; and Michael D. Friedman, '"O, Let Him Marry Her!": Matrimony and Recompense in *Measure for Measure*'.
5. William Shakespeare: all citations of Shakespeare are from *The New Oxford Shakespeare: Modern Critical Edition*, ed. Gary Taylor et al.
6. There is a great deal written on this topic, but good starting points are John Lyons, 'Deixis, Space, and Time' and Geoffrey Nunberg, 'Indexality and Deixis'.
7. See further Keir Elam, *The Semiotics of Theatre and Drama*; Erika Fischer-Lichte, *The Semiotics of Theatre*; Patrice Pavis, *Languages of the Stage* and 'Performance Analysis: Space, Time, Action'.
8. Kevin Curran, 'Shakespearean Comedy and the Senses'.
9. Thomas Blundeville, *The Arte of Logicke* (London, 1599), p. 1; Quentin Skinner, *Forensic Shakespeare*, pp. 11–25, and Henry S. Turner, *The English Renaissance Stage*, pp. 45–55.
10. Cicero, *On Duties*, p. 145. This paragraph draws on Turner, *The English Renaissance Stage*, pp. 230–1 and Neal Wood, 'Cicero and the Political Thought of the Early English Renaissance'.
11. Cicero, *On Duties*, p. 147.

12. See further, Turner, *The English Renaissance Stage*, pp. 45–55; Jon Hesk, 'Types of Oratory,' pp. 150–6; and Skinner, *Forensic Shakespeare*, pp. 11–25.
13. Peter Mack, *Elizabethan Rhetoric*, pp. 11–47; Skinner, *Forensic Shakespeare*, pp. 25–41.
14. See further, Kevin Curran, 'Prospero's Plea: Judgment, Invention, and Political Form in *The Tempest*'.

Chapter 7

Then Face to Face: Timing Trust in *Macbeth*

Jennifer Waldron

In a recent essay, Julia Lupton argues that theatre offers a 'laboratory and clinic for exploring trust' (p. 156). Trust falls, blind man's
buff and other theatrical games educate 'practitioners and audiences in the practice of trust as a political virtue and cognitive skill
that carries the memory of face-to-face encounters into a world of
increasingly mediated intentions and expert knowledges.'[1] Yet how
exactly does the phenomenology of trust shift as we move from a live
encounter like a trust fall to more extended social, technical, political
or even supernatural environments? My focus on the timing of trust
in *Macbeth* helps to show the intricate relationships in early modern
England among theatrical, political and theological modes of trust.
Shakespeare's Macbeth violates Duncan's 'double trust' (I, vii, 12)
when he kills his king/kin in the guest bed he has provided.[2] The
horror of the murder is tied to the taboo on killing one's kinsman or
guest, and the shock waves of 'treason' (II, iii, 67) follow from this
more basic violation of personal trust. Yet in *Macbeth*, these deeply
personal, physical violations of trust simultaneously seem to rupture natural temporal bonds and what we might call preternatural
or supernatural ones. Most striking are the play's many allusions
to an apocalyptic time frame, which begin to appear right after
Duncan's murder with Malcolm's reference to 'the great doom's
image' (II, iii, 71). Rather than setting present, face-to-face human
interactions in opposition to the 'end times' of apocalypse and divine
judgement, this essay shows how intricately they are connected in the
theatrical timing of Shakespeare's *Macbeth*.

Occupying one end of a spectrum of temporal systems, trust
in this theological 'promised end' operates over a long haul that
extends far beyond the natural bounds of life. Richard Hooker's

sermon on assurance gives a sense of the vast scales at which this form of trust is understood to operate: 'The earth may shake, the pillars of the world may tremble under us; the countenance of the heaven may be appalled, the Sun may lose his light, the moon her beauty, the stars their glory', but none of that will shake the faith of 'the man that trusteth in God.'[3] The play's references to an apocalyptic time frame offer an important example of trust imaginatively extended over vast reaches of time and space. Yet in *Macbeth*, these larger scales insistently impinge on the face-to-face interactions of the theatrical 'instant'.[4] This brings us back to the other end of the spectrum: the fine-grained physical timing that is essential to theatrical games and stage play, as in slapstick comedy – a chair removed just as someone sits down; a roundhouse swing that misses; a glance given while the other's face is turned away. In *Macbeth*, the play itself becomes a type of trans-scalar device that juxtaposes the timing of physical trust in the present moment with the apocalyptic time of 'then face to face', as imagined in the terms of Paul's first letter to the Corinthians.[5]

Macbeth resembles *King Lear*, *Hamlet* and other Shakespearean tragedies that play these long and short temporalities of trust against each other in striking ways. Take, for instance, the strangely inverted 'trust fall' to which Edgar subjects his father in *Lear*.[6] Gloucester believes he falls thousands of feet through space, putting a decisive end to worldly time. The audience witnesses something more mundane: an actor moving from a standing position to a fallen one. The two modalities coincide without ever resolving. As Edgar puts it, 'Had he been where he thought, / By this had thought been past' (IV, vi, 44–5). In the same way, the participants in a trust fall have an asymmetrical relation to time. For the one who is trusted with the catch, the partner falls in a split second. Yet those moments seem like an eternity to the person falling, uncertain of whether they will be caught. It's a very long second. Most people stop and turn around at least once before tilting backward off the heels – to make assurance double sure. In *King Lear*, Gloucester is of course doing the exact opposite, trusting Edgar's word that he is in fact on the brink of a cliff with nothing to catch him. But the precarious balance of incompatible time schemes is the same. Gloucester's fall constitutes 'this' present moment in relation to an imagined end of all thought and all time for him – the conditional tense of 'by this had thought been past'. With the scene's impossible invitation to juxtapose 'this' present with one that Gloucester would not experience at all (a temporal 'view from nowhere'), the performance space of *King Lear* becomes polychronic, capable of holding together incompatible time schemes as they approach each other but never meet.[7]

In light of this counter-factual dimension of trust, we can revisit systems theorist Niklas Luhmann's contrast between face-to-face encounters and their more extended and abstract counterparts. Even in the face-to-face encounter of a trust fall, small temporal gaps can expand and contract with infinite variety. Time and space are discontinuous, both with respect to the asymmetries of 'faller' and 'catcher' and with respect to the phenomenology of trust itself. During the instantaneous act of rocking back off the heels, the two possible outcomes (caught/not-caught) are experienced almost simultaneously right up until the last moment. And trust must be extended over that seconds-long but still great and wide 'gap of time' in which the catcher's hands are not yet felt.[8]

As Lupton observes, these kinds of absences are constitutive of all systems of trust. This means that there is no such thing as what King Duncan calls 'absolute trust' (I, iv, 14), which 'belongs to an imagined idyll that denies the controlled absences out of which trust is built.'[9] Not coincidentally, this reference to 'absolute trust' occurs in the same speech where Duncan fails to imagine an 'art' to 'find the mind's construction in the face' (I, iv, 11–12). As a spatial surface, the face has a particular relationship with trust that is well documented in the play's many references to the face as untrustworthy. Macbeth complains before the banquet scene that he and Lady Macbeth must make their 'faces vizards to' their hearts, 'disguising what they are' (III, ii, 35–6). Duncan's infamous comments about the 'mind's construction in the face' thus suggest the homology between spatial and temporal gaps as they both relate to trust. To claim that the (sur)face has no relation to what lies underneath is just as 'absolute' as the assertion of a necessary relationship between the two things. In this light, as much as Macbeth is often imagined as a scheming counterpart to the naive Duncan, Macbeth's fatalistic 'trust' (IV, i, 137) in the witches' prophecies can be understood as closely related to Duncan's 'absolute trust' in the traitorous Thane of Cawdor. And these failures on the part of two successive kings are not simply character flaws but are instead central to Shakespeare's investigation of sovereignty and time in this tragedy: both Duncan's artlessness and Macbeth's fatalism serve as foils for the play's highly theatrical demonstration of the relational quality of trust, its dependence on the contingency of human action within complex intersecting scales of time and space.

My focus on trust is therefore designed to counter both a positivist approach to the face-to-face interactions of theatre as an epistemological or ethical ground and to resist the opposite extreme, which tends to associate trust primarily with the capacity to overcome material constraints or to transcend contingencies of appearance. From a historical perspective, an advantage of this focus on the term 'trust' (as opposed to its more modern religious descendant 'faith') is that it reveals an important point where theology and early modern theatre intersect.[10] The religious dimensions of trust that Hooker describes were not imagined as necessarily removed either from physical presence or from the temporal present.

In *Macbeth*, end times become entangled with theatrical timing in several scenes, perhaps most strikingly at the moment when the ghost of Banquo displaces Macbeth from his stool. But at first the horrid visions of the dead rising from their graves are confined to descriptions of offstage entities – the murder itself and then Duncan's dead body. When MacDuff enters to report the death of Duncan, he hails the assembled lords as the dead whom he calls upon to arise from their graves to witness the Last Judgement:

> Up, up, and see
> The great doom's image. Malcolm, Banquo,
> As from your graves rise up, and walk like sprites
> To countenance this horror.
> *Bell rings.*
>
> (II, iii, 70–3)

MacDuff calls on Malcolm and Banquo to awake, as if they were themselves the dead rising from their graves. Lady Macbeth then describes the bell as a 'hideous trumpet', further reinforcing the Judgement Day imagery that Macbeth had earlier introduced. Macbeth had feared that Duncan's virtues would 'plead like angels, trumpet-tongued against / The deep damnation of his taking off' (I, vii, 19–20). Both recall 1 Corinthians 15: 'In a flash, in the twinkling of an eye, at the last trumpet. For the trumpet will sound, the dead will be raised imperishable, and we will be changed.'[11] A variety of theologically oriented readings of this apocalyptic language have been proposed by Adrian Streete, Hannibal Hamlin and others.[12] But a focus on the face-to-face helps to demonstrate the curious relationship between apocalyptic time and theatrical timing in this play. Macbeth refuses to 'countenance this horror', as MacDuff calls upon everyone to do. As he comments earlier, 'I am afraid to think what I have done. / Look on't again I dare not' (II, ii, 48–9). But his refusal to face what he has done turns out to entail a particular relation to time as much as it does to space.

The two are closely connected. Taking the question of space first, let's return to Hooker's description of heaven as a face. Hooker points to the 'countenance of the heaven' and promises assurance to the man who trusts in God beyond even seemingly major physical events such as the shaking of the pillars of the earth, or acts that might appall the face of heaven. These kinds of cosmic surfaces first appear in *Macbeth* among the reports of unnatural events that follow Duncan's murder. The Old Man includes the 'darkness' that 'does the face of earth entomb' (II, iv, 9), and MacDuff similarly shifts the scale of Scotland's suffering when he urges Malcolm to take action in Act IV: 'each new morn / New widows howl, new orphans cry, new sorrows / Strike heaven on the face, that it resounds / As if it felt with Scotland' (IV, iii, 4–7). These types of vast spatial scales converge with large temporal ones when MacDuff asks his fellows to rise up, as if from their graves, to 'countenance' the present horror of Duncan's murder. He calls upon his listeners to experience the present by jumping forward into the life to come, when they will be 'spirits' stalking the earth. In Macduff's dense set of references, there is thus a suggestion of apocalypse now: perhaps the scales of time might be reconfigured such that a very different kind of face might become visible in the present moment. The language is again from Paul's first letter to the Corinthians: 'For now we see through a glass, darkly; but then face to face.'[13] As with a Google map that jumps in discontinuous leaps across scales of space, here it is live theatre that holds out the promise of moving across scales of time, affording its audiences very particular modes of trust that work at different temporal scales.

Macbeth reinforces this apocalyptic imagery of the play with his insistence on 'assurance' and 'safety', terms that pervaded theological controversies at this time over how the faithful might have present assurance of their long-term fate on judgement day. 'Safe' and 'Safely' are versions of *salvus* or salvation, and are used in the Geneva Bible in just this way to speak of the 'safety' of the Protestant saints.[14] This version of 'safety' is perhaps as far from human control as could be. As Herbert puts it in 'The Hold-fast', 'Ev'n to trust in him, was also his.' Herbert alludes to the last things of Revelation 2: 25: 'Hold fast till I come.' The wait is potentially a very long one, and even the trust that the faithful might feel is understood to be a function of divine grace. Yet Macbeth's use of the terms 'trust' and 'safe' is decidedly worldly, and the friction between the two sets of meanings plays out as a form of situational irony. The first main cluster of references to 'safety' occurs just as Macbeth makes another decree suggesting human control of time: 'Let every man be master of his time' (III, i, 42). As Banquo leaves to 'fill up the time' before supper (III, i, 25), Macbeth begins his musings on safety: 'To be thus is nothing / But to be safely thus. Our fears in Banquo / stick deep' (III, i, 48–50). The perversity of this notion of safety reaches its height when Macbeth asks the murderer whether he has succeeded in killing Banquo: 'But Banquo's safe?' (III, iv, 24), to which the murderer responds, 'Safe in a ditch he bides' (25). Of course, Banquo is not quite so safe as this natural death might suggest. In the banquet scene, the temporality of apocalyptic return offers a highly theatrical counterpoint to Macbeth's efforts to establish sovereign control of both temporal and political 'succession'.

William Junker has recently demonstrated Shakespeare's similar deployment of apocalyptic spectacle for political ends in *Antony and Cleopatra*. While Octavian Caesar uses repetition to secure an 'eternal present' of imperial triumph, the scene of Cleopatra's suicide upends Octavian's temporal powers with its instantiation of apocalyptic time.[15] Octavian's imperial attempts to control time closely resemble Macbeth's. The young Caesar seeks to 'possess' time (II, vii, 93) and to align his reign with an eternal triumph. He comments of Cleopatra that 'her life in Rome / Would be eternal in our triumph' (V, i, 65–6). Macbeth, similarly, tries to use his secular power to establish 'eternal' temporal conditions.[16] After the witches' show of kings threatens Macbeth's success, Macbeth seeks to control time by decree: he first threatens that an 'eternal curse' (IV, i, 103) will fall on the witches if they don't reveal the fate of Banquo's 'issue' (IV, i, 100), and he then demands that the 'pernicious hour' of this revelation will 'stand aye accursèd in the calendar' (IV, i, 131–2).[17] On Macbeth's command, the pernicious hour will be isolated and lifted out of time; it will stand always accursed, its self-consistency tied to the spatial logic of the calendar. This is of course a curse-day, not a holy-day, but it follows the same pattern of banking time, laying it up in a way that prevents future change and ensures the constancy of succession – what Junker calls an 'eternal present' of sovereignty.[18]

By contrast, *Macbeth* offers several scenes that resemble Cleopatra's anti-imperial theatre in their capacity to reveal the polychronic quality of history. Cleopatra's suicide denies Octavian his 'eternal triumph': it is the 'mortal stroke' by which she 'defeats' him (V, i, 64–5). And when she describes her suicide, she envisions the moment of her death as a return to another time and space, one that she shared with Antony in the past and may again share at some future time. Junker comments:

> Cleopatra's being 'again' for Cydnus is performed not as the static reduplication of her past so much as the repetition, or retrieval, of her past into a present that changes and is changed by it. It is precisely the confluence of these two times in Cleopatra's dramatic performance that generates the dilated 'Now' of her theater.

This theatrical 'now' can be understood both through Christian apocalyptic and Jewish messianic thinking, including Walter Benjamin's discussion of the 'now-time' or messianic time of the interim.[19] As I have begun to suggest, *Macbeth* stages a similar conflict between imperial control of time and its apocalyptic opening through figures such as Banquo and the show of eight kings. Having murdered Duncan in order to become king, Macbeth believes he must murder Banquo in order to be 'safely' king, or to make 'assurance double sure' (IV, i, 81). Macbeth also seems to want to pre-empt Banquo's return at any future time, no matter how distant. But the 'now' time of the play's performance seems to be a time when no ends – not even those of mortal life – are 'safe' in this sense. As Macbeth notes, it is a time when 'charnel houses and our graves must send / Those that we bury back' (III, iv, 69–70). In this way, the language of short-term safety and assurance that Macbeth uses to describe his vision of political success (and succession) ironically conflicts with the theological resonances of the word, which depend upon the very apocalyptic temporal framework that Macbeth resists so entirely. Macbeth's battle for what his queen refers to as 'solely sovereign sway and masterdom' is depicted as a battle to isolate segments of time, taking them both out of short-term chronological sequence and out of any longer temporal system, such as the 'promised end' in which Hooker and Herbert put their trust.

To turn to a well-known example, Macbeth initially introduces in the conditional tense the notion that the assassination might 'trammel up the consequence and catch / With his surcease, success' (I, vii, 3–4):

> That but this blow
> Might be the be-all and the end-all, here,
> But here, upon this bank and shoal of time,
> We'd jump the life to come.
>
> (I, vii, 4–7)

The image of the net or trammel begins the spatialisation of time such that it might be possessed, bound up, the be-all and the end-all 'here, / But here.' The word 'here', as opposed to 'now', suggests how Macbeth's substantivisation of time becomes part of a bid to create an eternal present of sovereignty.[20] In this passage we can see not only the spatialisation of a long stretch of 'consequence' as something that could be made present, fished out of a river and safely landed on a 'bank and shoal of time'. We also see the grammatical conversion of temporal verbs into nouns: 'with his surcease, success'. The use of 'surcease' as a noun was relatively new (dating from 1590) when the play was first performed. This conversion of 'surcease' from a verb of endings to a noun, an end, offers an atemporal and agentless version of Duncan's death. Macbeth's act of murder becomes 'his surcease'. The same is true for 'success', used in this passage as a noun to mean 'succession', or that which follows the 'surcease'. Here 'success' also suggests the meaning of a concrete thing – any 'issue' from an action, good or bad. 'Surcease' and 'success' mirror each other in chiastic form that stands outside of any temporal succession, pulled from the flow of time and isolated on its bank. In other words, we could hear in the double meaning of 'success' the way in which Macbeth tries to turn the substantivised noun against its temporal origins, isolating his sovereign 'success' as the be-all and end-all of temporal succession itself. The future is possessed by the instant.[21]

It is worth noting that earlier uses of the word 'success' support this reading, establishing the noun as closely related to personal possession of and control over complex temporal events. 'Success' first appears in relation to Macbeth's military victories and the verbal reports that the King has received. Here success belongs to Macbeth, as Ross describes it: 'The King hath happily received, Macbeth / The news of thy success' (I, iii, 84–5). This digested form of success also appears in the letter that Lady Macbeth reads aloud. She learns that the witches met Macbeth in the 'day of success' (I, v, 1). Yet the play's references to 'success' begin almost immediately to move away from this sense of fullness. The temporality of 'success' takes on the uncertainty of a promise when Macbeth begins to doubt the 'supernatural soliciting' that has given him 'earnest of success' (I, iii, 128). Here the relationship of temporal succession to trust is especially clear: 'success' no longer belongs to Macbeth as a closed past action but exists in a temporal sequence that is beyond his control.[22] The phrase 'earnest of success' is especially suggestive, since the word 'earnest' again turns an act of trust into an object that has been given to Macbeth rather than an action or a relation. This sense of 'earnest of' as money paid 'for the purpose of securing a bargain or contract' (*OED*) is one that Shakespeare also uses to humorous effect in *Much Ado*, when Beatrice satirises the idea of a marriage contract: she will take 'sixpence in earnest of the bearherd, and lead his apes into hell' (II, i, 29–30).

As *Macbeth* proceeds, theatrical events turn these closed and object-like versions of 'success' inside-out, opening out into poly-chronic spectacles such as the appearance of Banquo's ghost. As a bookend for Macbeth's earlier conditional wish that his blow against Duncan might be the be-all and end-all, consider Macbeth's reaction to the witches' final show of eight kings in Act IV. When the line first appears, Macbeth complains, 'What, will the line stretch out to th' crack of doom?' (IV, i, 115). And when the witches dis-appear, he laments his trust in them: 'Infected be the air whereon they ride, / And damned all those that trust them!' (IV, i, 136–7). In this moment of disappointment, Macbeth regrets his trust in the witches and seems to recognise the error of taking their prophecies as present security. Yet he counters this visual demonstration of his powerlessness over temporal and political succession with continu-ing attempts to 'trammel up the consequence' – to contain future events within the present prophecies. Hearing the prophecy of the third apparition, Macbeth comments:

> Rebellious dead, rise never till the wood
> Of Birnam rise, and our high-placed Macbeth
> Shall live the lease of nature, pay his breath
> To time and mortal custom.
>
> (IV, i, 95–8)

That is to say, 'Rebellious dead, *never rise.*' According to Macbeth, the oscillations of apocalyptic time should stop here, but here, and remain enclosed in the safety of Dunsinane castle. The political dimensions of the scene are also important: these are the 'rebellious' dead because they threaten Macbeth's sovereign control of time; he displaces God in this apocalypse as he imagines putting down the rebellion of the dead rising against him. A similar moment occurs just after he promises to 'make assurance double sure / and take a bond of fate' (IV, i, 81–2). He speaks to the absent Duncan in the form of a divine commandment cast into the future: 'Thou shalt not live' (IV, i, 82).

Macbeth's aspirations to political sovereignty thus mimic divine sovereignty in ways that implicitly undercut his project. When what he refers to as the 'imperial theme' (I, iii, 125) begins to swell, Macbeth imagines that his act of killing Duncan might be the 'be-all and the end-all' (I, vii, 5). He then suggests that the act itself will occupy no temporal duration: 'I go, and it is done' (II, i, 62). His language resonates with perverse echoes of Creation and Judgement, juxtaposing the actions of a human subject, caught in the web of time, with the God-like capacity to mark the beginning or the end of time itself.[23] The language of sovereignty appears again and again in the play in relation to this kind of imagined temporal collapse, as in Lady Macbeth's preternatural sense that she can feel now 'The future in the instant' (I, v, 54). She tellingly uses the possessive 'our' and the language of sovereignty to describe temporal succession when she tells her husband to leave the night's great business to her: 'Which shall to all our days and nights to come / Give solely sovereign sway and masterdom' (I, v, 65–6). Her language turns the temporal succession of the future into object-like 'days and nights', and figuratively grants the agency of 'sovereign sway' to these days and nights. Macbeth echoes these links between sovereignty and time at several points, addressing Time itself in the moments leading up to his murder of Macduff's family:

> Time, thou anticipat'st my dread exploits.
> . . .
> From this moment
> The very firstlings of my heart shall be
> The firstlings of my hand; and even now,
> To crown my thoughts with acts, be it thought and done.
>
> (IV, i, 143–8)

Macbeth's effort to do away with temporality as a condition for his human actions again sounds the imperial theme: like Lady Macbeth's 'sovereign sway' for the days and nights to come, Macbeth's 'even now' wraps the future deed into the present thought and depicts their co-presence as a 'crowning' of these thoughts. Certainly, 'crown' in this sense means 'add the finishing touch' (*OED* v. 9), but it does so with the suggestion that thoughts from now on will exert a kind of sovereign control over acts: 'Be it thought and done.'[24]

By contrast with Macbeth's imperial bids to contain and command time, several apocalyptic spectacles use the complex 'now' time of theatrical performance to break it back open. The witches' final show is an example of the very kind of revelation that he had feared. The 'horrible sight' (IV, i, 120) brings him face-to-face not only with countenances of the future but also those of the past. Fore-most among these horrors is the smile of Banquo himself (IV, i, 121) as he rises from the dead and demands that Macbeth countenance him as Macbeth had not been able to do with Duncan. Even the political lineage is imagined in terms of facial characteristics: the 'gold-bound brow[s]' (IV, i, 112) of Banquo's line metonymically restore 'succession' to time. Yet this is not the simple time of chrono-logical progress or even securely royal succession. If the line merely led to James and ended there, that would be one thing, but the line that the theatre audience observes threatens to stretch to the crack of doom through the device of the mirror, which makes the show neither securely past nor merely prophetic. It is instead disorienting with respect to historical chronology: when exactly is the 'here' of this theatrical time? Temporal markers cannot be securely fixed, and the faces of these kings gain the capacity to reorient time and space for those who face them.

Perhaps the best example of the play's experiments with tim-ing trust is the apocalyptic physical comedy of the empty stool in the banquet scene. When Macbeth's stool is figuratively pulled out from under him by Banquo, the timing of this face-to-face theatrical encounter seems to coincide with the time of apocalyptic encounter – the 'then face to face' that Macbeth has been avoiding all along. After the ghost enters and sits in Macbeth's place, Lennox invites Macbeth to sit, drawing audience attention to the stool and to the actor playing the ghost. Macbeth does not sit down but instead speaks in the conditional tense about Banquo's presence: 'Here had we now our country's honour roofed / Were the graced person of our Banquo present' (III, iv, 39–40). Within the stage history in which an actor plays the ghost, Macbeth's conditional invocation plays against the visceral shock of the bloodied actor who moves across the stage and occupies Macbeth's seat. Macbeth only begins to notice what is happening when Ross invites him to grace the table with his royal company. Macbeth replies: 'The table's full' (III, iv, 45). Only when Lennox points to the place reserved for Macbeth does Macbeth finally see the ghost and respond to it: 'Which of you have done this?' (47). He then turns to Banquo's ghost, 'Thou canst not say I did it. Never shake / Thy gory locks at me' (49). Lady Macbeth takes him aside and reminds him, 'You look but on a stool' (66).

There is of course a long stage history here and much variation, but I want to make the fairly simple point that the stool on which the ghost does or does not sit becomes the site for a complex theat-rical constellation: contrasting systems of trust and their divergent

modes of timing converge on this stage property. Macbeth understands the banquet from the perspective of personal systems of face-
to-face trust: although he laments to Lady Macbeth the fact that they
need to make their faces 'vizards to' their hearts (III, ii, 36), he plans
to undermine this system from within, not fundamentally questioning the system of table fellowship or its founding on human face-to-
face interactions. All Macbeth sees is a common table that is full, all
stools equal. He does not expect his conditionally present Banquo to
move from grave to table.

My point is not only that table fellowship enacts systems of personal trust that are imagined to anchor larger political and religious
formations such as the Lord's Supper or the King's band of brothers.
This scene introduces at the same time and in the same space a very
different and anti-positivist system of trust: when it is occupied by
Banquo's ghost, the joint stool now affords an eschatological frame
that plays against Macbeth's continuing attempts to seal off time, to
contain Banquo and Duncan in their graves, and to avoid facing his
own acts of murder. Macbeth's appeal to a positivist system appears
here to be comically improbable: in the interim between the appearances of the ghost, Macbeth turns to historical precedent to establish
a time that should be free from the walking dead – a time when murder was common:

> The time has been,
> That when the brains were out the man would die,
> And there an end; but now they rise again
> With twenty mortal murders on their crowns,
> And push us from our stools.
>
> (III, iv, 76–80)

The 'now' time of this performance is no longer the 'olden time'
when the man 'would die / and there an end' (otherwise known as
'the good old days'). This is the time when the dead rise again, and
'push us from our stools'. In a version of the slapstick physical comedy of the chair pulled out or a game of musical chairs where timing
is everything, here the King is pushed out of his place at the communal table by a theatrical ghost who is ex-temporal.

While *Macbeth*'s approach to royal succession is often taken as
an implicit endorsement of the Augustan pretensions of King James,
who traced his bloodline to the figure of Banquo, the play's introduction of non-human temporal scales and disorienting polychronic
spectacles instead underlines the limited scope of all temporal power.

No man is 'master of his time'.[25] Perhaps more importantly, the scalar technics of live theatre here tend to explode the pretensions of temporal rulers to 'eternal' forms of sovereignty. A contemporary production that translates this politics of scale into a modern idiom is Rupert Goold's 2010 TV film, adapted for the BBC from his 2007 stage production. One of the film's dominant images is of the face of Macbeth (played by Patrick Stewart), blown up to Herculean proportions and displayed as a red Soviet-style banner. The banner features Macbeth's face in a three-quarter profile view, with a moustache and soldier's collar tab with rank insignia in the Stalinist style. But despite its distinctively modern political references, the banner's particular approach to spatial and temporal scale brilliantly captures the politics of temporal 'succession' in *Macbeth*. Much like the 'news' of Macbeth's 'success' that makes its way to Duncan in the opening act (I, iii, 85), the image of Stewart captures a moment of military success and transports it beyond historical time. In this sense, modern autocratic images such as Stalinist ones parallel Macbeth's approach to temporal order when he attempts to 'trammel up the consequence, and catch / with his surcease, success' (I, vii, 3–4) and then to eliminate Banquo's line of 'succession' to the throne. Both the modern autocrat and the early modern absolutist isolate a particular historical moment of 'success', rendering it object-like and attempting to establish it as a repeating event, forever 'in the calendar' (IV, i, 132).

In terms of spatial scale, the image is similarly non-human. Both its size and its visual replicability help to generate a type of eternal present of political power – power that cannot be addressed or 'countenanced' at the human scale. The impossibility of face-to-face trust in Goold's rendering of the banquet scene thus resonates with the politics of 'absolute trust' discussed at the opening of this essay: there is no relationship between the face printed on the surface of the banner and the temporal actions of the ruler himself. The colossal heroic image can never be forced to countenance any of the political horrors that might be carried out under its aegis. Goold's banquet scene is so chilling partly because it translates the scalar technics of the face from Shakespeare's anti-imperial apocalyptic theatre into a secular register. Just as Patrick Stewart's Macbeth finishes his lines about the dead who 'push us from our stools', the giant banner briefly appears behind him. It is now blurred and fragmentary, with only the lower half of the face visible within the frame. By showing how the momentary fears of the changeable man dislocate the heroic constancy of the banner, the shot underscores the impossibility of Macbeth's static conception of his 'success'. As with the delicate timing of Macbeth's displacement from his stool in theatrical performances, here the contingencies of camera movement help to demonstrate the relational quality of trust.

Yet in this film, Macbeth's death and Malcolm's political succession do not finally deliver on their promise of a new regime in which the ruler might face either his people or any kind of larger-scale reckoning. Goold makes this point by fixing the camera on Macbeth's still and disembodied face just as Malcolm refers to his own installation as King. After the assembled company all-hails him, Malcolm pointedly turns his back to the upturned faces of these 'thanes and kinsmen' (V, vii, 92). Holding Macbeth's severed head in his hands, Malcolm delivers the play's final lines as he backs down the dingy hallway through the ranks of his men. Despite his promise to counter Macbeth's reign of 'tyranny' (97), Malcolm's failure to address his men face-to-face signals a continuation of Macbeth's many efforts to avoid facing those he has harmed. Even more tellingly, as Malcolm delivers his final invitation to all to see him 'crowned at Scone' (105), he turns the severed head around and holds it aloft so that the film audience can finally see it. In Goold's brilliant rendering of this modern imperial triumph, the camera centres in on Macbeth's bloody face and holds it in the viewer's gaze for several seconds. But the eyes are shut, and all promise of a face-to-face reckoning is foreclosed.

Notes

1. Julia Lupton, 'Trust in Theater', p. 156.
2. See Julia Lupton, 'Climates of Trust in *Macbeth*'. All citations of Shakespeare come from *The New Oxford Shakespeare: Modern Critical Edition*, ed. Gary Taylor et al.
3. See Richard Hooker, 'A learned and comfortable sermon on the certainty and perpetuity of faith in the elect', p. 471. Thanks to Kim Hedlin for pointing me to this sermon.
4. On messianic time in Shakespeare, see Ken Jackson, '"Grace to boot": St. Paul, Messianic Time, and Shakespeare's *The Winter's Tale*'.
5. 1 Corinthians 13: 12, in the English of the King James Bible.
6. See Lupton's discussion of 'Blind Man's Bluff at Dover Cliff', in 'Trust in Theater', pp. 164–71.
7. In this sense, the theatrical laboratory of trust could be aligned with seventeenth-century experimental science. As Joanna Picciotto has pointed out, the paradisal 'view from nowhere' could be achieved

through collective efforts. See Picciotto, *Labors of Innocence in Early Modern England*, p. 559.

8. See *Winter's Tale*, V, iii, 185 and *Antony and Cleopatra*, I, v, 5. The great or wide 'gap of time' can be discontinuous with the temporality of the performance on either side of the scale: for Cleopatra, the seconds spent apart from Antony feel far longer than they do for those around her, while the 'gap of time' spanned in *The Winter's Tale* is far longer than the theatre audience has experienced.
9. Lupton, 'Trust in Theater', p. 5.
10. See Lupton on the more secular, modern direction of 'trust' as opposed to 'faith': Trust in Theater', p. 156.
11. 1 Corinthians 15: 52, in the English of the King James Bible.
12. See Adrian Streete, 'What bloody man is that?': Questioning Biblical Typology in *Macbeth*'; and Hannibal Hamlin, *The Bible in Shakespeare*.
13. 1 Corinthians 13: 12, in the English of the King James Bible.
14. On this point and for all references to the bible, see *The Geneva Bible: A Facsimile of the 1560 Edition*.
15. Junker, 'The Image of Both Theaters: Empire and Revelation in Shakespeare's *Antony and Cleopatra*'.
16. See Bryan Lowrance, '"Modern Ecstasy": *Macbeth* and the Meaning of the Political'.
17. This is reminiscent of Elizabeth's secular appropriation of holy days. See Shapiro, 'Is this a Holiday.'
18. Junker, 'Image of Both Theaters', p. 177.
19. Junker, 'Image of Both Theaters', p. 181.
20. See William Junker, 'Tomorrows at the End of Time: Eschatology, Sovereignty, and *Macbeth*'.
21. On Macbeth's 'unnatural relations to time', see David Norbrook, '*Macbeth* and the Politics of Historiography', p. 101.
22. On *Macbeth* as governed by a complex Calvinist conception of Providence, see Kristen Poole, *Supernatural Environments in Shakespeare's England*.
23. On James, the gunpowder plot and temporal claims to absolute power, see Junker, 'Tomorrows at the End of Time: Eschatology, Sovereignty, and *Macbeth*'.
24. This is what Cavell calls 'a wish for there to be no human action'. See Cavell, 'Macbeth Appalled', p. 233.
25. On explosive time in *Macbeth*, see Jonathan Gil Harris, *Untimely Matter in the Time of Shakespeare*.

Part IV

Moving Pictures

Chapter 8

The Man of Sorrows: Edgar's Disguise and Dürer's Self-portraits

Hanna Scolnicov

In the sub-plot of *King Lear*, the fugitive Edgar decides to disguise himself as a poor beggar escaped from the Bedlam mental asylum. Transforming himself into the folkloric figure of Poor Tom, Edgar strips off his fine clothes, remaining naked but for a 'blanket'. With his distinctive facial features grimed over with filth, Edgar turns into Poor Tom, a representative of suffering humanity. From a young nobleman, he turns into an unaccommodated man (III, iv, 84), a figure of 'houseless poverty' (III, iv, 26). From Gloucester's legitimate son, he turns into a nameless, faceless beggar, a generic Poor Tom. The whole play turns around the idea of the mutability of the individual under changed social circumstances,[1] or as Lear himself puts it: 'change places and handy-dandy, which is the justice, which is the thief?' (IV, vi, 148–50).[2]

The beggar's outfit will be shown to characterise Edgar as a Christ figure, naked except for the loincloth wrapped around his private parts, a figure practising the Imitation of Christ. The radical shift from young aristocrat, the son of the Earl of Gloucester, to the poor, crazed beggar taking on Christ's suffering will be elucidated through a comparison with the self-portraits of Albrecht Dürer (1471–1528), in which the artist moves from portraying himself as a flamboyant young aristocrat to shaping himself as the Man of Sorrows. The force and function of these different images will be traced back to the Renaissance ideas of Christian humanism that underlie both these representations of the self in the guise of the suffering Christ.

Elsewhere, I have expanded on the verbal pointers to Edgar's appearance as the Cynic philosopher Diogenes, the philosopher with whom Lear would like to converse in the storm.[3] But I also indicated the intersection of that theme with the equally important *imitatio Christi* motif inherent in the figure of the suffering, naked man, wearing the loincloth, and in Lear's gesture of imitating him, in his own turn. In the present essay I would like to develop further the strangely overlooked image of the Man of Sorrows that imposes itself on the figure of Edgar as Poor Tom, replacing both the person and the disguise with a religious and humanist visual icon of suffering humanity.

Shakespeare often uses disguises in his plays for dramatic effect. Face-to-face meetings gain an edge when, despite the clearly evident intimate acquaintance between the characters, one of them is disguised and becomes unrecognisable to the other. The disguised character clearly recognises the other, but there is no reciprocity in the relationship. Edgar and Kent, the two disguised characters in *King Lear*, generate a host of powerful scenes that depend on their being unrecognised by the characters who face them.

Exemplary in this respect is the encounter between Lear and the disguised Kent in Act I, scene iv. The scene opens with a short soliloquy, in which Kent informs the audience that 'I razed my likeness' (I, iv, 4). In what amounts to a job interview, Lear questions his familiar, Kent:

> What art thou? . . . What dost thou profess? . . . [and again] What art thou? . . . What wouldst thou? . . . Who wouldst thou serve? . . . Dost thou know me, fellow? . . . What services canst thou do? . . . How old art thou? . . . (I, iv, 9–36)

All these are interrogations that try to discover the identity of the interlocutor. The most direct of these questions is 'Dost thou know me', which refers back to the interrogator, the 'me', and probes the reciprocal relationship between the self and the person facing him. Observing the interchange from the sidelines, the spectator is allowed to appreciate the unequal meeting, in which Lear does not recognise Kent. However, the spectator must accept that, within the world of the play, Kent is no longer recognisable. Even if it contradicts his own experience, the spectator must submit to this anomalous state of affairs, because this is the given dramatic situation, upon the acceptance of which his aesthetic enjoyment depends.

The strong effect of such an encounter is dependent on the audience being aware simultaneously of both the true identity of the disguised character and his deceptive appearance to his interlocutor. Our superior knowledge as audience must be assured through verbal references as well as visual clues. The risk of disclosure creates dramatic tension and makes us follow closely every word and every move.

The most extreme instance of lack of recognition in *King Lear*, and one that stretches our willing suspension of disbelief, is Gloucester's failure to recognise his own son Edgar, disguised as Tom o'Bedlam, when facing him. Attuned as we are today to the nuances of realism, we may feel uneasy with the artificiality of this dramatic scene. But the heightened theatricality of this face-to-face scene has so powerful an expressive force that it can perhaps best be seen as an early form of Expressionist art.

Both Edgar and Kent announce in soliloquies the alteration of their identity, thus alerting the audience to their changed appearance. The lack of recognition by those who meet with them face-to-face creates dramatic irony: the spectator experiences, together with the disguised character, the full significance of the meeting, while the other character is unaware of his interlocutor's true identity. One of the functions of this dramatic irony is to ensure the continuity, cohesion or unity of the character, despite his changed appearance. The unity of character, not one of the traditional 'dramatic unities', but taken for granted in almost all traditional forms of drama, is at stake, on the brink. But it is protected by the spectator's awareness that the character is merely playing a role. Revealing his identity within the dramatic world will endanger him, but it is imperative that the spectator recognise the character throughout, despite his disguise.

Disguise is a basic feature of theatre, where the actor assumes a character, so that the act of disguising within the compass of the play is a highly theatrical gesture, a double-tiered disguise. Shakespeare manipulated such scenes effectively in his comedies, especially in cross-gender disguises, but their use in tragedy is more restricted.[4] The layered acting of the disguised character, especially the facial expression demanded of the actor, should convey to the audience the character's duplicity, while his changed clothing and overall appearance prevents his dramatic antagonist from recognising him. The multi-layered personification blocks the ability of the dramatic interlocutor to decipher the face.

In a virtuoso scene, in a soliloquy of only twenty-one verse lines (II, iii),[5] Edgar transforms himself on the stage, in front of our eyes, into the mad beggar, Tom o'Bedlam.[6] He has become a threatened fugitive – 'no port is free, no place that . . . does not attend my taking.' In order to 'preserve' himself, he takes on 'the basest and most poorest shape that ever penury in contempt of man / Brought near to beast'. He grimes his face with filth and blankets his loins and 'outface[s]' the elements 'with presented nakedness'. Edgar ends his soliloquy of transformation with the striking declaration that he has now annihilated his former self: 'Edgar I nothing am' (II, iii, 21). The nobly born Edgar has altered himself from a young aristocrat, the son of the Earl of Gloucester, into a Bedlam beggar, both mad and poor. Shedding his fine clothes, his changed appearance expresses a total, inner transformation.

In addition to this declaratory soliloquy, Edgar also uses a number of asides to remind the audience of who he is. These also serve to reveal his inner thoughts and feelings, so that we don't judge his behaviour towards his blinded father as callous. While the spectator sees Poor Tom, he is also made aware of Edgar's 'real' face and 'real' feelings, thus enjoying a double view of the character. This double take is typical of the whole play, beginning with the scene of the division of the kingdom, where we are able to see through the flattery and hypocrisy of Lear's evil daughters and to discern Cordelia's true nature through her asides.

By smearing his face with dirt, Edgar becomes faceless, both literally and metaphorically. He strips himself of his customary apparel, and changes his familiar behaviour, shedding his previous identity, as though this were, together with his actual clothing, merely an assumed garment to be worn or discarded at will. The unity of his character, an unacknowledged, but taken for granted, dramatic unity, is assured not only by the continuing identity of the actor performing his different disguises, but even more so through the enduring unity of 'Edgar's' selfhood, so presenting a real challenge for the actor performing the steadfast sameness, as well as the change and difference.

Our appreciation of the performance of the play is dependent on our ability as audience to perceive the persistent, underlying sameness, as well as the superimposed changes or variations. Unlike us, Gloucester cannot discern the common denominator between the different appearances of Edgar. The pathos of Gloucester's inability to recognise his disguised son is stressed even further after he loses his eyesight, when he acknowledges, 'I stumbled when I saw' (IV, i, 21). He now regrets his mistreatment of Edgar, declaring:

> Might I but live to see thee in my touch,
> I'd say I had eyes again.
>
> (IV, i, 25–6)

The realisation of his grave mistake and his ensuing regret are stretched to the limit by the dramatic setting, as they are voiced in the presence of Poor Tom, both subject and victim of Gloucester's misjudgement, but also his loving and sensitive son. The encounter between the unrecognisable son and the unrecognising father is stretched to the limit with the blinded father physically unable to recognise Edgar. Gloucester recalls 'the naked fellow' he saw in last night's storm, who made his son come into his mind (IV, i, 34–6). One of the insights he reaches in his blindness is that ''Tis the time's plague when madmen lead the blind' (IV, i, 49).

The theme of the madman leading the blind is developed in a series of variations, with Edgar assuming more disguises, now, due to his father's loss of sight, based on a change of voice and manner rather than clothing. The variations become increasingly fantastic, as Poor Tom undertakes to lead Gloucester to the brink of the overhanging cliffs of Dover. The spectator and reader too are led to the dizzying heights of this bravura scene, in which a magnificent and deceptive landscape is conjured up in a poetic passage – only to be annulled by the dramatic action, as Gloucester falls flat on the stage boards. Anything is possible in this improbable scene, when the 'naked soul' (IV, i, 46) leads the man who has no eyes (IV, vi, 60). Tom's earlier mad incantations to the devils prove to be the means by which we have been ushered into this world of fantasy, where there is a fiend with a thousand noses and two full moons as eyes (IV, vi, 69–70), a world in which Gloucester can be led to believe he is climbing a steep hill and throwing himself into the abyss.

According to Aristotle, in the *Poetics*, recognition (*anagnorisis*) is of crucial importance to the plot of tragedy, leading to reversal (*peripeteia*). Whether understood as recognition of the other, or the self, or both, this is a key term in his conception of the structure of tragedy as a whole and in the intimate correspondence of character and plot. Edgar's deliberate change of face, signalling a change of persona, delays such recognition and underlines the importance of the characters' ability to recognise each other. By preventing his recognition, Edgar's disguise postpones the reversal of the plot-line. This retardation creates a counter-movement in the sub-plot of the play. Instead of the action moving forward towards its resolution, it seems to take the opposite direction, getting more and more entangled.

There is no mutuality or symmetry in the relations between the disguised Edgar, who recognises his father, and Gloucester, who cannot recognise his disguised son. The effect of this asymmetry is dependent on the audience's recognition of the disguised character, on their superior knowledge and understanding of the situation. One can discern here another, theatrical convention, a visual one that is derived from the oral conventions of the aside and the soliloquy. As in these more familiar Elizabethan conventions, the characters on stage remain unaware of what the spectators, who are further removed, can see happening. The disguise functions as a theatrical trick, a theatrical convention that serves to complicate the development of the plot. Having been previously informed through the characters' soliloquies of their disguises, the audience recognise the disguised character and are aware of the lack of recognition by his interlocutor, so achieve a wider perspective than the characters involved. Though unrealistic, these sophisticated dramatic and theatrical conventions are highly expressive and effective.

Edgar assumes in the play multiple identities. He is not only himself as well as Mad Tom, but also the different faceless characters he pretends to be when leading his blinded father. Gloucester's blindness permits the pretence of further characters, depending on Edgar's changed voice, accent and speech – although Gloucester is not totally fooled, saying later that there was something in the poor beggar that reminded him of his son (IV, i, 34–7). Lastly, Edgar's face is completely hidden by the visor he puts on for the final heraldic duel with his brother, the usurping Edmund. The visor serves him as a mask. Only when he finally puts his visor up is Edgar's 'true' face restored, and he celebrates this by announcing: 'My name is Edgar', i.e. he regains his name and, with it, his true identity and title (V, iii, 170).

Paradoxically, it is in his nakedness that Edgar becomes completely unrecognisable.[7] His disguise consists of taking off his clothes rather than putting on new garments. But he is not totally naked. As he has announced in his disguising soliloquy, he 'blanket[s] his loins' (II, ii, 181). The blanket, the cloth around his loins, is referred to again by the Fool, who insists that 'he reserved a blanket, else we had been all shamed' (III, iv, 61). In other words, this blanket hides his private parts.[8]

Strikingly, on top of his self-declared transformation into the Bedlam beggar, the figure Edgar assumes also contains the image of the crucified Christ, the Man of Sorrows, despised and rejected by society, naked except for the traditional loincloth. The image of the Man of Sorrows is based on the Christian reading of Isaiah 53: 3 as referring to the coming of Christ:

> He is despised and rejected of men; a man of sorrows, and acquainted with grief: and we hid as it were *our* faces from him; he was despised, and we esteemed him not. (King James Bible, Isaiah 53: 3)[9]

This icon of the Man of Sorrows is familiar from countless medieval and renaissance paintings, and I am suggesting that Shakespeare uses this traditional visual image, lifting it from its strictly religious context and giving it a humanist significance.

Many Christian overtones can be heard in the play and have been discussed over the years by various critics, notably by Roy Battenhouse.[10] More recently, Edgar's Christian aura has been pointed out by Simon Palfrey in his book dedicated to *Poor Tom*. Palfrey sees Poor Tom as some kind of 'a Christ allegory', noticing that 'an aureole of Christian historicity clearly hedges the Edgar-part's experience' He thinks that Edgar's 'fury and vexation in the hovel might suggest the harrowing of hell, when Christ descended to the prison of condemned souls and released them from limbo.' But, to my mind, the harrowing of hell suggestion has nothing to support it in the text. Perhaps this claim represents a groping for textual evidence that will support the justified general feeling of the author that 'Tom adumbrates Christ . . . a look alike that is not alike.'[11] I believe that it is rather Edgar's striking appearance on stage, naked but for his loin-cloth, that is iconic, pointing to the long tradition of Christological representations, and that he assumes the practice of the imitation of Christ.

'Sorrows' is the revealing word used by Edgar to describe himself, in response to his blinded father's inquiry: 'Now, good sir, what are you?' (IV, v, 211). He answers in an evasive manner:

> A most poor man made tame to fortune's blows,
> Who by the art of known and feeling sorrows
> Am pregnant to good pity.
>
> (IV, v, 212–14)

The mere evocation of 'Fortune's blows' transposes the 'sorrows' into the humanist context, welding the iconography of Fortuna, derived from the Roman conceptual goddess, with Renaissance Christology, in which Jesus' humanity, rather than his divinity, is stressed through his bodily suffering, through his Passion. The harrowing of hell is out of place in the humanist Christianity expressed in this play, in which neither crucifixion nor resurrection are mentioned.

Edgar's appearance in the figure of the Man of Sorrows is crucial to his encounter with Lear in the storm, where Lear recognises 'the uncovered body' of Poor Tom as 'the thing itself', and attempts to emulate this 'unaccommodated man' by ripping off his own 'lendings' (III, iv, 91–6). Thus the question of what the disguised Edgar looks like is of overwhelming importance to the way the play is produced and understood.

Lear questions Poor Tom about his past: 'What hast thou been?' (III, iv, 76). In his former life, he tells Lear, he has been 'a servingman, proud in heart and mind, that curled his hair, wore gloves in [his] cap', and so on (III, iv, 77–86). Clearly, this is not an actual confession of his own past misconducts, but a homiletic picture of himself as a typical courtier, guilty of the deadly sin of vanity. In the words of the German preacher Thomas à Kempis (1379–1471), in his *Imitation of Christ*, 'It is vanity to seek after, and to trust in, the riches that shall perish . . . It is vanity to follow the desires of the flesh and be led by them.'[12] Poor Tom is now differentiated from his former self as Edgar, the young nobleman who was a dandy dedicated to cultivating his own looks, spending his time in illicit and multiple sexual relations, in drink and dicing, lascivious and prodigal, and a breaker of oaths (III, iv, 77–83). In his own words, by living in court, he has been guilty of all these vices and more.

But if this is what Edgar has been, what is he now? The answer to this aspect of his persona is provided by Lear. Observing him face-to-face, Lear comments on what he sees, on the 'un-covered body' exposed to the 'extremity of the skies' (III, iv, 92). Lear ponders the naked body of Edgar and reflects on its general philosophical meaning, asking the ultimate humanist question: 'Is man no more than this?' (III, iv, 92). The individual dramatic character of Edgar is thus abstracted into a general symbol of mankind.[13]

Having left behind his courtly attributes, the beggar facing Lear is no longer protected from the world by borrowings from the animal world, borrowings that emphasise the vulnerability of man as compared with the beasts. In Lear's eyes, Edgar is now 'a poor, bare, forked animal', so 'the thing itself' (III, iv, 95). Edgar's double figure as both a young nobleman and mad beggar loses its individualising traits and personal history and turns into a generalised representation of suffering humanity.[14]

Gaining this new insight of the human condition, Lear tears off his own clothing, his own lendings from the animal world, in what is, to this day, the most powerful of theatrical gestures, the gesture of undressing, the gesture of stripping.[15] At this point, the King's small company is joined by Gloucester, who not only fails to recognise his naked son, but also, ironically, reprimands the King gently: 'What, hath your grace no better company?' (III, iv, 126).

Representing Edgar as becoming unrecognisable even to his father doesn't work on a realistic level, but it should be understood on the symbolic level, removing him from his immediate circumstances and identifying him with the wider context of human misery. This movement from the particular to the general and representative, which endows the dramatic character with a depth that his individual persona cannot have, is a familiar Shakespearian strategy. A whole cultural tradition thus enriches the particular dramatic situation and the individual dramatic character.

The realisation that wearing a blanket around his private parts makes Edgar assume the appearance of the Man of Sorrows suggests what he may have looked like on the Elizabethan stage, and also the pathos and significance conveyed by his figure. There are plenty of Renaissance visual representations of Christ as the Man of Sorrows that can be related to Edgar's person, but perhaps the most pertinent are those striking images in which Albrecht Dürer (1471–1528) depicted himself as the Man of Sorrows. In his *Self-Portrait as The Man of Sorrows* (1522) (see Figure 8.1),[16] he drew himself in a highly naturalistic and easily recognisable manner, but also as naked except for the cloth wrapped around his loins, adding the instruments of the Passion, such as the scourge and fasces, so as to leave no doubt about his self-identification with Christ.

Figure 8.1 Dürer: Self-portrait as the Man of Sorrows (1522), drawing with lead pencil on blue-green primed paper, 408 × 290 mm (Kunsthalle, Bremen).

Figure 8.2 Dürer: Self-portrait as Christ (1521), coloured pen drawing, 127 × 117 mm (Kunsthalle, Bremen).

Dürer's own, physical suffering is indicated in another drawing, his *Self-portrait as Christ* (1521), in which he is recognisably both himself and Christ at one and the same time (see Figure 8.2).[17] In this small picture, he is pointing at his ailing body, to the painful area in his side. As art historian Joseph Leo Koerner reads the picture, this is both a realistic pointer to the spleen as the locus of his own physical pain, and to the spleen as the source of melancholy, that is his psychological state of mental suffering. But, furthermore:

> There is another aspect of the Bremen self-portrait that could not have been overlooked by a contemporary viewer of the sketch. Pointing to his side and gazing out of the picture, Dürer assumes the traditional pose of Christ as Man of Sorrows . . . Christ's sidewound was an object of special devotion in the Middle Ages.[18]

In the present comparative study of Shakespeare's characterisation of Edgar and Dürer's self-depiction as Christ, it is perhaps not irrelevant to remember that Edgar comments on the appearance of Lear who has gone out of his mind and is crowned with a wreath of flowers as a 'side-piercing sight' (IV, vi, 85), referring in this terse expression to Christ's agony on the cross, when one of the Roman soldiers pierced his side with a spear (John 19: 34).[19] This concise phrase alerts us to the physical aspects of both the viewer and the viewed victim, transferring the side-piercing from the victim to the viewer's sight, referring to the effect on the onlooker of viewing the victim of torture, all this while evoking the cultural and religious referent, the account of torture and pain inflicted in the course of the Passion. It taps the strong emotion associated with the New Testament story, without, however, mentioning the story itself and its protagonist, he whose side has been pierced. The force of the phrase derives from its compacting together all these different ideas into three words. Shakespeare makes use of the most extreme traditional Christian expression of suffering for his characterisation of his two protagonists, Edgar and Lear. Like the image of the loincloth hiding from sight the genitals of the naked Edgar, the side-piercing too provides a direct reference to Christ's Passion, without so much as naming it. Shakespeare need not, and cannot, go any further than that. The medieval image of suffering is lifted from of its original religious context and inserted into the Renaissance, humanist context.

Even within Dürer's body of works, his Christ-like images are exceptional self-portrayals, both particular and general, affecting us on both levels. In his earlier *Self-Portrait in the Nude* (1509),[20] Dürer depicted himself as totally naked (see Figure 8.3). His complete nakedness

Figure 8.3 Dürer: Self-portrait in the nude (1509), pen and brush, black ink with white lead on green prepared paper, 29 × 15 cm (Weimarer Stadtschloss).

distinguishes this picture from those other self-portraits where, in the guise of the Man of Sorrows, his private parts are covered. The effect and meaning of this change in his self-depiction are immense.[21]

In his even earlier self-portraits of 1493[22] and 1498,[23] Dürer appears as a handsome young man, well-dressed and carefully coiffed, reminding us of what Poor Tom says to Lear about his own past as a frivolous courtier (see Figures 8.4 and 8.5).

Like Edgar, Dürer has recorded his two faces – first, the good-looking young man, then the Man of Sorrows. Dürer's self-perception may seem at first remote in time and place from Shakespeare's characterisation of Edgar, but one should remember that Dürer's prints made him famous across Europe due to the availability and ease of transporting such prints. As Erwin Panofsky wrote:

> [I]n Germany, in the fifteenth century, book printing, engraving and woodcuts for the first time enabled the individual to disseminate his ideas all over the world. It was by means of the graphic arts that Germany finally attained the rank of a Great Power in the domain of art, and this chiefly through the activity of one man who,

Figure 8.4 Dürer: Portrait of the Artist Holding a Thistle (1493), oil on parchment pasted on canvas, 56 ×17.3 cm (Louvre, Paris).

Figure 8.5 Dürer: Self-portrait (1498), oil on panel, 52 × 41 cm (Prado, Madrid).

though famous as a painter, became an international figure only in his capacity of engraver and woodcut designer: Albrecht Dürer. His prints set a new standard of graphic perfection for more than a century, and served as models for countless other prints, as well as for paintings, sculptures, enamels, tapestries, plaques and faïences, and this not only in Germany, but also in Italy, in France, in the Low Countries, in Russia, in Spain and indirectly even in Persia.[24]

Although the representations of himself as Christ are not prints, so not available in multiple copies, Dürer's fame all over Europe assured the spread of his innovative visual ideas. Furthermore, the Man of Sorrows was already a familiar subject of religious painting in the Middle Ages.

That Dürer was also well-known in England in Shakespeare's time and highly regarded can be learned, for example, from a reference to him in the essay 'On Beauty' by Francis Bacon:

There is no excellent beauty that hath not some strangeness in the proportion. A man cannot tell whether Apelles or Albert Dürer were the more trifler; whereof the one would make a personage by geometrical proportions: the other, by taking the best parts out of divers faces, to make one excellent. Such personages, I think, would please nobody but the painter that made them.[25]

Despite its dismissive tone, one can learn from this passage that Dürer is considered by Bacon as on a par with no less than the celebrated Apelles! Although it is unlikely that Shakespeare ever saw the said drawings, it is certainly the case that Dürer's pictorial world influenced the visual world of the Renaissance in general, including that of England, and that the visual associations are therefore similar. Furthermore, art historians speak of 'The so-called Dürer Renaissance of around 1600',[26] indicating his relevance to the humanist ideas circulating at the period.

Dürer's religious paintings reflect his espousal of the northern theology of the *Devotio Moderna*, the Modern Devotion, emphasising the humanity of Jesus, stressing his human body, expressing his suffering as a human being, thus leading the way to identify emotionally with Christ and his Passion, to imitate Christ. In this he was following the teachings of Thomas à Kempis, mentioned above, a member of the *Devotio Moderna* movement, who had composed the *Imitatio Christi* (*c.*1418–27), a Latin manual of devotion. It has been said, 'With the exception of the Bible, no Christian writing has had so wide a vogue or so sustained a popularity as this.'[27] The book was translated into several languages, among them English, and printed a number of times in the sixteenth and seventeenth centuries, proving highly influential.[28] Like the proliferation of Dürer's prints, the advent of the printing press also allowed the spreading of this book and its ideas.

I am not arguing for any direct connection between the German painter and Shakespeare. Instead, what I am suggesting is that the motif of the imitation of Christ is one of the elements comprising Shakespeare's characterisation of Edgar, and that unravelling the significance of Dürer's presentation of himself in the image of Jesus can help us understand this important component in Edgar's complex figure.

Not only is there the parallel between Edgar's description of himself as young courtier and Dürer's self-portraits as young dandy, but they both also take upon themselves the imitation of Christ. Like Shakespeare's superimposition of the Christ figure on Poor Tom, so also Dürer's self-portraits offer a double vision of the realistic self-image and the spiritual figuration. Art historian Gertrud Schiller dismisses the criticism that, in depicting himself as God, Dürer was guilty of hubris, arguing rather that, 'Compassion to the point of identification is expressed repeatedly in Dürer's art when he gives the Man of Sorrows his own features.'[29] In portraying himself as a representative of suffering humanity, Dürer was joining his humanist perception to his Christian faith, thus expressing the core idea of Christian humanism, which is ultimately based on the Biblical story that man was created in the image of God. In depicting himself in the image of Christ, Dürer shifts the religious emphasis from the traditional story of the Passion to the abstracted suffering of humanity. The humanist ideas explored in *King Lear* are basically those expressed by Dürer. Shakespeare likewise circumvents the traditional medieval Passion plays, incorporating Christian images and ideas into his humanist play, a play that asks, in the words of the protagonist himself: 'Is man no more than this?' (III, iv, 101). The question about the nature of man is the ultimate humanist question, and his encounter with Edgar in the storm initiates its discussion by Lear, who reaches the insight that 'thou art the thing itself', that man is nothing but 'a bare, forked animal' like Poor Tom (III, iv, 104–6).

Beyond his more literal transformation into the folkloric figure of Tom o'Bedlam, Edgar's disguising-soliloquy offers a verbal parallel to Dürer's visual self-fashioning as the Man of Sorrows. Through his *imitatio Christi*, Edgar is no longer merely himself, but an embodiment of the idea of the Man of Sorrows, and it is as such that he is no longer recognisable to his father. Intriguingly, the two disguised characters, Kent and Edgar, face each other in the storm without recognising each other.

The lack of recognition among those surrounding him serves to point to the wider significance of the character of Edgar as the representative of suffering humanity. He assumes an importance that goes far beyond his function in the plot, expressive of the humanist implications of the traditional Christian iconography. There is no redemptive power in the suffering of either Edgar or Lear. The Christian world of images within which Shakespeare writes is a humanistic rather than religious world. Shakespeare uses the available Christian image but removes it from its immediate Christian context. The image of the naked man with a loincloth is there, as are the sorrows, but these remain as delicately traced outlines, and there is no direct verbal reference to Christ and his Passion. Literally effacing himself, the figure of Edgar can assume different and constantly changing guises, further reinforcing his ability to encompass and represent suffering humanity.

Notes

1. Edgar's selfhood is preserved throughout. It is his lower forms of social identity as individual and subject that are affected by his external transformation. See Hanna Scolnicov, '"Who is it that can tell me who I am?": Individual, Subject and Self in *King Lear*'.
2. All textual references are to the Arden Shakespeare edition: *King Lear*, ed. R. A. Foakes.
3. Hanna Scolnicov, 'Lear's Conversation with the Philosopher'.
4. For an excellent survey of Shakespeare's use of disguises and masquerading, see P. V. Kreider, 'The Mechanics of Disguise in Shakespeare's Plays'.
5. Foakes discusses the editorial insertion of the scene breaks, see notes to I, ii, 171 and I, ii, 192.
6. This is a matter of interpretation. As Foakes notes, 'it has become customary for Edgar to . . . transform himself in front of the audience', but he also puts forward the option that the change occurs in between scenes (note to II, ii, 180–92).
7. On nakedness in Elizabethan drama, see Maurice Charney, '"We put fresh garments on him": Nakedness and Clothes in *King Lear*'.
8. Maria de Grazia focuses on the function of the loincloth as a codpiece that accentuates Edgar's phallic power. See her 'The Ideology of Superfluous Things: *King Lear* as Period Piece', pp. 22, 29.
9. The 'man of sorrows' translates the Hebrew 'איש מכאובות', referring to both pain and sorrow.
10. Roy W. Battenhouse, *Shakespearean Tragedy: Its Art and Its Christian Premises*.
11. Simon Palfrey, *Poor Tom: Living* King Lear, pp. 213–14. I am indebted to Julia Lupton for directing me to the Christian interpretation in Palfrey's book.
12. Thomas à Kempis, *The Imitation of Christ*, vol. 7, part 2, p. 214 (The First Book, Chapter 1, paragraph 4). Available at https://books.google.com/books?id=mBqFj_ZoLy0C&lpg=PA208&ots=E8Y1J2dys9&dq=' (last accessed 10 July 2018).
13. Lear's dismal view of man is echoed, even more bleakly, by Primo Levi in his Holocaust memoir, *Se questo è un uomo* (*If This Is a Man*).
14. For more on Shakespeare's dual exposure of realism and symbolism in *King Lear*, see Michael Mooney, '"Edgar I nothing am": 'Figurenposition' in *King Lear*', p. 153; see also Maynard Mack, *King Lear in Our Time*.
15. For more on stage-stripping, see Hanna Scolnicov, 'Stripping as Gesture'.
16. Self-portrait as the Man of Sorrows (1522). Drawing with lead pencil on blue-green primed paper, 40.8 × 29 cm (Kunsthalle, Bremen).
17. Self-portrait as Christ (1521). Coloured pen drawing, 127 × 117 mm (Kunsthalle, Bremen).

18. Joseph Leo Koerner, *The Moment of Self-Portraiture in German Renaissance Art*, p. 179.

19. This phrase summarises the theme so brilliantly that it was used by Peter Travis as his title for an essay on the medieval Chester Passion play. See Peter W. Travis, 'The Dramatic Strategies of Chester's Passion Pagina: "O thou side-piercing sight!" – *King Lear*', pp. 275–89.

20. Self-portrait in the nude (1509), pen and brush, black ink with white lead on green prepared paper, 29 × 15 cm (Weimarer Stadtschloss).

21. Brian Cummings, *Mortal Thoughts: Religion, Secularity and Identity*, has this painting on the cover of his book. On pp. 26–7 he analyses this painting, without, however, referring to Dürer's daring self-exposure, which distinguishes it from his self-portraits as Christ.

22. Portrait of the Artist Holding a Thistle (1493), oil on parchment pasted on canvas, 56 × 17.3 cm (Louvre, Paris).

23. Self-portrait (1498), oil on panel, 52 × 41 cm (Prado, Madrid).

24. Erwin Panofsky, *The Life and Art of Albrecht Dürer*, pp. 3–4.

25. Francis Bacon, 'Of Beauty', in *Essays, Civil and Moral*, pp. 111–12. Originally published in 1612.

26. See Joseph Leo Koerner, 'Dürer's Model: Reflections on Dürer and His Legacy', Exhibition held at the British Museum 2002–2003. Available at https://www.britishmuseum.org/pdf/4%20Durer%20Model1.pdf (last accessed 29 December 2017).

27. See Introductory Note to the English translation in the Harvard Classics, note 12 above, presumably by the translator, Rev. William Benham.

28. See the long list of entries in EEBO (Early English Books online) of the printed translations.

29. Gertrud Schiller, *Iconography of Christian Art*, p. 198.

Chapter 9

The Face as Rhetorical Self in Ben Jonson's Literature

Akihiko Shimizu

One of the fundamental aspects of a face-to-face encounter is its generation of an immediate demand to decipher the character of the other. Sociologist Erving Goffman once explained that a face 'may be defined as the positive social value a person effectively claims for himself by the lines others assume he has taken during a particular contact.'[1] As the term 'face-to-face' communication suggests, then, the face is, in one sense, the very image of a person's self that we consider fixed and trustworthy. At the same time, it is also an image that circulates within society and is shared and interpreted by others through constraints outside the realm of our perception. This ambiguity was particularly of concern for English citizens who observed the rise of urbanisation and mobilisation of society in the 1580s and 1590s. The necessity of perceiving the social attributes and credibility of incognitos through facial expression, appearance and manners sparked a vogue of character writing which served both as popular entertainment and courtesy book.[2] While recent Shakespeare scholarship and early modern literary studies have witnessed a revival of character criticism and recognised it 'as a valid analytic category', scholars working on Ben Jonson appear to be less interested in the subject.[3] There are only a handful of studies discussing Jonson and character exclusively, several of which were published more than a century ago.[4] However, when we consider the validity of E. C. Baldwin's claim that 'Jonson was the first to recognize' the kinship 'between the drama and the character-sketch' and Benjamin Boyce's acknowledgement of Jonson's use of 'character' throughout his literary career (he notes the sketches in *Cynthia's Revels* (1601) as '[the] "first" English "Characters"'), it appears that the subject's lack of attention in modern Jonson scholarship requires reassessment.[5]

This chapter, then, attempts to offer an update on the examination of Jonsonian character in several aspects. First, I situate Jonson within the contexts of contemporary cultures of the comedy of humours and rhetorical education that drew on classical rhetorical theories of character. Second, I observe the uses and effects of the face as an external index of selfhood in Jonson's *Every Man Out of His Humour* (1599) and the prose commonplace book, *Discoveries* (1634), and juxtapose the findings to Thomas Overbury's character writing to clarify important aspects of the face's performance of inwardness and outwardness. Third, by comparing Jonson's and Shakespeare's references to characters' faces in plays, I argue that character is essentially intersubjective, and that it should be understood as an effect of performative interaction between *dramatis personae* in plays as well as between players and the audience. In conclusion, I suggest that Jonson treats the face both as an identifying trait and as a rhetorical instrument, thus revealing his interest in the social construction of character not only at behavioural but also rhetorical and performative levels.

Jonson as the creator of 'perfect characters'

The current critical view of Jonson's contribution to literary characterisation results from biases in the historical reception of Jonson's literary merit generally. The earliest acknowledgements of Jonson's technique of characterisation appear in the context of the so-called 'War of the Theatres', which was a response to the 'Bishop's Ban'.[6] In John Weever's *The Whipping of the Satyre* (1601), for example, Jonson is ridiculed as 'Monsieur Humourist': 'had you been but so mean a philosopher as [to] have known *mores sequuntur humores* [i.e. moral behaviour derived from the observation of humours], you would questionless have made better humours, if it had been but to better our manners, and not, instead of a moral medicine, to have given them a mortal poison.'[7] Thomas Dekker follows this and ridicules Jonson's obsession with humours in *Satiromastix, or The Untrussing of the Humourous Poet* (1602). Assuming that the audience in the theatre recognises the character of Horace as Jonson himself, Dekker has him prosecuted in public: 'that's he, that's he, that's he, that pennes and purges Humours and diseases' (V, ii, 306–7).[8] These references, however disparaging they might appear, establish Jonson's public reputation as the author of humours.

Following Jonson's establishment as the author of the comedy of humours, the seventeenth and earlier eighteenth-century concept of 'character' tends towards an appreciation of Jonson's art. Thomas Shadwell praises Jonson as 'the onely person that appears to me to have made perfect Representations of Humane life' and lamented that no contemporary playwright managed to create 'near so perfect Characters as the admirable Johnson alwayes made, who never wrote Comedy without seven or eight excellent Humours.'⁹ Shadwell's acknowledgement of Jonson's ability to present particular characters by 'confining' them to individual persons is shared by John Dryden:

> [H]umour is meant some extravagant habit, passion, or affection; particular [. . .] to some person: By the oddness of which, he is immediately distinguish'd from the rest of men [. . .] The description of these humours, drawn from the knowledge and observation of particular persons, was the peculiar genius and talent of *Ben Johnson*.¹⁰

As Shadwell's and Dryden's appreciation underlines, within the seventeenth-century literary context Jonson's dramatic merit resided in his superb representation of particular characters on stage through the depiction of humours.

Compared with these positive appreciations of Jonsonian characters of humours, Victorian critics show their disparagement of Jonson's art in their veneration of what they understand to be the Shakespearean literary mode. Perhaps one of the most widely accepted views is the critical contrast drawn between Jonson's 'flat' characters and Shakespeare's 'round' ones, which is established by Samuel Johnson and reinforced by Samuel Taylor Coleridge, A. C. Bradley and E. M. Forster.¹¹ Focusing on the cultural construction of the concept of 'character', Deirdre Shauna Lynch has shown a shift in reading practices in the late eighteenth century that resulted in an equation of 'character' with the reader's capacity to discover hidden depths in the fictional person. The reader who could dive beneath the surface to detect inner meanings proved herself a superior reader and person, one who could discern moral depth.¹² As a result of this shift, which began with an interest in the depth of Shakespeare's dramatic characterisation, readers from the nineteenth century and onwards found Jonson's characters to be lacking.

Anne Barton draws on these contrasting views of Shakespeare's and Jonson's characters for her argument that, in *Volpone*, as in other Jonsonian plays, the characters 'sometimes strike readers (although rarely theatre audiences) as perplexingly flat, outlines as opposed to individuals.'[13] She goes on, however, to comment that 'most of the characters who struggle through this welter of objects seem to be animated less by souls or natural affections than by a strange lust for material possessions.'[14] One might argue, in our present crisis of later capitalism, that this is not at all a 'strange' phenomenon, since people have 'lust' for material possessions in modern consumer society – and that Jonson's analysis of character-construction in the emergence of capitalism is therefore salient.[15] Moreover, as Barton herself concedes, the way critics see Jonson's characters as 'flat' tends to be the consequence of an overtly 'literary' reading of the play – especially by drawing a comparison between Jonson and Shakespeare. Jonson's characters 'are far less self-aware than most of Shakespeare's' as they 'do not fully understand, let alone find themselves able to articulate, why they act as they do.'[16]

This apparent lack of self-awareness seems to be an important element in understanding face-to-face encounters of Jonson's characters of humours as they rely on 'inference and suggestion' rather than revelation to deduce knowledge of the persons they encounter.[17] The characters' dependence on inference and suggestion in processing random information concurs with Lorna Hutson's summary that the early modern character is 'the product not of coherence and depth, but of discontinuities in codes that make up the legibility of the speaking subject, and of the perceived "surplus" of information that these generate.'[18] This view of character as a product of 'surplus' and 'discontinuous' information within seemingly coherent sign systems endorses the necessity for the acting body and its face to fundamentally be open for interpretation. Oscillating incessantly between outward appearance and internal speculation, Jonson's characters are the effect of a simultaneous process of rhetorical self-concealment and self-exposure. As these impersonators attempt to depict their own worth by affecting humours, their interlocutors use rhetorical conjecture to expose what lies beneath this verbal disguise.[19] As a result of this dynamic of rhetorical concealment and rhetorical investigation or exposure, the characters reside in their endless discursive interaction with one another, alternating between the display of who they want to look like and other people's observation and estimation of who they really are. Hence in comprehending a rhetorical dialectic between a character's concealment/performance and another character's attempt to read through that performance through inference, we ought to examine the first layer of this dialectical exchange in the face as key to reading Jonson's characterisation. The following sections will attest to the face's role in the rhetorical and performative construction of Jonson's characters.

Humours, the face and the classical rhetorical theory of 'character'

In order to understand Jonson's distinctively performative approach to dramatic characters as a means of representing rhetorical exchange on stage, it is useful to examine the classical rhetorical theory of character in such terms as *descriptio, decorum* and *ekphrasis* – rhetorical techniques adapted for representing a person verbally. Jonson's rhetorical theory of character, which aims to persuade the readers and audience by delineating the *ethos*, or the characteristic spirit and manners of the times, is indeed based on Aristotle's *Rhetoric* which argues:[20] 'neither does rhetoric theorize about each opinion – what may seem so to Socrates or Hippias – but about what seems true to people of a certain sort, as is also true with dialectic' (Book 1, Chapter 2).[21] As Jonson's characters are designed as types, it is clear that his theory of character draws heavily on Aristotle's who attributes the various oppositional emotions such as anger and calmness, or fear and boldness (Book 2, Chapters 2–11) to some basic types of men, such as the young, the old, the rich and the miser (Book 2, Chapters 12–17).[22] In going 'through the kinds of character, considering what they are like in terms of emotions and habits and age of life and fortune', Aristotle observes the typical actions, motives and passions of these types of men and avoids individualising them.[23] This rhetorical theory of character becomes a foundation shared and adapted by the writers of later periods, including Theophrastus and Jonson.

In his *Characters* Theophrastus lays a foundation for character writing – a literary sub-genre in short prose writing that describes the typical manners and actions of various different types of men of professions.[24] As Boyce and Peter Womack explain, Theophrastan characters are developed in association 'with the figure of *descriptio* which plays an important part in the Ciceronian *argumentum ad hominem*, and its rather short-lived popularity reflects the almost total control exercised over pre-university education in the Renaissance by the rhetorical categories of invention and style.'[25] Using this pedagogic technique, Theophrastan characters aimed at assimilating seemingly random features of social behaviour and reducing them 'into the generalised discourse of official culture' in which they 'are able to function as signs'.[26] Preoccupied with offering the idiosyncratic details of a person, character writing was only concerned with the phenomenological acknowledgement and recognition of its subject in their outward manifestations, and not with the epistemological understanding of human nature.

Utilising type characters and focusing on showcasing their idio-syncrasy, *Every Man Out of His Humour* indicates Jonson's interest in a Theophrastan representation of the social manners and interac-tions which are endorsed by the fashion of his times. As Asper nar-rates, the term 'humour' is acknowledged not only as a metaphorical discourse of medical knowledge (Induction, 86–100) but also as a social phenomenon that is applied to the actions and behaviours of the individuals (100–12).[27] Thus the rebellious abuse of humours encourages the audience to censure the individuals' affectation as 'ridiculous' since the eccentricity of socially misfit characters is 'the time's deformity' reflected in 'a mirror' (112, 116–18). The reference to a mirror, moreover, suggests Jonson's application of the classical rhetorical topos of *ut pictura poesis* and the technique of *ekphrasis* – a rhetorical exercise explicated in Aphthonius' *Progymnasmata* for creating graphic and dramatic description of visual art as 'the verbal emblem'.[28] As *ekphrasis* originates in the Greek word *ekphrazein*, meaning to 'speak out' or call things by their names, it was used in literature as an authorial voice 'to persuade and move and audi-ence to believe in the verisimilitude of a textual reality' and there-fore was closely linked to Aristotle's idea of *enargeia* – 'a style that is made dynamic through a pathetic visual vividness of representa-tion'.[29] Underpinned by the 'persuasive efficacy' of *enargeia*, which is also the key to face-to-face communication, the Jonsonian concept of character should be understood predominantly as a rhetorical effect of interaction and not as a manifestation of consciousness, a view sometimes implied by those who dismiss or neglect to take Jonson's characters seriously as persons.[30]

Jonson's insistence about the rhetorical representation of the sig-nifier (i.e. character) over the signified (i.e. self) informs his attempt to highlight the gap between the idea that forms the plot and the char-acters whose actions materialise the idea on stage. Thus, as Womack points out, his characters are often 'divisive, actor-oriented, explo-sive rather than organic'.[31] Essentially, Jonson's characters showcase their moral judgements incurred through the negotiations between the generalisation and particularisation of a person, as is discussed in *Discoveries*:

Whilst I name no persons, but deride follies, why should any man confess or betray himself? [. . .] Is it such an inexplicable crime in poets, to tax generally; and no offence in them who, by their excep-tion, confess they have committed them particularly? [. . .] Some vices (you will say) are so foul, that it is better they should be done than spoken. But they that take offence where no name, character or signature doth blazon them seem to me like affected as women, who, if they hear anything ill spoken of the ill of their sex, are presently moved, as if the contumely respected their particular; and on the contrary, when they hear good of good women, conclude that it belongs to them all. (1634–50)

Jonson's concern about rhetorical representation of a generalised person is a kind of approbation, while his concern about people's misunderstanding and abusive imitation of particularised characters is critical. For this reason, Jonson holds a robust understanding of the notion of character as a reflections of a person's mirror image in rhetoric and dramatic action: 'Language shows a man: speak, that I may see thee. It springs out of the most retired and inward parts of us, and is the image and the parent of it, the mind. No glass renders a man's form or likeness so true as his speech' (*Discoveries*, 1439–41).

Jonson's attention to language and rhetoric, especially in terms of *ekphrasis* as character making, leads to the success of *Every Man Out* in 1599.[32] Composed between the two publications of Issac Casaubon's Latin translation of Theophrastus's *Characters*, *Characteres Ethici, sive Descriptiones Morum* in 1592 and 1599, *Every Man Out* indicates Jonson's attempt in supplementing the dramatic characters by the Theophrastan satiric prose description in 'Characters'.[33] This operation is evident in the sketch of Puntarvolo's character:

A vainglorious knight, over-Englishing his travels and wholly consecrated to singularity [. . .] Of presence good enough, but so palpably affected to his own praise that, for want of flatterers, he commends himself to the floutage of his own family. He deals upon returns and strange performances, resolving, in despite of public derision, to stick to his own particular fashion, phrase, and gesture. (*Every Man Out*, 'Characters', 11–17)

Like Theophrastus, Jonson depicts Puntarvolo's character in a detached and concise narrative that describes the outward features and the typical conduct of a 'particular' sort of person and aims to appeal to the reader's common understanding of the type in their society.[34] Puntarvolo's 'over-Englishing' humours suggests, however, a more complex process of imitation: his 'strange performances' stem from his fixation with the 'returns' – bets on his safe return from a foreign travel. In this context, 'performances' refers not only to 'the doing

of an action or operation' (*Oxford English Dictionary*, 'performance', *n.* 1a) but also to '[t]he carrying out, discharge, or fulfilment
of a command, duty, promise, purpose, responsibility, etc.; execution, discharge. Freq. opposed to *promise*' ('performance', *n.* 3).[35]
Puntarvolo's self-conscious affectation of his allegedly unique character is constituted by socio-legal interaction and contract, derived
from *promise* and its *execution* between the two parties. Thus he is
actively impersonating a humorous character rather than passively
or naturally expressing his inner urges.

The performativity of Jonson's characters is enacted not only
through a character's embodiment of social customs but also,
reflectively, through a character's desire to be the object of rhetorical appraisal. Puntarvolo's preoccupation with 'particular fashion,
phrase and gesture' indicates a characteristic of his inner desire to
be the subject of praises and flatteries, which urges him to imitate
gentlemanly behaviour in rhetoric and action. Indeed Jonson's view
of 'character' predominantly problematises people's desire for the
rhetorical imitation as part of the performative process.[36] This was
a concern significant enough for him to revisit in *Discoveries*:

> I have considered our whole life is like a play: wherein every man,
> forgetful of himself, is in travail with expression of another. Nay,
> we so insist in imitating others, as we cannot (when it is necessary)
> return to ourselves; like children, that imitate the vices of stammer-
> ers so long, till at last they have become such, and make the habit to
> another nature, as it is never forgotten. (784–8)

Jonson acknowledges that the individual 'self' is constituted by
our urge for verbal and gestural expression with another and is
therefore essentially rhetorical/fictional. The pessimistic view of
the negation of 'self' reveals the underlying Aristotelian concept
of the human being, processed via John of Salisbury's *Policraticus*.
The process of the loss of self is initiated by man's natural inclination for 'imitation' – of the vices in most cases – and reinforced by
'habit' until it becomes 'nature'. Since every person is essentially
'forgetful of himself', the self becomes an effect of rhetorical imitation. Accordingly, there will be something stylised and generic
about these acquired 'selves'.

In the scenes of Paul's Walk in *Every Man Out*, this imitative performativity of type characters facilitates both the characters' observations of and their conversations about other people's faces and
appearances especially in asides, which in return initiate their own

participation in the display. As Helen Ostovich writes, this three-dimensional perspective that allows us to see the characters' manipulative self-representation as habitus calls upon the audience/reader's 'faculty of judgement by focusing on the fact of plurality and diversity as the guide to responsible comprehension of the human condition' that Hannah Arendt discusses.[37]

This malleability of the self-as-humours appealed tremendously to the young writers of the 1590s who were less preoccupied with the description of the in-depth consciousness of individuals than with delineating identities in such ways that anticipate modern forensic discourse and tabloid papers. Thus, between the publication of Issac Casaubon's Latin translation of Theophrastus's *Characteres Ethici, sive Descriptiones Morum* in 1592/99 and John Healey's English translation that came out in 1616, there appeared works like Joseph Hall's *Characters of Virtues and Vices* (1608) which, according to J. W. Smeed, 'created the vogue, almost the craze for character-writing that lasted throughout the seventeenth century England.'[38] As Boyce sums up, 'Not that there were actual Characters in English before 1608. But some, though not all, of the literary intentions of the Character-writer can be seen operating in numerous authors of earlier date.'[39] As a close friend to Sir Henry Wotton who met Casaubon in Geneva in 1593, Jonson certainly knew Casaubon's work; he inscribed a copy of Casaubon's 1605 edition of Persius to Sir John Roe.[40] Jonson's adaptation of Theophrastan character writing in *Every Man Out* is thus one of the earliest attempts among early modern English writers at assimilating this tradition, and it certainly contributed to setting up a framework for exhibiting social norms and customs rhetorically and through face-to-face interaction.[41]

Jonson's contribution to the understanding of character as an effect of interaction might well have inspired contemporary character writers like Thomas Overbury. Overbury's *A Wife* (1614) adapted Theophrastan *Characters* for Jacobean court culture; this trend involved many other authors such as Thomas Dekker, John Webster, Sir Henry Wotton, Sir Thomas Roe and Sir Henry Goodyer, many of whom Jonson knew well.[42] Favoured by the men of the Inns of Court around 1610, the volume's definition of a character as an established norm reveals the early modern understanding of personhood in correlation with the face:

> If I must speake the Schoole-Masters language I will confesse that Character comes of this infinitiue moode χαράξω which signifieth to ingraue, or make a deepe Impression. And for that cause, a letter (as A. B.) is called a Character.

Character is also taken for an Egiptian Hierogliphicke, for an impress, or shorte Embleme; in little comprehending much.

To square out a Character by our English levell, it is a picture (reall or personall) quaintlie drawne in various collours, all of them heightened by one shadowing.

It is a quicke and soft touch of many strings, all shutting vp in one musicall close: It is wits descant on any plaine song.[43]

As Overbury writes, character in the original Greek, Latin and Egyptian contexts is a letter or symbol in a very general sense; anything to engrave (or to be engraved as) a sign or stamp (or to be stamped) onto wax is considered to be character. As character is both simultaneously a signifier (that is, things to actively engrave or impress) and a signified (things that are passively engraved or impressed), it achieves the Emblematic goal of 'in little comprehending much'. In this sense, character is analogous to the epigram, which originated in epigraph and epitaph and embodied its complexity *on the surface*.

Establishing a metaphor of portrait painting of 'a picture (*reall or personall*)', Overbury's definition of an interactive character sublimates Aristotle's and Theophrastus's rhetorical theory of character into the previously mentioned topos of *ut pictura poesis* that Horace argued in *Ars Poetica* – a work Jonson studied eagerly and translated for the second time, after the fire in 1623 had destroyed the first copy.[44] Horace's *Ars Poetica* draws on Aristotle's concept of *mimesis* in *Poetics* and describes the need for poets to find the fit style to the matter, a rhetorical principle known as *decorum*. This was a relevant technique in drama as well as poetry; as David Wiles writes, *decorum* in the theatrical context 'means that the actor will fit his performance to whatever character he is given, good or bad, while in public life the citizen must conform to the *persona* or "mask" that nature has given him, with temperance and restraint moderated by more individual traits.'[45] Thus, reciprocating Goffman's understanding of face-to-face communication, *decorum* mediates the face that reconciles the conflicts between public and private, actor and audience, and type and individual in character.[46] In this sense, it is logical that Overburian character – which recognises the split in the 'real and personal' pictures of a person – acknowledges the need for literacy, or wit, in reading the representational crux in the face.[47]

Drawing on Plutarch's *Parallel Lives*, Overbury's theory of character construction, like portrait painting, finds its ultimate goal in the revelation of *ethos* – or spirit – of the absent subject. As Edward Burns argues, character writers, portrait painters and actors were all aware that a person's likely appearance (*eidos*) is most 'perceivable in human face'.[48] Indeed as the *OED* definition suggests, the 'face' may be essentially understood as the most convincing register of a person: it is defined primarily as 'In a person (or personified being) (esp. as a principal feature in recognition)' which develops into 'The countenance as having particular qualities or attributes' and thus '[r]egarded as expressive of feeling or character, or as having a specified expression' ('face, n.', entry 1.a; 2.a).[49] Thus, despite the awareness of the potential danger of deceit in an over-trusting face, early modern citizens sought for proof of character in the face. Jonson's consciousness of the significance of the face in terms of character is epitomised in *Discoveries*: 'A man is read in his face: God in his creatures' (377).

It is within this conceptual framework of *decorum* that Overbury and Jonson produced their characters on stage, in prose and in poetry.[50] For Jonson, character is the idea and method of depicting a person that not only fits into the combination of categorical types (rich/poor and so forth), but also represents the poet's trustworthy knowledge of the world, human nature and manners in a suitable style.[51] To be able to offer a convincing *ekphrasis* as a rhetorical reproduction of characters placed in real society, the Jonsonian comedy of humours is attuned to face-making as a forthrightly and self-consciously performative approach to characterisation that is manifestly aware of its performative status as non-natural or non-mimetics.[52]

Performative character and the face in Jonson and Shakespeare

This classical rhetoric of character, understood as a largely verbal practice, is embodied in Jonson's comedy of humours such as *Cynthia's Revels* (1600) as a symbiotic relationship in 'his poesy' which 'affords / Words above action, matter above words' ('Prologus', 19–20). This view was based on Quintilian's understanding of *enargeia* as the power of *phantasia* or imagination, through which the absent emotions of somebody else 'are presented to the mind in such a way that we seem actually to see them with our eyes and have them physically present to us.' Through the impressions derived from agents (or characters), the reader or audience member associates himself with 'things, words and actions' in a realistic manner (*Institutio Oratoria*, VI, ii, 29–34).[53] In the classic rhetorical theory of character, then, imagination is only an auxiliary means for the orator to present the fictional character as part of the trustworthy reproduction of *likelihood* in his discourse. Thus naturally, the pragmatic effect of *enargeia* is materialised in its use of *prosopopoeia* (or 'face-making' as translated literally) as an *active* impersonation of 'fictitious speeches of other persons' put into the mouth of his client' (VI, i, 25) to literally impress the court: 'Not only words, but some actions are used to produce tears [. . .] These things [i.e. evidential props that display the deed of crime] commonly make an enormous impression, because they confront people's minds directly with the facts' (VI, i, 30–1).[54]

In *Cynthia's Revels*, Jonson applies this *prosopopoeic* theory to the characterisation of Amorphus who plans to create a portrait gallery by collecting 'the particular, and distinct face of every your most noted species of persons' (II, iii, 12–14).[55] Amorphus's interest lies in the superficial outward features of men and he slights the moral aspect of characters which are condemned by Mercury and Cupid. Amorphus's accumulation of faces, I think, not merely provides 'descriptive detail' that helps 'reveal what inner identities they possess', as Beecher argues; it is also to reveal the praxis of interpretation whereby he gathers patterns of characterisation through a process of inference.[56] Amorphus's obsession with superficial appearance is epitomised in Act II, scene iii, where he instructs Asotus to 'observe' him making faces of such types as 'your merchant's, or city-face' (II, iii, 16), 'student's, or academic face' (18), 'soldier's face' (20), 'lawyer's face' which is the 'anti-face to' the former one (22), 'statist's face' (25), and above all, 'your face of faces, or courtier's face' (28), which 'according to our subdivision of a courtier' breaks down to 'elementary, practic, and theoric' sorts (29–30). Being Amorphus's zany who 'doth most of these tricks after him, sweats to imitate him in everything to a hair' (78–80), Asotus is assured by his master that it is the face-making performance that produces a person: '[I]n any rank or profession whatsoever, the most general or major part of opinion goes with the face, and simply respects nothing else. Therefore, if that can be made exactly, curiously, exquisitely, thoroughly, it is enough' (42–5). In essence, their focus is on how to take advantage of the manipulative reproduction of the face as a means to become a person they are not.

This comical scene is reinforced by asides from Mercury and Cupid who observe with critical eyes. Indeed Mercury, who mocks Amporphus as 'some excellent painter, to have ta'en the copy of all these faces' (54–5), describes him to Cupid by adopting the Theophrastan rhetoric of characterisation that Amorphus uses:

> He walks most commonly with a clove or pick-tooth in his mouth.
> He's the very mint of compliment; all his behaviours are printed,
> his face is another volume of essays, and his beard an Aristarchus.
> (67–70)

In Mercury's view, neither Amorphus's behaviour nor his face reveal
his inner identity; they are understood as 'minted' or 'printed' repli-
cas of conduct books that circulated in early modern London. This
interchangeability of characters and their faces is further developed
in the following scene in which Cupid offers 'to help to paint' Lady
Argurion, and 'another character or two' (139–40). Mercury's
response, 'What, lay colour upon colour? That affords but an ill
blazon' (120), shows that the courtiers' manipulation of the faces
is mutually shared with the ladies, who apply layers of paints as
make-up on their faces, and who, as the pun suggests, own dubious heraldry as 'it is a solecism to have a heraldic shield which
lays a colour on top of another colour, as colours must always be
laid over a metal.'[57] Thus the faces in *Cynthia's Revels* become a
currency of Puntarvolo-esque performance: like blazons, they are
circulated, collected and used for social contracts. As lordship and
ladyship became more easily purchasable by the new rich, so did the
face raise certain doubts in the early modern mindset regarding its
straightforward authenticity in correlation to the bearer's identity.[58]

Later in Act IV, Jonson creates a scene with four ladies: Phantaste,
Philautia (who, according to Cupid, 'has a good superficial judgement
in painting' (II, iv, 32–3)), Argurion and Moria. They 'run over' the
portraits of male courtiers to decide '[w]hich is the properest man
amongst them' (IV, i, 36–8). Their judgement is based on the superficial features of the courtiers, and naturally their faces come to the
centre of the ladies' attention. For example, Anaiades, who Mercury
criticises earlier that '[h]is fashion is not to take knowledge of him
that is beneath him in clothes' (II, ii, 71–2), is dismissed for having 'a
very imperfect face' which is '[l]ike a squeezed orange: sour, sour' (IV,
i, 51–2). The same focus on the face applies for their view of Asotus,
who is compared with Hedon. Argurion, who dotes on Asotus, challenges other ladies as follows:

> Hedon, in troth, no. Hedon's a pretty slight courtier, and he wears his
> clothes well and sometimes in fashion; marry, his face is but indiffer-
> ent, and he has no such excellent body. No, th'other is a most delicate
> youth, a sweet face, a straight body, a well-proportioned leg and foot,
> a white hand, a tender voice. (73–7)

It shows, then, that the face is, of all body parts, the most com-modified feature in the play. By delineating the charms of Asotus, Argurion is mocked by the ladies for 'bestowing a copy (i.e. por-trait) of him upon us' (79–80). This notion of the face as commodity highlights Jonson's impression of the snobbery and moral blind-ness in his society, which threatens the view of blood as proof of true nobility's inner virtue as addressed in such plays as *Catiline*.[59] Thus, in response to the commodification of nobility that could undermine the established moral values of his time, Jonson uli-tised, as Annette Drew-Bear and Farah Karim-Cooper have expli-cated, the characters' cosmetic deceit of face-painting in such plays as *Sejanus*, *Catiline*, *Cynthia's Revels*, *Volpone*, *Epicene* and *The Devil's an Ass*.[60] Although Jonson shared the medieval view of 'facial alternation' as 'the devil's attempt to disguise himself to deceive and seduce mankind', he did make use of this image in his comedy 'in a peculiarly Jonsonian way to dramatize pretence in all its forms.'[61] Indeed, face-painting scenes in Jonson's plays are operative for revealing the disguises of characters to the audience. His frequent utilisation of such scenes leads Drew-Bear to conclude that 'no playwright uses cosmetics so extensively as Jonson.'[62] For Jonson, the controversial issue of face-manipulation was more a social phenomenon than a personal moral hazard.

This notion of the face as a topos of the social construction of character is pervasive in Jonson's literary career. In the 'Character' of Fallace in *Every Man Out*, for example, she is described as: 'Deliro's wife and idol, a proud mincing peat, and as perverse as he is officious. She dotes as perfectly upon the courtier as her husband doth on her, and only wants the face to be dishonest' ('Character', 45–7). Fallace's face is her audacity; she keeps her secret because of the absence of the face that manifests her faithless character. In this sense, Fallace's untrustworthy wantonness is rhetorically rep-resented in her concealment of the face which is supposed to show her credibility. Jonson juxtaposes Fallace's perverse nature to her 'officious' husband, Deliro, who is 'of the common council for his wealth' and hence a public figure who deals with the circulation and transference of money ('Character', 36–7). Thus for Fallace and Deliro, the face not only expresses individual inward emotion but also functions as a public place to display, feign, interpret and negotiate.

In this sense, the face is a topos for the malleability of the human subject, and the socially interactive and changeable nature of the human in society. At the beginning of *Sejanus* (1603), on the other hand, Sabinus laments the corruption of the court and tells Silus how their lack of face-shifting skills proves their moral character: 'we are no good engineers; We want the fine arts, and their thriving use / Should make us graced or favoured of the times. / We have no shift of faces, no cleft tongues' (Actus Primus, 4–7). Later in Jonson's literary career, the abuse of the malleability of the face is epitomised in the main character in *The Alchemist* (1612): Face. The ever-shifting nature of Face as a dishonest servant is represented both physically and metaphorically: he puts various faces in front of different characters, and eventually 'loses his face' when his conning plot fails in the end. Thus, in Jonson's works, the need for discerning the typical behaviours of men of certain types was nurtured by the vogue of the anti-social exhibitionism of humours and the counterfeiting use of tropes recognised as gallantry. The commendation of good actions as exemplary and the vituperation of vicious actions as ludicrous found in the comedy of humours, satire and character writing all contributed to the early modern concern with the civilising process.[63]

The awareness of the face as a place to negotiate and share inward self and outward appearance is, of course, not exclusively Jonsonian; it appears in Shakespeare's comedy as well. In *Twelfth Night* (1602), for example, Viola judges the Captain as a person of good character because she sees his 'fair behaviour' (I, ii, 43).[64] This reflects the trust in outwardness as a proof of inner virtue: 'I will believe thou hast a mind that suits / With this thy fair and outward character' (I, ii, 46–7). *As You Like It* (1623) further develops this notion of outward character by making Celia and Rosalind consult about how to disguise themselves in order to escape from court. In response to Celia's suggestion that 'I'll put myself in poor and mean attire, / And with a kind of umber smirch my face' (I, iii, 100–1), Rosalind speaks of her thoughts:

> Were it not better,
> Because that I am more than common tall,
> That I did suit me all points like a man?
> A gallant curtel-axe upon my thigh,
> A boar-spear in my hand, and in my heart,
> Lie there what hidden womans' fear there will.
> We'll have a swashing and a martial outside,
> As many other mannish cowards have
> That do outface it with their semblances.
>
> (I, iii, 103–11)

Facing and outfacing separate the characters of Celia and Rosalind with regard to their understanding of disguise.[65] For Celia, face painting does enough to disguise her character, whereas for the taller Rosalind, she could 'outface' the feigned manliness with a 'semblance' by wearing men's costume and affecting 'a martial outside', which would eventually hold back the emotion of fear in her 'heart'.[66] Yet, Rosalind's plan for her disguise is disrupted by her suitor, Orlando, who seeks her character by waywardly tagging his poems on the trees in the Forest of Arden to 'character' his thought into the barks: 'O Rosalind, these trees shall be my books, / And in their barks my thoughts I'll character, / That every eye which in this forest looks / Shall see thy virtue witnessed everywhere' (III, ii, 5–8).

Trying to establish the public image of Rosalind in the Forest of Arden, Orlando reveals his curious fetishism of her face: 'All the pictures fairest lined / Are but black to Rosalind. / Let no face be kept in mind, / But the fair of Rosalind' (III, ii, 75–8). Torn between the desire to privatise her face in his memory and 'to character' her name and face and make them publicly accessible, Orlando ends the poem by disaggregating Rosalind as a collection of better parts taken from all the human beings in the world: 'Thus Rosalind of many parts / By heavenly synod was devised / Of many faces, eyes, and hearts, / To have the touches dearest prized' (III, ii, 129–32). As his poem unconsciously asserts the public ownership of Rosalind, it ends up being discovered not by Rosalind but by Celia.

Orlando's view of the face as a public space seems to be a response to the scene that precedes the wooing in the forest, in which Duke Senior discovers the status and the person of Orlando when he sees his face:

> If that you were the good Sir Rowland's son,
> As you have whispered faithfully you were,
> And as mine eye doth his effigies witness
> Most truly limned and living in your face,
> Be truly welcome hither. I am the Duke
> That loved your father.
>
> (II, vii, 194–9)

Orlando inherits the noble character of his father in his face, but this is invalid until others activate the recognition. This reminds us of Burns's argument that 'no one can see their face unaided', and therefore 'we are all helplessly in thrall to offered accounts of our identity.'[67] In this sense, the face becomes a topos of the social recognition and realisation of heritable character.

These examples suggests that both Jonson and Shakespeare share an interest in acknowledging the impersonated character as intersubjective and also in prompting the audience to participate in deciphering the character from the face.[68] Just as we discern the emotions of the second self by looking at the expressions of emojis and avatars, reading/representing one's character in a face was a valid social phenomenon in early modern England. Indeed, as Burns claims, character 'is a two-way process' which 'allows a double articulation of character, as a process of seeing, and a process of being seen, as a transaction between two human subjects.'[69] This view of character in terms of the exchange of appearance and gaze explains why Jonson's characters are attracted to public spheres of display, exchange and transaction, such as Paul's Walk in *Every Man Out*, the Market in *Bartholomew Fair* and the Piazza in *Volpone*.[70] As we saw in *As You Like It*, when Celia remakes her identity by smirching the umber on her face, Shakespeare's characters have the ability to reconstitute their virtual selves by actively controlling their expressions and impressions according to the customs of Jacobean society. If Jonson's representation of the 'humours' character was also recurrent in Shakespeare's comedy, we can revise Samuel Johnson's praise of Shakespeare as 'the poet of nature' whose universal 'characters are not modified by the customs of particular places [. . .] by the peculiarities of studies or professions [. . .] or by the accidents of transient fashions or temporary opinions.'[71]

Conclusion

The examples I discussed above bring to light the early modern awareness of the face as a place to negotiate between inward self and outward appearance, and this awareness draws upon the classical rhetorical understanding of personhood and character. Along with writers such as Shakespeare and Overbury, Jonson contributed immensely to the cultural achievement of character writing through his establishment of 'humours' as a literary device and for his rhetorical and dramaturgical representation of characters' faces. By predicating and highlighting the ambivalence of the faces of the characters through the rhetoric of humours, Jonson devoted himself to representing inherently processual persons who gather information and assimilate it based on inferences. While the passive reader, observer and collector of faces lacks a fundamentally fixed self and therefore remains socially mobile and potentially subversive, the active impersonator of characters uses and exploits the split images of their faces in an effect of economic and cultural exchange.[72] It is the contradictory dimension of the face that made it an indispensable tool for Jonson and his contemporaries in developing performative characters.

Notes

1. Erving Goffman, *Behaviour in Public Places: Notes on the Social Organization of Gathering*, p. 5. Some parts of this essay first appeared in Akihiko Shimizu, 'Passions, Acting and Face in Early Modern Characters: An Alternative View on the Avatar', *Integrative Psychological and Behavioral Science* 46 (2012): 569–83. I thank the editors for permission to reuse them.
2. See Anna Bryson, *From Courtesy to Civility: Changing Codes of Conduct in Early Modern England.*
3. Paul Yachnin and Jessica Slights, 'Introduction', in *Shakespeare and Character: Theory, History, Performance, and Theatrical Persons*, p. 3. For other recent work on character, see, for example, Christy Desmet, *Reading Shakespeare's Characters: Rhetoric, Ethics, and Identity*; Lloyd Davis, *Guise and Disguise: Rhetoric and Characterization in the English*; Elizabeth Fowler, *Literary Character: The Human Figure in Early English Writing*; Yu Jin Ko and Michael W. Shurgot (eds), *Shakespeare's Sense of Character: On the Page and from the Stage*; John E. Curran Jr, *Character and the Individual Personality in English Renaissance Drama.*
4. See, Edward Chauncey Baldwin, 'Ben Jonson's Indebtedness to the Greek Character-Sketch'; Edward K. Graham, 'Ben Jonson and the Character-Writers'. For recent criticisms on Jonson and character, see Peter Womack, *Ben Jonson*, Chapter 2; Richard A. McCabe, 'Ben Jonson, Theophrastus, and the Comedy of Humours'; Helen Ostovich, 'Introduction,' in Ben Jonson, *Every Man Out of His Humour*; Ian Donaldson, *Ben Jonson: A Life*, pp. 1–21.
5. Baldwin, 'Ben Jonson's Indebtedness to the Greek Character-Sketch', p. 394; Boyce, Benjamin Boyce, *Theophrastan Character in England to 1642*, pp. 105–8.
6. For recent discussions of Jonson's role in the 'Wars of the Theatres', see Matthew Steggle, *Wars of the Theatres: The Poetics of Personation in the Age of Jonson*; James P. Bednarz, *Shakespeare and the Poets' War*; Edward Gieskes, '"Honesty and Vulger Praise": The Poet's War and the Literary Field'; Charles Cathcart, *Marston, Rivalry, Rapproachment, and Jonson*; Donaldson, *Ben Jonson: A Life*, pp. 150–74; Jay Simons, 'Stinging, Barking, Biting, Purging: Jonson's *Bartholomew Fair* and the Debate on Satire in the Poetmachia'.

7. John Weever, *The Whipping of the Satyre* (London: 1601), sig. A4.
8. Thomas Decker, *The Dramatic Works of Thomas Dekker*, vol. 1, p. 382. On Jonson's reception, see C. H. Herford and Percy Simpson (eds), *Ben Jonson*, Vol. 11, pp. 307–569. Hereafter, the edition is referred to as *H&S*.
9. Thomas Shadwell, 'The Preface' to *The Sullen Lovers: Or, The Impertinents*, in *The Complete Works of Thomas Shadwell*, Vol. 1, p. 11.
10. John Dryden, *Of Dramatick Poesie, an Essay*, pp. 52–3.
11. Samuel Johnson, 'The Preface to Shakespeare' (1765), in *The Yale Edition of the Works of Samuel Johnson*, Vol. 7; Samuel Taylor Coleridge, *Coleridge's Shakespeare Criticism*; A. C. Bradley, *Shakespearean Tragedy: Lectures on Hamlet, Othello, King Lear, Macbeth*; E. M. Forster, *Aspects of the Novel*. On the origin of character criticism, Brian Vickers, 'The Emergence of Character Criticism, 1774–1800'. For Jonson's reception in the Romantic period, see Tom Lockwood, *Ben Jonson in the Romantic Age*.
12. Deidre Shauna Lynch, *The Economy of Characters: Novels, Market Culture, and the Business of Inner Meaning*.
13. Anne Barton, *Ben Jonson, Dramatist*, p. 108.
14. Ibid., p. 110.
15. For a discussion on the development of proto-capitalist culture in late sixteenth-century England, see Richard Halpern, *The Poetics of Primitive Accumulation: English Renaissance Culture and the Genealogy of Capital*.
16. Barton, *Ben Jonson*, p. 108.
17. Ibid., p. 108.
18. Lorna Hutson, *The Invention of Suspicion: Law and Mimesis in Shakespeare and Renaissance Drama*, p. 112. Hutson's summary follows Catherine Belsey's and Alan Sinfield's view of the early modern character.
19. On disguise and Jonson, see Davis, *Guise and Disguise*; Peter Hyland, *Disguise and Role-Playing in Ben Jonson's Drama*; Hyland, *Disguise on the Early Modern Stage*; Kevin A. Quarmby, *The Disguised Ruler in Shakespeare and His Contemporaries*. On impersonation, see Stephen Orgel, *Impersonations: The Performance of Gender in Shakespeare's England*.
20. On Jonson's use of classical rhetorical theory in his character creation, see, for example, Katherine E. Maus, *Ben Jonson and the Roman Frame of Mind*; Womack, *Ben Jonson*, chapter 2.
21. Aristotle, *On Rhetoric: A Theory of Civil Discourse*, p. 41.
22. Ibid., pp. 116–56.
23. Ibid., p. 149.
24. On Theophrastan characters in early modern English literature, see Boyce, *Theophrastan Character in England*; J. M. Smeed, *The Theophrastan Character: The History of a Literary Genre*, pp. 1–46.

25. Womack, *Ben Jonson*, pp. 53–4. See also Boyce, *Theophrastan Character in England*, pp. 16–52.

26. Womack, *Ben Jonson*, pp. 53–4.

27. David Bevington et al. (eds), *Cambridge Edition of Works of Ben Jonson*, Vol. 1, p. 265. Hereafter, all the quotations of Jonson's works are from *CWBJ*.

28. Murray Krieger, *Ekphrasis: The Illusion of the Natural Sign*, pp. 115–42, 196–231.

29. Mack Smith, *Literary Realism and Ekphrasis Tradition*, p. 37. See also Walter Bernhart, 'Functions of Description in Poetry', p. 134.

30. Robert Cockcroft, *Rhetorical Affect in Early Modern Writing: Renaissance Passions Reconsidered*, p. 47. On early modern understanding of *enargeia*, see also Katherine A. Craik, *Reading Sensations in Early Modern England*; Heinrich F. Plett, *Enargeia in Classical Antiquity and the Early Modern Age: The Aesthetics of Evidence*.

31. Womack, *Ben Jonson*, p. 75.

32. See David Kay, *Ben Jonson: A Literary Life*, p. 51.

33. On Jonson's use of Theophrastan character, see McCabe, 'Ben Jonson, Theophrastus, and the Comedy of Humours', pp. 25–37.

34. For a recent study on the use of type characters in Stuart England, see Mario DiGangi, *Sexual Types: Embodiment, Agency, and Dramatic Character from Shakespeare to Shirley*.

35. 'performance, n.,' *OED Online*. Oxford University Press. On Jonson's use of 'performance', see Mary Thomas Crane, 'What Was Performance'.

36. On Jonson's performativity, see James Loxley and Mark Robson, *Shakespeare, Jonson, and the Claims of the Performative*, p. 13. For recent Shakespeare criticisms on performance/performative, see, for example, Robert Weimann, *Author's Pen and Actor's Voice: Playing and Writing in Shakespeare's Theatre*; Barbara Hodgdon, and W. B. Worthen (eds), *A Companion to Shakespeare and Performance*; Bridget Escolme, *Talking to the Audience: Shakespeare, Performance, Self*; David Mann, *Shakespeare's Women: Performance and Conception*; Matthew James Smith, *Performance and Religion in Early Modern England: Stage, Cathedral, Wagon, Street* (Notre Dame: University of Notre Dame Press, 2018); Paul Menzer, 'Character Acting'; Robert Weimann and Douglas Bruster, *Shakespeare and the Power of Performance: Stage and Page in Elizabethan Theatre*; W. B. Worthen, *Shakespeare Performance Studies*.

37. Helen Ostovich, '"To Behold the Scene Full": Seeing and Judging in *Every Man Out of His Humour*', p. 92, n. 11.

38. Smeed, *The Theophrastan Character*, p. 6.

39. Boyce, *Theophrastan Character in England*, p. 54. On this point, see also Jacques Bos, 'Individuality and Inwardness in the Literary Character Sketches of the Seventeenth Century', p. 150.

40. See *H&S*, Vol. 8, p. 663. On Wotton and Jonson, see Donaldson, *Ben Jonson: A Life*, pp. 233, 384–7.

41. On Thomas Coryate's reference to Casaubon in his *Coryats Cruidities* (1611), see Donaldson, *Ben Jonson: A Life*, pp. 298–302; O'Callaghan, Michelle, *The English Wits: Literature and Sociability in Early Modern England*, p. 130.

42. For discussion on the possible contributors, see Donald Beecher, 'Appendix IV', in Overbury, *Characters*, pp. 116–290.

43. Thomas Overbury, *A vvife novv the vvidovv of Sir Thomas Ouerburie Being a most exquisite and singular poeme, of the choyse of a wife. Whereunto are added many witty characters, and conceyted newes; written by himselfe, and other learned gentlemen his friendes*, sigs. S2v–S3r.

44. On the legal meaning of 'real' and 'personal' characters with regards to immovable (real) and movable (personal) property, see Edward Burns, *Character: Acting and Being on the Pre-Modern Stage*, p. 124. On Jonson's special interest in Horace, see Stanley Stewart, 'Jonson's Criticism'; Victoria Moul, *Jonson, Horace and the Classical Tradition*.

45. David Wiles, *Theatre and Citizenship: The History of a Practice*, p. 55.

46. As Boyce argues, decorum as an art of finding the fit style to the subject was an indispensable part of rhetorical education. See *Theophrastan Character in England*, pp. 26–36, 47–52, 113.

47. On the rhetoric of wit, see Adam Zucker, *The Places of Wit in Early Modern English Comedy*, pp. 1–22.

48. Burns, *Character*, p. 3. For Jonson's acknowledgement of Plutarch's comparison between poetry and painting, see *Disc.*, 1074–82.

49. 'face, n.,' *OED Online*. Oxford University Press.

50. On *decorum*, *ethopoesis* and character making, see Davis, *Guise and Disguise*, p. 6. For Jonson's sonnet, see *CWBJ*, Vol. 2, p. 501.

51. Ibid., p. 501.

52. On the relationship of *ethos*, *pathos* and *mores* to emotion, see Quintilian, *The Orator's Education*, 6.3.8–31, pp. 49–61. Hereafter, the reference to *Insitutio Oratoria* is from this edition. On dramatic use of *enargeia* and *narratio*, see Hutson, *The Invention of Suspicion*, chapter 3.

53. On Quintilian's interest in the pragmatic uses of *enargeia*, particularly in politico-legal orations to display evidence, see Brian Vickers, *In Defence of Rhetoric*, pp. 76–8.

54. On active impersonation of character and Quintilian, see Davis, *Guise and Disguise*, pp. 6–7, 30–5.

55. All my quotes from *Cynthia's Revels* are from the Quarto version in *CWBJ*, Vol. 1.

56. Beecher, 'Introduction', in Overbury, *Characters*, ed. Beecher, p. 53.

57. *CWBJ*, Vol. 1, p. 481, note to line 120.

58. Matthew James Smith points out the increase of performative characters 'who really believe their passions to be essential to their existence' in the early modern period, whose 'misidentification of the self' marks an ontological shift which makes sincerity and self-coherence 'a point

of dramatic conflict'. See Smith, 'w/Sincerity, Part I: The Drama of the Will from Augustine to Milton', p. 23.

59. See, for example, Blair Worden, 'Politics in *Catiline*: Jonson and his Sources'.
60. Annette Drew-Bear, 'Face-Painting Scenes in Ben Jonson's Plays'; Farah Karim-Cooper, *Cosmetics in Shakespearean and Renaissance Drama*, Ch. 5.
61. Annette Drew-Bear, *Painted Faces on the Renaissance Stage: The Moral Significance of Face-Painting Conventions*, pp. 35, 81.
62. Drew-Bear, 'Face-Painting Scenes in Ben Jonson's Plays', p. 401.
63. On the early modern civilising process, see Norbert Elias, *The Civilizing Process*; Bryson, *From Courtesy to Civility*.
64. William Shakespeare, all citations of Shakespeare are from *The New Oxford Shakespeare: Modern Critical Edition*, ed. Gary Taylor et al., and are cited in the text by act, scene and line numbers.
65. For a discussion of outfacing, see Bruce Smith's essay in this volume.
66. *OED* defines 'outface, *v.*' 3.a. as 'To maintain (something false or shameful) with boldness or effrontery; to brazen out'.
67. Burns, *Character*, p. 130.
68. See Leanore Lieblein, 'Embodied Intersubjectivity and the Creation of Early Modern Character'.
69. Burns, *Character*, p. 2.
70. On the site of exchange in seventeenth-century London, see Linda Levy Peck, *Consuming Splendor: Society and Culture in Seventeenth-Century England*, pp. 188–229; James Mardock, *Our Scene is London: Ben Jonson's City and the Space of the Author*; Julie Sanders, *The Cultural Geography of Early Modern Drama, 1620–1650*, pp. 133–77.
71. Johnson, *The Yale Edition of the Works of Samuel Johnson*, Vol. 7, p. 62.
72. In this sense, my approach to Jonsonian character shares its perspective with Lynch who aimed to 'address character's changing conditions of legibility' throughout eighteenth- and nineteenth-century England. See Deidre Shauna Lynch, *The Economy of Character*, p. 1.

Chapter 10

Hamlet's Face

W. B. Worthen

Petrification

I want to open with a scene from *Hamlet*: Lars Eidinger crouching downstage right, projecting his image in video on a beaded curtain dividing the upstage banquet table from the downstage thrust dirt-box that forms the principal playing area of Thomas Ostermeier's production, still in rep at the Schaubühne in Berlin (premiere 2008) (Figure 10.1). Jan Kott's Hamlet of 'late autumn, 1956, read only newspapers',[1] and Hamlet today is typically involved in the inter-mediality of performance, perhaps even the digital remediation of theatre. Of course, Hamlet was always fascinated by the media of recording – the 'Words, words, words' of the book he uses to torment Polonius – and by the media of display as well, clothing, gesture, games and the stage. As Mark Poster notes, the body 'is configured in its practices', positioned 'in relation to material objects, machines, other humans', perhaps nowhere as significantly as in the theatre.[2] *Hamlet* evokes the technicity of theatre, where the theatrical body is always already technologised; in the theatre, the actor's body is always a body in acting.

In theatre today, then, digital projection takes its place in an already reflexively remediating space, one which works 'to remind the viewer of the medium'.[3] After all, Eidinger's massive face is hardly unique as an emblem of *Hamlet*. From Ethan Hawke filming himself, other characters, and sampled files in Michael Almereyda's 2000 film to David Tennant toying around with his film camera in the *Mousetrap* scene in Greg Doran's 2008 RSC production, Hamlet in the new century occupies the intersection of the mediatised and the mediated, the fond records of digital record-ing and the apparent – and perhaps only apparent – immediacy of liveness.

Figure 10.1 Lars Eidinger, left, as Hamlet in *Hamlet*, dir. Thomas Ostermeier, Schaubühne, Berlin. Photo Credit: © Arno Declair.

The contemporary theatre's incorporation of recording and projection technology is part of the theatre's ongoing intermedial development, an important historical dimension of the theatre as technology.[4] In several books, Bernard Stiegler explores the negotiated, dynamic relation between the agencies of the human and the technical, between the *who* and the *what* – 'the one, bio-anthropological, the other, techno-logical' – in which 'the dynamic of the *who* itself redoubles that of the *what*: conditioned *by* the *what*, it is equally conditional *for* it.[5] In the theatre the *who* is a function of technological mediation, and like other productions, Ostermeier's *Hamlet* suggests a complex, theatrical version of the dialectic between the technologised externality of acting and the apparition of identity it creates or gestures toward, between the *what* of the mask and the *who* of the face.

Eidinger's double, doubly mediated face throws into relief the ethical charge of contemporary theatrical technicity, a problematic that can be, albeit delicately, associated with Emmanuel Levinas. Though Peggy Phelan asks whether 'the face-to-face encounter' of the theatre '*might* speak to philosophy with renewed vigor', it can do so only from the eccentric, provisional, vanishing point of the theatre's particular technologies of mediation.[6] There are any number of reasons to resist an easy assimilation of the casually interactive relations of the theatre to the ethical mystery of Levinas's encounter with the Other, not least the sense in which the Other demands a response that seems 'infinite', to go beyond the aesthetic warrant of theatre, to awaken us, as Judith Butler suggests, 'to what is precarious in another life or, rather, the precariousness of life itself'.[7] The relations of theatre are always mediated, conditional and conditioned by a rich sociability, a sociability in which to *see* is precisely to be protected from the *seen*, the *scene*.[8] The dynamic dependence of the actor's (and the spectator's) face on technologised embodiment seems to militate against the more absolute encounter with the *face* demanded by Levinas's sense of that encounter.[9]

What I want to consider here is the possibility that Levinas's meditation, while perhaps misleading about stage acting, nonetheless provides a perspective on one challenge essential to theatricality and, in different ways, to the technicity of performance: the technology of the face, a technology which is not analogous to the mask but is the technology of the mask itself. Levinas is notably dubious about the ethical claims of art, a resistance in which the theatre figures prominently and negatively. In 'Reality and Its Shadow', Levinas describes artforms as complicit in a gesture – 'art consists in substituting for the object its image'[10] – which, as Jill Robbins puts it, encodes Levinas's objection 'to the possibility of theatrical representation itself',[11] especially what Levinas calls in 'Persons or Figures', 'the petrification of our faces', arising from acting as though one were 'on the stage'.[12] In 'Reality and Its Shadow', Levinas illustrates the hold of the image on the reader in strikingly physiological, performance-like terms, as a function of *rhythm*, which 'represents a unique situation where we cannot speak of consent, assumption, initiative or freedom, because the subject is caught up and carried away by it', becoming the rhythm, 'part of its own representation', even while recognising that 'in rhythm there is no longer a oneself, but rather a sort of passage from oneself to anonymity'. Rhythm takes up, grooms and governs the subject to its beat, '*involving*', identifying the subject '*among* things which should have had only the status of objects': the subject, then, 'is among things as a thing, as part of the spectacle. It is exterior to itself.'[13] When the world-as-imaged touches us rhythmically, 'musically', it engages 'sensation free from all conception, that famous sensation that eludes introspection, appeared with images'.[14] Much as the Puritan anti-theatrical pamphleteer Stephen Gosson wrote in 1579, images 'ravish the sense', rather than appealing to conceptualising reason.[15] The image displaces the order of the real, becoming something fixed, a statue or a mask, or, with all that this word entails for Levinas, an idol,[16] and in its rhythmic grasp on the reader or spectator, it thingifies the subject as well. Spectators are 'prisoners', immobilised outside the channels of ethical contact.[17]

Rendering the real as a 'spectacle', Levinas's art transforms potentially ethical relations into empty, theatrical ones. The resemblance through which even poetry 'bewitches our gestures' and so prevents ethical recognition is dangerous precisely in its likeness to the experience of seeing acting.[18] Any person 'bears on his face, alongside of its being, with which he coincides, its own caricature, its picturesqueness'.[19] This *picturesqueness* (which seems to mean something like its ability to be imitated, to be reproduced as *resemblance*, *caricature*, the fixed features of a concealing mask), like an actor, both is 'the person and is the thing'. And since this caricature, this mask 'is what it is and it is a stranger to itself', the face in its auto-caricature both 'reveals itself in its truth, and, at the same time, it resembles its own image'.[20] In this regard, then, even as 'the very structure of the sensible as such',[21] resemblance threatens our captivity to a petrified 'lesser world, of appearances only',[22] a shadow seized as an idol, a statue out of time, addressed in sensation but not through conception.

Nonetheless, as *Hamlet* perhaps argues, theatre, like social life, can only articulate, approximate, remediate ethical relations through its distinctive technicity, its fashioning of encounters with others whose faces are attentive, attention seeking, made and remade as theatrical, faces exposed to one another as the masks they are and as strangers to themselves. Nicholas Ridout observes that it is precisely 'around the ethical, aesthetic and political problems of such encounters that the wrongness of theatre appears and organizes itself';[23] these encounters are organised through the specific technical dimensions of performance. The encounter with the *face* of the Other is also mediated, an act of interlocution facilitated by speech, which in Levinas's thinking both 'proceeds from absolute difference' and 'cuts across vision', presumably the seductive vision that display shares with picturesque caricature.[24] 'For the face to operate as a face', Judith Butler remarks, 'it must vocalize or be understood as the workings of a voice'.[25] The encounter with the *face* requires a proximity that is ethical rather than purely spatial; and yet, insofar as Levinas's conception of the recognition of the Other requires speech, discourse, it also requires spatial and temporal mediation, which restates the dialectic between fixity and changeability, between the known and the immanent, between what Levinas calls the *said* or the *already said* ('a fixity of assertions and relations') and the *saying*, 'a continuous interaction that remains open to change and difference'.[26]

For Levinas, then, theatre appears to hollow out the scene of *saying*, to transform the conceptualising force of the ethical encounter with the *face* of the Other to the illusory subjection to the petrified picturesqueness of the actor's phiz. The ethical etiolation of the theatre's faciality recalls a symmetry with the claims of another theorist of action also gesturally removed from, and inextricably bound to, the stage. I am thinking, of course, of J. L. Austin's famous remark that

> a performative utterance will, for example, be *in a peculiar way* hollow or void if said by an actor on the stage, or if introduced in a poem, or spoken in soliloquy. [. . .] Language in such circumstances is in special ways – intelligibly – used not seriously, but in ways *parasitic* upon its normal use – ways which fall under the doctrine of the *etiolations* of language.[27]

Austin is instructive here. Austin's performative acts are, in the theatre, hollow *in a peculiar way*, but they also have force in ways *peculiar* to the theatre, too. After all, performatives do *do things* onstage, conditioned, as all performatives are, by the scene and conventions – what Austin calls the 'procedures' – of their utterance, here the double scene of dramatic and theatrical performativity. An actor making a promise 'in character' represents a promise that is liable to all the ills of any promise *in the fictive world of the play*. Think of the threatening chill of Prince Hal's promise in *1 Henry IV*: 'I do. I will' (II, v, 394).[28] But Austin is worried about the interface between two performative frames, the dramatic and the theatrical. When the character promises 'I love you', or perhaps that 'Thy husband is thy lord, thy life, thy keeper', perhaps the two actors are in love, so the *saying* has a coy double force, the dramatic action working to enable and complicate a non-dramatic performative (animating the pleasure of seeing well-known couples playing romantic comedies, Richard Burton and Elizabeth Taylor in *The Taming of the Shrew*, or friends like John Gielgud and Ralph Richardson – or, more recently, Ian McKellan and Patrick Stewart – verbally fencing in Harold Pinter's *No Man's Land*). In the theatrical frame, delivering the line 'I love you' while craftily upstaging one's scene partner, the actor's 'I love you' might actually perform 'I own you', or 'I can't stand you', or 'I'll show *you!*' to the other actor, an act that the merest glance between them will drive home, make happen *for them*, but not perhaps for the audience, who are outside the structure of that performative utterance. This promise will have force as a performative utterance, a force that's unusual – if it is unusual – only in being distinct from the semantic value of the words it uses. Much as the repetitive structure of the theatrical conditions the possibility of the performative (from which Austin nervously attempted to exclude it), the forms of ethical encounter may share some reciprocity with the complexity of faciality in the theatre. To seize this opportunity requires an attention less to the *said* than to the *saying, how* the potential for encounter is structured by the technicities of theatre, the technicities *peculiar to theatre*.[29]

What an utterance performs as a *saying* – or perhaps as an *acting* – to spectators is conceptually rich in the theatre in ways that simply exceed the discourse of the *said*, the text. Making that theatrical complex of events take place is what *acting* does with the *said* of the dramatic script, using it to frame a mobile, active relation to a theatre audience. As Robbins suggests, though, Levinas is opposed to figuration, in which to 'represent the rapport between persons is to "freeze" it', turning 'what ought to be an ethical relationship into a theatrical pageant'.[30] This choice of terms precisely captures how Levinas reductively misrepresents the interactivity of performance, petrifying it as the frozen tableaux of the pageant, an emblem, much as Austin sees theatre as a parasite on the ordinary circumstances of utterance rather than as its distinctive (and for Derrida determining) case. When Levinas notes that 'We can attend to the puppet in the personages of a tragedy', he expresses an insensitivity to how theatre conceptualises, thinks *through* its embodied participants, and how they change in their dynamic tactics of embodiment, or if you like, their peculiar means of participating in the staging of some kind of other.[31] Like actors, puppets move – they are not statues – and are animated by the attribution of the performers' own bodily delicacy, their nuanced expression of bodily being in the world to the puppets' attitudes, postures, movements; as Tzachi Zamir remarks of actors, 'bits and pieces' of body language are '*given over*' to the puppet.[32]

The marionette tossed in a corner is a tangle of string and sticks; suspended from the hands of the puppeteer, it remediates and so extends the puppeteer's human, physical tact and dexterity. In many forms of puppet theatre, *bunraku* for example, the puppeteer and his virtuosity remain fully visible. The role of Hamlet is a string of verse, a set of marked-up pages, perhaps a few audio files and PDFs on an iPad, stashed in a backpack in the dressing room; in the theatre it becomes the instrument of the actor's work, part of what he or she is doing in the play, before and with other actors, before and with the audience as well. Not a statue in sight: the ethical encounter of the theatre is mediated by the forms, moods and shapes of its contemporary theatricality.

I am trying to read Levinas against himself, for what his work might open for our thinking about the thinking of theatrical technicity, possibilities he surely never intended, perhaps in part because his understanding of theatre was so fully channelled by a richly antitheatrical tradition, in which acting is not a form of *doing* but a making of images, statues, idols, a tradition which perhaps screens out the possibility for the articulation of the *face* in the mask of the Other.[33] With regard to Austin, while the duplicity of theatre cannot be either dismissed or directly aligned with 'ordinary' performativity, it might be said that the performativity of acting is not so much void as *peculiar* in and to the stage. In the theatre, the ethical dynamics, the dynamics of the *face* and the Other, are similarly not so much the imposition of a statuesque and imprisoning idolatry as a suggestive relationality in which those terms are *peculiarly* operative: the person and the thing, intellectual and sensory apprehension, a structure in which participants are what they are and are rendered as strangers to themselves and especially to us. Much as theatrical performatives are, in their own way, *peculiar*, so the face-to-face encounter in the theatre is 'compromised' in specific ways, perhaps, as Ridout implies, nearly reversing the dynamics of the performative: 'Something fails to take place amid what does take place.'[34] Theatrical performance evokes a peculiar *faciality* peculiar to the theatre.

The mask is part of the mediality of theatre though different theatres technologise it in different ways: to that extent, theatre can perhaps never seize the nakedness of the Other, but only what Pirandello thought of as the nakedness of the mask. And yet while for Levinas treating the *face* as an image 'is to turn it into a caricature, frozen, petrified, a mask', an inherent act of violence,[35] the theatre's potentially *facialising* technology, *acting*, depends precisely on the assertion and the failure of this caricature, its failure to petrify, so to speak: we never really *see* Macbeth or Desdemona, after all. The virtuosity of acting is always visible, its *caricature* mask or role never really obscures the actor and so provides the condition of our engagement with each other: it is what it is and is also a stranger to itself. In performance, while the mask may seem to petrify the image of a face, it actually does something quite different, articulating its other, an abyss that it conceals, reveals, mystifies and summons into view. Like the puppet evoking a vitality which it expresses but cannot inhabit, the actor's mask, whether literal or not, 'is always there to create the contrastive nudity' of something else, a nudity, depth, talent construed by the mask itself.[36]

Acting is a technological process of using the mask to disclose an other who is also the actor as an other, an actor, someone making something. The actor's face both exceeds and falls short of the idol of picturesque caricature, of 'character'. Perhaps, as a prosthetic of the human, acting constitutes the human by showing its failure to be what it shows: the technicity of acting constitutes a human by asserting what ritually evades it. As Butler remarks of Levinas, 'For representation to convey the human, then, representation must not only fail, but it must *show* its failure'.[37] While the realist theatre tends to privilege the actor's 'disappearance' into the character, this impossible vanishing act sustains the showing off that is always visibly part of acting, part of what is attractive and sometimes offputting about acting, a virtuosity that drives the appetite for the spectacle of acting as a technology of difference, of showing, not concealing.[38] The technology of acting is, in the theatre, always visible: it's what people love, and some people don't, about, say, Meryl Streep.

While not the *face* of the Other, the mask of the actor nonetheless evokes an ethical complexity of seizing a face, the ceaseless interplay between what Butler calls 'humanization and dehumanization' that characterises the domain of representation.[39] This ceaseless interaction is shaped differently by different theatres historically, and shaped differently today by different technologies, different forms of mediation. Theatrical acting is sustained by the body, film acting is the art of the face; theatrical acting, embodied acting, is an art of addition, the display of skill, film acting is the art of subtraction, of nonchalance, of stepping back, of letting the camera do the work of finding what the face might say, which is, in the end, what the face says.

Perhaps Ostermeier's *Hamlet* registers the disjunction between the theatrically mediated body and the cinematically mediated face. And yet even this distinction tends, instructively enough, to evaporate, as when Levinas describes the shape and posture of women waiting in line in Vassili Grossman's *Life and Fate*, their 'particular way of craning their neck and their back, their raised shoulders with shoulder blades tense like springs, which seemed to cry, sob, and scream', seemed to become a *face*.[40] As Butler remarks here, the body becomes a face, and the face, 'if we are to put words to its meaning, will be that for which no words really work; the face seems to be a kind of sound, the sound of language evacuating its sense, the sonorous substratum of vocalization that precedes and limits the delivery of any semantic sense'.[41] A speaking as *saying* that transcends the *said*, recalling another face, one not quite seen, or not seen clearly, a face that emerges as not quite a face, 'all body like gone', just a Mouth babbling from the dark, speaking something that swells briefly into 'words', at least into 'certain vowel sounds'; refusing to be identified with them, she, it, merely a mouth, recedes again into the muttering dark. There was 'nothing she could tell' after all.[42] It's perhaps not surprising that the theatre finds something approaching – and evacuating – Levinas's *face* in Beckett, who deploys a precisely technologised set of bodily relations: actress bound and blindfolded, audience across the proscenium, also in the dark, eyes fixed on that flickering spot. The machine of *Not I* precisely stages a rigorous attention to the possibility of perceiving that evanescent Other through the modern theatre's technologies of relation. *What? Who?*

If, as I am suggesting, the actor's face is a *peculiar* application of Levinasian relations in a *way peculiar to* theatre, how might we use the specific technicity of contemporary theatre to ask how the mediating technologies of the face pose an ethical question, and pose it between the body and the screen?

Facing screening

Ostermeier's *Hamlet* is drastically cut, and unusually reliant on the physicality of his Hamlet, Lars Eidinger. Eidinger is a peculiar presence: tall, lean, energetic and unpredictable, not least because of his relatively deadpan expression.[43] Moreover, this *Hamlet* foregrounds Eidinger's relation to the house: he speaks to and confides in the audience, spends a good section of the *Mousetrap* scene clambering around in the seats. He is clothed and naked; he puts on a fatsuit; he is splattered with mud; he clowns around in the duel scene; he eats mud. And his face is projected: he is here and there, small and large, embodied and screened, remediated and, well, remediated.

In many respects, Ostermeier's *Hamlet* evokes a relatively traditional modern sense of theatre technicity. At the Schaubühne, at least, the house is dark, the audience seated on a steeply raked set of risers facing the stage, the ideological relations of the modern theatre, the spectator's 'invisible' privacy insisting on a more internalised experience, a concentration not on the contagious spectacle infecting the other faces in the house, but on the signification of the actor's – or the character's – face as the constitutive object of aesthetic experience. Of course, the spectators' faces are always visible to the actors, a fact that this *Hamlet* explores in several ways: by turning the camera on the audience (the image projected on the upstage bead curtain) and notably in the long *Mousetrap* scene in which Hamlet (Player Queen) and Horatio (Player King) strip to their underwear (Eidinger in heels, stockings, aviator sunglasses and a blonde wig, resembling Gertrude), don cardboard crowns and climb around among the seated spectators, engaging in an extensive improvisation, their mostly naked, sweaty, dirty bodies at work on and through the house. The assertion of the spectators' ethical absence from the spectacle, a distinctive dimension of the design and spatial rhetoric of modern theatre, is compromised in this production, as the actors go well beyond 'original practices' of quipping to and leering at the audience – though Eidinger does plenty of that, too: '"Leave me alone", he orders Rosencrantz and Guildenstern. "I have to deliver a monologue now."'[44] On one occasion, a spectator during a performance at the Schaubühne got up politely during the show and carefully made her way down the side aisle to the exit. Eidinger stopped and addressed her, asking where she was going (the toilet), how long she would be, saying that we would wait. And wait we did, while he stood quietly, for the most part, gazing around the house, occasionally commenting to a couple of elderly women in the front row, who audibly complained about the delay. It's an illustrative moment: as Ridout suggests in his analysis of stage fright and embarrassment, the woman here is 'locked in a structure' in which she is summoned for a face-to-face encounter in which she can only be as she appears, distinguished from Eidinger who, commanding the house, has the many forms of amplified appearance at his control. The moment of address stages the theatrical power of the actor's virtuoso disappearance, while confining her to a single apparition, her face frozen in the mask of shame.[45]

This corrosive *Hamlet* foregrounds what is usually seen as the purchase of *liveness* in the theatre, in which the actor's physical work articulates with a sense of surrender to the audience, a surrender that – in the relations of modern theatricality – the audience sees but cannot really acknowledge in a Levinasian sense: it's up there, but we are here, removed from responsibility for our purchased line of sight by the conventional aesthetics of this mode of (theatrical) production. Symbolic distance etiolates ethical proximity. Eidinger's performance marks the different kind of access – or non-access, failed access, illusory access – promised by theatrical acting. A relation and a means to relation, the performance is like Levinas's *face* to the extent that it coordinates, intermittently at least, a moment of seeing as a moment of undecidable, if modest, precarity – what else might he/they/it do? to me? to himself? to himself for me? It's not so much that Eidinger is *live* but that he is working, physically making the performance on and with the public, sometimes seeming to hang back 'in' the scene, 'in' character, sometimes seeming to step out, step closer, more proximally, though even that language underscores the utter inadequacy of our critical language here, our ways of accounting of what the actor does (with and through the role). It is work. In *Hamlet,* the actors are also stagehands: they push the trestle stage forward and back; they point a water hose in the air, making the 'rain' that transforms Old Hamlet's funeral (with which the evening begins) into a sodden mess. It may be stage mud, but it's mud nonetheless, covering, marking, entering Eidinger's body, perhaps most audaciously when he eats it, sticking out his brown tongue to the camera.

While Eidinger's physical performance ranges from the moribund to the manic, his projected face strikes a different relation to the public, a void gesture of relation, of seeing, the faciality of 'character' as a thing. When Eidinger thrusts a fistful of mud into his mouth, everyone gasps, but I don't think we gasp at the projected image upstage, for even in live-feed, the video face is already a record, a petrified caricature, a replayable playing of 'Hamlet'; as Lyn Gardner shrewdly notes, the 'more he stares into the camera, the more he disappears'.[46] In the intermediality specific to Ostermeier's *Hamlet,* acting and video assert different forms of relation between actor and spectator: the screen provides 'information' – about the face we see in great and subtle, entirely unnatural detail – that is not responsive to us, however much we respond to it; it is, perhaps, more akin to Levinas's image. Eidinger's face registers our reaction. And yet while Richard Hornby remarks that a mud-eating Hamlet is 'obviously not a Hamlet we could identify with', Hamlet (whether we identify with him or not, whether theatre is a medium for identification) is never in our vicinity.[47] Perhaps we are more proximate to Eidinger, caught, arrested by an act of physical work that vividly figures the humanising/dehumanising moment of the actor's maskey face.

The Ostermeier *Hamlet* can be profitably contrasted with another production, Toneelgroep Amsterdam's 2007 *Roman Tragedies,* directed by Ivo van Hove. This production, which combines shortened versions of *Coriolanus, Julius Caesar* and *Antony and Cleopatra* into one intermissionless performance, occupies the technological interface of the contemporary *mise-en-scène* in a distinctive manner.

Figure 10.2 *The Roman Tragedies*, Brooklyn Academy of Music. Photo: W. B. Worthen.

When *Roman Tragedies* is staged in a theatre, at the outset – in some venues at least – the audience watches the play from the auditorium. The actors perform mainly downstage before what looks like a cross between an airport lounge and a modern hotel bar behind them: there is in fact a bar stage left, makeup stations for the actors stage right, and a labyrinth of modular sofas and seats, grouped 'conversation-ally' around a panoply of flat-screen monitors, on which the actors' live performances are simultaneously broadcast (Figure 10.2).[48]

Above this corporate, interchangeable, modular, nowhere space, a large screen hosts a live Twitter feed on which audiences, presum-ably on their phones, engage, review, comment on the production and on one another; when no one is speaking onstage, the supertitle bar is also accessible for live commentary from a bank of laptops stage left. At various points in the evening, the audience is invited to leave the auditorium, occupying this vast upstage area. What hap-pens then is fascinating. Sometimes the actors enter the space, acting alongside the spectators but markedly not interacting with them; sometimes the actors do not spatially reorient their performance and act from the front of the stage out across the proscenium to the variably empty house. To the public getting drinks, bumping into friends and colleagues, gathering around the flatscreens, socially mediatising, the live is almost always over there: it has its back to us, not facing us at all, except on the screens. As an instance, an allegory of the ethical relations of theatre today, *Roman Tragedies*, perhaps like the Wooster Group *Hamlet*, poses the actor's face as more directly accessible through the mask of mediatisation. Here, though, the production seems to imply that the fault is not in our stars, or our smartphones, but in ourselves that it is thus: we choose to go onstage, to 'see' the performance in live-feed video rather than full-size and in the flesh. At a performance in New York in 2012 I was reminded of Pieter Breughel's *Landscape with the Fall of Icarus*. Caught up in the attractions of our world – the infinitely reproduced sofa and manufactured flatscreen replacing the plowman's furrow, the sailing ship, the flock of sheep, the horse's behind, all gathered in the newly discovered excitement of a realist painterly medium, a surface seen from an immersive, drone-like perspective we seem to share with airborne Daedalus – caught up in that surface, we, too, ignore the spectacular, embodied tragedy in flight, catching it perhaps only from the corner of an eye, as we scope out a seat, attention flitting around the crowd onstage.

The spatiality of *Roman Tragedies* bears directly on its framing of theatrical, and ethical relations. Rather than a scene of ethical engagement, the production feels to some people just like 'wandering and participation' which becomes 'both fragmented and passive',[49] while for others, the enforced or invited summons to occupy the space of performance denied 'audience members' the 'comfort of the outsider's perspective and the illusion of interpretive closure'.[50] But what this range suggests from a Levinasian perspective is perhaps an alternative observation having to do with the disjunction of ethical and spatial proximity. The ability to see the face (usually difficult in the theatre) is a function of its mediation, of the conventions through which a given form of mediation asserts *immediacy*, thereness, *proximity*. Eidinger seems to evacuate the face onscreen, which is nonetheless absorbing, while his manic liveness articulates a proximity that nonetheless refuses identification, signifying the theatrical dimension of Levinas's ethics too: the other remains other. The traditional proscenium stage perhaps guarantees an interpretive closure that's false from the perspective of an immersive aesthetic, but that – within its own perspective, inscribed in an ideological structure of representation reaching back to Giotto if not to Vitruvius – marks the distance required to seize the actor's face in a meaningful, mediated *relation*.

For this reason, perhaps like the Wooster Group, what *Roman Tragedies* stages is not a dialectic between true and false faces, enacted and imagined, mobile and petrified, the Other and merely distracting others. *Roman Tragedies* illustrates the notion that mediation is all we have, and that the projected close-up does provide 'information', something like the actor's headshot, a moment of complex intermedial proximity that *we* – and I mean *us*, here and now – are learning to negotiate, much as the nineteenth-century technicity of proscenium frontality eventually required a different technology of acting, the complex, proximal distance of Stanislavsky's 'public solitude'. I think one word captures this unsettled, mediated proximity for us today, though it's a word that originates in the nineteenth-century, too: tweet.

Theatre offers the space for a certain kind of meditation on medial relations, on the different forms of proximity theatrical performance enables. I want to close with a pendant image from the Wooster Group *Hamlet*. The Wooster *Hamlet* transpires in a fully mediatised space, littered with screens and cameras. Its central *gestus* – re-enacting the 1964 Gielgud-Burton Electronovision film, live-degraded during the Wooster performance – overtly locates acting in a dialogue with recorded and recording media, much as Scott Shepherd/Hamlet is in dialogue with the booth throughout the evening, and all actors physically reproduce the movements and intonations of the actors in the film projected upstage. Just moments before the end of the performance, Laertes – in both the Wooster action and on the screen of the Gielgud/Burton film running upstage – helps the wounded, dying Hamlet to a chair, where he slumps, eventually closing his eyes. In the Wooster production, Scott Shepherd sits, eyes open, then closes his eyes, while the video screen upstage freezes on a shot with his eyes open. It's a complex moment, the live video at once recording and stopping, petrifying the action, and also interrupting the seriality between film and live performance. Whose face is active here? Hamlet's face, Shepherd's live face, eyes closed, or Shepherd's screen face, slightly larger than life-size, eyes open, a recorded image of the very recent past? Which is the ethically petrified, idolatrous mask, and which the ethically rewarding face? In one sense, it seems that the audience is summoned by the recording, which, in whatever qualified a manner, seems to 'see' us when the actor does not. After a few seconds, Shepherd's eyes close on the screen as well, and then both the large screen of the Burton film and the small screen of the live video fade to snow. Then both screens fade out, leaving Shepherd/Hamlet seated in a dim pool of light. Then, just before the blackout – so close to the blackout that it's hard to capture – Shepherd/Hamlet opens his eyes, and, as Beckett might have put it '*fixes the audience*' (*Catastrophe*; Beckett 1986: 461), a *look* that lasts less than a second, perhaps less than that, a look in which the actor *sees us*, or seems to ('Am I as much as being seen?').[51] In the decomposing stage of the Wooster Group, a feedback between histories, instruments, media and performances, *Hamlet* ends on a signal moment: the actor *looks* and seems to create, or to invite, or merely to stage, a moment of ethical obligation, a moment sustained by, defined by, *this* overwrought apparatus, a moment of the evanescent face beyond the masks of Hamlet.[52]

Notes

1. Jan Kott, 'Hamlet of the Mid-Century', p. 68
2. Mark Poster, 'Desiring Information and Machines', p. 87.
3. Jay David Bolter, and Richard Gruisin, *Remediation: Understanding New Media*, p. 272.
4. See Mark B. N. Hansen's brief but illuminating discussion in '"New Media"', pp. 176–7.
5. Bernard Stiegler, *Technics and Time, 2: Disorientation*, p. 7.
6. Peggy Phelan, 'Marina Abamović: Witnessing Shadows', p. 577. My emphasis.
7. Judith Butler, *Precarious Life: The Powers of Mourning and Violence*, p. 132. For a sceptical perspective on the assimilation of Levinas to theatre, see Alan Read, *Theatre, Intimacy and Engagement*, p. 227 and Nicholas Ridout, *Theatre and Ethics*, pp. 54–5, as well as a more watered-down version in Helena Grehan, *Performance, Ethics and Spectatorship in a Global Age*, p. 31. My sincere thanks to Hana Worthen for inspiring this engagement with Levinas, for suggesting this text, and for the discipline of her example.
8. As Nicholas Ridout observes, the stage often works to protect its spectators from the means of production itself, as when actors in the modern Stanislavskian tradition 'are paid to produce, in the perspective stage and through the tools of psychological illusionism' the 'fully rounded autonomous character, rich with the complex subjectivity which is the birthright of bourgeois subjective autonomy', a structure which precisely conceals the 'means of production: we see plays, not work.' See Ridout, *Stage Fright, Animals, and Other Theatrical Problems*, p. 100.

9. Wade suggests that theatrical representation 'may enact violence upon otherness by "fitting" the Other to the theatrical frame' – as, for instance, may be the case in the representation of women in theatres (classical Greek, early modern English) in which playwrights and performers are all male. See Leslie A. Wade, 'Sublime Trauma: The Violence of Ethical Encounter', p. 16.

10. Emmanuel Levinas, 'Reality and Its Shadow', p. 3.

11. Jill Robbins, *Altered Reading: Levinas and Literature*, p. 50. My thanks to Hana Worthen for bringing this text to my attention.

12. Emmanuel Levinas, 'Persons or Figures', p. 121. In *Altered Reading*, Jill Robbins makes a detailed case for Levinas's antipathy to art, in which the 'petrification of the face' would be 'a violence directed *at* the face'. See *Altered Reading*, p. 49.

13. Levinas, 'Reality and Its Shadow', p. 4

14. Ibid., p. 5.

15. Although Levinas speaks specifically of literature and painting, his own theatrical vocabulary re-enacts familiar tropes of anti-theatrical discourse, not least the notion that theatre sets forth, as Stephen Gosson put it in his 1579 *Schoole of Abuse*, 'straunge consortes of melody, to tickle the eare; costly apparel, to flatter the sight; effeminate gesture, to rauish the sence; and wanton speache, to whet desire too inordinate lust', sensations which are not 'ended in outward sense', but 'by the priuie entries of the eare, slip downe into the hart, & with gunshotte of affection gaule the minde, where reason and virtue should rule the roste.' See Stephen Gosson, *The Schoole of Abuse, Conteining a plesaunt inuectiue against Poets, Pipers, Plaiers, Iesters, and such like Caterpillers of a Comonwelth*, B6r–B7r.

16. Levinas, 'Reality and Its Shadow', p. 8.

17. Ibid., p. 10.

18. Levinas, 'Persons or Figures', p. 121.

19. Levinas, 'Reality and Its Shadow', p. 6.

20. Ibid., p. 6.

21. Ibid., p. 8.

22. Ibid., p. 7.

23. Ridout, *Stage Fright*, p. 28.

24. Levinas, *Totality and Infinity: An Essay on Exteriority*, pp. 194–5.

25. Butler, *Precarious Life*, p. 161 note 6. Also see Butler, *Precarious Life*, p. 138.

26. See Wade, 'Sublime Trauma', p. 24.

27. J. L. Austin, *How to Do Things with Words*, p. 22.

28. William Shakespeare, all citations of Shakespeare are from *The New Oxford Shakespeare: Modern Critical Edition*, ed. Gary Taylor et al.

29. The notion that the *performative* depends on a citational iterability akin to the structure of theatre stands at the centre of Jacques Derrida's

familiar reading of Austin; see Derrida, 'Signature Event Context', pp. 324–8.

30. Robbins, *Altered Reading*, p. 48.
31. Levinas, 'Reality and Its Shadow', p. 9.
32. Tzachi Zamir, *Acts: Theater, Philosophy, and the Performing Self*, p. 25.
33. For a similar effort to read Levinas against the grain of his own politics, see Butler, *Notes Toward a Performative Theory of Assembly*, pp. 106–7. My thanks to Hana Worthen for suggesting the relevance of this text.
34. Ridout, *Stage Fright*, p. 31.
35. Robbins, *Altered Reading*, p. 84.
36. Jon Erickson, 'The Face and the Possibility of an Ethics of Performance', p. 18.
37. Butler, *Precarious Life*, p. 144.
38. As Sherman suggests, it is also associated with a certain kind of shame, to the extent that 'In order to recognize or identify the virtuoso, attendants must accept their own sense of falling short of the virtuoso's abilities, imagined to reside uniquely "in" the virtuoso him or herself.' Yet these 'standards and expectations clearly belong to the attendants; they are the ones casting someone at the end of an unbridgeable distance as an object'; Jon Foley Sherman, *A Strange Proximity: Stage Presence, Failure, and the Ethics of Attention*, pp. 107–8.
39. Butler, *Precarious Life*, p. 140.
40. Emmanuel Levinas, 'Peace and Proximity', p. 167.
41. Butler, *Precarious Life*, p. 134.
42. Samuel Beckett, *Not I*, in *Complete Dramatic Works*, pp. 382, 379, 382.
43. Not everyone would agree with this characterisation of Eidinger's physicality; though recognising that Eidinger wears a fatsuit for much of the evening, Richard Hornby finds that with his 'pasty skin, flabby face, and shaggy hair, he is the most ordinary-looking person imaginable.' See Richard Hornby, 'Two Hamlets', p. 127; Leo Robson, on the other hand, notes an 'athletic' Hamlet. See Leo Robson, 'Hamlet, Barbican, London'.
44. Robson, 'Hamlet, Barbican, London'.
45. Ridout, *Stage Fright*, p. 92.
46. Lyn Gardner, Rev. Hamlet; Benjamin Fowler takes this moment straight, suggesting that 'We in the audience were Hamlet, looking through his lens', a reading which seems to violate the optics of the scene. See Fowler, Rev. of *Hamlet*.
47. Hornby, 'Two Hamlets', p. 128.
48. The set is variously described as 'antiseptic' (James R. Ball, 'Staging the Twitter War', p. 168), one of the 'interchangeable' spaces of modern life, a nowhere of 'Modular configurations' (Natalie Corbett and Keren Zaiontz, 'The Politics of Distraction', p. 117) like the nowhere

of the 'corporate convention space' (Christian M. Billing, '*The Roman Tragedies*', p. 417).

49. Bridget Escolme, 'Shakespeare, Rehearsal and the Site-Specific', p. 518.
50. Christophe Collard, 'On the Dynamic Equilibrium of Embodied Adaptations: Contextualizing Ivo van Hove's *Roman Tragedies*', pp. 4, 9.
51. Samuel Beckett, *Catastrophe*, p. 461.
52. Sarah Werner notes that the video 'catches his opened eyes during Fortinbras's final speech. Shepherd is only pretending his death, but the absence of his Hamlet erases the rest of the "live" performance'. See Werner, 'Two Hamlets: Wooster Group and Synthetic Theater', p. 327.

Afterword: Theatre and Speculation

William N. West

To come face to face is, literally, to confront another. To think of coming upon another face to face is to imagine an encounter that is direct. To speak of coming face to face, whether in ordinary language (and the list of languages that have naturalised this expression is long) or in the more specialised discourses of philosophy, theology or theatre, is to give such an encounter a figure. When it appears, it is a promise of perfect and perfectly mutual access.

'Face to face' is an expression with a long past. If its history does not begin with Paul's first letter to the Corinthians, it certainly passes through it. The King James translation is more familiar ('For now we see through a glass, darkly; but then face to face: now I know in part; but then shall I know even as also I am known'), but the Latin of the Vulgate is closer to Paul's Greek: '*Videmus nunc per speculum in aenigmate: tunc autem facie ad faciem. Nunc cognosco ex parte: tunc autem cognoscam sicut et cognitus sum*'.[1] The *glass* of the first sentence in English is a mirror, *per speculum*, literally an instrument by which one sees; *darkly* is expressed in Latin (and Greek) by another mediation, 'in a riddle' or 'puzzle', *in aenigmate*, and qualifies the seeing not visually but cognitively or logically. The rhetorical structure of the Latin further suggests the greater immediacy of the face to face.[2] The verb *videmus*, 'we see', governs two isocola, evenly structured clauses of ten syllables each, mirroring each other and enacting in language the symmetrical confrontation they describe. The *nunc* (now) that introduces the first clause of each sentence is echoed by the rhyming *tunc* (then) that introduces the second clauses. In the first sentence, the mediations of the first clause disappear in the second, both the represented mediations of the mirror (*speculum*) and the riddle (*aenigma*) and the lexical ones, the prepositions *per* (through) and *in* (in), that represent their relation to perception.[3] They resolve into the balanced image of one face turned towards another, *facie ad faciem*, naming for the first time, with the same word, both what sees and what is seen. The *speculation in a riddle* of the present moment becomes – what? τότε δὲ πρόσωπον πρὸς πρόσωπον, *tunc autem facie ad faciem*, but then face to face. We cannot even call this *theoria*, that Greek word for clear vision so readily adopted by philosophers. Not even a verb intervenes in this phrase, so perfectly does one face confront the other. To see face to face promises a perfect immediacy and mutuality to come, a transparency unclouded by reflections or riddles expressed rhetorically by polyptoton, the repetition of multiple inflections of the same word: '*Nunc <u>cognosco</u> ex parte: tunc autem <u>cognoscam</u> sicut et <u>cognitus</u> sum*' ('Now <u>I know</u> in part: but then <u>shall I know</u> even as <u>I am known</u>').[4] In the second sentence, too, Paul becomes lonelier, as first person plural changes to first person singular: *we see* but *I know, I shall know*. In the first clause, the present tense of *cognosco* ('I know') stands alone. It is in the second clause, when the part has been made whole and the mirror is no more, that mutuality is enacted in language. Loneliness is overcome by the presence of the second person, only however implied in the unnamed agent of the passive verb. The flawed present *cognosco* ('I know') is fulfilled as the future by the tense of *cognoscam* ('I shall know'), when the act of *knowing* (*cognosco, cognoscam*) will be inverted and balanced against the passive *being known* (*cognitus sum*). I will know then that I have been known all along.

Paul's account of seeing face to face anticipates it resolving as epiphany. His language recalls the conversation of God with Moses, whom God distinguishes as one to whom he speaks 'mouth to mouth' (rather than 'face to face') and 'not in riddles' (Numbers 12: 8, in the Septuagint, οὐ δι' αἰνιγμάτων). His tone echoes the ambivalence and sureness of Job's triumphant lament '*et rursum circumdabor pelle mea, et in carne mea videbo Deum meum.*' Job's second clause unambiguously means 'in my flesh I shall see my God', but the first clause has been translated from Hebrew as both 'again I shall be compassed with my skin' and 'after my skin has been thus stripped away'.[5] But about the other face before whom this subject will know and is known, Paul has little to say. The knower who knows me, whose knowledge of me models my hoped-for knowledge of it, goes undesignated by any word. The perfection of my knowledge then can only be represented by the perfection of the knowledge of me, unknown to me now, whether in a particular now or perhaps a timeless present: I shall know as I am known, already or always. Paul's account of epiphany is also an eschatology, which is to say that the mutual presence of regards that mirror each other, although it is not achieved now (*nunc*), is promised achievement in some analogous then (*tunc*). But part of this promise is thus also that there is no *here* and *now* in which it will be realised. Although we are told elsewhere that Moses spoke to God 'face to face', lines later God tells Moses that no human will look upon his face and live (Exodus 33: 11, 20).

Paul's account does not and cannot (and probably would not) render its seeing face to face in the present. But Paul's account is a single moment in a discontinuous genealogy of coming face to face. Other thinkers have explored the encounter face to face as a way of being in the world of here and now, and their accounts have taken the form of a phenomenology. Following Descartes' radical recentring of knowledge in the self, other thinkers have repeatedly returned to the figure of coming face to face in order to restore thinking to the world from its seclusion in introspection, to express the presence to the face of the world towards which it is intent but which it continually loses, and to overcome the threat of solipsism and to seek community, whether with the world or with other selves in the world. This genealogy might be that of phenomenology itself.[6] Hegelian dialectic sought in part to repair the divorce of matter and mind in Cartesian dualism by staging a series of encounters in which Spirit recognises itself in the semblance of another. But Hegelian thinking could seem to be a trick of rediscovering everywhere and forever the self, and other thinkers responded in a series of propositions and negations about coming face to face. In 1901 Edmund Husserl declared 'We want to go back to the "things themselves".'[7] Husserl's phenomenological minimum for ensuring that the self is not merely interrogating itself but encountering the world turned out to be something like coming face to face. In his later *Cartesian Meditations*, he proposed that at its barest, phenomenology and the evidence on which it is constructed are a refusal of abstraction, an embrace of experience and, literally, 'a spiritual coming-to-face with It itself' (*ein Es-selbst-geistig-zu-Gesicht-bekommen*).[8] Heidegger's explorations of Being turn away from the attempted immediacy of Husserl's phenomenology, seeing in Husserl's intent facing towards particular beings a blindness to Being.

Emmanuel Levinas's *Totality and Infinity* is perhaps the most fully developed phenomenology of the face (*visage*, like *Gesicht* both what is seen and the power of sight, a face and the action of seeing) and of the face-to-face (*face-à-face*, the same as French translations of Corinthians). Its first lines – '"The true life is absent." But we are in the world.' – take up the crux of feeling the pang of what seems the loss of access to life while within the world that sustains us as living.[9] Levinas is responding to, without acknowledging, a passage from Rimbaud's *A Season in Hell*, 'The true life is absent. We are not in the world.'[10] Life and world alike are lost to Rimbaud, perhaps tautologically. Levinas transforms Rimbaud's despairing cry into an intention towards a true life from the midst of the world. He thus corrects both Husserl and Heidegger, each of whom in different ways tried to strike that which was most intimate to experience and each of whom, for Levinas, strayed from it in different ways. Husserl fails to acknowledge what is truly alien when it comes-to-face with what it initially takes as its object; Heidegger acknowledges otherness but grounds both the self and the other in their relation to Being.[11] *Totality and Infinity* seeks to bring its subjects fully into each other's presence, face to face – a presence that as an absolute demand would fall before or pre-empt the different failures of mediation that characterise phenomenology and ontology.

Levinas takes the face-to-face as a first philosophy, prior to either the Cartesian epistemology reformed by Husserl or Heidegger's ontology, a metaphysics of transcendence that is the matrix of existence and experience. It is 'a relation whose terms do not form a totality', the bounded whole for which 'the "otherwise" and the "elsewhere" that they desire still belong to the here below that they refuse.'[12] This contrasts the linear symmetry of *nunc* and *tunc* in 1 Corinthians, the balancing of the *now* when I do not see in mirrors and riddles and the *then* when I will know and be known. In Levinas's account of coming face to face, something appears and interrupts the predictable flow of the quotidian. True strangeness adventures into the familiar world: 'The way in which the other presents himself, exceeding the idea of the other in me, we here name face (*visage*).'[13] In what is literally their confrontation, neither face can be reduced to the other, despite how each seems to mirror the other. The pellucid glass of the future unexpectedly shatters, riddles, tesserates with infinite potentiality into crazy opacity. For Levinas, the 'transcendence' of the face-to-face 'designates a relation with a reality infinitely distant from my own reality, yet without this distance destroying the relation and without this relation destroying the distance.'[14] The confrontation offers a model for both perfect strangeness and perfect knowledge. The advent of the face of the other 'makes possible the description of the notion of the immediate . . . The immediate is the face-to-face (*face-à-face*).'[15]

Levinas's face-to-face is not a catching-sight-of but a moment of address-towards the notice of 'meaning prior to my *Sinngebung* [lit. 'sense-giving'] and thus independent of my initiative and my power.

It signifies the philosophical priority of the existent over Being.'[16] The other opposes the self not by resistance, but in 'the very unforeseeableness (*imprévisibilité*) of its reaction.'[17] The excess and unforeseeability of the face-to-face is what opens it to infinity, from which alone a future that is not the same as the past can emerge.[18] Coming face to face is both radical openness to an encounter and radical exposure to its risks, a moment before those alternatives (or others) are decided, primed with potential, the confrontation itself before negation or opposition or reconciliation, before even recognition.

From one perspective, then, Levinas comes at the end of a genealogy of thinking about the face-to-face. It is possible, though, that part of imagining the face-to-face is to understand it as not having a history. Levinas seemed to understand so. 'When man truly approaches the Other,' concludes one section of *Totality and Infinity*, 'he is uprooted from history.'[19] But if the face-to-face approaches transcendence, it also represents a loss of the world that Levinas had tried to remedy. The face in Levinas's account of the face-to-face appears without commonality and without context. For Levinas, as for Paul, the figure of the face-to-face allowed for a critique of less perfect forms of knowing as evasions of presence. But for Levinas, as for Paul, the rigour with which the exteriority of the self to the face of the other was defined abstracted both from each other and from any imaginable world. 'The infinitely Other can only be Infinity,' observes Derrida in his long animadversion on Levinas's thought.[20] Accounts from Paul to Levinas took the face-to-face as a figure for mutual presence. Derridean deconstruction challenged these very terms, although it remained captivated by the critique of both ontology and phenomenology that Levinas's discussion of the face-to-face offered. Nevertheless, 'the other cannot be what it is, infinitely other, except in finitude and mortality (mine *and* its).'[21] Levinas' account of the face-to-face ends up far from where it begins, '"The true life is absent." But we are in the world.' As he tries to characterise the face-to-face, though, the finitude and mortality of the world in which we are rooted slip further into abstraction. The cost of imagining that absolute confrontation, transcending every expectation, is any past or present, any history or context. Absolute, absolved from history and the world, incapable of particularisation or relation, it is no wonder that the face in Levinas's face-to-face can only appear, like Paul's, as that of God.[22]

But we might also recognise that there are other kinds of face to face encounters besides epiphany, and that not all such encounters share the intention to perfect presence. To speculate into a glass and seek into riddles, there is, in particular, the theatre, which Stanley Cavell has remarkably described as a place in which we can escape the fearful symmetry of the face-to-face. In a powerful reading of *King Lear* and *Othello*, Cavell observes that theatrical characters cannot be aware of us attending to them:

1. . . . I will say: We are not in their presence.
2. They are in our presence.[23]

Cavell's theatre engages us because it demands that we allow what we are looking at its difference from us, like the face to face encounter in Levinas or in Paul, and it does so very differently than phenomenologies of the face-to-face propose. Cavell is also concerned with failures of knowledge and imagination in the face of the other, but like Derrida he does not think they can be addressed 'except in finitude and mortality (mine *and* its).' While the face to face encounter promises immediacy and absoluteness (and perhaps absolution) to that which is closest to and therefore hardest for us, theatre does not.

Theatre and *theory* both derive from another Greek word for seeing, neither the one that Paul used nor the one he seems to have avoided (see note 4). But etymology is not destiny, and *theatre* seems to offer a different kind of perception than that of *theory* or the face-to-face. As W. B. Worthen observes, 'The relations of theatre are always mediated, conditional, and conditioned by a rich sociability . . .'[24] While the face-to-face as a figure for the intimate and difficult process of encountering the other tends towards an apocalypse outside of time, *theatre* happens all the time, in time, in the world. And these asymmetries and mediations are not shortcomings or failures on the way towards a face to face encounter that would be absolute. They are what theatre is made of and the source of its powers. What we encounter and seek to encounter in theatre is not the face abstracted, but many faces and their many worlds: 'I will say: We are not in, and cannot put ourselves in the presence of the characters; but we are in, or can put ourselves in, their *present*.'[25] Theatre is not outside of contexts, but deeply within them; better yet, it is revelatory of contexts and contingencies, productive of them.[26] Where *theory* seems to strive for the perfect mutuality of the face-to-face, then finds it out of bounds, *theatre* speculates and riddles in its presents and revels in its gifts.

For Levinas or Paul the face-to-face is radically singular, a moment that breaks absolutely with all else. In Shakespearean drama and in performance, it is instead radically particular and radically elusive and infinitely productive in how I, equally elusive and particular, come into relation with it. Levinas specifies that the attention towards otherness which he finds in the face and the face-to-face, in which there is a transcendent imperative, differs from the attention towards something that is simply given to attention.[27] But while Levinas examines the first kind of attention, the essays in this collection detail the second, not the empty, unspecified alterities, asymmetries and asynchronies of Levinas, but their particular manifestations.

The essays in this volume explore some of these particularities, their contexts and histories, asymmetries, asynchronies and mediations of all kinds. Such particularities make the face-to-face encounter essentially impossible if we want to understand it to be a kind of zero-degree of relation, but that in fact give it its significance in the world we inhabit and make together through myriad partial encounters with each other. Like Paul or Levinas, many of them involve descriptions or performances of fantasies of transparency or mutuality. But rather than simply acknowledging them as fantasies, as deconstructive criticism risks doing, the precision of their fantasies means that we can concentrate on their productivity rather than on their misprisions of presence. 'What *we* do', proposed Wittgenstein in a passage that Devin Byker quotes in this volume, 'is to bring words back from their metaphysical to their ordinary use.'[28] What these essays do is to bring back the face-to-face meeting from theory to its ubiquitous, irreducible enactments. The face to face encounters in the plays of Shakespeare and his contemporaries, and in these essays that think through them, are the physical translations of the metaphysics of presence. They return us to the actual physics of individual encounters that bring full characters face to face, letting slip the promise of the absolute face-to-face, bearing with them their other relations and histories, showing the myriad positivities, particularities, differences that arise in each such confrontation. Unsurprised by the theatre's failure to render presence as symmetrical, perfect, immediate, complete, the essays here take up the gestures towards face-to-face encounters that theatre can cultivate as actions undertaken in the world. The contributors demonstrate in part what Shakespeare and performance and spectation can contribute to the structure of a philosophy of the Other by bootstrapping an infinity out of finitude – or in less airlessly theoretical terms, how theatre as a practice models the infinite variety of encounters we have and might have. Refusing the absoluteness, the absolution, of the face-to-face as a reduction, these essays take up the play itself as a form of finitude that engenders a surplus, a limited space of infinite potentiality. In so doing, they show that there is no simple, perfect face-to-face in the world we share. There is no need for it.

What these essays demonstrate in vibrant particularity, in fact, is how on Shakespeare's stages there is no absolute face to face. There are many face-to-face confrontations in which one of any number of relations might appear and develop. These Shakespearean face-to-face encounters are part of a world or worlds, and sometimes may even be its origin, but they are not the only possible one. Paul Kottman has argued that for the history of Western thought from Homer onwards, the pre-eminent model of initiation into mutual recognition was the duel. A worldly manifestation of the Pauline face-to-face, the duel figured how one demanded recognition from another by staking its life against another's acknowledgement. Kottman notes that one of Shakespeare's particularly theatrical insights was to de-essentialise the duel. Shakespeare does not see the duel, or any other face-to-face encounter, as the existential matrix. Rather, Shakespeare's plays represent multiple moments in varying relations of existential determination, any of them irreducible.[29] In Levinas's terms, such scenes show how totality is replaced by the infinity of possible configurations of relation between finite beings.

Cavell's theatre is explicitly a theatre of tragedy. It may be that, unlike Cavell's exploration of the face-to-face, or Levinas's, Shakespeare's theatre – if we can even speak so abstractly about something so rooted in its mediations and relations and histories – is comic, and often comical. Levinas's face is Other. Shakespeare's faces are Like. They can see in each other similarity as well as epiphany or alienation, negotiate as well as confront. The rich partialities of their worlds, though they are also incomplete, offer resources that draw them together into a future beyond any face to face encounter that might be complete.[30] This is as true of Lady Macbeth and Duncan or Othello and Iago as it is of Lear and Cordelia or Viola and Sebastian and Orsino and Olivia. Part of tragedy is its irrevocability, a decisiveness of event or action that can only be made comic by a certainty like Paul's or Dante's, which can take the world as divine comedy. But Shakespeare's theatre frames its encounters differently. Worlds of perfect vision and perfect knowledge, total worlds, must be either tragic or comic, because in them all accounts will be settled. The infinity of relations in Shakespeare's plays, cobbled from partialities and imperfections, are comic not because they promise that the worst returns to laughter but because the relations they speculate upon can always be revised – seen again and transformed.

The Introduction to this volume begins in rehearsal, a repeated, exploratory finding-out of how a relation works. Shakespeare's theatre, even when it is tragic, is often something like that. Each encounter face to face with another counts, each matters, each changes every encounter that follows – but each also holds the possibility that future encounters can follow and that the relation that each encounter inaugurates can be transformed in that future. Of that future we can scarcely say more than that it will come, in its infinite potentiality. What's to come is still unsure. The readiness is all. The wholeness and immediacy pledged in the face-to-face is never certain and never permanent but always and from everywhere imaginable. It is rendered comic because it may rise from worse to better, and potentially comical, because it cannot fully escape the humbling particularities of the world. From this vantage, Shakespearean tragedy looks something like a species of Shakespearean comedy, the contingent disappointment of what could be rather than the inevitability of what must. In place of the apocalyptic relation of the face-to-face, the contingencies of Shakespearean theatre constitute a kind of variorum of actual relations. From their finite parts, they open an infinity of possibilities.

Shakespeare's plays show the world through a glass darkly, and in them we encounter each other and our shared world. We do not need to deprecate that understanding in favour of the promise of coming face to face with something greater. They embrace the imperfect knowledge and the mediated desires of the mirror for its sureness that life goes on and is going on. The part of this theatre is to look and act where it cannot fully see or know. It addresses others in the world in its speculations through the mirror and in riddles, incomplete, mediate, imperfect, confused. But it recognises that to change these conditions of partiality is also to forego what it looks to meet, face to face.

Notes

1. 1 Corinthians 13: 12, in the English of the King James Bible. Paul's original Greek is 'βλέπομεν γὰρ ἄρτι δι' ἐσόπτρου ἐν αἰνίγματι τότε δὲ πρόσωπον πρὸς πρόσωπον· ἄρτι γινώσκω ἐκ μέρους τότε δὲ ἐπιγνώσομαι καθὼς καὶ ἐπεγνώσθην.' See Jennifer Waldron's discussion in this volume of how Shakespeare calls upon this passage in two particular theatrical encounters.
2. The Greek has these features as well as others. The Greek for 'face to face' suggests another immediacy; the words for *face* are in the same

case, and the preposition that relates them is repeated from the word for face: *prosōpon pros prosōpon.*

3. See Matthew Smith in this volume on 'thinking with the preposition'; see also Bruce Smith's essay here, as well as his 'E/loco/com/motion'.

4. There is a suppressed pun in the Greek, for which the present tense of a different word for *know*, οἶδα, is supplied by a form derived from the perfect tense of a verb meaning *see* – so that *I know* can be expressed by a form that means literally *I have seen.*

5. Job 19: 26, lightly modifying Wycliffe's translation for the first interpretation and quoting the Revised Standard translation for the second. I have used a modern translation because both the Geneva and King James versions interpolate material to make better sense of a confusing passage. Notes to the Revised Standard edition suggest that the Hebrew is also ambiguous. Both interpretations were current in Shakespeare's lifetime. The Latin Vulgate is more easily taken in the sense of the Wycliffite translation, that Job will again be clothed in skin, but the Geneva and King James versions emphasise the destruction of Job's skin.

6. See, for instance, Paul Ricoeur's incisive summary in *The Course of Recognition.* I am grateful to Matthew Smith for pointing me towards this text.

7. Husserl, 'Wir wollen auf die "Sachen selbst" zurückgehen', in *Logische Untersuchungen,* 2 vols, 2: 7.

8. The German is from *Cartesianische Meditationen und Pariser Vorträge,* Husserliana v.1, p. 52. My translation here is so literal as to be nearly illegible. German *zu Gesicht bekommen* is an expression like English 'lay eyes on', where *Gesicht* is both the power of *sight* and the *face,* as is French *visage,* used later by Husserl's student and translator Emmanuel Levinas. More comprehensibly, it is 'a mental seeing of something itself' (Husserl, *Cartesian Meditations: Introduction to Phenomenology,* p. 12). In Levinas' French translation of 1931, there is no sign of the word *face (Gesicht)*: 'c'est donc qu'eu elle le regard de notre esprit atteint la chose elle-même', *Méditations Cartésiennes: Introduction à la Phenomenologie,* trans. Gabrielle Peiffer and Emmanuel Levinas, p. 10. But Husserl's influence appears in Levinas's choice of *visage* for the face, and Husserl's 'coming-to-face' is felt in Levinas's own 'face-to-face'.

9. '"La vraie vie est absente." Mais nous sommes au monde.' *Totalité et Infini: Essai sur l'Extériorité,* p. 3; *Totality and Infinity: An Essay on Exteriority,* p. 3.

10. 'La vraie vie est absente. Nous ne sommes pas au monde', *Une saison en enfer, Delires I.*

11. *Totality and Infinity,* 67; *Totalité et Infini,* 39. In *The Course of Recognition,* Ricoeur contrasts Husserl and Levinas as two complementary poles in thinking through the problem of mutual recognition, Husserl

from the point of view of the ego, Levinas from the point of view of the Other. We might add Heidegger as the thinker of recognition as a problem of Being.

12. *Totalité et Infini*, pp. 9, 11; *Totality and Infinity*, pp. 39, 41. I have modified the translation of the second passage slightly for clarity. *Passim*, I have also inserted hyphens into the translation *face-to-face* for *face-à-face*.

13. *Totality and Infinity*, p. 50. *Totalité et Infini*, p. 21: 'La manière dont se présente l'Autre, dépassant *l'idée de l'Autre en moi*, nous l'appelons, en effet, visage.' I discuss the secular force of acknowledging that another exceeds the idea of the other in me in different terms in 'Titus' Infinite Jest'.

14. *Totalité et Infini*, pp. 12; *Totality and Infinity*, p. 41.

15. *Totality and Infinity*, pp. 51–2; *Totalité et Infini*, pp. 22–3.

16. *Totality and Infinity*, p. 51; *Totalité et Infini*, p. 22. *Sinngebung* is Husserl's term for the active intending of thought towards an object; *existents* and *Being* recall Heidegger.

17. *Totality and Infinity*, pp. 199; *Totalité et Infini*, p. 173.

18. In her contribution to this volume, Emily Shortslef cites some other figures for the advent of novelty in the world, among them what Hannah Arendt calls *action*, and Michael Witmore's discussion of theatre as a tracing of the unexpected patterns of diffusion from converging lines of causality. On performance and what may be, see also Daniel Sack, *After Live: Possibility, Potentiality, and the Future of Performance*, who distinguishes the openness of *potentiality* from the implied teleologies of *possibility*.

19. *Totality and Infinity*, p. 52; *Totalité et Infini*, p. 23.

20. 'Violence and Metaphysics: An Essay on the Thought of Emmanuel Levinas', p. 104; 'Violence et Métaphysique: Essai sur la pensée d'Emmanuel Levinas', *Revue de Métaphysique*, p. 349.

21. 'Violence and Metaphysics', pp. 114–15; 'Violence et Métaphysique', p. 430.

22. Levinas does assert that the face is not that of God; my argument is that Levinas nevertheless figures it the same way, almost inevitably given his conditions. Derrida argues that the face (*visage*) in Levinas is neither the face (*Face*, capitalised) of God nor the figure of man, but their resemblance, 'Violence et Métaphysique', p. 354; 'Violence and Metaphysics', p. 109. Stanley Cavell has noted that 'the problem of the other' has replaced many of the positions formerly occupied by questions of 'the problem of god' (*The Claim of Reason: Wittgenstein, Skepticism, Morality, and Tragedy*, p. 489, quoted in Hent de Vries. 'From "Ghost in the Machine" to "Spiritual Automaton": Philosophical Meditation in Wittgenstein, Cavell, and Levinas', p. 77.

23. Cavell, 'The Avoidance of Love: A Reading of *King Lear*', in *Disowning Knowledge in Seven Plays of Shakespeare* [updated], p. 103. I have preserved the striking typography of Cavell's paragraph break in this quotation.

24. Worthen, this volume.
25. 'The Avoidance of Love', 108.
26. See Lawrence Manley's contribution to this volume here, which explores how increasingly complex interferences in the face to face encounter make correspondingly richer theatre. I discuss theatrical performance specifically as an activity that creates contexts in 'Playing in Context, Playing out Context'.
27. *Totalité et Infini*, 20; *Totality and Infinity*, 49.
28. *Philosophical Investigations*, p. 116; Byker, this volume.
29. Paul Kottman, 'Duel'.
30. In this sense, the bed trick that Devin Byker discusses is an example of how the 'fantasy of facelessness' is overcome by waking up the next morning.

Notes on Contributors

Devin Byker is Assistant Professor of English at the College of Charleston. His work has appeared in the *Journal of Medieval and Early Modern Studies* and *Shakespeare Studies*. He is currently working on a book project about how early English drama explores the forms of life that are possible within one's dying moments.

Kevin Curran is Professor of Early Modern Literature at the University of Lausanne in Switzerland and editor of the book series Edinburgh Critical Studies in Shakespeare and Philosophy. He is the author of *Shakespeare's Legal Ecologies: Law and Distributed Selfhood* (Northwestern University Press, 2017) and *Marriage, Performance, and Politics at the Jacobean Court* (Ashgate, 2009). He is the editor of *Shakespeare and Judgment* (Edinburgh University Press, 2016).

Julia Reinhard Lupton is Professor of English at the University of California, where she has taught since 1989. She is the author or co-author of five books on Shakespeare, including *Shakespeare Dwelling: Designs for the Theater of Life, Thinking with Shakespeare: Essays on Politics and Life* and *Citizen-Saints: Shakespeare and Political Theology*.

Lawrence Manley is William R. Kenan, Jr Professor of English at Yale University and the author, with Sally-Beth MacLean, of *Lord Strange's Men and Their Plays* (2014). His other works include *Literature and Culture in Early Modern London* (1995) *and Convention, 1500–1750* (1980), as well as being the editor of *London in the Age of Shakespeare: An Anthology* (1986) and *The Cambridge Companion to London in English Literature (2011)*.

Hanna Scolnicov is Professor Emerita of Theatre Studies and former Head of the School of Graduate Studies of the Faculty of Arts at Tel-Aviv University, and Life Member of Clare Hall, Cambridge. Her publications include *Experiments in Stage Satire* (Peter Lang, on Ben Jonson) and *Woman's Theatrical Space* (Cambridge University Press). She has co-edited, with Peter Holland, *The Play Out of Context* and *Reading Plays* (Cambridge University Press), and, with Martin Procházka, Michael Dobson and Andreas Höfele, *Renaissance Shakespeare, Shakespeare Renaissances*.

Akihiko Shimizu is a Lecturer in Japanese Studies at Cardiff University. He has published articles on Ben Jonson, early modern character and legal rhetoric. He is currently working on the representations of the face in early modern English and Japanese literatures.

Emily Shortslef is an Assistant Professor of English at the University of Kentucky. Her work has appeared in the *Journal for Early Modern Cultural Studies* and *Exemplaria*, and is forthcoming in *ELH*. She is currently completing a book manuscript entitled *Shakespeare and the Drama of Complaint*, which explores the intersections between Shakespearean drama, moral philosophy and early modern discourses of complaint.

Bruce R. Smith, Dean's Professor of English and Theatre at the University of Southern California, is the author of seven books on Shakespeare, including most recently *Shakespeare | Cut: Rethinking Cutwork in an Age of Distraction*.

Matthew James Smith is Associate Professor of English at Azusa Pacific University. He is the author of *Performance and Religion in Early Modern England: Stage, Cathedral, Wagon, Street* which offers a comparative study of theatricality across performance genres. He also serves as Associate Editor of *Christianity and Literature* and has guest-edited special issues entitled 'Sincerity' and 'The Sacramental Text Reconsidered'.

William N. West is Associate Professor of English, Classics, and Comparative Literary Studies at Northwestern University where he teaches and thinks about early modern literature and performance. His books include *Theatres and Encyclopedias in Early Modern Europe* (Cambridge University Press, 2002) and *As If: Essays in* As You Like It (punctum, 2016). He also edits the scholarly journal *Renaissance Drama*.

W. B. Worthen is Alice Brady Pels Professor in the Arts at Barnard College, where he chairs the Department of Theatre; he is also Professor of English and Comparative Literature at Columbia University, and co-chair of the PhD in Theatre. He is recently the author of *Shakespeare Performance Studies*, and *Theatre, Technicity, Shakespeare* is forthcoming from Cambridge University Press.

Bibliography

'A late discourse . . . Touching the cure of wounds by the powder of sympathy' (1658), in Richard Hunter and Ida Macalpine (eds), *Three Hundred Years of Psychiatry, 1535–1860* (London: Oxford University Press, 1963).

Adelman, Janet, 'Bed Tricks: On Marriage and the End of Comedy in *All's Well That Ends Well* and *Measure for Measure*', in Norman H. Holland, Sidney Homan and Bernard J. Paris (eds), *Shakespeare's Personality* (Berkeley: University of California Press, 1989), pp. 151–74.

Adelman, Janet, 'Marriage and the Maternal Body: On Marriage as the End of Comedy in *All's Well that Ends Well* and *Measure for Measure*', in *Suffocating Mothers: Fantasies of Maternal Origin in Shakespeare's Plays, Hamlet to The Tempest* (New York: Routledge, 1992), pp. 76–102.

Adelman, Janet, *Suffocating Mothers: Fantasies of Maternal Origin in Shakespeare's Plays, Hamlet to The Tempest* (New York: Routledge, 1992).

Agamben, Giorgio, *Means without End: Notes on Politics*, trans. Vincenzo Binetti and Cesare Casarino (Minneapolis: University of Minnesota Press, 2000).

American Psychiatric Association, *Diagnostic and Statistical Manual of Mental Disorders: DSM-IV*, 4th edn (Washington, DC: American Psychiatric Association, 1994).

American Psychiatric Association, *Diagnostic and Statistical Manual of Mental Disorders: DSM-5*, 5th edn (Washington, DC: American Psychiatric Publishing, 2013).

Arendt, Hannah, 'Personal Responsibility Under Dictatorship', in Jerome Kohn (ed.), *Responsibility and Judgment* (New York: Random House, 2003), pp. 17–48.

Arendt, Hannah, 'Some Questions of Moral Philosophy', in Jerome Kohn (ed.) *Responsibility and Judgment* (New York: Random House, 2003), pp. 49–146.

Arendt, Hannah, 'The Crisis in Culture', in *Between Past and Future: Eight Exercises in Political Thought* (London: Penguin Books, 1993), pp. 197–226.

Arendt, Hannah, 'Truth and Politics', in *Between Past and Future: Eight Exercises in Political Thought* (London: Penguin Books, 1993), pp. 227–64.

Arendt, Hannah, *The Human Condition* (Chicago: University of Chicago Press, 1958).

Arendt, Hannah, *The Human Condition*, 2nd edn (Chicago: University of Chicago Press, 1998).

Arendt, Hannah, *The Life of the Mind* (San Diego, CA: Harcourt, 1978).

Aristotle, *Aristotle in 23 Volumes*, vol. 23, trans. W. H. Fyfe (Cambridge, MA: Harvard University Press, 1932). *Perseus Digital Library*, ed. Gregory R. Cane. Tufts University. Accessed here: http://www.perseus.tufts.edu (accessed 5 August 2017).

Aristotle, *On Rhetoric: A Theory of Civil Discourse*, trans. George A. Kennedy (Oxford: Oxford University Press, 2007).

Armstrong, Nancy and Warren Montag, 'The Figure in the Carpet', *PMLA* 132 (3) (2017), pp. 613–19.

Ascham, Roger, *Toxophilus* (London, 1545).

Austin, J. L., *How to Do Things with Words*, ed. J. O. Urmson (Cambridge, MA: Harvard University Press, 1962).

Austin, J. L. *How to Do Things with Words*, ed. J. O. Urmson and Marina Sbisà (Cambridge, MA: Harvard University Press, 1975).

Austin, Norman, *Archery at the Dark of the Moon: Poetic Problems in Homer's Odyssey* (Berkeley: University of California Press, 1975).

Bacon, Francis, 'Of Beauty', in Charles W. Eliot (ed.), *Essays, Civil and Moral*, Harvard Classics Vol. 3, XLIII (New York: Collier, 1909).

Bacon, Francis, *The Major Works*, ed. Brian Vickers (Oxford: Oxford University Press, 1996).

Baldwin, Edward Chauncey, 'Ben Jonson's Indebtedness to the Greek Character-Sketch', *Modern Language Notes*, 16 (7) (1901), pp. 193–8.

Ball, James R., III, 'Staging the Twitter War: Toneelgroep Amsterdam's *Roman Tragedies*', *TDR: The Drama Review – The Journal of Performance Studies*, 57 (4) (2013), pp. 163–70.

Barber, C. L., *Shakespeare's Festive Comedy* (Princeton: Princeton University Press, 1959).

Barret, J. K., 'The Crowd in Imogen's Bedroom: Allusion and Ethics in *Cymbeline*', *Shakespeare Quarterly*, 66 (4) (2015), pp. 440–62.

Barton, Anne, *Ben Jonson, Dramatist* (Cambridge: Cambridge University Press, 1984).

Bates, Jennifer Ann, *Hegel and Shakespeare on Moral Imagination* (Albany, NY: State University of New York Press, 2010).

Battenhouse, Roy W., *Shakespearean Tragedy: Its Art and Its Christian Premises* (Bloomington: Indiana University Press, 1969).

Baumbach, Sibylle, '"Thy face is mine": Faces and Fascination in Shakespeare's Plays', in James A. Knapp (ed.), *Shakespeare and the Power of the Face* (Farnham: Ashgate, 2015).

Beckerman, Bernard, 'Shakespeare's Dramaturgy and Binary Form', *Theatre Journal*, 33 (1) (1981), pp. 5–17

Beckerman, Bernard, 'Shakespeare's Industrious Scenes', *Shakespeare Quarterly*, 30 (2) (1979), pp. 138–50.

Beckerman, Bernard, *Shakespeare at the Globe, 1599–1609* (New York: Macmillan, 1962).

Beckerman, Bernard, *Theatrical Presentation: Performer, Audience, and Act*, ed. Gloria Brim Beckerman and William Coco (New York: Routledge, 1990).

Beckett, Samuel, *Catastrophe*, in *Complete Dramatic Works* (London: Faber, 1986), pp. 455–61.

Beckett, Samuel, *Not I*, in *Complete Dramatic Works* (London: Faber, 1986), pp. 373–83.

Beckwith, Sarah, *Shakespeare and the Grammar of Forgiveness* (Ithaca: Cornell University Press, 2011).

Bednarz, James P., *Shakespeare and the Poets' War* (New York: Columbia University Press, 2001).

Beecher, Donald, 'Appendix IV', in Thomas Overbury, *Characters*, ed. Donald Beecher (Ottawa: Dovehouse Editions, 2003).

Beecher, Donald, 'Introduction', in Thomas Overbury, *Characters*, ed. Donald Beecher (Ottawa: Dovehouse Editions, 2003).

Belfiore, Elizabeth, *Tragic Pleasures: Aristotle on Plot and Emotion* (Princeton: Princeton University Press, 1992).

Benveniste, Émile, 'Active and Middle Voice in the Verb', in *Problems in General Linguistics*, trans. Mary Elizabeth Meek (Coral Gables: University of Miami Press, 1971), pp. 145–52.

Bernhart, Walter, 'Functions of Description in Poetry', in Werner Wolf and Walter Bernhart (eds), *Description in Literature and Other Media* (Amsterdam and New York: Rodopi, 2007).

Bernstein, Jay, *Torture and Dignity: An Essay on Moral Dignity* (Chicago: University of Chicago Press, 2015).

Best, Stephen and Sharon Marcus, 'Surface Reading: An Introduction', *Representations*, 108 (1) (2009), pp. 1–21.

Bevington, David, et al. (eds), *Cambridge Edition of Works of Ben Jonson*, 7 vols (Cambridge: Cambridge University Press, 2012).

Billing, Christian M., 'The Roman Tragedies', *Shakespeare Quarterly*, 61 (3) (2010), pp. 415–39.

Blundeville, Thomas, *The Arte of Logicke* (London, 1599).

Bloom, Gina, *Gaming the Stage: Playable Media and the Rise of English Commercial Theatre* (Ann Arbor: University of Michigan Press, 2018).

Bodi, Russel, 'Lessons from a Street-fighter: Reconsidering *Romeo and Juliet*.' Forthcoming in *Shakespeare 401*, ed. Kenneth Graham (McGill-Queen's University Press, 2019).

Boitani, Piero, *The Gospel According to Shakespeare*, trans. Vittorio Montemaggi and Rachel Jacoff (Notre Dame: University of Notre Dame Press, 2013).

Bolter, Jay David and Richard Grusin, *Remediation: Understanding New Media* (Cambridge, MA: MIT Press, 2000).

Bos, Jacques, 'Individuality and Inwardness in the Literary Character Sketches of the Seventeenth Century', *Journal of the Warburg and Courtauld Institutes*, 61 (1998).

Bourdieu, Pierre, *Distinction: A Social Critique of the Judgment of Taste*, trans. Richard Nice (London: Routledge, 1984).

Boyce, Benjamin, *Theophrastan Character in England to 1642* (Cambridge, MA: Harvard University Press, 1947).

Bradley, A. C., *Shakespearean Tragedy: Lectures on Hamlet, Othello, King Lear, Macbeth* (London: Macmillan, 1904).

Brandom, Robert, 'From Autonomy to Recognition', in C. H. Krijnen (ed.), *Recognition – German Idealism as an Ongoing Challenge* (Leiden: Brill, 2013).

Brann, Eva, *Homeric Moments: Clues to Delight in Reading 'The Odyssey' and 'The Iliad'* (Philadelphia: Paul Dry Books, 2002).

Briggs, Julia, 'Shakespeare's Bed-Tricks', *Essays in Criticism*, 44 (4) (1994), pp. 293–314.

Bryson, Anna, *From Courtesy to Civility: Changing Codes of Conduct in Early Modern England* (Oxford and New York: Clarendon Press, 1998).

Budick, Sanford, 'Shakespeare's Secular Benediction: The Language of Tragic Community in *King Lear*', in Arthur Marotti and Chanita Goodblatt (eds), *Religious Diversity and Early Modern English Texts: Catholic, Judaic, Feminist, and Secular Dimensions* (Detroit: Wayne State University Press, 2013).

Budra, Paul, 'Affecting Desire in Shakespeare's Comedies of Love', in Karen Bamford and Ric Knowles (eds), *Shakespeare's Comedies of Love* (Toronto: University of Toronto Press, 2008).

Burns, Edward, *Character: Acting and Being on the Pre-Modern Stage* (New York: St. Martin's Press, 1990).

Butler, Judith, *Giving an Account of Oneself* (New York: Fordham University Press, 2005).

Butler, Judith, *Notes Toward a Performative Theory of Assembly* (Cambridge, MA and London: Harvard University Press, 2015).

Butler, Judith, *Precarious Life: The Powers of Mourning and Violence* (London and New York: Verso, 2004).

Carnicke, Sharon Marie, 'Acting Techniques', in Bruce R. Smith (ed.), *The Cambridge Guide to the Worlds of Shakespeare* (Cambridge: Cambridge University Press, 2016).

Cathcart, Charles, *Marston, Rivalry, Rapprochement, and Jonson* (Aldershot: Ashgate, 2008).

Cave, Terence, *Recognitions: A Study in Poetics* (Oxford: Clarendon, 1990).

Cavell, Stanley, 'Macbeth Appalled', *Disowning Knowledge in Seven Plays of Shakespeare* [updated] (Cambridge: Cambridge University Press, 2003).

Cavell, Stanley, 'Othello and the Stake of the Other', *Disowning Knowledge in Seven Plays of Shakespeare* [updated] (Cambridge: Cambridge University Press, 2003).

Cavell, Stanley, 'The Avoidance of Love: A Reading of *King Lear*', *Must We Mean What We Say: A Book of Essays*, 2nd edn (Cambridge: Cambridge University Press, 2002).

Cavell, Stanley, 'The Avoidance of Love: A Reading of *King Lear*', in *Disowning Knowledge in Seven Plays of Shakespeare* [updated] (Cambridge: Cambridge University Press, 2003), pp. 39–124.

Cavell, Stanley, *Disowning Knowledge in Seven Plays of Shakespeare* [updated] (Cambridge: Cambridge University Press, 2003).

Cavell, Stanley, *Philosophy the Day after Tomorrow* (Cambridge, MA: Harvard University Press, 2005).

Cavell, Stanley, *The Claim of Reason: Wittgenstein, Skepticism, Morality, and Tragedy* (New York: Oxford University Press, 1979).

Cersano, S. P., 'Edward Alleyn, the New Model Actor, and the Rise of the Celebrity in the 1590s', *Medieval and Renaissance Drama in England*, 18 (2005), pp. 47–58.

Charney, Maurice, '"We put fresh garments on him": Nakedness and Clothes in King Lear', in Rosalie S. Colie and F. T. Flahiff (eds), *Essays in Prismatic Criticism* (London: Heinemann, 1974).

Cicero, *On Duties*, trans. Walter Miller, Loeb Classical Library (Cambridge, MA: Harvard University Press, 1913).

Clyomon and Clamydes: A Critical Edition, ed. Betty J. Littleton (The Hague: Mouton, 1969).

Cockcroft, Robert, *Rhetorical Affect in Early Modern Writing: Renaissance Passions Reconsidered* (New York: Palgrave, 2003).

Coleridge, Samuel Taylor, *Coleridge's Shakespeare Criticism*, ed. Thomas Middleton Raysor (London: Constable, 1930).

Collard, Christophe, 'On the Dynamic Equilibrium of Embodied Adaptations: Contextualizing Ivo van Hove's *Roman Tragedies*', *Theatre Annual*, 66 (2013), pp. 1–16.

Common Conditions, ed. Roberta Barker (Oxford: Malone Society Reprints, 2004).

Cooke, William, *Memoirs of Samuel Foote, Esq. with a Collection of His Genuine Bon-Mots, Anecdotes, Opinions, &c.* (New York, 1806).

Corbett, Natalie, and Keren Zaiontz, 'The Politics of Distraction: Spectatorial Freedom and (dis)Enchantment in Toneelgroep's *Roman Tragedies*', *Canadian Theatre Review*, 147 (2011), pp. 117–20.

Craik, Katherine A., *Reading Sensations in Early Modern England* (Basingstoke and New York: Palgrave Macmillan, 2007).

Crane, Mary Thomas, 'What was Performance', *Criticism*, 43 (2) (2001), pp. 169–87.

Critchley, Simon, *The Problem with Levinas* (Oxford: Oxford University Press, 2015).

Cummings, Brian, *Mortal Thoughts: Religion, Secularity and Identity* (Oxford: Oxford University Press, 2013).

Curran, John E. Jr, *Character and the Individual Personality in English Renaissance Drama* (Newark: University of Delaware Press, 2014).

Curran, Kevin, 'Feeling Criminal in *Macbeth*', *Criticism*, 54 (3) (2012), pp. 391–401.

Curran, Kevin, 'Prospero's Plea: Judgment, Invention, and Political Form in *The Tempest*', in Kevin Curran (ed.), *Shakespeare and Judgment* (Edinburgh: Edinburgh University Press, 2016), pp. 157–71.

Curran, Kevin, 'Shakespearean Comedy and the Senses', in Heather Hirschfeld (ed.), *The Oxford Handbook of Shakespearean Comedy* (Oxford: Oxford University Press, 2018).

Davis, Lloyd, *Guise and Disguise: Rhetoric and Characterization in the English Renaissance* (Toronto: University of Toronto Press, 1993).

de Grazia, Maria, 'The Ideology of Superfluous Things: *King Lear* as Period Piece', in Margareta de Grazia, Maureen Quilligan and Peter Stallybrass (eds), *Subject and Object in Renaissance Culture* (Cambridge: Cambridge University Press, 1996).

de Vries, Hent, 'From "ghost in the machine" to "spiritual automaton": Philosophical meditation in Wittgenstein, Cavell, and Levinas', *International Journal for Philosophy of Religion*, 60 (2006), pp. 77–97.

Debes, Remy (ed.), *Dignity: A History* (Oxford: Oxford University Press, 2017).

Dekker, Thomas, *The Dramatic Works of Thomas Dekker*, Vol. 1, ed. Fredson Bowers (Cambridge: Cambridge University Press, 1953–61).

Deleuze, Gilles and Félix Guattari, '1837: The Refrain', in *A Thousand Plateaus: Capitalism and Schizophrenia*, trans. Brian Massumi (Minneapolis: University of Minnesota Press, 1987), pp. 310–50.

Derrida, Jacques, 'Signature Event Context', *Margins of Philosophy*, trans. Alan Bass (Chicago: University of Chicago Press, 1982).

Derrida, Jacques, 'Violence and Metaphysics: An Essay on the Thought of Emmanuel Levinas', in *Writing and Difference*, trans. and intro. Alan Bass (Chicago: University of Chicago Press, 1978), pp. 79–153.

Derrida, Jacques, 'Violence et Métaphysique: Essai sur la pensée d'Emmanuel Levinas', *Revue de Métaphysique et de Morale*, 69 (1964), pp. 322–54, 425–73.

Desens, Marliss C., *The Bed-Trick in English Renaissance Drama: Explorations in Gender, Sexuality, and Power* (Newark: University of Delaware Press, 1994).

Desmet, Christy, *Reading Shakespeare's Characters: Rhetoric, Ethics, and Identity* (Amherst: University of Massachusetts Press, 1992).

Dessen, Alan C. and Leslie Thomson, *A Dictionary of Stage Directions in English Drama, 1580–1642* (Cambridge: Cambridge University Press, 1999).

DiGangi, Mario, *Sexual Types: Embodiment, Agency, and Dramatic Character from Shakespeare to Shirley* (Philadelphia: University of Pennsylvania Press, 2011).

Donaldson, Ian, *Ben Jonson: A Life* (Oxford: Oxford University Press, 2011).

Drew-Bear, Annette, 'Face-Painting Scenes in Ben Jonson's Plays', *Studies in Philology*, 77 (4) (1980), pp. 388–401.

Drew-Bear, Annette, *Painted Faces on the Renaissance Stage: The Moral Significance of Face-Painting Conventions* (London and Toronto: Associated University Presses, 1994).

Dryden, John, *Of Dramatick Poesie, an Essay*, ed. Yuji Kaneko (London: Routledge, 1996).

Ekman, Paul (ed.), *Emotion in the Human Face* (Los Altos: Mahor Books, 2013).

Elam, Keir, *The Semiotics of Theatre and Drama*, 2nd edn (London: Routledge, 2002).

Elias, Norbert, *The Civilizing Process*, trans. Edmund Jephcott (Oxford: Basil Blackwell, *c.*1978–82).

Elkins, James, *The Object Stares Back: On the Nature of Seeing* (Orlando, FL: Harcourt, 1996).

Ellerbeck, Ellen, 'Adoption and the Language of Horticulture in *All's Well That Ends Well*', *Studies in English Literature, 1500–1900*, 51 (2) (2011), pp. 305–26.

Empson, William, *The Structure of Complex Words* (Ann Arbor: University of Michigan Press, 1967).

Erasmus, *The Praise of Folly*, trans. Betty Radice, in A. H. T. Levi (ed.), *The Collected Works of Erasmus* (Toronto: University of Toronto Press, 1989).

Erickson, Jon, 'The Face and the Possibility of an Ethics of Performance', *Journal of Dramatic Criticism and Theory*, 13 (2) (1999), pp. 5–21.

Ernst I, Johann, 'Pictures and Other Works of Art in the Royal Palaces, in the Year 1613', in William Brenchley Rye (ed.), *England as Seen by Foreigners in the Days of Elizabeth and James the First* (New York: Benjamin Blom, 1967).

Escobedo, Andrew, '"Unlucky Deeds" and the Shame of Othello', in Michael D. Bristol (ed.), *Shakespeare and Moral Agency* (London: Continuum, 2010), pp. 159–70.

Escobedo, Andrew, 'On Sincere Apologies: Saying "Sorry" in *Hamlet*', *Philosophy and Literature*, 41 (1) (2017), pp. 155–77.

Escolme, Bridget, 'Shakespeare, Rehearsal and the Site-Specific', *Shakespeare Bulletin*, 30 (4) (2012), pp. 505–22.

Escolme, Bridget, *Talking to the Audience: Shakespeare, Performance, Self* (London: Routledge, 2005).

Ferguson, Margaret, 'Translation and Homeland Insecurity in Shakespeare's *The Taming of the Shrew*', in Karen Newman and Jane Tylus (eds), *Early*

Modern Cultures of Translation (Philadelphia: University of Pennsylvania Press, 2015), pp. 117–52.

Fernyhough, Charles, *The Voices Within: The History and Science of Howe Talk to Ourselves* (New York: Basic Books, 2016).

Fischer-Lichte, Erika, *The Semiotics of Theatre*, trans. Jeremy Gaines and Doris L. Jones (Bloomington: Indiana University Press, 1992).

Forman, Simon, 'The Bocke of Plaies and Notes therof per forman for Common Pollicie', 1611. Accessed at www.shakespearedocumented.org.

Forster, E. M., *Aspects of the Novel* (London: E. Arnold, 1927).

Foucault, Michel, *Discipline and Punish: The Birth of the Prison*, trans. Alan Sheridan (London: Vintage Books, 1977).

Fowler, Benjamin, Rev. *Hamlet. Shakespeare Bulletin*, 31 (4) (2013), pp. 737–45.

Fowler, Elizabeth, *Literary Character: The Human Figure in Early English Writing* (Ithaca and London: Cornell University Press, 2003).

Freedberg, David, *The Power of Images: Studies in the History and Theory of Response* (Chicago: University of Chicago Press, 1991).

Friedman, Michael D., '"O, Let Him Marry Her!": Matrimony and Recompense in *Measure for Measure*', *Shakespeare Quarterly*, 46 (1995), pp. 54–64.

Garber, Marjorie, *Shakespeare's Ghost Writers: Literature as Uncanny Causality* (New York: Methuen, 1987).

Gardner, Lyn, Rev. *Hamlet. Guardian* 3 December 2011.

Geneva Bible: A Facsimile of the 1560 Edition (Peabody, MA: Hendrickson, 2007).

Giddens, Anthony, *The Constitution of Society* (Berkeley: University of California Press, 1986).

Gieskes, Edward, '"Honesty and Vulgar Praise": The Poet's War and the Literary Field', *Medieval and Renaissance Drama in England*, 18 (2005), pp. 75–102.

Girard, René, 'Hamlet's Dull Revenge', *A Theatre of Envy: William Shakespeare*, 2nd edn (Exeter: Short Run Press, 2000), pp. 271–89.

Goffman, Erving, *Behaviour in Public Places: Notes on the Social Organization of Gathering* (New York: Free Press, 1963).

Gold, Moshe and Sandor Goodheart (eds), *Of Levinas and Shakespeare: 'To See Another Thus'* (West Lafayette: Purdue University Press, 2018).

Goldstein, David B., 'Facing *King Lear*', in James A. Knapp (ed.), *Shakespeare and the Power of the Face* (Burlington, VT: Ashgate, 2015), pp. 75–91.

Gosson, Stephen, *The Schoole of Abuse, Conteining a plesaunt inuectiue against Poets, Pipers, Plaiers, Iesters, and such like Caterpillers of a Comonwelth* [originally published in 1579] (London: Thomas Woodcocke), Early English Books Online.

Graham, Edward K., 'Ben Jonson and the Character-Writers', *Sewanee Review*, 14 (3) (1906), pp. 299–305.

Grehan, Helena, *Performance, Ethics and Spectatorship in a Global Age* (Basingstoke: Palgrave Macmillan, 2009).

Gumbrecht, Hans Ulrich, *Production of Presence: What Meaning Cannot Convey* (Stanford: Stanford University Press, 2004).

Haines, Simon, 'Recognition in Shakespeare and Hegel', in R. S. White, Mark Houlahan and Katrina O'Louglin (eds), *Shakespeare and Emotions: Inheritances, Enactments, Legacies* (New York: Palgrave Macmillan, 2015), pp. 218–30.

Halpern, Richard, *The Poetics of Primitive Accumulation: English Renaissance Culture and the Genealogy of Capital* (Ithaca and London: Cornell University Press, 1991).

Hamlin, Hannibal, *The Bible in Shakespeare* (Oxford: Oxford University Press, 2013).

Hampton-Reeves, Stuart, 'Fighting', in Stuart Hampton-Reeves and Bridget Escolme (eds), *Shakespeare and the Making of Theatre* (New York: Palgrave Macmillan, 2012), pp. 146–64.

Hansen, Mark B. N., 'New Media', *Critical Terms for Media Studies*, ed. W. J. T. Mitchell and Mark B. N. Hansen (Chicago and London: University of Chicago Press 2010), pp. 172–85.

Harris, Jonathan Gil, *Untimely Matter in the Time of Shakespeare* (Philadelphia: University of Pennsylvania Press, 2008).

Hentzner, Paul, *Itinerarium Germaniae, Galliae, Angliae, Italiae . . .* trans. Richard Bentley, in Henry Morley (ed.), *Travels in England during the Reign of Queen Elizabeth* (London: Cassell, 1901).

Herford, C. H. and Percy Simpson (eds), *Ben Jonson*, Vol. 11 (Oxford: Oxford University Press, 1952).

Hesiod, *Catalogues of Women, fragment 68.21–7*, in *Homeric Hymns, Epic Cycle, Homerica*, trans. Hugh G. Evelyn-White (Cambridge: Loeb Classical Library, 1914).

Hesk, Jon, 'Types of Oratory', in Erik Gunderson (ed.), *The Cambridge Companion to Ancient Rhetoric* (Cambridge: Cambridge University Press, 2009), pp. 145–61.

Hodgdon, Barbara, and W. B. Worthen (eds), *A Companion to Shakespeare and Performance* (London: Blackwell, 2005).

Honneth, Axel, *The Struggle for Recognition: The Moral Grammar of Social Conflicts*, trans. Joel Anderson (Oxford: Polity, 1995).

Hooker, Richard, 'A learned and comfortable sermon on the certainty and perpetuity of faith in the elect', sermon one in *The Works of that Learned and Judicious Divine, Mr. Richard Hooker*, Vol. 3, ed. John Keble, 6th edn (Oxford: Clarendon Press, 1874).

Hornby, Richard, 'Two Hamlets', *Hudson Review*, 65 (1) (2012), pp. 122–8.

Hunt, Maurice, *The Divine Face in Four Writers: Shakespeare, Dostoevsky, Hesse, and C. S. Lewis* (New York: Bloomsbury, 2015).

Husserl, Edmund, *Cartesian Meditations: Introduction to Phenomenology*, trans. Dorion Cairns (The Hague: Martinus Nijhoff, 1960).

Husserl, Edmund, *Cartesianische Meditationen und Pariser Vorträge*, Husserliana vol. 1 (The Hague: Martinus Nijhoff, 1950).

Husserl, Edmund, *Logische Untersuchungen*, 2 vols (Halle: Max Niemayer, 1900/1).

Husserl, Edmund, *Méditations Cartésiennes: Introduction à la Phenomenologie*, trans. Gabrielle Peiffer and Emmanuel Levinas (Paris: J. Vrin, 1966).

Hutson, Lorna, *The Invention of Suspicion: Law and Mimesis in Shakespeare and Renaissance Drama* (Oxford: Oxford University Press, 2007).

Hyland, Peter, *Disguise and Role-Playing in Ben Jonson's Drama* (Salzburg: Institut für Englische Sprache und Literatur, 1977).

Hyland, Peter, *Disguise on the Early Modern Stage* (Farnham: Ashgate, 2011).

Jackson, Ken, '"Grace to boot": St. Paul, Messianic Time, and Shakespeare's *The Winter's Tale*', in Paul Cefalu and Brian Reynolds (eds), *The Return of Theory in Early Modern English Studies* (London: Palgrave Macmillan, 2011), pp. 192–210.

Jakobson, Roman, 'Linguistics and Poetics', in T. Sebeok (ed.), *Style in Language* (Cambridge, MA: MIT Press, 1960), pp. 350–77.

James, Heather, 'Shakespeare's Learned Heroines in Ovid's Schoolroom', in Charles Martindale and A. B. Taylor, *Shakespeare and the Classics* (Cambridge: Cambridge University Press, 2004), pp. 66–85.

Jonson, Ben, *The English Grammar,* Chapter 16 ('Of a Verb'), in David Bevington, Martin Butler and Ian Donaldson (eds), *The Cambridge Edition of the Works of Ben Jonson Online* (Cambridge: Cambridge University Press, 2012), http://universitypublishingonline.org/cambridge/benjonson/ (last access 29 November 2017).

Johnson, Samuel, 'The Preface to Shakespeare' (1765), in *The Yale Edition of the Works of Samuel Johnson*, Vol. 7, ed. Arthur Sherbo (New Haven: Yale University Press, 1968), pp. 59–113.

Junker, William, 'The Image of Both Theaters: Empire and Revelation in Shakespeare's *Antony and Cleopatra*', *Shakespeare Quarterly*, 66 (2) (2015), pp. 167–87.

Junker, William, 'Tomorrows at the End of Time: Eschatology, Sovereignty, and *Macbeth*', unpublished paper presented at the Shakespeare Association of America seminar, 'Shakespeare, Phenomenology, and Periodization' (March 2013).

Karim-Cooper, Farah, *Cosmetics in Shakespearean and Renaissance Drama* (Edinburgh: Edinburgh University Press, 2006).

Kastan, David Scott, '"His semblable is his mirror": *Hamlet* and the Imitation of Revenge', *Shakespeare Studies*, 19 (1987), pp. 111–24.

Kay, David, *Ben Jonson: A Literary Life* (New York: St. Martin's Press, 1995).

Kearney, James, '"This is above all strangeness": *King Lear*, Ethics, and the Phenomenology of Recognition', *Criticism*, 54 (3) (2012), pp. 455–67.

Kempis, Thomas à, *The Imitation of Christ*, vol. 7, part 2, p. 214 (The First Book, Chapter 1, paragraph 4). Available at https://books.google.com/books?id=mBqFj_ZoLy0C&lpg=PA208&ots=E8Y1J2dys9&dq=' (last accessed 10 July 2018).

Kerrigan, John, *Revenge Tragedy: Aeschylus to Armageddon* (Oxford: Clarendon Press, 1996).

Kerrigan, John, *Shakespeare's Binding Language* (Oxford: Oxford University Press, 2016).

Kerrigan, William, 'The Personal Shakespeare', in Norman N. Holland, Sidney Homan and Bernard J. Paris (eds), *Shakespeare's Personality* (Berkeley: University of California Press, 1989).

Kierkegaard, Søren, *Fear and Trembling*, ed. Stephens Evans and Sylvia Walsh, trans. Sylvia Walsh (Cambridge: Cambridge University Press, 2006).

Knapp, James A. (ed.), *Shakespeare and the Power of the Face* (Farnham: Ashgate, 2015).

Ko, Yu Jin, 'The Comic Close of *Twelfth Night* and Viola's *Noli me Tangere*', *Shakespeare Quarterly*, 48 (4) (Winter, 1997), pp. 391–405.

Ko, Yu Jin and Michael W. Shurgot (eds), *Shakespeare's Sense of Character: On the Page and from the Stage* (Aldershot: Ashgate, 2012).

Koerner, Joseph Leo, 'Dürer's Model: Reflections on Dürer and his Legacy', Exhibition held at the British Museum 2002–2003'. Accessed at https://www.britishmuseum.org/pdf/4%20Durer%20Model1.pdf (last accessed 29 December 2017).

Koerner, Joseph Leo, *The Moment of Self-Portraiture in German Renaissance Art* (Chicago: University of Chicago Press, 1993).

Koerner, Joseph Leo, *The Reformation of the Image* (Chicago: University of Chicago Press, 2008).

Kott, Jan, 'Hamlet of the Mid-Century', *Shakespeare Our Contemporary*, trans. Boleslaw Taborski (New York: W. W. Norton, 1974), pp. 57–73.

Kottman, Paul A., 'Duel', in *Early Modern Theatricality* (Oxford Twenty-First Century Approaches to Literature), ed. Henry S. Turner (Oxford: Oxford University Press 2013), pp. 402–22.

Kottman, Paul A., *Love as Human Freedom* (Stanford: Stanford University Press, 2017).

Kottman, Paul A., *Tragic Conditions in Shakespeare: Disinheriting the Globe* (Baltimore: Johns Hopkins University Press, 2009).

Kreider, P. V., 'The Mechanics of Disguise in Shakespeare's Plays', *Shakespeare Association Bulletin*, 9 (4) (1934), pp. 167–80.

Krieger, Murray, *Ekphrasis: The Illusion of the Natural Sign* (Baltimore: Johns Hopkins University Press, 1992).

Kyd, Thomas, *Solimon and Perseda*, in F. S. Boas (ed.), *The Works of Thomas Kyd* (Oxford: Clarendon Press, 1901).

Kyd, Thomas, *The Spanish Tragedy*, ed. David Bevington (Manchester: Manchester University Press, 1996).

Kyd, Thomas, *The Spanish Tragedy*, ed. Clara Calvo and Jesús Tronch (London: Arden, 2013).

Lacan, Jacques, 'Desire and the Interpretation of Desire in *Hamlet*', *Yale French Studies*, 55/56 (1977), pp. 11–52.

Lakoff, George and Mark Johnson, *Philosophy in the Flesh: The Embodied Mind and Its Challenge to Western Thought* (New York: Basic Books, 1999).

Lawrence, Sean, 'The Two Faces of Othello', in James A. Knapp (ed.), *Shakespeare and the Power of the Face* (Burlington, VT: Ashgate, 2015), pp. 61–74.

Leggatt, Alexander, 'Introduction', *All's Well That Ends Well* (New Cambridge edition), ed. Russell Fraser (Cambridge: Cambridge University Press, 2003), pp. 1–43.

Lehnhof, Kent R., 'Relation and Responsibility: A Levinasian Reading of *King Lear*', *Modern Philology*, 111 (3) (2014), pp. 485–509.

Leifer, Eric, *Actors as Observers: A Theory of Skill in Social Relationships* (New York: Garland, 1991).

Lemon, Rebecca, 'Scaffolds of Treason in *Macbeth*', *Theatre Journal*, 54 (1) (2002), pp. 24–53.

Levey, Satina M. and Peter Thornton, *Of Household Stuff: The 1601 Inventories of Bess of Hardwick* (London: National Trust, 2001).

Levi, Primo, *Se questo è un uomo* (*If This Is a Man*) (Torino: Einaudi, 1947).

Levin, Richard, 'Hamlet, Laertes, and the Dramatic Function of Foils', in Arthur F. Kinney (ed.), *Hamlet: New Critical Essays* (New York: Routledge, 2002), pp. 215–30.

Levinas, Emmanuel, 'Peace and Proximity', *Emmanuel Levinas: Basic Philosophical Writings*, ed Adriaan T. Peperzak, Simon Critchley and Robert Bernasconi (Bloomington: Indiana University Press, 1996), pp. 161–9.

Levinas, Emmanuel, 'Persons or Figures', *Difficult Freedom: Essays on Judaism*, trans. Seán Hand (Baltimore: Johns Hopkins University Press, 1997), pp. 119–22.

Levinas, Emmanuel, 'Reality and Its Shadow', *Collected Philosophical Papers* (Dordrecht: Martinus Nijhoff, 1987), pp. 1–13.

Levinas, Emmanuel, 'Transcendence and Height', in Adriaan T. Peperzak, Simon Critchley and Robert Bernasconi (eds), *Emmanuel Levinas: Basic Philosophical Writings* (Bloomington: Indiana University Press, 1996), pp. 11–31.

Levinas, Emmanuel, *Entre Nous*, trans. Michael B. Smith and Barbara Harshav (New York: Columbia University Press, 1998).

Levinas, Emmanuel, *Otherwise than Being or Beyond Essence*, trans. Alphonso Lingis (Pittsburgh: Duquesne University Press, 1998).

Levinas, Emmanuel, *Totalité et Infini: Essai sur l'Extériorité* (The Hague: Martinus Nijhoff, 1961).

Levinas, Emmanuel, *Totality and Infinity*, trans. Alphonso Lingis (Pittsburgh: Duquesne University Press, 1969).

Levinas, Emmanuel, *Totality and Infinity: An Essay on Exteriority*, trans. Alphonso Lingis (Pittsburgh: Duquesne University Press, 1961).

Lewis, Cynthia, '"Dark Deeds Darkly Answered": Duke Vincentio and Judgment in *Measure for Measure*', *Shakespeare*, 34 (1983), pp. 271–89.

Lieblein, Leanore, 'Embodied Intersubjectivity and the Creation of Early Modern Character', in Paul Yachnin and Jessica Slights (eds), *Shakespeare and Character*, pp. 117–35.

Lin, Erika T., *Shakespeare and the Materiality of Performance* (London: Palgrave Macmillan, 2012).

Lockwood, Tom, *Ben Jonson in the Romantic Age* (Oxford and New York: Oxford University Press, 2005).

Lowrance, Bryan, '"Modern Ecstasy": *Macbeth* and the Meaning of the Political', *English Literary History*, 79 (4) (2012), pp. 823–49.

Loxley, James and Mark Robson, *Shakespeare, Jonson, and the Claims of the Performative* (New York and London: Routledge, 2013).

Lynch, Deidre Shauna, *The Economy of Character: Novels, Market Culture, and the Business of Inner Meaning* (Chicago: University of Chicago Press, 1998).

Lyons, John, 'Deixis, Space, and Time', *Semantics*, 2 (1977), pp. 636–724.

Lupton, Julia Reinhard, '*All's Well that Ends Well* and the Futures of Consent', in *Thinking with Shakespeare: Essays on Politics and Life* (Chicago: University of Chicago Press, 2011), pp. 97–129.

Lupton, Julia Reinhard, 'Climates of Trust in *Macbeth*', in Craig Bourne and Emily Caddick (eds), *The Routledge Companion to Shakespeare and Philosophy* (London: Routledge, 2019).

Lupton, Julia Reinhard, 'Judging Forgiveness: Hannah Arendt, W. H. Auden, and *The Winter's Tale*', *New Literary History*, 45 (2014), pp. 641–63.

Lupton, Julia Reinhard, 'Macbeth Against Dwelling', in *Shakespeare Dwelling* (Chicago: University of Chicago Press, 2018), pp. 85–116.

Lupton, Julia Reinhard, 'Shakespeare's Social Work: From Displacement to Placement in *Twelfth Night*', forthcoming in Kenneth Graham (ed.), *Shakespeare 401* (Montreal: McGill-Queen's University Press, 2019).

Lupton, Julia Reinhard, 'Trust in Theater', in Donald Wehrs and Thomas Blake (eds), *Palgrave Handbook of Affect Studies and Textual Criticism* (New York: Palgrave, 2017).

Lupton, Julia Reinhard, *Thinking with Shakespeare: Essays on Politics and Life* (Chicago: University of Chicago Press, 2013).

McCabe, Richard A., 'Ben Jonson, Theophrastus, and the Comedy of Humours', *Hermathena*, 146 (1989), pp. 25–37.

McElroy, Mary, and Kent Cartwright, 'Public Fencing Contests on the Elizabethan Stage', *Journal of Sport History*, 13 (3) (1986), pp. 193–211.

Mack, Maynard, *King Lear in Our Time* (Berkeley: University of California Press, 1965).

Mack, Peter, *Elizabethan Rhetoric: Theory and Practice* (Cambridge: Cambridge University Press, 2002).

MacKay, Ellen, *Persecution, Plague, and Fire: Fugitive Histories of the Stage* (Chicago: University of Chicago Press, 2011).

McMillin, Scott, 'The Sharer and His Boy: Rehearsing Shakespeare's Women', in Peter Holland and Stephen Orgel (eds), *From Script to Stage in Early Modern England* (Basingstoke: Palgrave, 2004).

Manley, Lawrence, 'Shakespeare and the Golden Fleece', in Ellen Rosand (ed.), *Readying Cavalli's Operas for the Stage* (Farnham: Ashgate, 2013), pp. 187–98.

Mann, David, *Shakespeare's Women: Performance and Conception* (Cambridge: Cambridge University Press, 2008).

Marchitello, Howard, 'Speed and the Problem of Real Time in *Macbeth*', *Shakespeare Quarterly*, 64 (4) (2013), pp. 425–48.

Mardock, James, *Our Scene is London: Ben Jonson's City and the Space of the Author* (New York and London: Routledge, 2008).

Marston, John, 'Prologue', accessed at Early English Books Online, https://quod.lib.umich.edu/e/eebogroup/.

Menzer, Paul, 'Character Acting', in Farah Karim-Cooper and Tiffany Stern (eds), *Shakespeare's Theatres and the Effects of Performance* (London: Arden Shakespeare, 2013), pp. 141–67.

Milton, John, *Paradise Lost*, in Merritt Y. Hughes (ed.), *Complete Poems and Major Prose* (Indianapolis: Hackett. 1957).

Moi, Toril, *Revolution of the Ordinary: Literary Studies After Wittgenstein, Austin, and Cavell* (Chicago: University of Chicago Press, 2017).

Mooney, Michael, '"Edgar I nothing am": "Figurenposition" in *King Lear*', *Shakespeare Survey*, 38 (1985).

Morley, Thomas, *A Plaine and Easie Introduction to Practicall Musicke* [originally published in 1597), Early English Books Online.

Morris, David, *The Sense of Space* (Albany: State University of New York Press, 1999).

Moul, Victoria, *Jonson, Horace and the Classical Tradition* (Cambridge: Cambridge University Press, 2010).

Munday, Anthony, *John a Kent and John a Cumber*, ed. Arthur E. Pennell (New York: Garland, 1980).

Norbrook, David, '*Macbeth* and the Politics of Historiography', in Kevin Sharpe and Steven N. Zwicker (eds), *Politics of Discourse: The Literature and History of Seventeenth-Century England* (Berkeley: University of California Press, 1987), pp. 78–116.

Nunberg, Geoffrey, 'Indexality and Deixis', *Linguistics and Philosophy*, 19 (1993), pp. 1–43.

Nussbaum, Martha, *Upheavals of Thought* (Cambridge: Cambridge University Press, 2003).

Nuttall, A. D., 'Action at a Distance: Shakespeare and the Greeks', in Charles Martindale and A. B. Taylor, *Shakespeare and the Classics* (Cambridge: Cambridge University Press, 2004), pp. 209–22.

O'Callaghan, Michelle, *The English Wits: Literature and Sociability in Early Modern England* (Cambridge: Cambridge University Press, 2007).

Olson, Paul A., *Beyond a Common Joy: An Introduction to Shakespearean Comedy* (Lincoln: University of Nebraska Press, 2008).

Orgel, Stephen, *Impersonations: The Performance of Gender in Shakespeare's England* (Cambridge: Cambridge University Press, 1996).

Ostovich, Helen, 'Introduction', in Ben Jonson, *Every Man Out of His Humour*, ed. Helen Ostovitch (Manchester: Manchester University Press, 2001), pp. 1–95.

Ostovich, Helen, '"To Behold the Scene Full": Seeing and Judging in *Every Man Out of His Humour*', in Martin Butler (ed.), *Re-Presenting Ben Jonson* (London: Palgrave Macmillan, 1999).

Overbury, Thomas, *A vvife novv the vvidovv of Sir Thomas Ouerburie Being a most exquisite and singular poeme, of the choyse of a wife. Whereunto are added many witty characters, and conceyted newes; written by himselfe, and other learned gentlemen his friendes* (London: Printed by T. C[reede] for Lawrence Lisle, 1616).

Ovid, *Ovid: Heroides and Amores*, trans. Grant Showerman, Loeb Classical Library (Cambridge, MA: Harvard University Press, 1914).

Oxford English Dictionary [online], 'bravery', http://www.oed.com.ezproxy.uky.edu/view/Entry/22798?redirectedFrom=bravery#eid (last accessed 30 November 2017).

Oxford English Dictionary [online], 'crown', https://vpn.uci.edu/+CSCO+10756767633A2F2F6A6A6A2E6272712E70627A++/view/Entry/45060?rskey=NE9cul&result=2&isAdvanced=false#eid (last accessed 31 July 2018).

Oxford English Dictionary [online], 'earnest', https://vpn.uci.edu/+CSCO+10756767633A2F2F6A6A6A2E6272712E70627A++/view/Entry/59001?rskey=ZRF1Nn&result=1&isAdvanced=false#eid (last accessed 31 July 2018).

Oxford English Dictionary [online], 'face', https://vpn.nacs.uci.edu/+CSCO+10756767633A2F2F6A6A6A2E6272712E70627A++/view/Entry/67426?rskey=KKIqBK&result=2&isAdvanced=false#eid (last accessed 8 July 2018).

Oxford English Dictionary [online], 'gallery', www.oed.com/view/Entry/76266 (last accessed 29 November 2018).

Oxford English Dictionary [online], 'outface', http://www.oed.com.ezproxy.uky.edu/view/Entry/133589?rskey=xyJMJK&result=2&isAdvanced=false#eid (last accessed 30 November 2018).

Oxford English Dictionary [online], 'performance', https://vpn.uci.edu/+CSCO+10756767633A2F2F6A6A6A2E6272712E70627A++/view/Entry/140783?redirectedFrom=performance#eid. *Oxford English Dictionary Online*, 'performance' (last accessed 30 November 2018).

Oxford English Dictionary [online], 'repair', https://vpn.uci.edu/+CSCO+10756767633A2F2F6A6A6A2E6272712E70627A++/view/Entry/162630?rskey=rKA3j2&result=3&isAdvanced=false#eid. *Oxford English Dictionary Online*, 'repair' (last accessed 30 November 2018).

Palfrey, Simon, *Poor Tom: Living* King Lear (Chicago: University of Chicago Press, 2014).

Panofsky, Erwin, *The Life and Art of Albrecht Dürer*, rev. edn (Princeton: Princeton University Press, 2005 edn).

Pausanias, *The Description of Greece*, trans. W. H. S. Jones (Cambridge, MA: Harvard University Press, 1992).

Pavis, Patrice, 'Performance Analysis: Space, Time, Action', trans. Sinéad Rushe, *Gestos*, 22 (1996), pp. 11–32.

Pavis, Patrice, *Languages of the Stage: Essays in the Semiology of the Theatre* (New York: Performing Arts Journal Publications, 1982).

Peck, Linda Levy, *Consuming Splendor: Society and Culture in Seventeenth-Century England* (Cambridge: Cambridge University Press, 2005).

Pfister, Manfred, *The Theory and Analysis of Drama*, trans. John Halliday (Oxford: Oxford University Press, 2013).

Phelan, Peggy, 'Marina Abamović: Witnessing Shadows', *Theatre Journal*, 56 (2004), pp. 569–77.

Picciotto, Joanna, *Labors of Innocence in Early Modern England* (Cambridge, MA: Harvard University Press, 2010).

Platter, Thomas, *Englandfahrt im Jahre 1599*, ed. Hans Hect (Halle: Max Niemeyer, 1929).

Plett, Heinrich F., *Enargeia in Classical Antiquity and the Early Modern Age: The Aesthetics of Evidence* (Leiden and Boston: Brill, 2012).

Poole, Kristen, *Supernatural Environments in Shakespeare's England* (Cambridge: Cambridge University Press, 2011).

Poole, Thomas, 'Judicial Review at the Margins: Law, Power, and Prerogative', *University of Toronto Law Journal*, 60 (1) (2010), pp. 81–108.

Poster, Mark, 'Desiring Information and Machines', *Data Made Flesh: Embodying Information*, ed. Robert Mitchell and Phillip Thurtle (London and New York: Routledge, 2004), pp. 87–101.

Prosser, Eleanor, *Hamlet and Revenge* (Stanford: Stanford University Press, 1967).

Puttenham, George, *The Art of English Poesy*, ed. Frank Whigham and Wayne A. Rebhorn (Ithaca: Cornell University Press, 2007).

Quarmby, Kevin A., *The Disguised Ruler in Shakespeare and His Contemporaries* (Farnham: Ashgate, 2012).

Quintilian, *The Orator's Education*, ed. and trans. Donald A. Russell (Cambridge, MA: Harvard University Press, 2001).

Quiring, Björn, *Shakespeare's Curse: The Aporias of Ritual Exclusion in Early Modern Royal Drama* (London: Routledge, 2013).

Raffnsøe, Sverre, 'Beyond rule: trust and power as capacities', *Journal of Political Power*, 6 (2) (2013), pp. 241–60.

Rankin, Patrice, 'Dignity in Homer and Classical Greece', in Remy Debes (ed.), *Dignity: A History* (Oxford: Oxford University Press, 2017), pp. 19–46.

Read, Alan, *Theatre, Intimacy and Engagement: The Last Human Venue* (Basingstoke: Palgrave Macmillan, 2008).

Rhie, Bernie, 'Wittgenstein on the Face of Work of Art', Nonsite.org (2011) http://nonsite.org/article/wittgenstein-on-the-face-of-a-work-of-art.

Ricoeur, Paul, *The Course of Recognition*, trans. David Pellauer (Cambridge, MA: Harvard University Press, 2005).

Ridout, Nicholas, *Stage Fright, Animals, and Other Theatrical Problems* (Cambridge: Cambridge University Press, 2006).

Ridout, Nicholas, *Theatre and Ethics* (Basingstoke: Palgrave Macmillan, 2009).

Rimbaud, Arthur, 'Délires I. Vierge Folle, L'Époux Infernal'. A Season in Hell. The Illuminations, trans. Enid Rhodes Peschel (London: Oxford University Press, 1974), pp. 66–75, at p. 68.

Roach, Joseph, *The Player's Passion: Studies in the Science of Acting* (Newark: University of Delaware Press, 1985).

Robbins, Jill, *Altered Reading: Levinas and Literature* (Chicago and London: University of Chicago Press, 1999).

Roberts, Sasha, '"Let Me the Curtains Draw": The Dramatic and Symbolic Properties of the Bed in Shakespeare', in Jonathan Gil Harris and Natasha Korda (eds), *Staged Properties in Early Modern English Drama* (Cambridge: Cambridge University Press, 2002), pp. 153–74.

Robson, Leo, '*Hamlet*, Barbican, London', FT.com, 4 December 2011.

Roszia, Sharon Kaplan and Deborah N. Silverstein, 'Adoptees and the Seven Core Issues of Adoption', *Adoptive Families*, 32 (1999), pp. 8–13.

Sack, Daniel, *After Live: Possibility, Potentiality, and the Future of Performance* (Ann Arbor: University of Michigan Press, 2015).

Sacks, Peter, 'Where Words Prevail Not: Grief, Revenge, and Language in Kyd and Shakespeare', *ELH*, 49 (3) (1982), pp. 576–601.

Sanders, Julie, *The Cultural Geography of Early Modern Drama, 1620–1650* (Cambridge: Cambridge University Press, 2011).

Schalkwyk, David, 'Cavell, Wittgenstein, Shakespeare, and Skepticism: *Othello* vs. *Cymbeline*', *Modern Philology*, 114 (3) (2017), pp. 601–29.

Schalkwyk, David, *Love and Language in Shakespeare* (Cambridge: Cambridge University Press, 2018).

Schalkwyk, David, *Speech and Performance in Shakespeare's Sonnets and Plays* (Cambridge: Cambridge University Press, 2002).

Schiller, Gertrud, *Iconography of Christian Art*, trans. Janet Seligman, Vol. 11 (London: Lund Humphries, 1972; 1st German edn 1968).

Schwarz, Kathryn, *What You Will: Gender, Contract, and Shakespearean Social Place* (Philadelphia: University of Pennsylvania Press, 2011).

Scolnicov, Hanna, '"Who is it that can tell me who I am?": Individual, Subject and Self in *King Lear*', *Shakespeare Jahrbuch*, 142 (2006), pp. 142–56.

Scolnicov, Hanna, 'Lear's Conversation with the Philosopher', in Randall Martin and Katherine Scheil (eds), *Shakespeare/Adaptation/Modern Drama: Festschrift for Jill Levenson* (Toronto: University of Toronto Press, 2011), pp. 218–31.

Scolnicov, Hanna, 'Stripping as Gesture', *Assaph: Studies in the Theatre*, 24 (2010), pp. 139–52.

Selleck, Nancy, *The Interpersonal Idiom in Shakespeare, Donne, and Early Modern Culture* (New York: Palgrave Macmillan, 2008).

Seneca, *Seneca. Vol. VIII: Tragedies*, trans. and ed. John G. Fitch (Cambridge, MA: Harvard University Press, 2002).

Serres, Michael, *Angels: A Modern Myth*, trans. Francis Cowper (Paris: Flammarion, 1995).

Shadwell, Thomas, 'The Preface' to *The Sullen Lovers: Or, The Impertinents*, in *The Complete Works of Thomas Shadwell*, Vol. 1, ed. Montague Summers (London: Fortune Press, 1927).

Shakespeare, William, *Comedies, Histories, and Tragedies* (London: Isaac Jaggard and Edward Blount, 1623), sigs. ᵖA1ᵛ, ᵖA1+1ʳ, d2ᵛ.

Shakespeare, William, *Hamlet: The Texts of 1603 and 1623*, ed. Ann Thompson and Neil Taylor, Third Series (London: Arden Shakespeare, 2006).

Shakespeare, William, *King Lear*, ed. R. A. Foakes, Arden Shakespeare Edition (London: Thomson Learning, 2000).

Shakespeare, William, *Macbeth*, ed. Sandra Clark and Pamela Mason, Arden Shakespeare 3rd edn (London and New York: Bloomsbury, 2015).

Shakespeare, William, *The New Oxford Shakespeare: Modern Critical Edition* (ed. Gary Taylor, John Jowett, Terri Bourus and Gabriel Egan) (Oxford: Oxford University Press, 2016).

Shapiro, James, 'Is This a Holiday', in *1599: A Year in the Life of William Shakespeare* (New York: Harper Collins, 2005).

Sherman, Jon Foley, *A Strange Proximity: Stage Presence, Failure, and the Ethics of Attention* (London and New York: Routledge, 2016).

Shimizu, Akihiko, 'Passions, Acting and Face in Early Modern Characters: An Alternative View on the Avatar', *Integrative Psychological and Behavioral Science* 46 (2012), pp. 569–83.

Maus, Katherine E., *Ben Jonson and the Roman Frame of Mind* (Princeton: Princeton University Press, 1985).

Silver, George. *Paradoxes of Defence* (London, 1599).

Simon, Eli, *Masking Unmasked: Four Approaches to Basic Acting* (New York: Palgrave Macmillan, 2003).

Simons, Jay, 'Stinging, Barking, Biting, Purging: Jonson's *Bartholomew Fair* and the Debate on Satire in the Poetmachia', *Ben Jonson Journal*, 20 (1) (2013), pp. 20–37.

Skinner, Quentin, *Forensic Shakespeare* (Oxford: Oxford University Press, 2015).

Smeed, J. M., *The Theophrastan Character: The History of a Literary Genre* (Oxford and New York: Clarendon Press, 1985).

Smith, Bruce R., 'E/loco/com/motion', in *From Script to Stage in Early Modern England*, ed. Peter Holland and Stephen Orgel (Basingstoke: Palgrave Macmillan, 2004), pp. 131–50.

Smith, Bruce R., 'Sermons in Stones: Shakespeare and Renaissance Sculpture', *Shakespeare Studies*, 17 (1985), pp. 1–23.

Smith, Mack, *Literary Realism and Ekphrasis Tradition* (University Park: Pennsylvania State University Press, 1995).

Smith, Matthew James, 'Tragedy *before* Pity and Fear', in Donald R. Wehrs and Thomas Blake (eds), *Handbook to Affect Studies* (Palgrave Macmillan, 2017), pp. 391–412.

Smith, Matthew James, 'w/Sincerity, Part I: The Drama of the Will from Augustine to Milton', *Christianity and Literature*, 67 (1) (2017), pp. 8–33.

Smith, Matthew James, *Performance and Religion in Early Modern England: Stage, Cathedral, Wagon, Street* (South Bend: University of Notre Dame Press, 2018).

Snyder, Susan, 'Erasmus' Colloquies', in Susan Snyder (ed.), *All's Well that Ends Well* (Oxford World's Classics, 1993), pp. 233–9.

Snyder, Susan, 'Introduction' in Susan Snyder (ed.), *All's Well That Ends Well* (Oxford World's Classics, 1993), pp. 1–67.

Soni, Vivasvan, 'Introduction: The Crisis of Judgment', in *The Eighteenth Century: Theory and Interpretation*, 51 (2010), pp. 261–88.

Staley, Gregory A., *Seneca and the Idea of Tragedy* (Oxford: Oxford University Press, 2010).

Steggle, Matthew, *Wars of the Theatres: The Poetics of Personation in the Age of Jonson,* English Literary Studies 75 (Victoria, BC: University of Victoria, 1998).

Stern, Daniel, *The Present Moment in Psychotherapy and Everyday Life* (New York: Norton, 2004).

Sterrett, Joseph, 'Confessing Claudius: Sovereignty, Fraternity, and Isolation at the Heart of *Hamlet*', *Textual Practice*, 23 (5) (2009), pp. 739–61.

Stewart, Stanley, 'Jonson's Criticism', in Richard Harp and Stanley Stewart (eds), *Cambridge Companion to Ben Jonson* (Cambridge: Cambridge University Press, 2000), pp. 175–87.

Stiegler, Bernard, *Technics and Time, 2: Disorientation*, trans. Stephen Barker (Stanford: Stanford University Press, 2009).

Streete, Adrian, '"What bloody man is that?": Questioning Biblical Typology in *Macbeth*', *Shakespeare*, 5 (1) (2009), pp. 18–35.

Strier, Richard, 'Excuses, Bepissing, and Non-being: Shakespearean Puzzles about Agency', in Michael D. Bristol (ed.), *Shakespeare and Moral Agency* (London: Continuum, 2010), pp. 55–70.

Thomas à Kempis, *The Imitation of Christ*, Harvard Classics (New York: P. F. Collier and Son, 1909).

Thompson, James, *Performance Affects: Applied Theatre and the End of Effect* 2nd edn (New York: Palgrave Macmillan, 2011).

Tompkin, Sylvan, *Exploring Affect: The Selected Writings of Silvan S. Tomkins*, ed. E. Virginia Demos (Cambridge: Cambridge University Press, 1995).

Travis, Keira, 'Wordplay and the Ethics of Self-Deception in Shakespeare's Tragedies', in Michael D. Bristol (ed.), *Shakespeare and Moral Agency* (London: Continuum, 2010), pp. 42–54.

Travis, Peter, 'The Dramatic Strategies of Chester's Passion Pagina: "O thou side-piercing sight!" – *King Lear*', *Comparative Drama*, 8 (3) (1974), pp. 275–89.

Tribble, Evelyn, 'Skill', in Henry S. Turner (ed.), *Early Modern Theatricality* (Oxford: Oxford University Press, 2013), pp. 173–88.

Tribble, Evelyn, *Early Modern Actors and Shakespeare's Theatre: Thinking with the Body* (London: Bloomsbury, 2017).

Turner, Henry S., *Early Modern Theatricality* (Oxford: Oxford University Press, 2013).

Turner, Henry S., *The English Renaissance Stage: Geometry, Poetics, and the Practical Spatial Arts* (Oxford: Oxford University Press, 2006).

Turner, Robert Y., 'Some Dialogues of Love in Lyly's Comedies', *ELH*, 29 (3) (1962), pp. 276–88.

'Two treatises (1644)' in Richard Hunter and Ida Macalpine (eds), *Three Hundred Years of Psychiatry, 1535–1860* (London: Oxford University Press, 1963).

Van Es, Bart, *Shakespeare in Company* (Oxford: Oxford University Press, 2013).

Vickers, Brian, 'The Emergence of Character Criticism, 1774–1800', *Shakespeare Survey*, 34 (1981), pp. 11–21.

Vickers, Brian, *In Defence of Rhetoric* (Oxford: Clarendon Press, 1988).

Wade, Leslie A., 'Sublime Trauma: The Violence of Ethical Encounter', *Violence Performed: Local Roots and Global Routes of Conflict*, ed. Patrick Anderson and Jisha Menon (Basingstoke: Palgrave Macmillan, 2009), pp. 15–30.

Weever, John, *The Whipping of the Satyre* (London: 1601).

Wehrs, Donald R., 'Ethical Ambiguity of the Maternal in Shakespeare's First Romances', in Gold et al. (eds), *Of Levinas and Shakespeare: 'To See Another Thus'* (West Lafayette, IN: Purdue University Press, 2018), pp. 203–36.

Wehrs, Donald R., 'Touching Words: Embodying Ethics in Erasmus, Shakespearean Comedy, and Contemporary Theory', *Modern Philology*, 104 (1) (2006), pp. 1–33.

Weimann, Robert, *Author's Pen and Actor's Voice: Playing and Writing in Shakespeare's Theatre* (Cambridge: Cambridge University Press, 2000).

Weimann, Robert and Douglas Bruster, *Shakespeare and the Power of Performance: Stage and Page in Elizabethan Theatre* (Cambridge: Cambridge University Press, 2008).

Werner, Sarah, 'Two *Hamlet*s: Wooster Group and Synthetic Theater', *Shakespeare Quarterly*, 59 (3) (2008), pp. 323–9.

West, William N., 'Playing in Context, Playing out Context', *Shakespeare in Our Time: A Shakespeare Association of America* Collection (London: Bloomsbury Arden, 2016), pp. 206–10.

West, William N., 'The Idea of a Theatre: Humanist Ideology and the Imaginary Stage in Early Modern Europe', *Renaissance Drama*, 28 (1997).

West, William N., 'Titus' Infinite Jest', *Re-Thinking the Secular in the Age of Shakespeare*, ed. Katherine Brokaw and Jason Zysk (Evanston: Northwestern University Press, forthcoming).

Wiles, David, *Theatre and Citizenship: The History of a Practice* (Cambridge: Cambridge University Press, 2011).

Wills, David, *Dorsality: Thinking Back through Technology and Politics* (Minneapolis: University of Minnesota Press, 2008).

Williams, Robert R., *Recognition: Fichte and Hegel on the Other* (Albany: State University of New York Press, 1992).

Witmore, Michael, 'Eventuality', in Henry S. Turner (ed.), *Early Modern Theatricality* (Oxford: Oxford University Press, 2013), pp. 386–401.

Wittgenstein, Ludwig, *Philosophical Investigations*, trans. G. E. M. Anscombe (Upper Saddle River, NJ: Prentice-Hall, 1953).

Wittgenstein, Ludwig, *Culture and Value*, trans. Peter Winch (Chicago: University of Chicago Press, 1980).

Wittington, Leah, *Renaissance Suppliants: Poetry, Antiquity, Reconciliation* (Oxford: Oxford University Press, 2016).

Worthen, W. B., *Shakespeare Performance Studies* (Cambridge: Cambridge University Press, 2014).

Womack, Peter, *Ben Jonson* (Oxford and New York: Basil Blackwell, 1986).

Wood, Neal, 'Cicero and the Political Thought of the Early English Renaissance', *Modern Language Quarterly*, 51 (1990), pp. 185–207.

Woodruff, Paul, *Reverence: Renewing a Forgotten Virtue*, 2nd edn (Oxford: Oxford University Press, 2014).

Worden, Blair, 'Politics in *Catiline*: Jonson and his Sources', in Martin Butler (ed.), *Re-Presenting Ben Jonson* (New York: Macmillan, 1999), pp. 152–73.

Yachnin, Paul and Jessica Slights, 'Introduction', in Paul Yachnin and Jessica Slights (eds), *Shakespeare and Character: Theory, History, Performance, and Theatrical Persons* (Basingstoke: Palgrave Macmillan, 2009).

Zamir, Tzachi, *Acts: Theater, Philosophy, and the Performing Self* (Ann Arbor: University of Michigan Press, 2014).

Zamir, Tzachi, *Double Vision: Moral Philosophy and Shakespearean Drama* (Princeton: Princeton University Press, 2007).

Zimmerman, Susan, *The Early Modern Corpse and Shakespeare's Theatre* (Edinburgh: Edinburgh University Press, 2005).

Zucker, Adam, *The Places of Wit in Early Modern English Comedy* (Cambridge: Cambridge University Press, 2011).

Index